MY HERO ACADEMIA
VIGILANTES
5

Writer / Letterer
Hideyuki Furuhashi

Penciller / Colorist
Betten Court

Original Concept
Kohei Horikoshi

【secret identity】

noun | se · cret iden · ti · ty
: the true person behind the mask of anonymity
worn by spies, superheroes, etc.

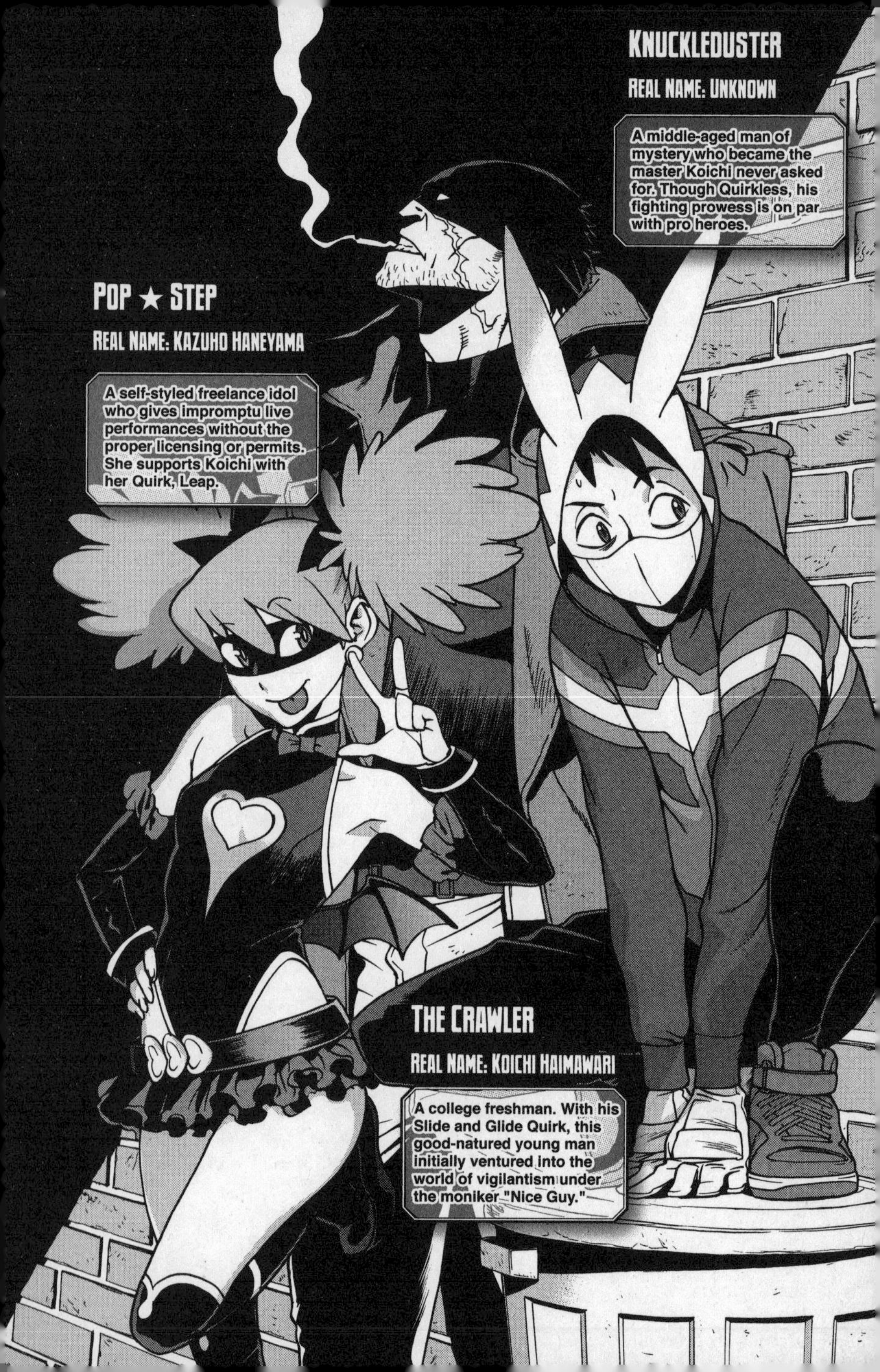
KNUCKLEDUSTER
REAL NAME: UNKNOWN
A middle-aged man of mystery who became the master Koichi never asked for. Though Quirkless, his fighting prowess is on par with pro heroes.
POP ★ STEP
REAL NAME: KAZUHO HANEYAMA
A self-styled freelance idol who gives impromptu live performances without the proper licensing or permits. She supports Koichi with her Quirk, Leap.
THE CRAWLER
REAL NAME: KOICHI HAIMAWARI
A college freshman. With his Slide and Glide Quirk, this good-natured young man initially ventured into the world of vigilantism under the moniker "Nice Guy."

CHARACTERS

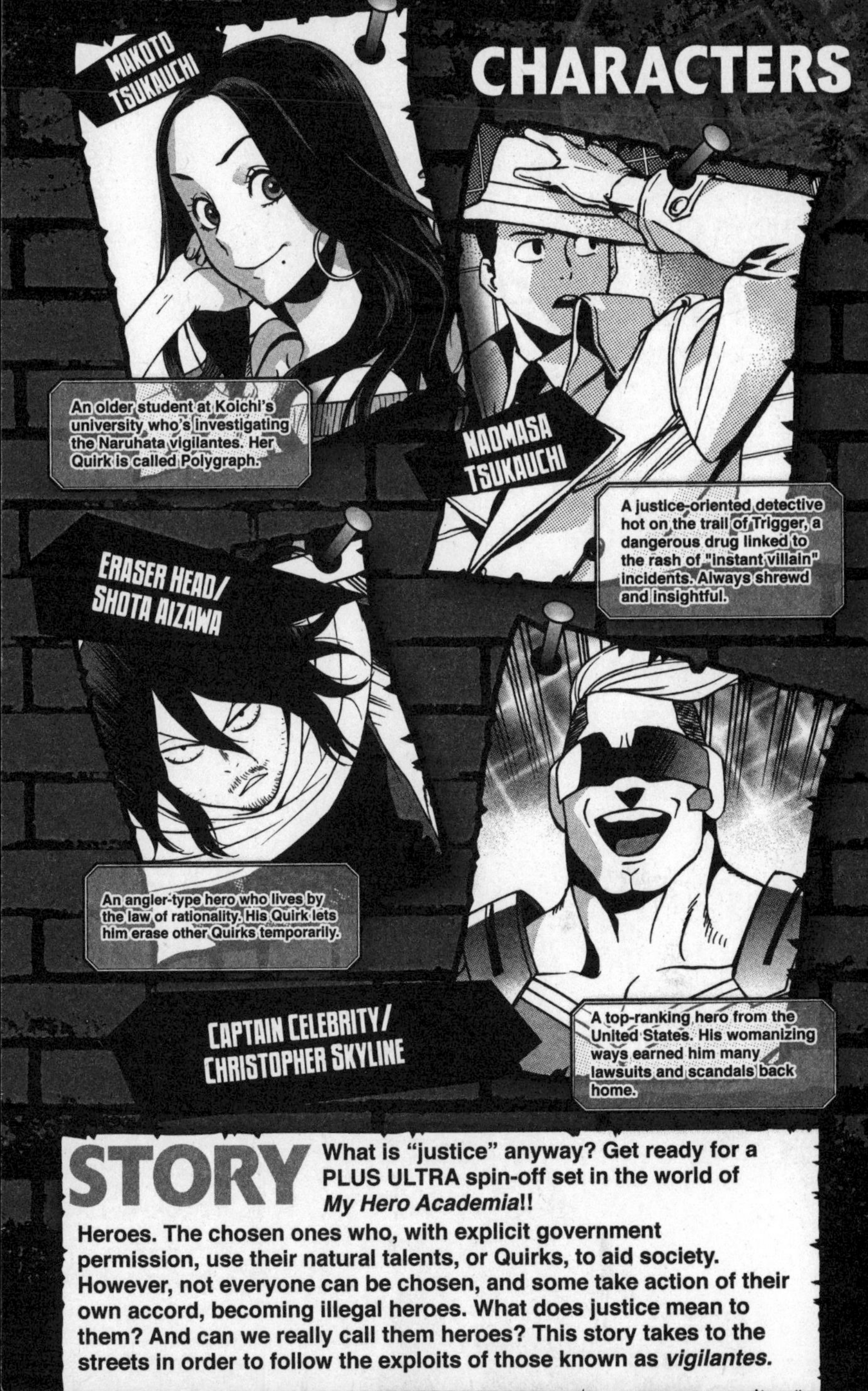

MAKOTO TSUKAUCHI
An older student at Koichi's university who's investigating the Naruhata vigilantes. Her Quirk is called Polygraph.
NAOMASA TSUKAUCHI
A justice-oriented detective hot on the trail of Trigger, a dangerous drug linked to the rash of "instant villain" incidents. Always shrewd and insightful.
ERASER HEAD/ SHOTA AIZAWA
An angler-type hero who lives by the law of rationality. His Quirk lets him erase other Quirks temporarily.
CAPTAIN CELEBRITY/ CHRISTOPHER SKYLINE
A top-ranking hero from the United States. His womanizing ways earned him many lawsuits and scandals back home.

STORY

What is "justice" anyway? Get ready for a PLUS ULTRA spin-off set in the world of *My Hero Academia*!!

Heroes. The chosen ones who, with explicit government permission, use their natural talents, or Quirks, to aid society. However, not everyone can be chosen, and some take action of their own accord, becoming illegal heroes. What does justice mean to them? And can we really call them heroes? This story takes to the streets in order to follow the exploits of those known as *vigilantes*.

MY HERO ACADEMIA VIGILANTES

5

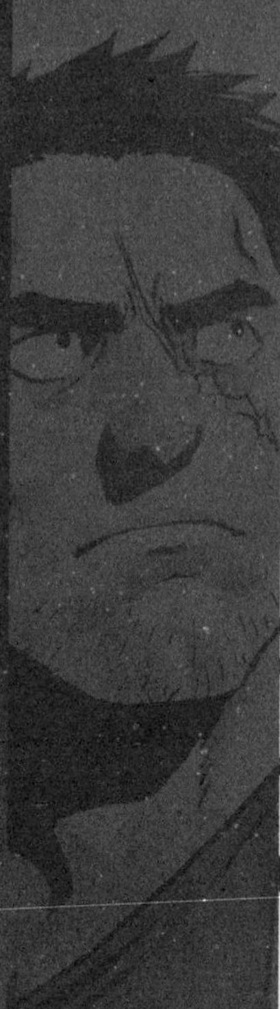

CONTENTS

Ep. 27 - Business as Usual

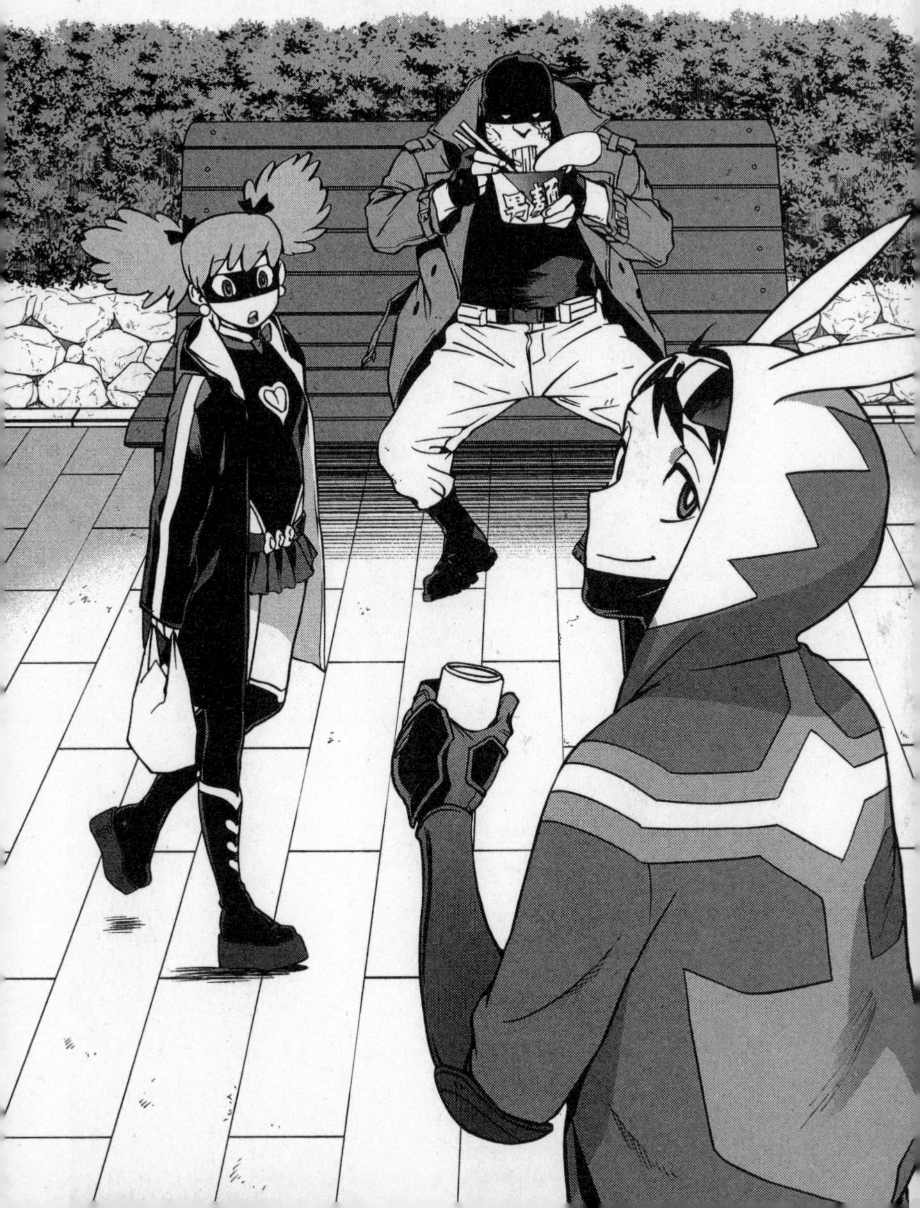

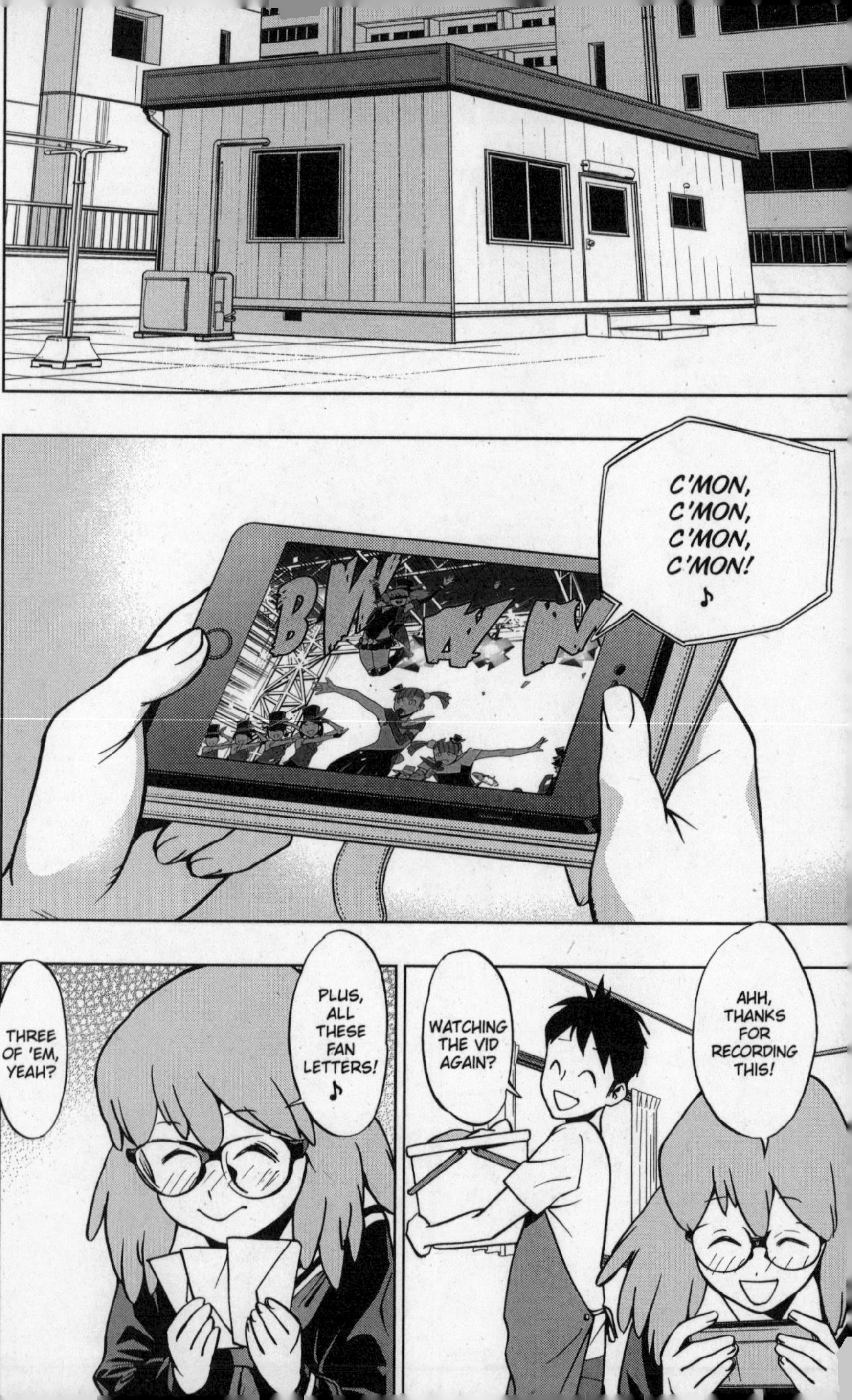
C'MON, C'MON, C'MON, C'MON! ♪
AHH, THANKS FOR RECORDING THIS!
WATCHING THE VID AGAIN?
PLUS, ALL THESE FAN LETTERS! ♪
THREE OF 'EM, YEAH?

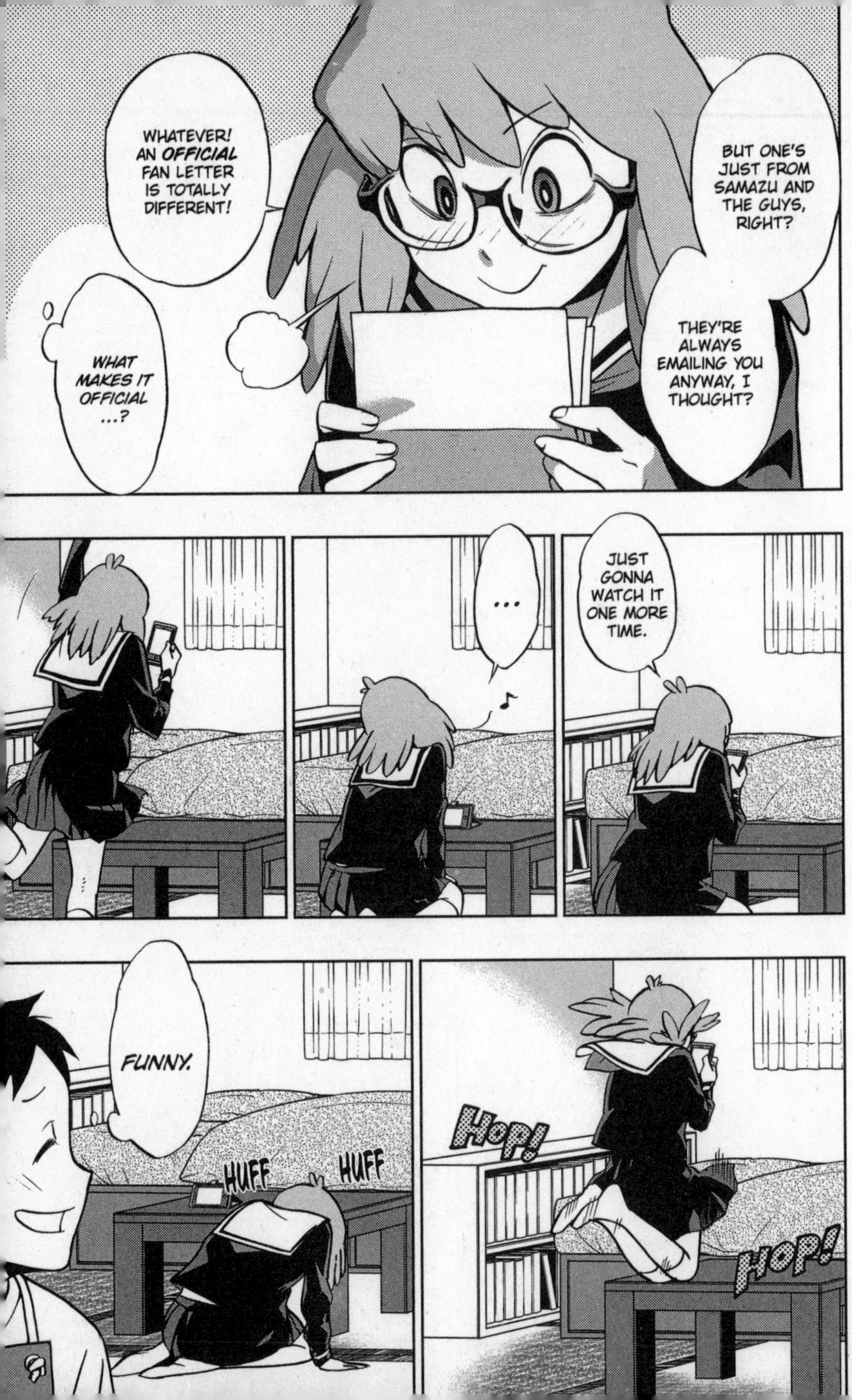
BUT ONE'S JUST FROM SAMAZU AND THE GUYS, RIGHT?
THEY'RE ALWAYS EMAILING YOU ANYWAY, I THOUGHT?
WHATEVER! AN *OFFICIAL* FAN LETTER IS TOTALLY DIFFERENT!
WHAT MAKES IT OFFICIAL ...?
JUST GONNA WATCH IT ONE MORE TIME.
...
HOP!
HOP!
FUNNY.
HUFF
HUFF

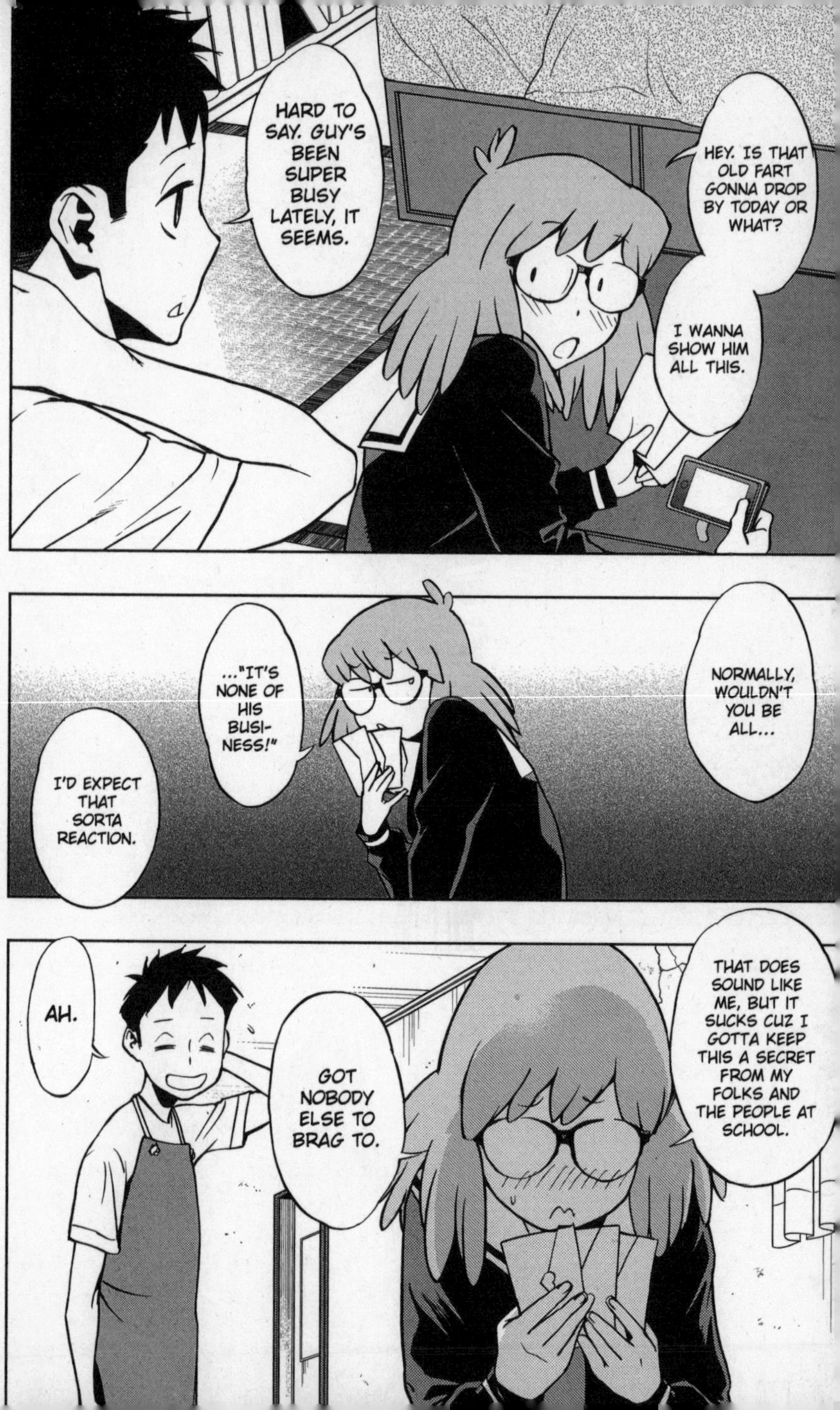
HEY. IS THAT OLD FART GONNA DROP BY TODAY OR WHAT?
I WANNA SHOW HIM ALL THIS.
HARD TO SAY. GUY'S BEEN SUPER BUSY LATELY, IT SEEMS.
NORMALLY, WOULDN'T YOU BE ALL...
..."IT'S NONE OF HIS BUSI-NESS!"
I'D EXPECT THAT SORTA REACTION.
THAT DOES SOUND LIKE ME, BUT IT SUCKS CUZ I GOTTA KEEP THIS A SECRET FROM MY FOLKS AND THE PEOPLE AT SCHOOL.
GOT NOBODY ELSE TO BRAG TO.
AH.

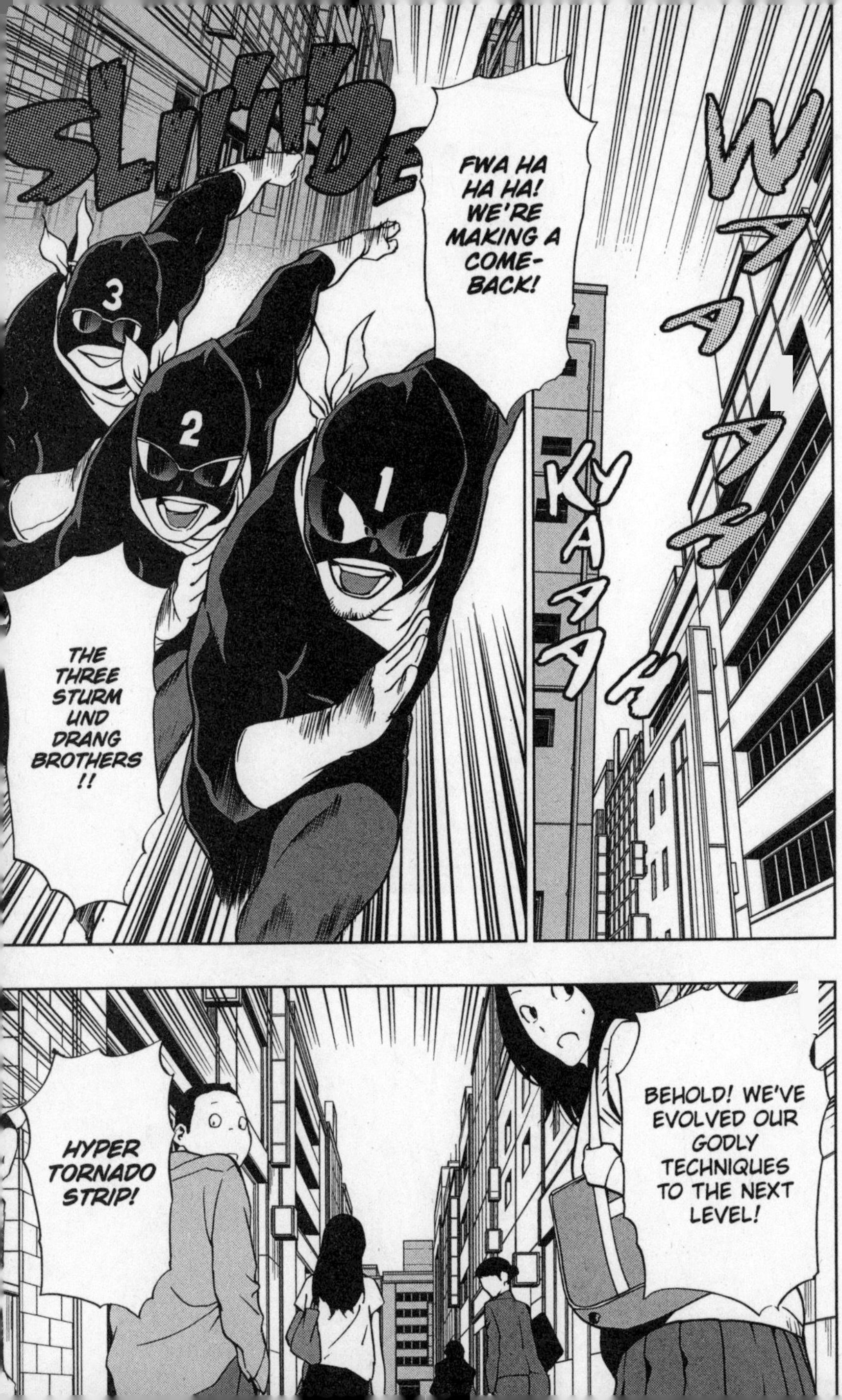
WAAAH
KYAAAH
SLIIIDE
FWA HA HA HA! WE'RE MAKING A COME-BACK!
THE THREE STURM UND DRANG BROTHERS !!
BEHOLD! WE'VE EVOLVED OUR GODLY TECHNIQUES TO THE NEXT LEVEL!
HYPER TORNADO STRIP!

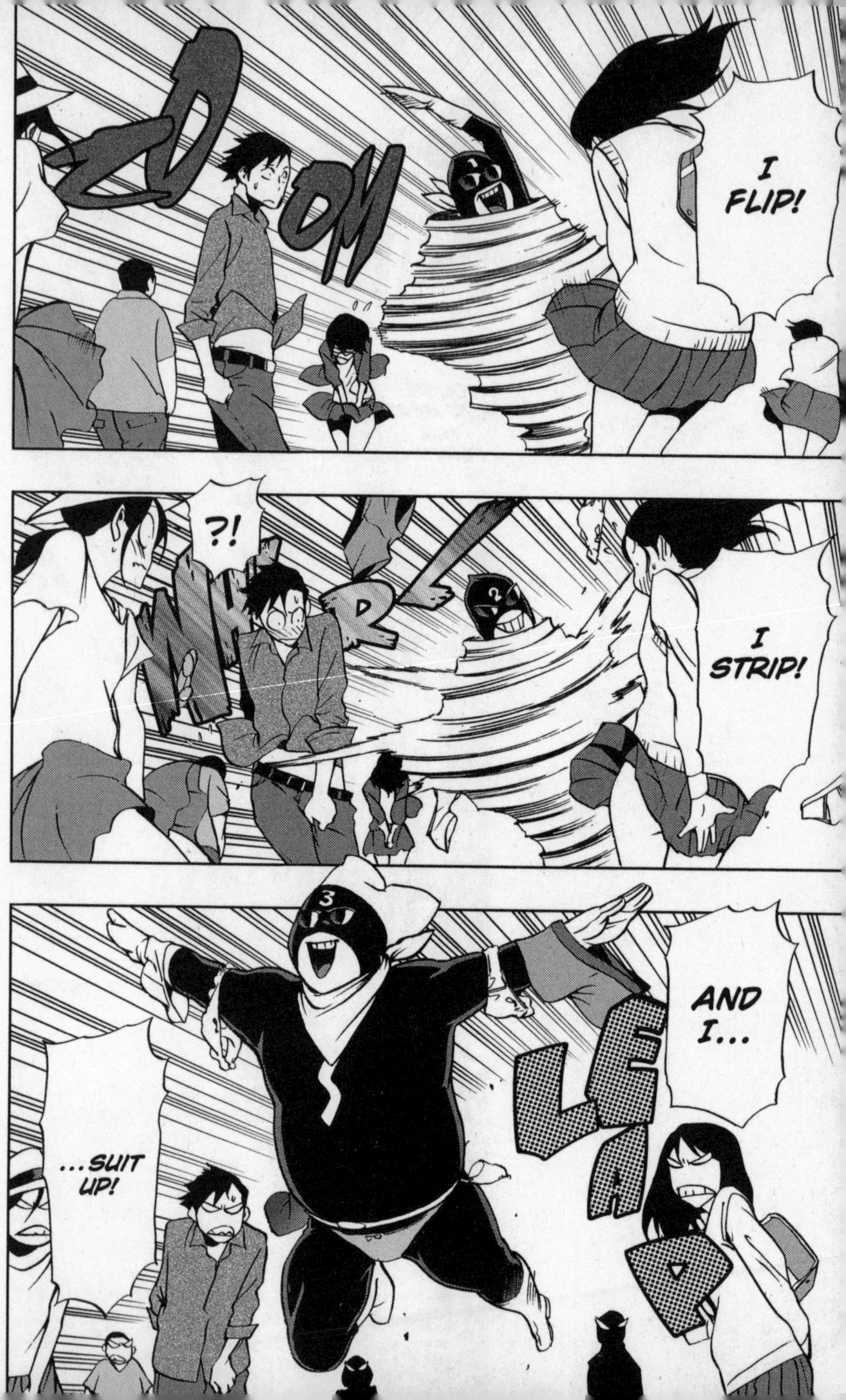
I FLIP!
ZOOM
I STRIP!
?!
AND I...
LEAP
...SUIT UP!

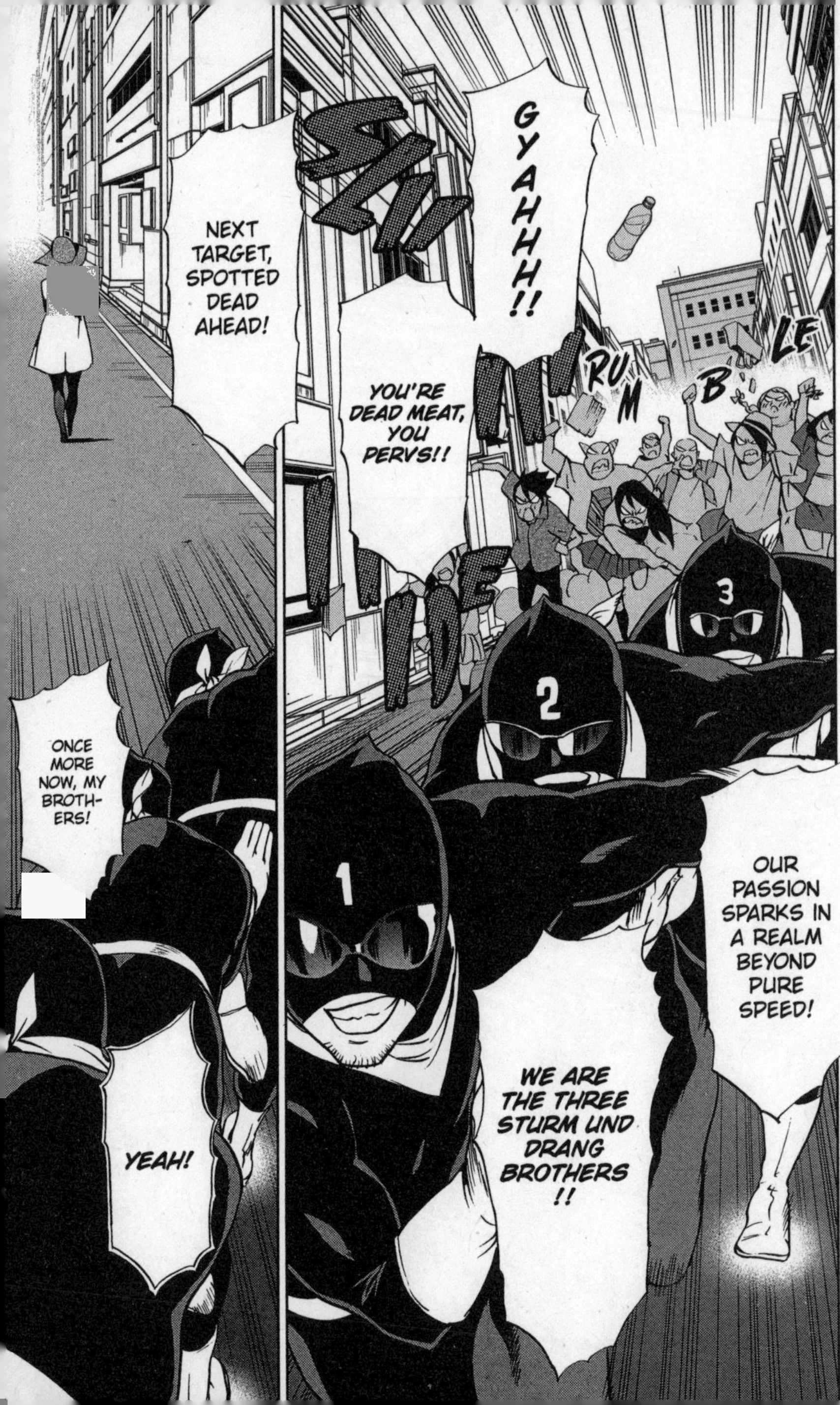
GYAHHHH!!
SHH
RUMBLE
YOU'RE DEAD MEAT, YOU PERVS!!
OUR PASSION SPARKS IN A REALM BEYOND PURE SPEED!
WE ARE THE THREE STURM UND DRANG BROTHERS!!
NEXT TARGET, SPOTTED DEAD AHEAD!
ONCE MORE NOW, MY BROTH-ERS!
YEAH!

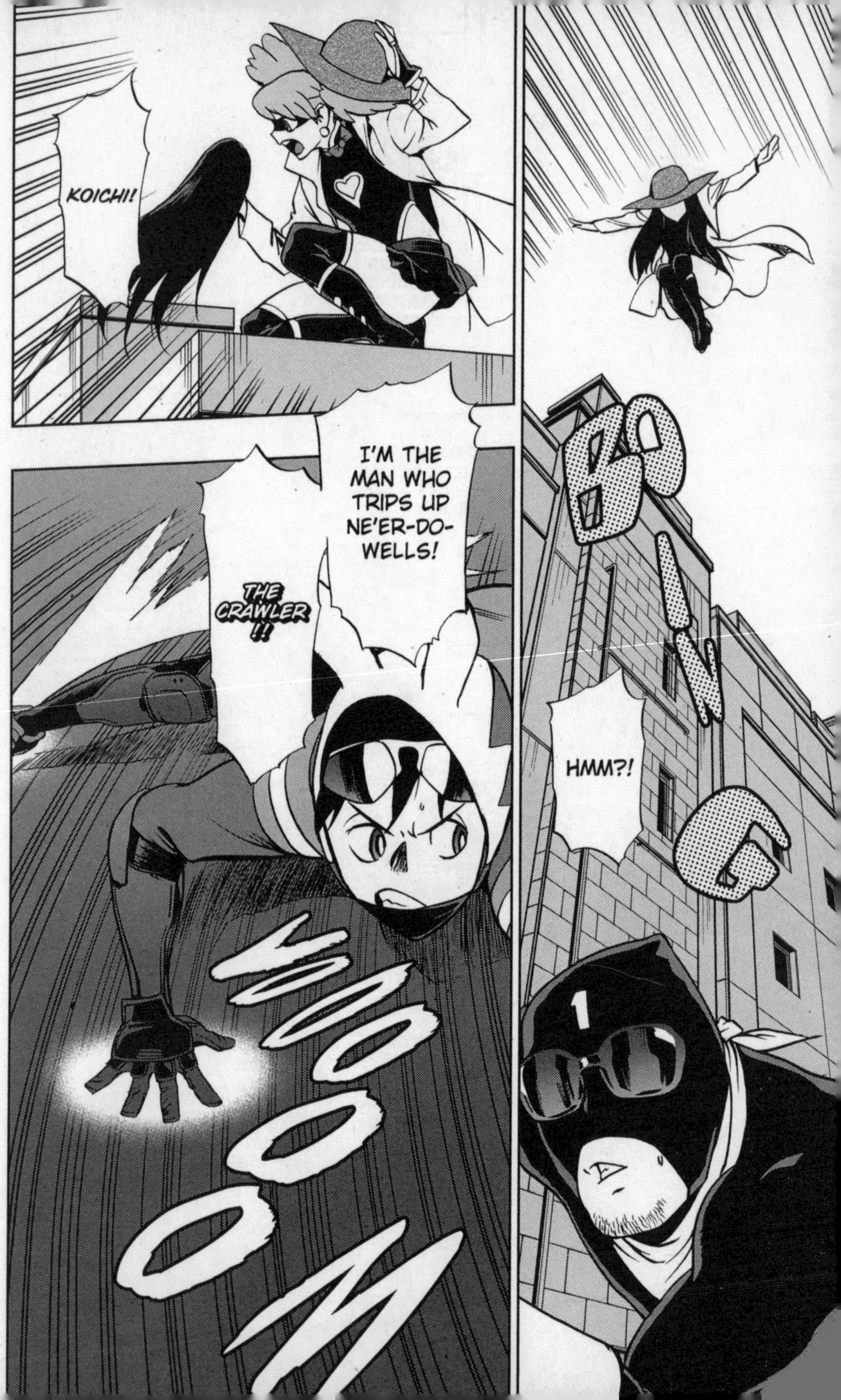
KOICHI!
BOING
HMM?!
I'M THE MAN WHO TRIPS UP NE'ER-DO-WELLS!
THE CRAWLER!!

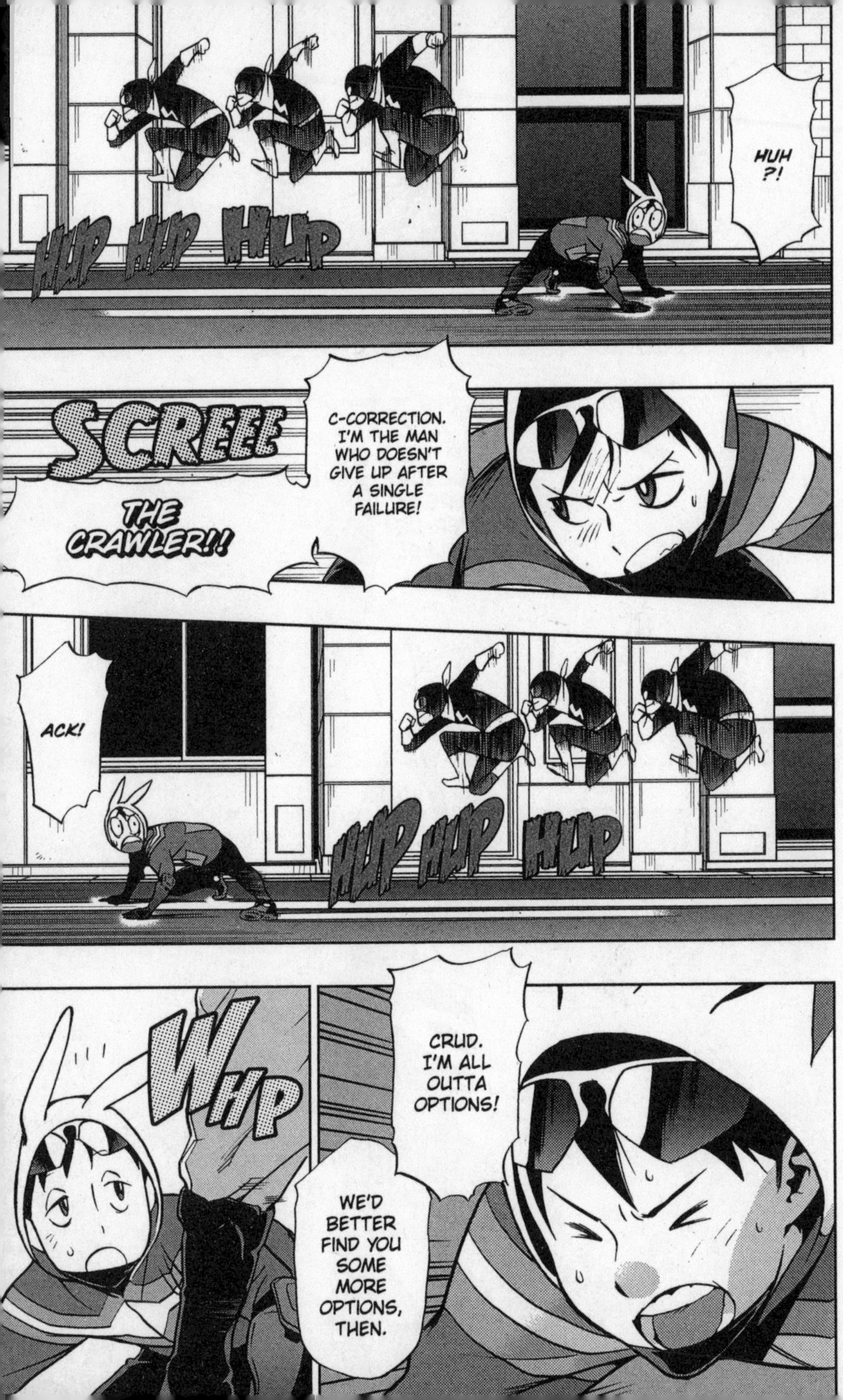
HUH ?!
HUP HUP HUP
C-CORRECTION. I'M THE MAN WHO DOESN'T GIVE UP AFTER A SINGLE FAILURE!
SCREEE
THE CRAWLER!!
HUP HUP HUP
ACK!
CRUD. I'M ALL OUTTA OPTIONS!
WHIP
WE'D BETTER FIND YOU SOME MORE OPTIONS, THEN.

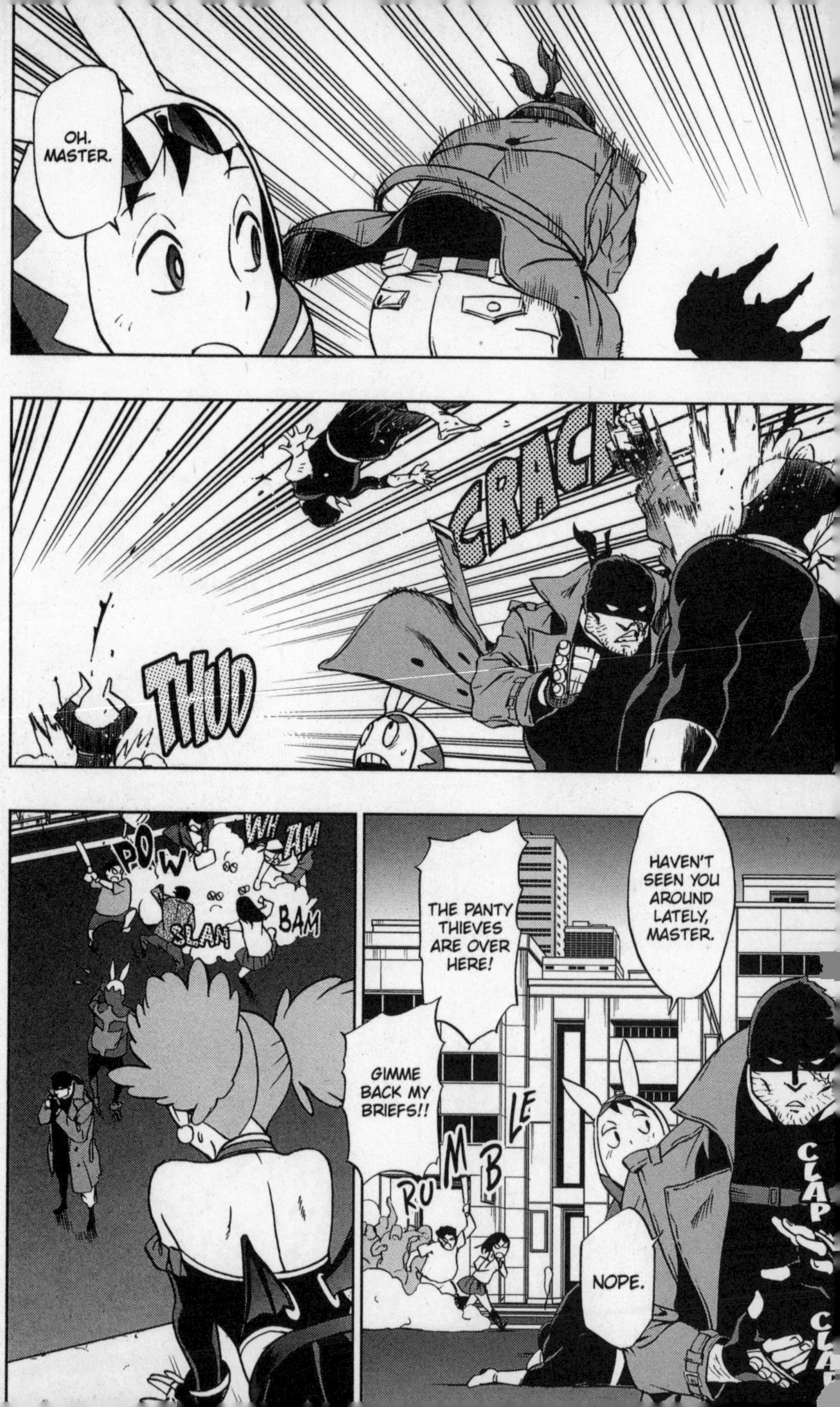
OH. MASTER.
CRACK
THUD
HAVEN'T SEEN YOU AROUND LATELY, MASTER.
CLAP
THE PANTY THIEVES ARE OVER HERE!
GIMME BACK MY BRIEFS!!
RUMBLE
NOPE.
CLAP
WHAM
POW
BAM
SLAM

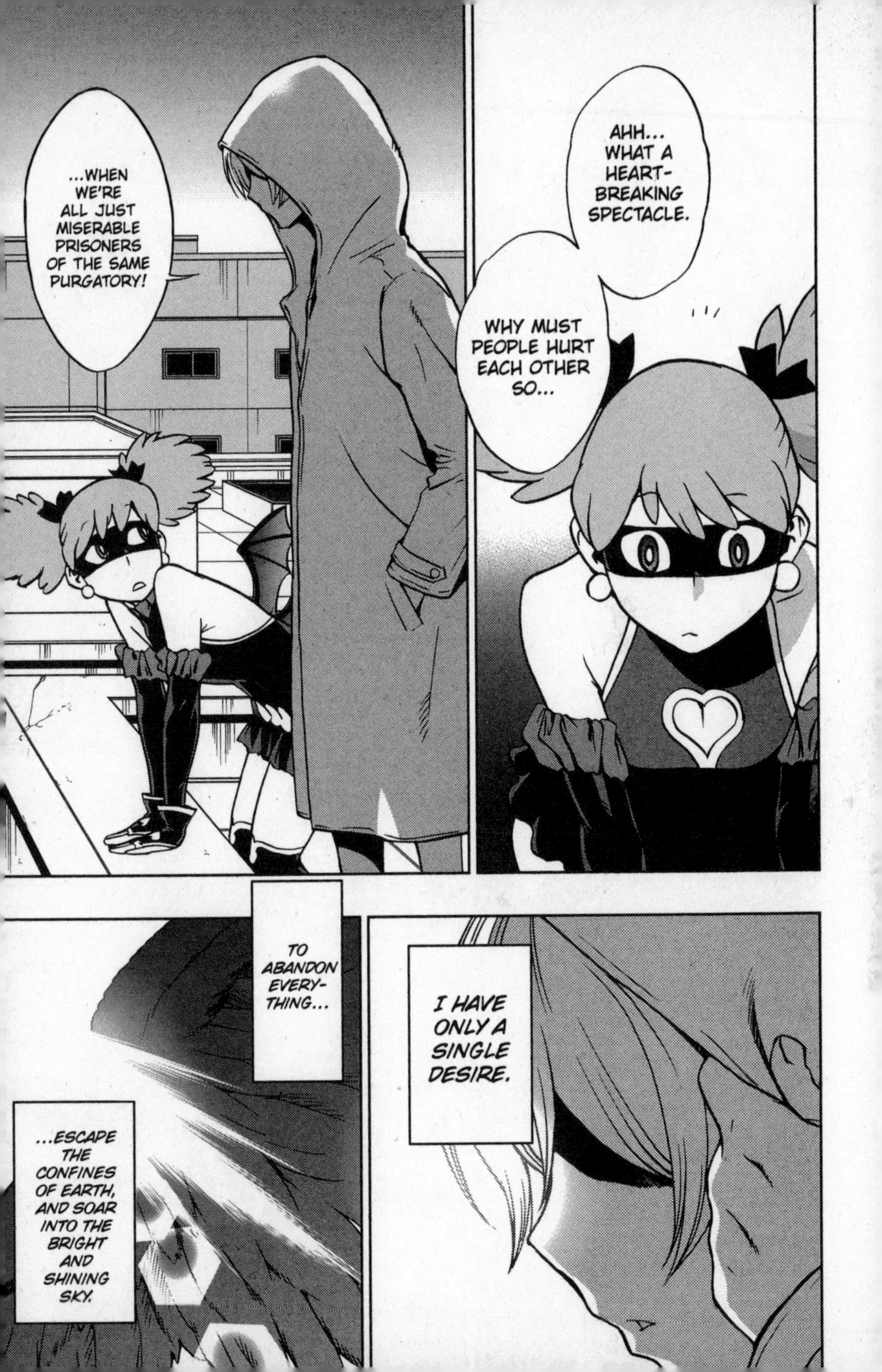
AHH... WHAT A HEART-BREAKING SPECTACLE.
WHY MUST PEOPLE HURT EACH OTHER SO...
...WHEN WE'RE ALL JUST MISERABLE PRISONERS OF THE SAME PURGATORY!
I HAVE ONLY A SINGLE DESIRE.
TO ABANDON EVERY-THING...
...ESCAPE THE CONFINES OF EARTH, AND SOAR INTO THE BRIGHT AND SHINING SKY.

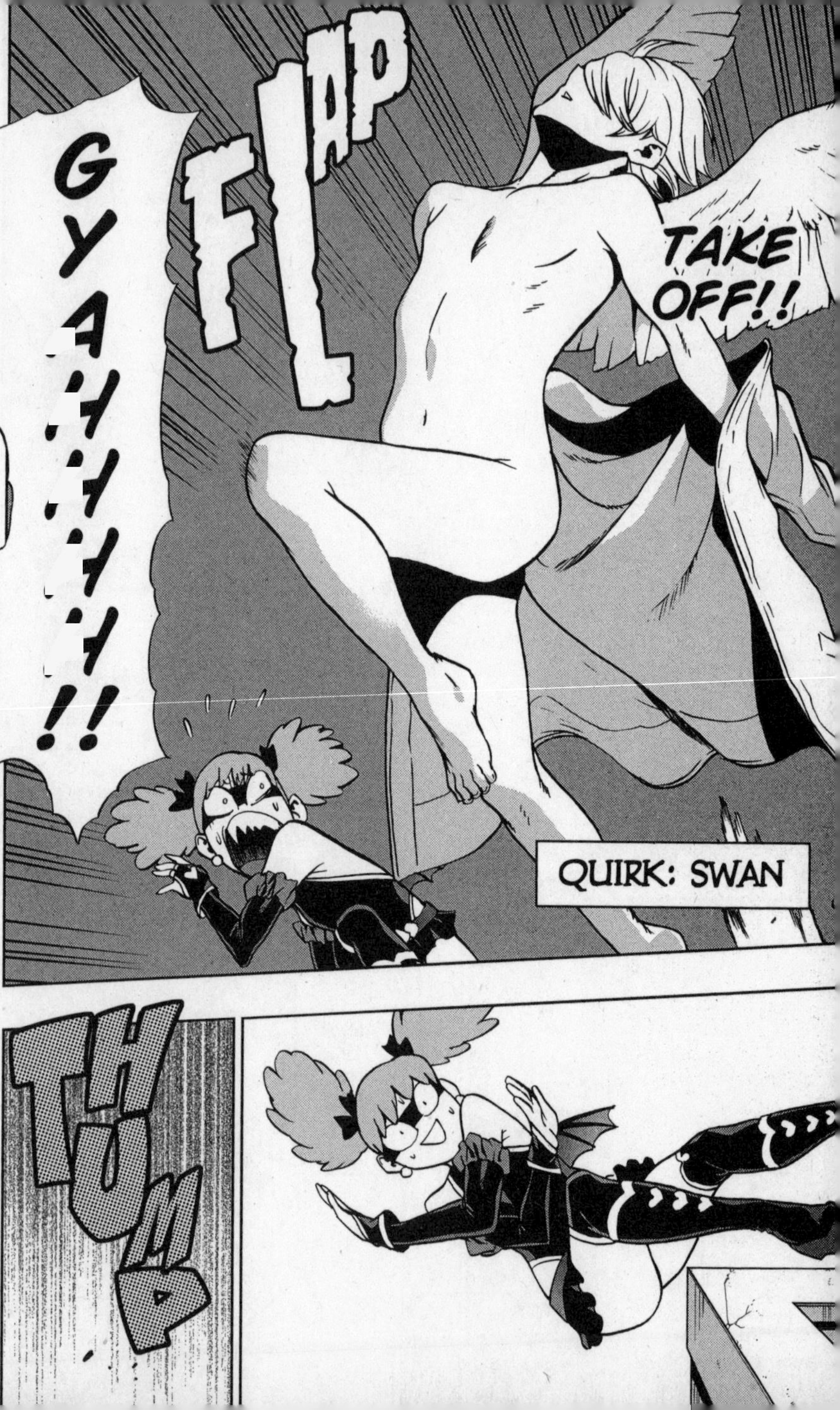
TAKE OFF!!
QUIRK: SWAN
FLAP
GYAHHHHH!!
THUMP

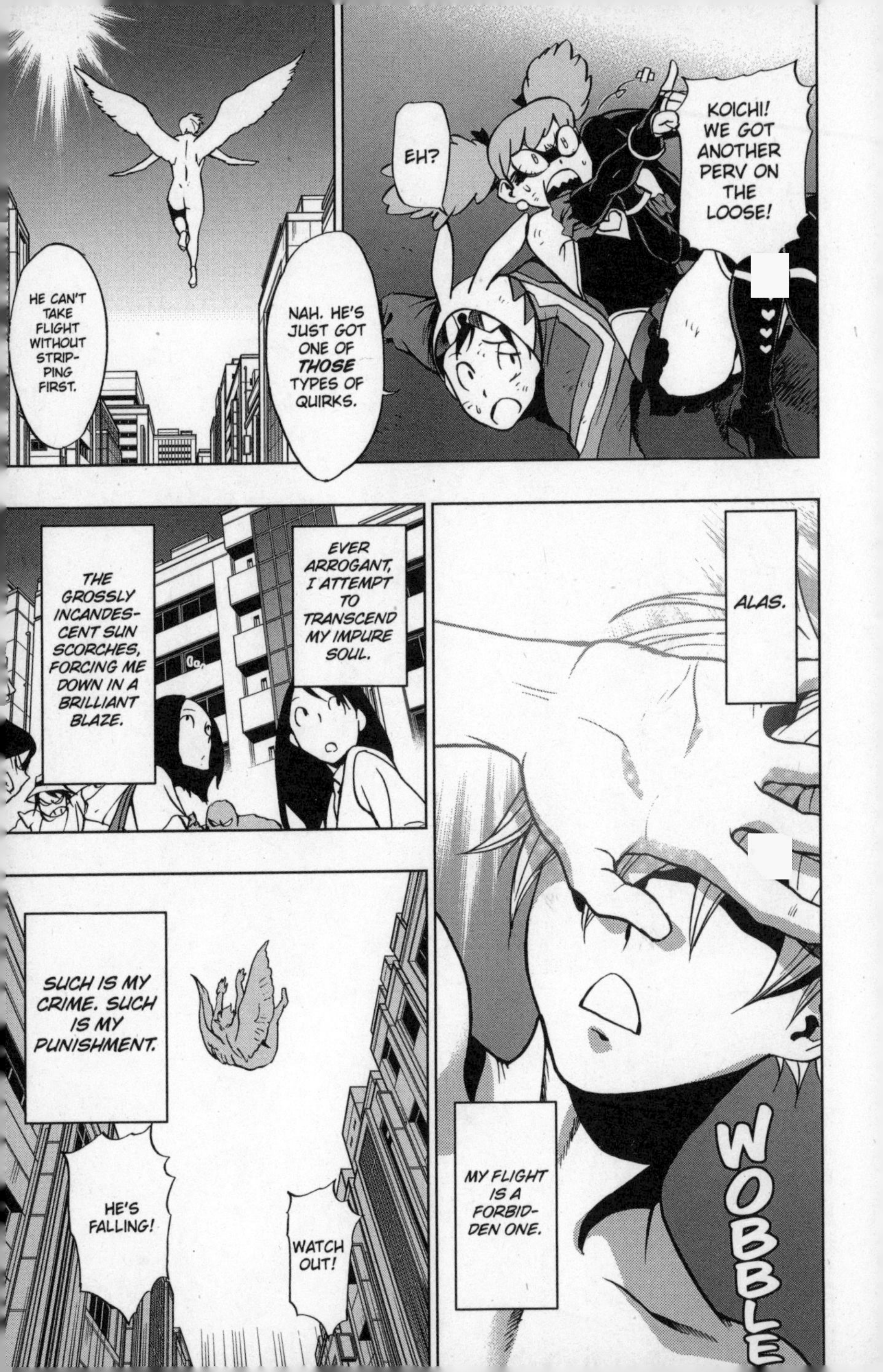
KOICHI! WE GOT ANOTHER PERV ON THE LOOSE!
EH?
NAH. HE'S JUST GOT ONE OF *THOSE* TYPES OF QUIRKS.
HE CAN'T TAKE FLIGHT WITHOUT STRIP-PING FIRST.
ALAS.
WOBBLE
MY FLIGHT IS A FORBID-DEN ONE.
EVER ARROGANT, I ATTEMPT TO TRANSCEND MY IMPURE SOUL.
THE GROSSLY INCANDES-CENT SUN SCORCHES, FORCING ME DOWN IN A BRILLIANT BLAZE.
SUCH IS MY CRIME. SUCH IS MY PUNISHMENT.
HE'S FALLING!
WATCH OUT!

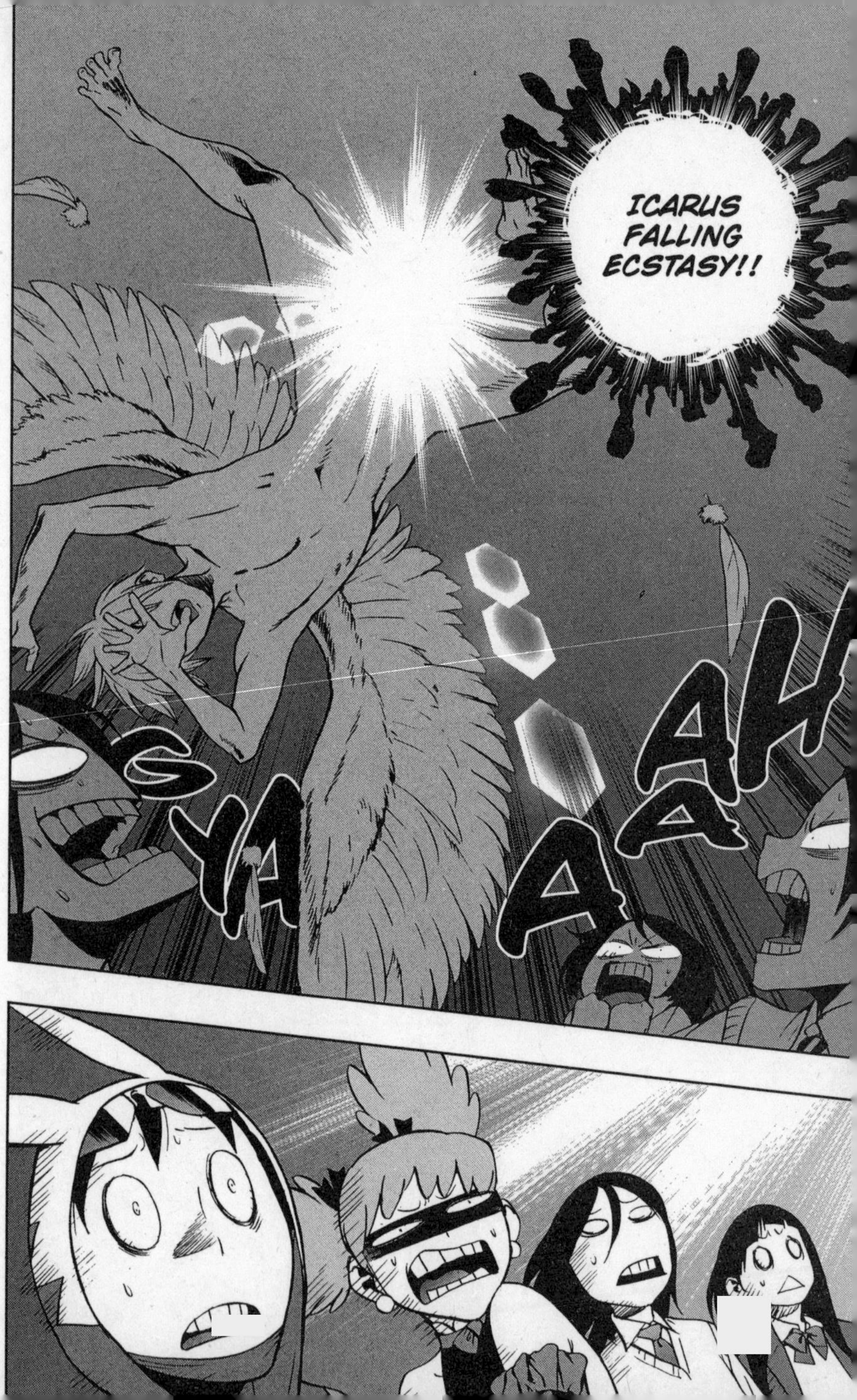
ICARUS FALLING ECSTASY!!
GYAAAAAH

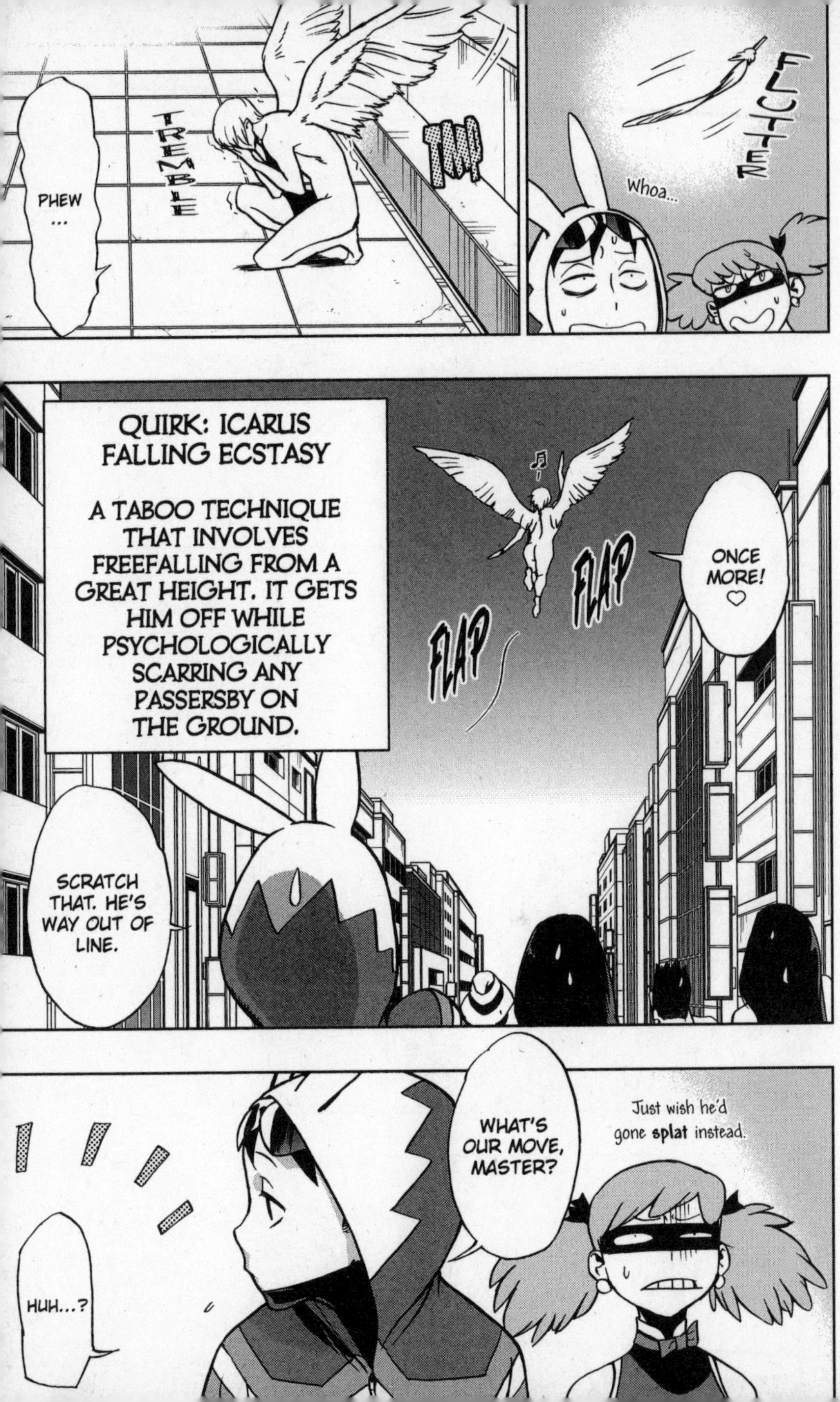
FLUTTER
Whoa...
TMP
TREMBLE
PHEW...
ONCE MORE! ♡
FLAP
FLAP
QUIRK: ICARUS FALLING ECSTASY
A TABOO TECHNIQUE THAT INVOLVES FREEFALLING FROM A GREAT HEIGHT. IT GETS HIM OFF WHILE PSYCHOLOGICALLY SCARRING ANY PASSERSBY ON THE GROUND.
SCRATCH THAT. HE'S WAY OUT OF LINE.
Just wish he'd gone splat instead.
WHAT'S OUR MOVE, MASTER?
HUH...?

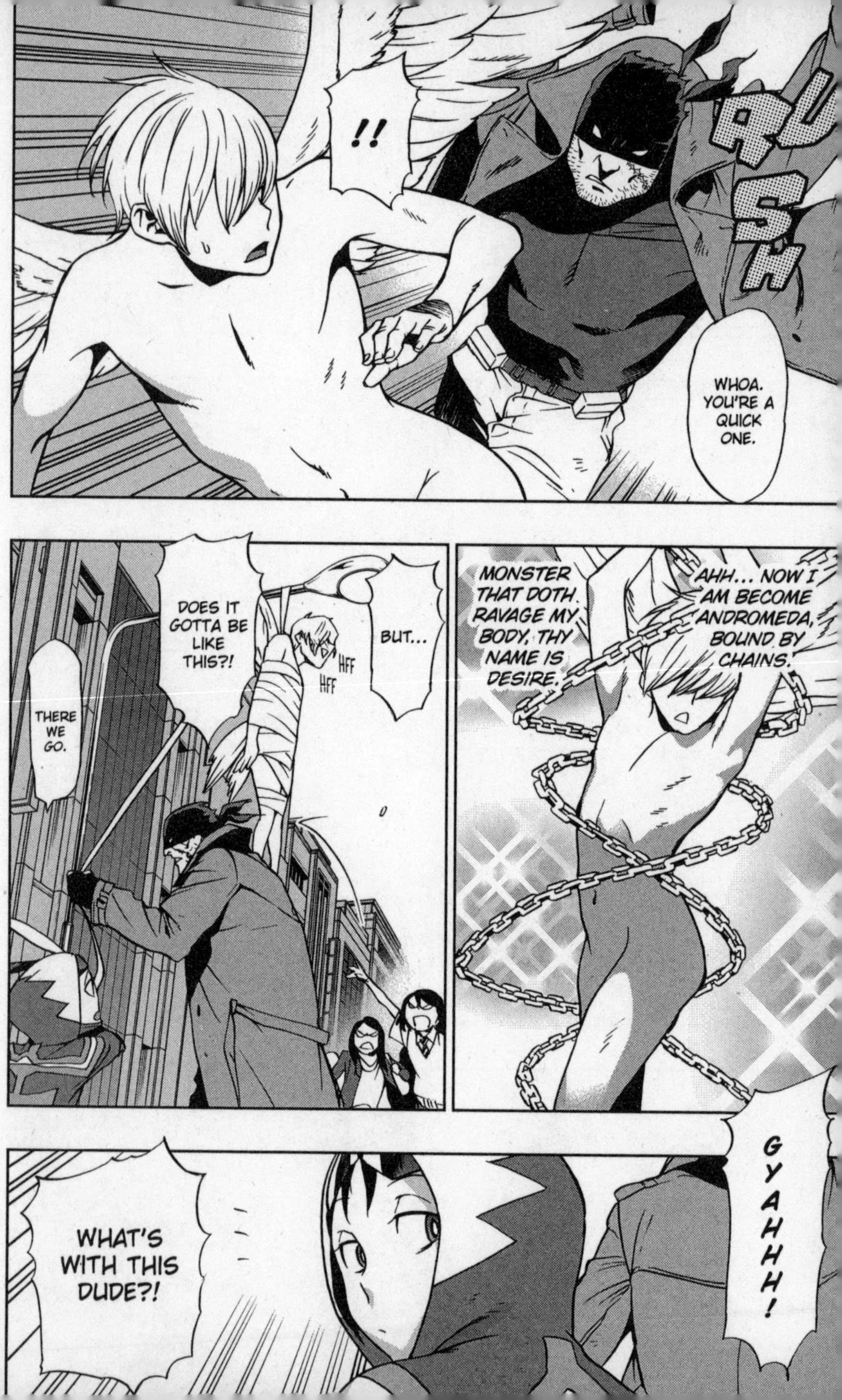
RUSH
!!
WHOA. YOU'RE A QUICK ONE.
AHH... NOW I AM BECOME ANDROMEDA, BOUND BY CHAINS.
MONSTER THAT DOTH RAVAGE MY BODY, THY NAME IS DESIRE.
BUT...
DOES IT GOTTA BE LIKE THIS?!
HFF HFF
THERE WE GO.
GYAHHH!
WHAT'S WITH THIS DUDE?!

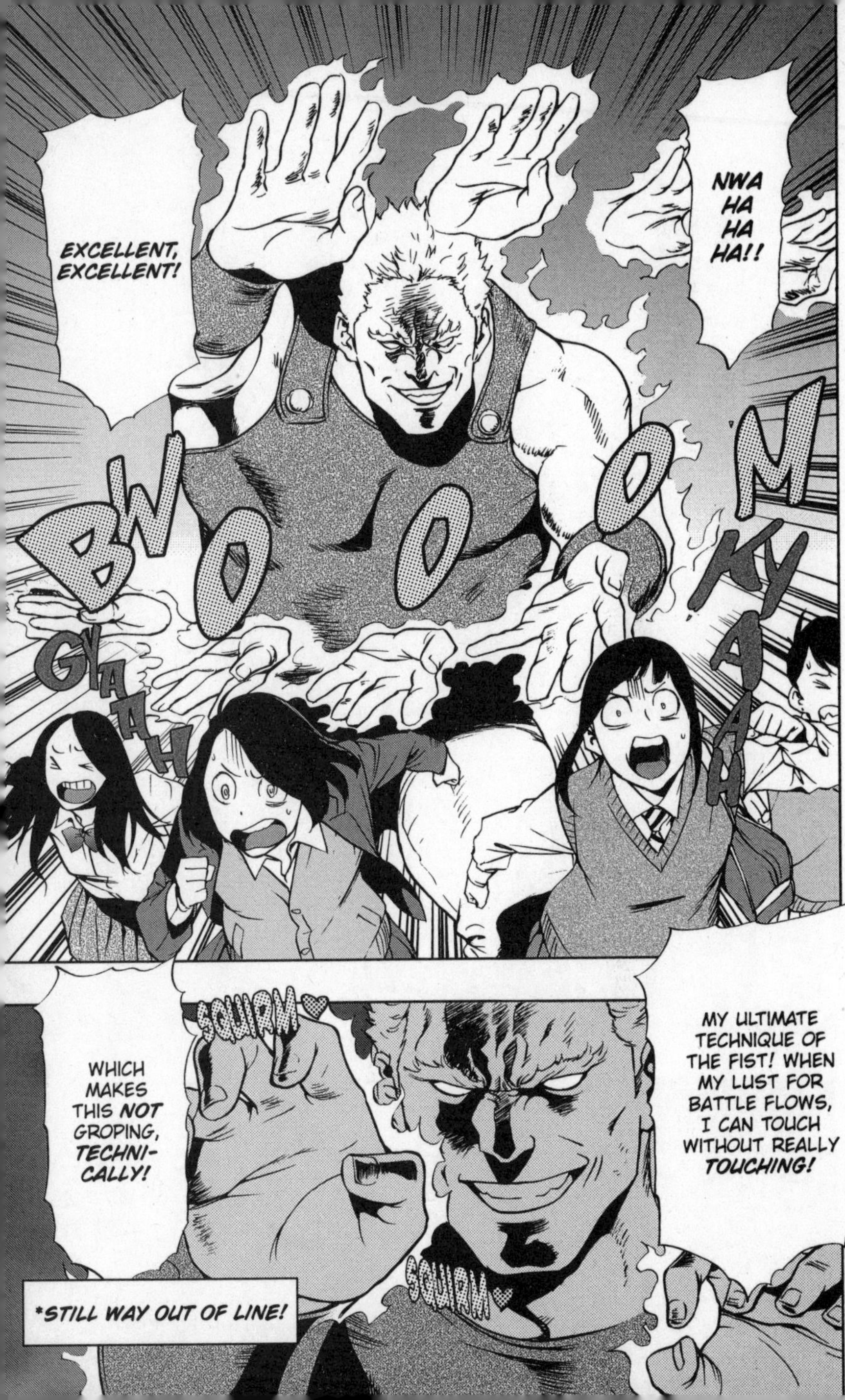
NWA HA HA HA!!
EXCELLENT, EXCELLENT!
BWOOOM
KYAAAH
GYAAAH
MY ULTIMATE TECHNIQUE OF THE FIST! WHEN MY LUST FOR BATTLE FLOWS, I CAN TOUCH WITHOUT REALLY TOUCHING!
SQUIRM♥
WHICH MAKES THIS NOT GROPING, TECHNICALLY!
SQUIRM♥
*STILL WAY OUT OF LINE!

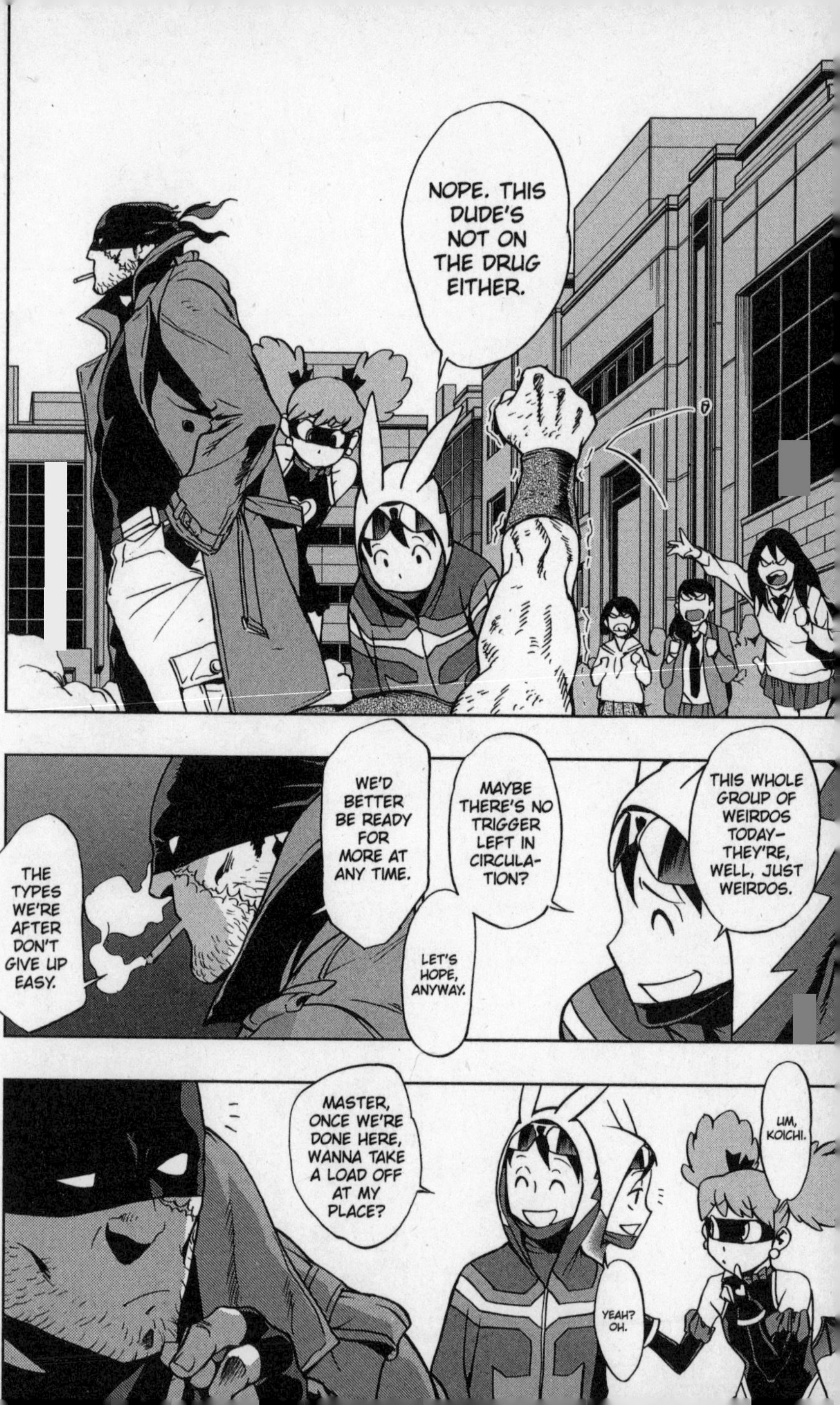
NOPE. THIS DUDE'S NOT ON THE DRUG EITHER.
THIS WHOLE GROUP OF WEIRDOS TODAY— THEY'RE, WELL, JUST WEIRDOS.
MAYBE THERE'S NO TRIGGER LEFT IN CIRCULA-TION?
LET'S HOPE, ANYWAY.
WE'D BETTER BE READY FOR MORE AT ANY TIME.
THE TYPES WE'RE AFTER DON'T GIVE UP EASY.
MASTER, ONCE WE'RE DONE HERE, WANNA TAKE A LOAD OFF AT MY PLACE?
UM, KOICHI.
YEAH? OH.

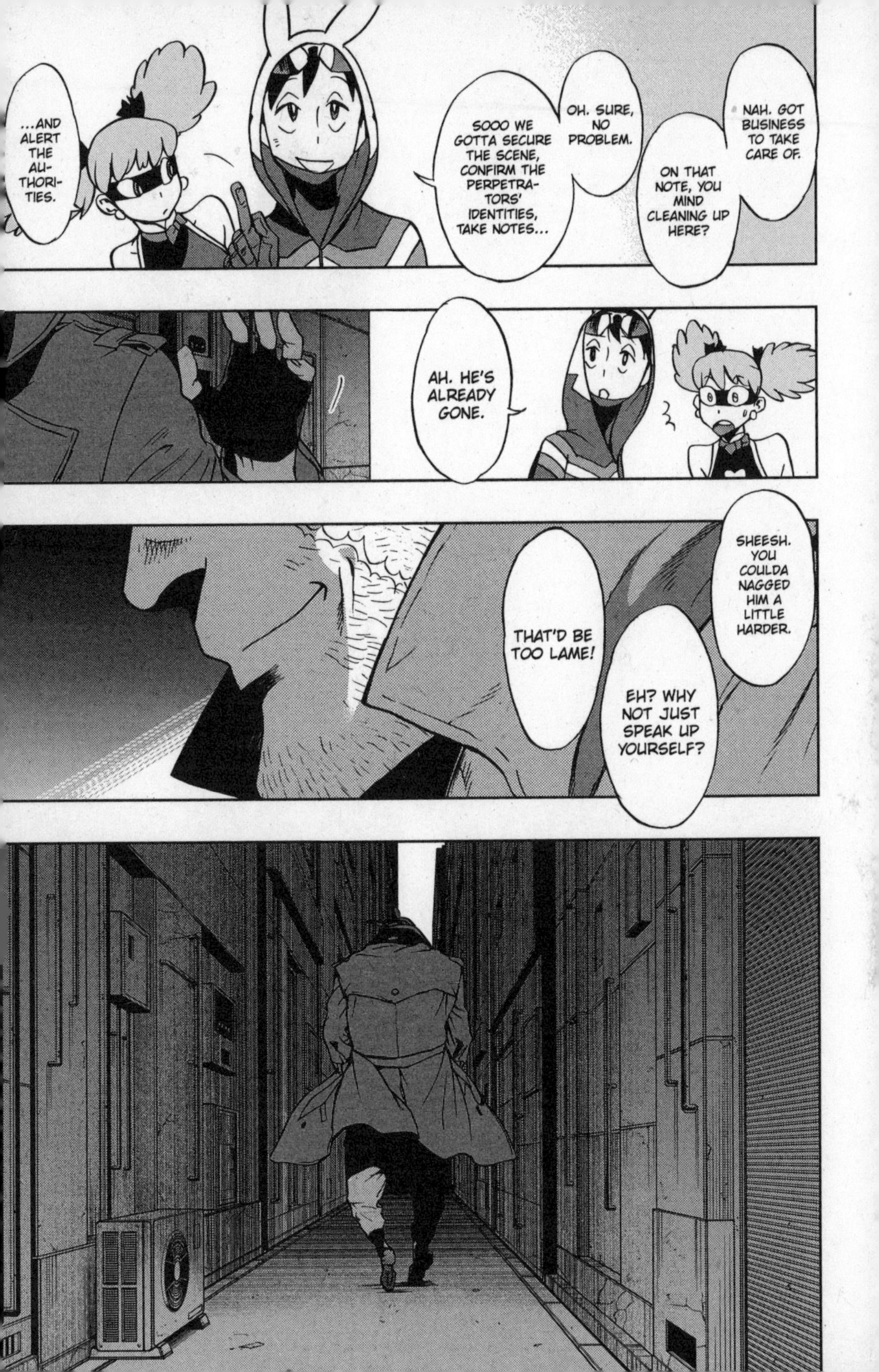
NAH. GOT BUSINESS TO TAKE CARE OF.
ON THAT NOTE, YOU MIND CLEANING UP HERE?
OH. SURE, NO PROBLEM.
SOOO WE GOTTA SECURE THE SCENE, CONFIRM THE PERPETRATORS' IDENTITIES, TAKE NOTES...
...AND ALERT THE AUTHORITIES.
AH. HE'S ALREADY GONE.
SHEESH. YOU COULDA NAGGED HIM A LITTLE HARDER.
EH? WHY NOT JUST SPEAK UP YOURSELF?
THAT'D BE TOO LAME!

THE COLUMN

MASTER AND KOICHI

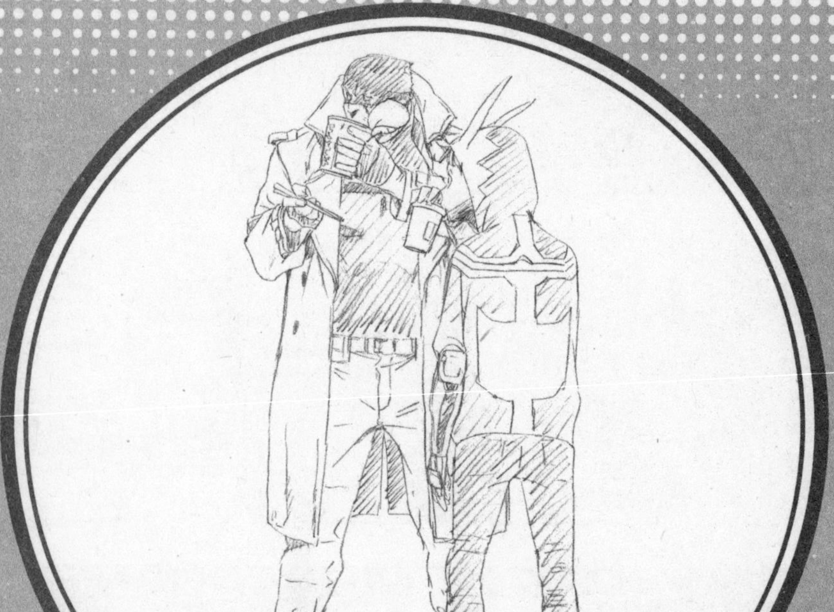

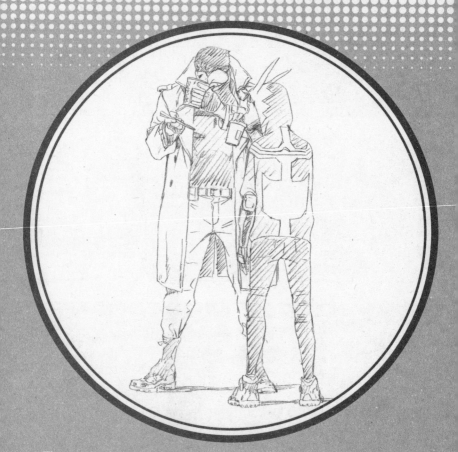

The so-called Team Vigilantes trio (Master, Koichi and Pop) struck a really nice balance, but that balance had to be rocked if Koichi was ever going to grow. With Master gone, there's no one to explain things, deal the finishing blow to enemies, etc., so while it feels like a big inconvenience plotwise, it also broadens the range of decisions that Koichi has to make.

—Furuhashi

Ep. 28 - What a Man Takes with Him

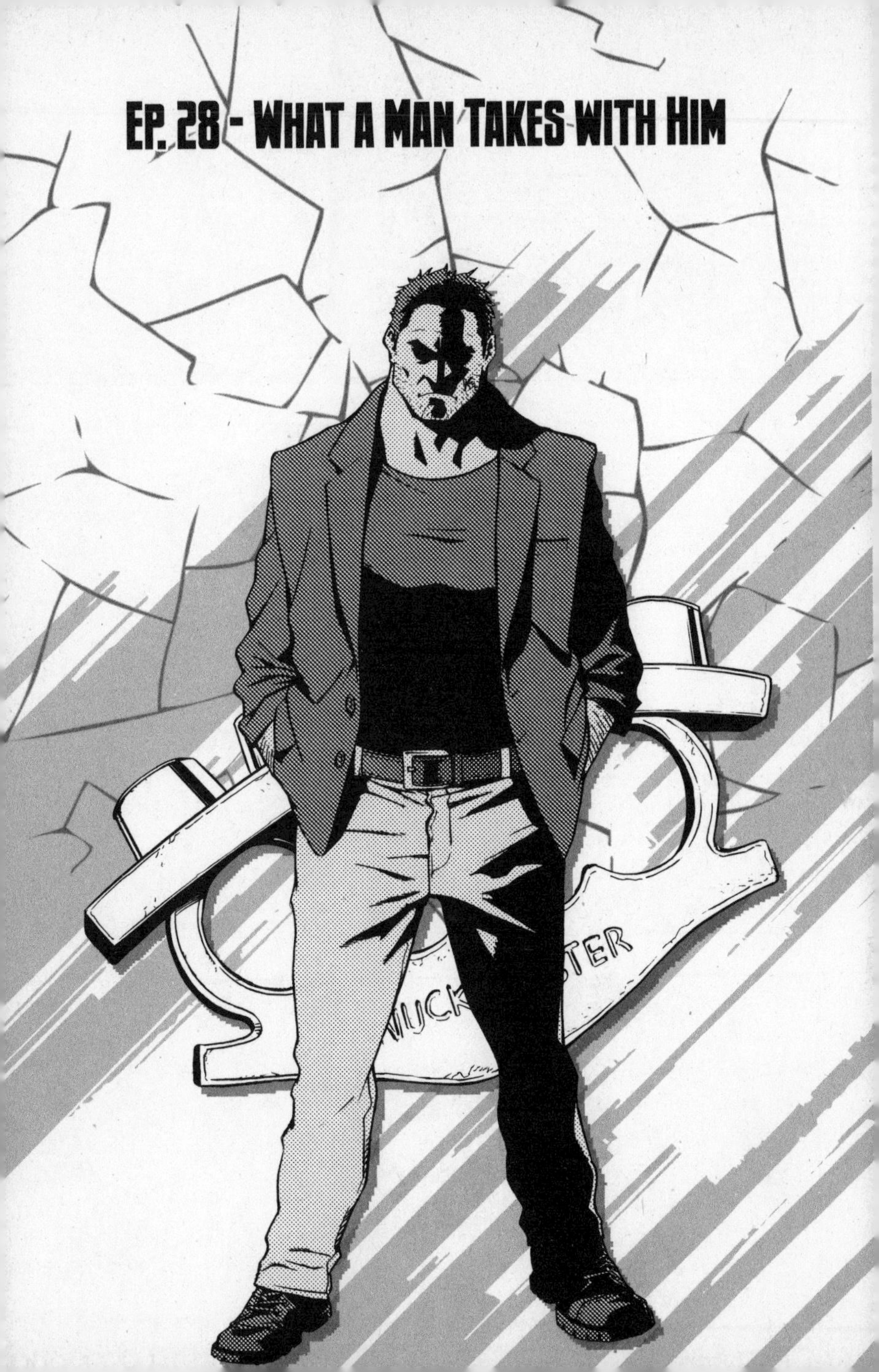

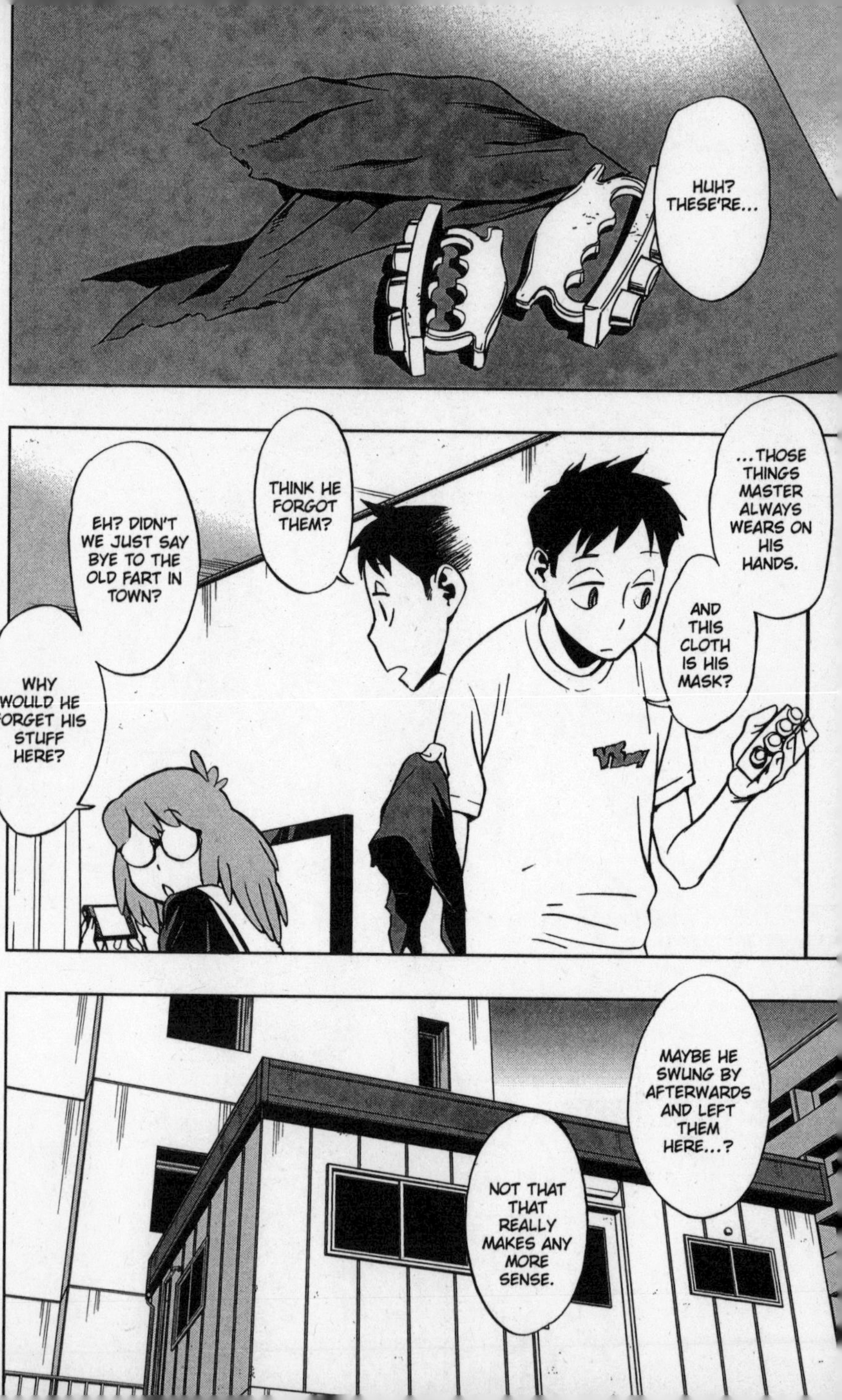
HUH? THESE'RE...
...THOSE THINGS MASTER ALWAYS WEARS ON HIS HANDS.
AND THIS CLOTH IS HIS MASK?
THINK HE FORGOT THEM?
EH? DIDN'T WE JUST SAY BYE TO THE OLD FART IN TOWN?
WHY WOULD HE FORGET HIS STUFF HERE?
MAYBE HE SWUNG BY AFTERWARDS AND LEFT THEM HERE...?
NOT THAT THAT REALLY MAKES ANY MORE SENSE.

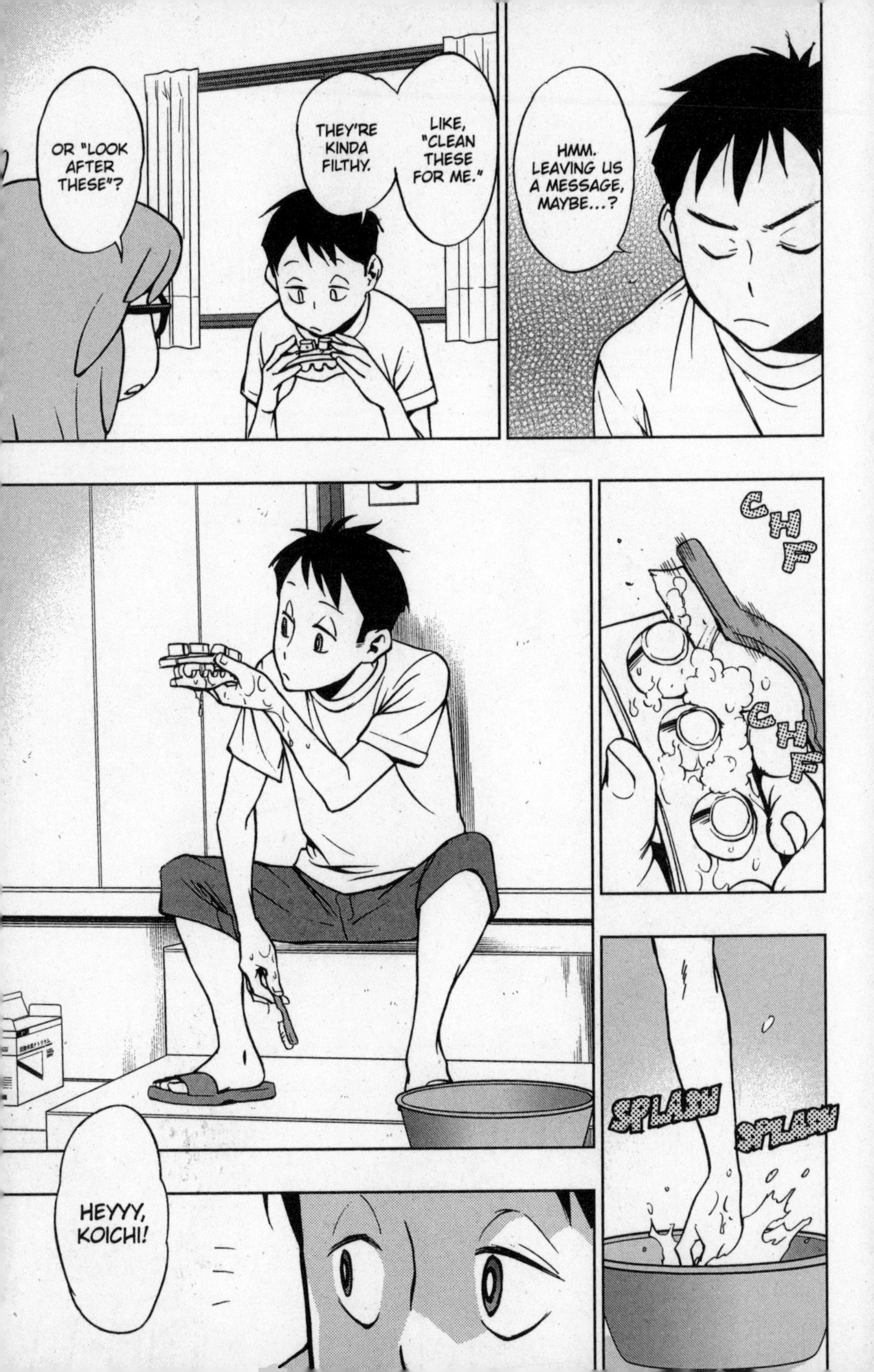
HMM. LEAVING US A MESSAGE, MAYBE...?
LIKE, "CLEAN THESE FOR ME."
THEY'RE KINDA FILTHY.
OR "LOOK AFTER THESE"?
CHF
CHF
SPLASH
SPLASH
HEYYY, KOICHI!

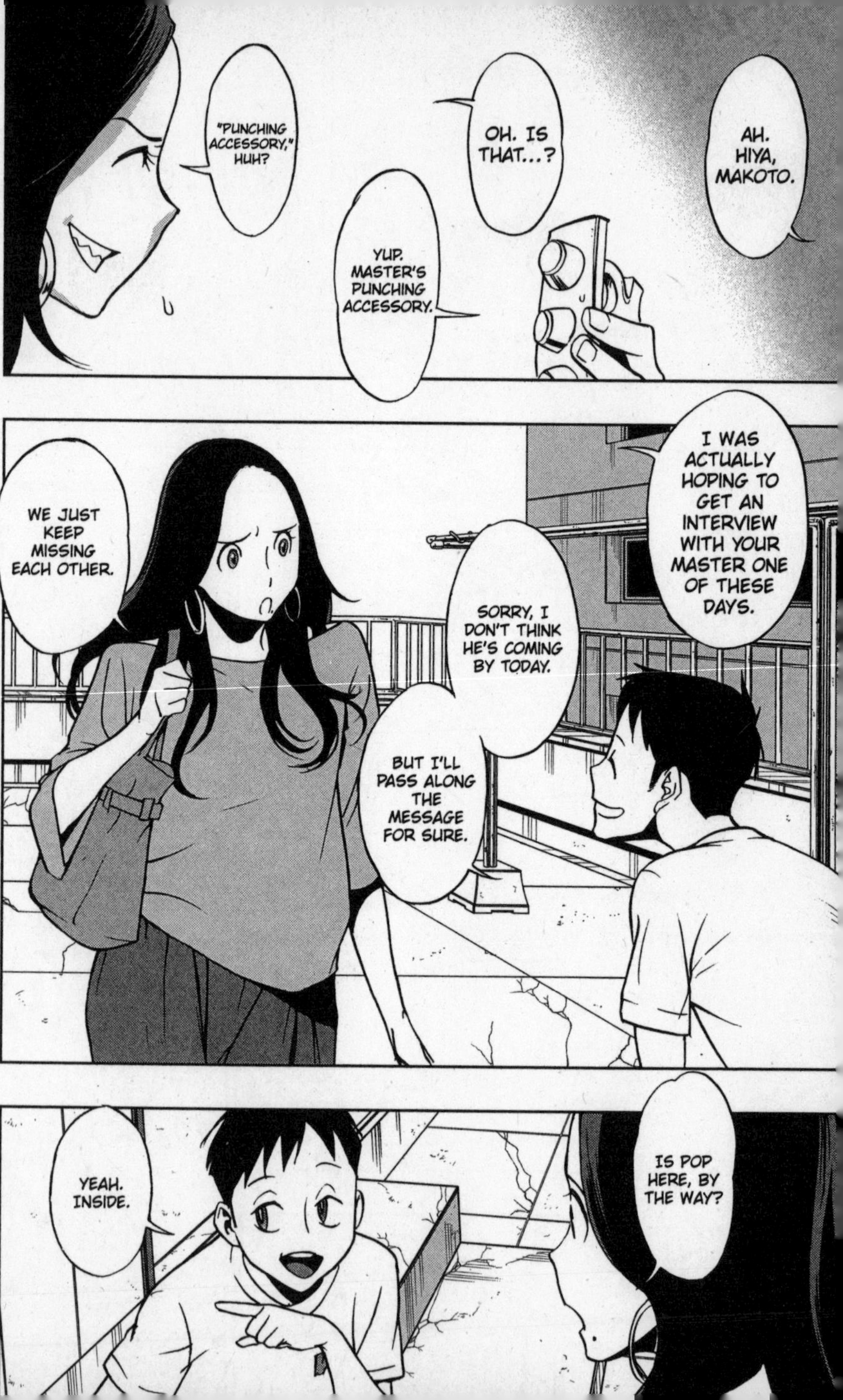
AH. HIYA, MAKOTO.
OH. IS THAT...?
YUP. MASTER'S PUNCHING ACCESSORY.
"PUNCHING ACCESSORY," HUH?
I WAS ACTUALLY HOPING TO GET AN INTERVIEW WITH YOUR MASTER ONE OF THESE DAYS.
SORRY, I DON'T THINK HE'S COMING BY TODAY.
BUT I'LL PASS ALONG THE MESSAGE FOR SURE.
WE JUST KEEP MISSING EACH OTHER.
IS POP HERE, BY THE WAY?
YEAH. INSIDE.

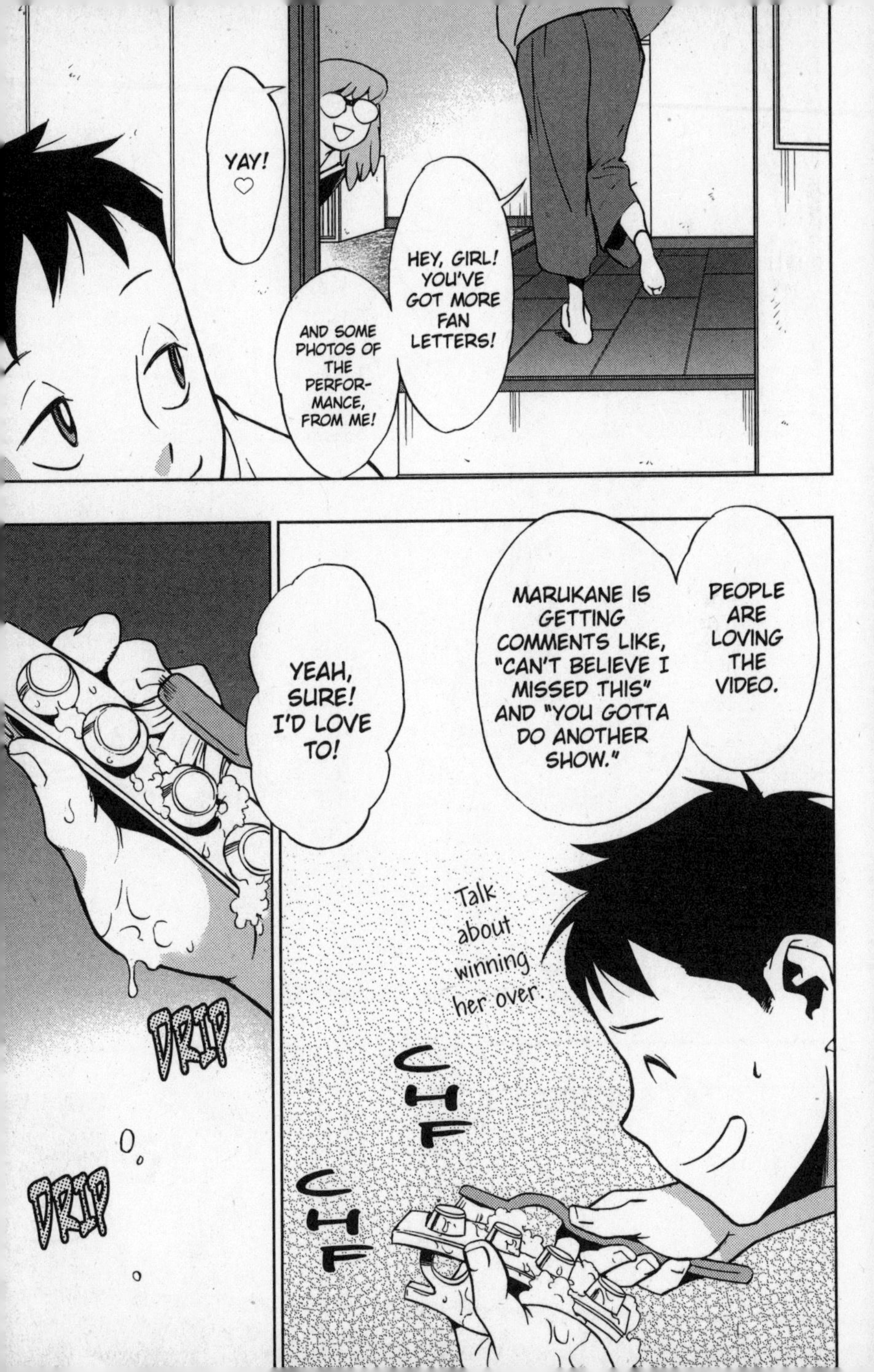
HEY, GIRL! YOU'VE GOT MORE FAN LETTERS!
AND SOME PHOTOS OF THE PERFORMANCE, FROM ME!
YAY! ♡
PEOPLE ARE LOVING THE VIDEO.
MARUKANE IS GETTING COMMENTS LIKE, "CAN'T BELIEVE I MISSED THIS" AND "YOU GOTTA DO ANOTHER SHOW."
Talk about winning her over.
CHF CHF
YEAH, SURE! I'D LOVE TO!
DRIP
DRIP

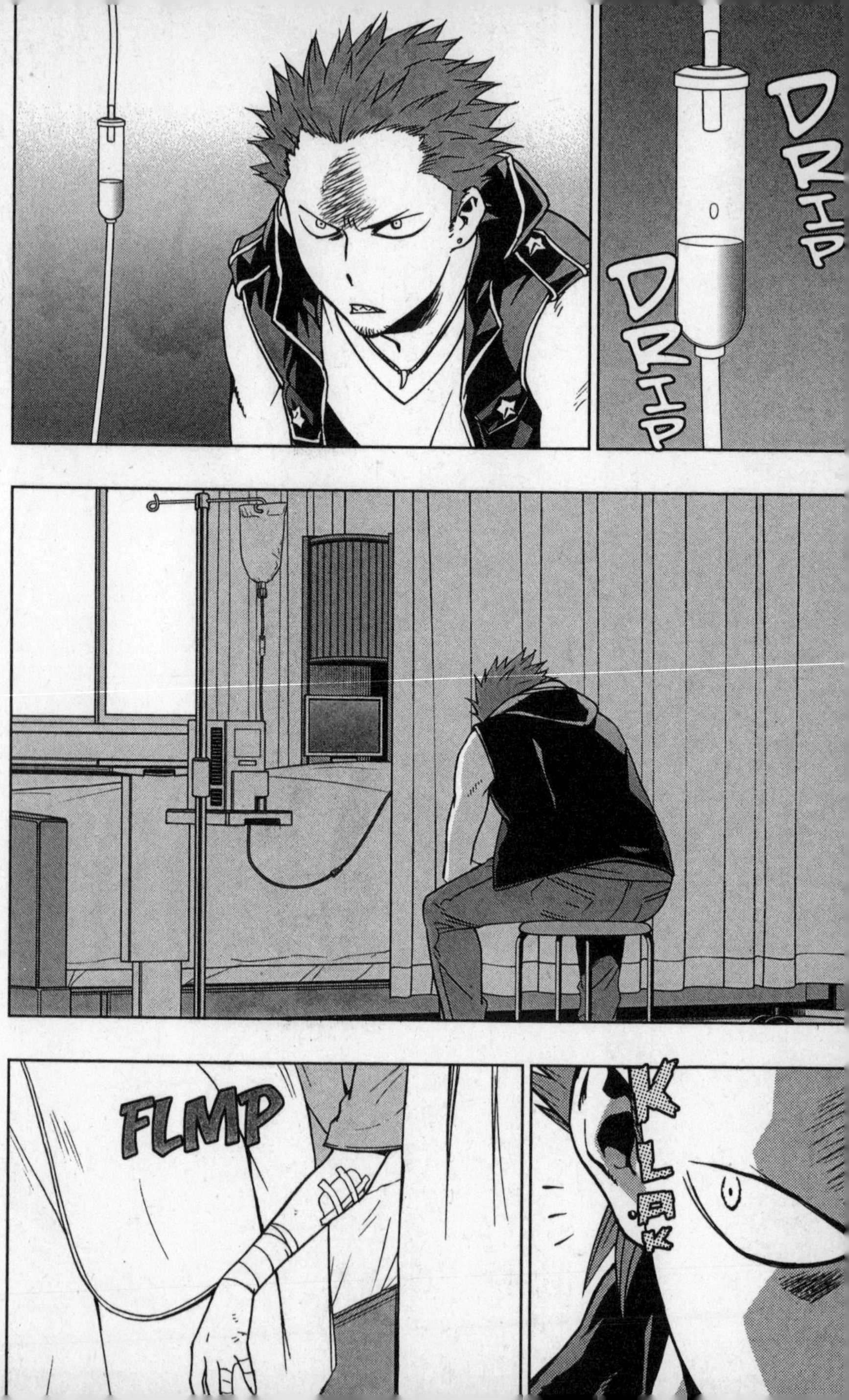
DRIP
DRIP
KLAK
FLMP

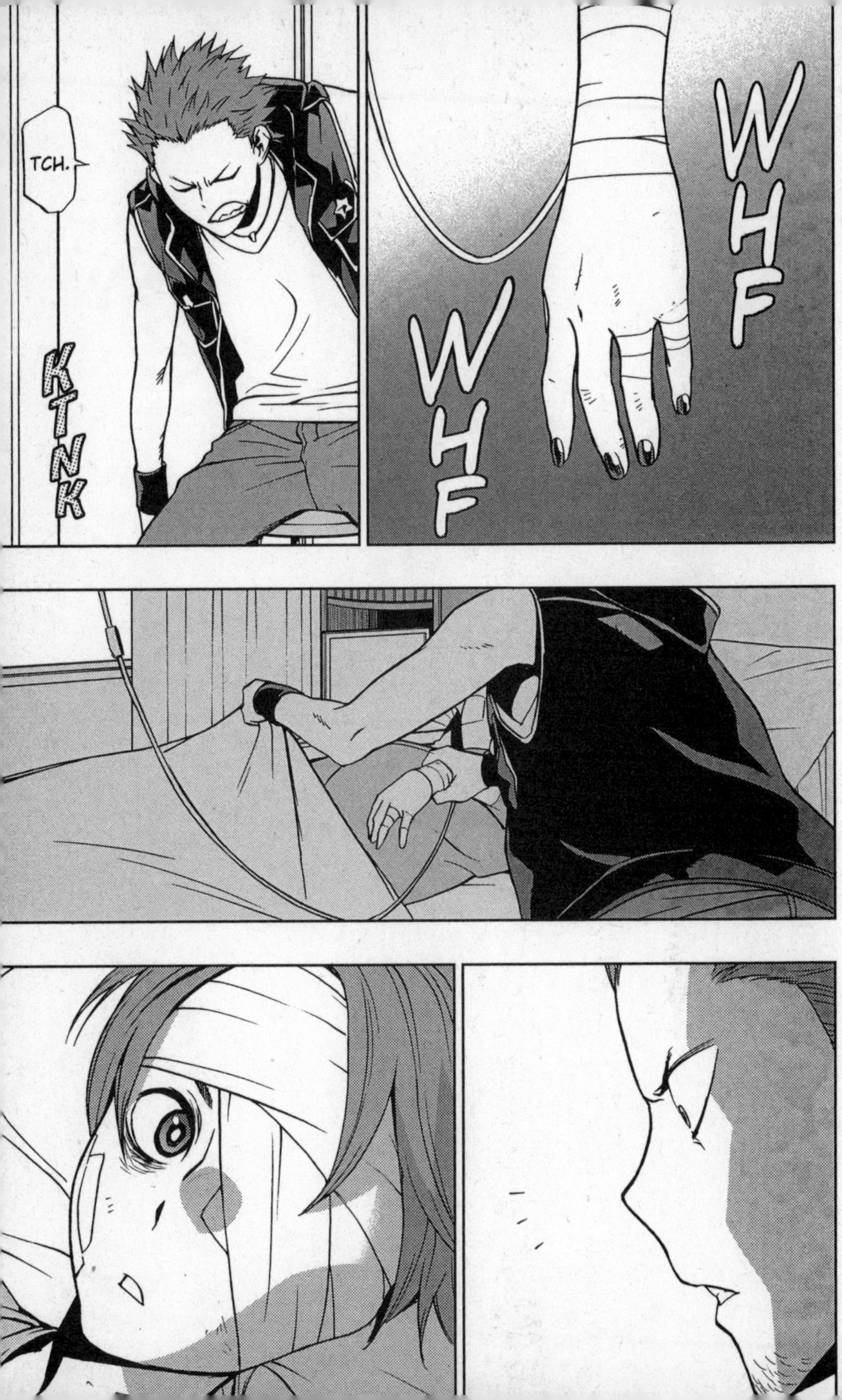
WHF
WHF
TCH.
KTNK

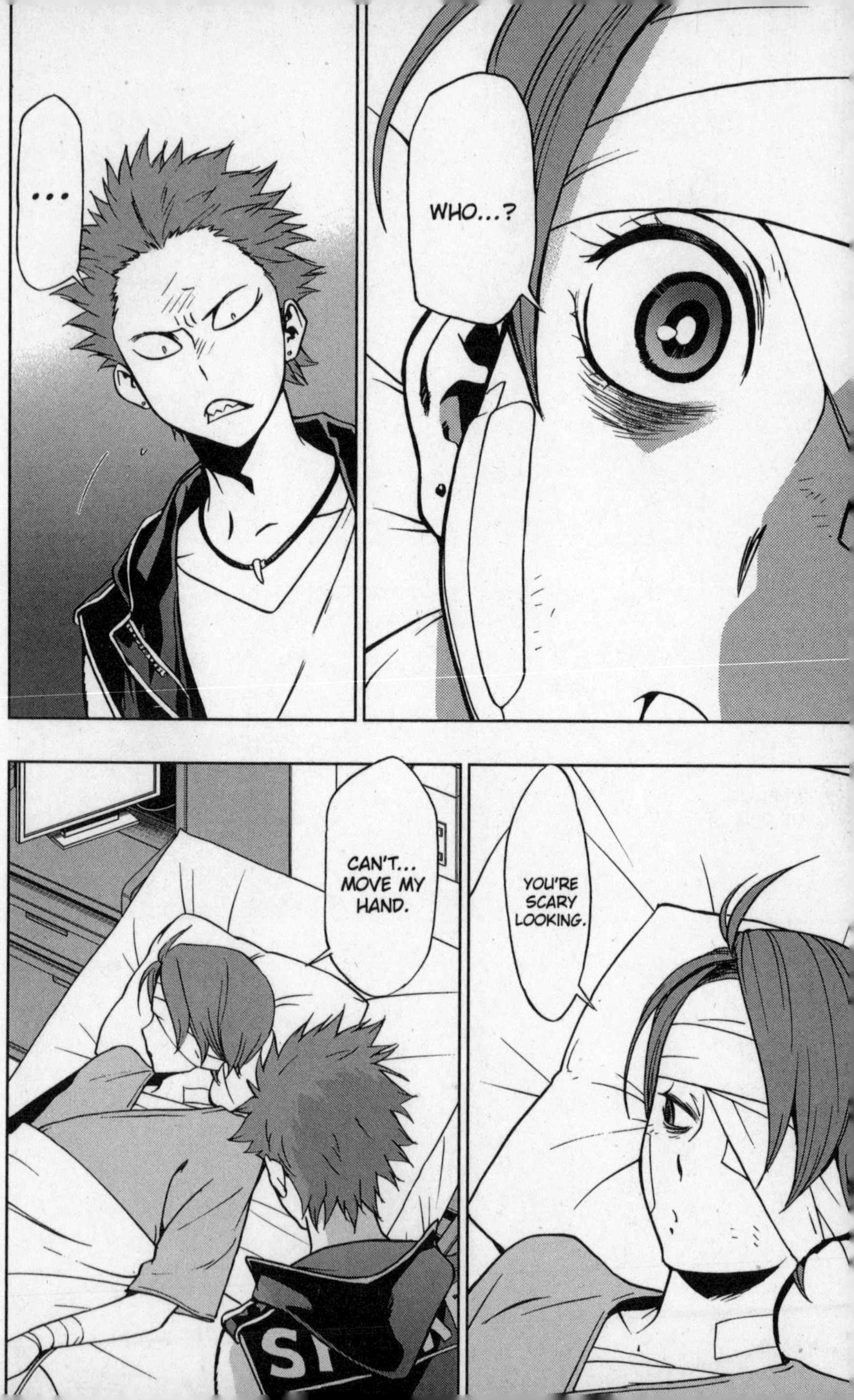
WHO...?
...
YOU'RE SCARY LOOKING.
CAN'T... MOVE MY HAND.

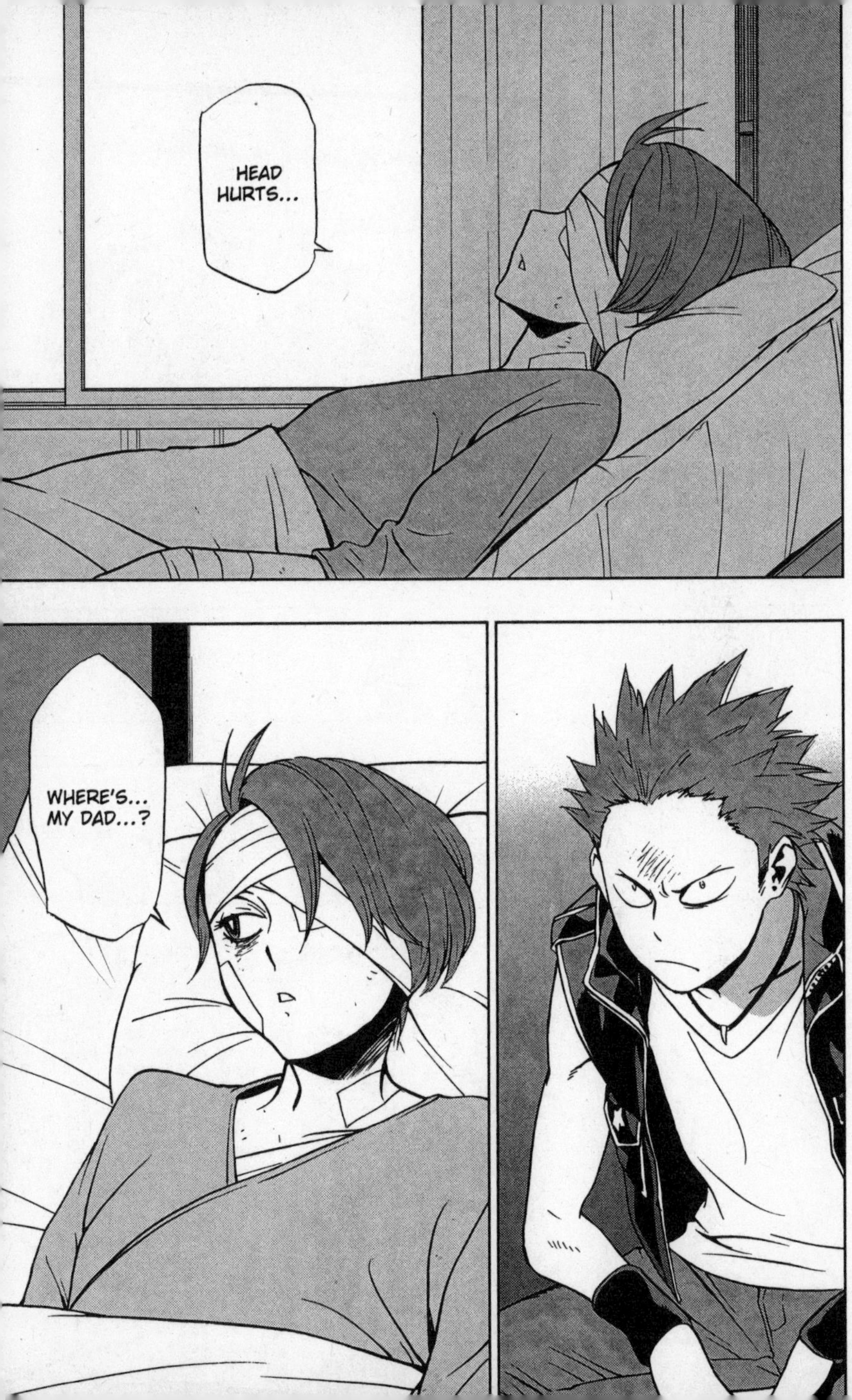
HEAD HURTS...
WHERE'S... MY DAD...?

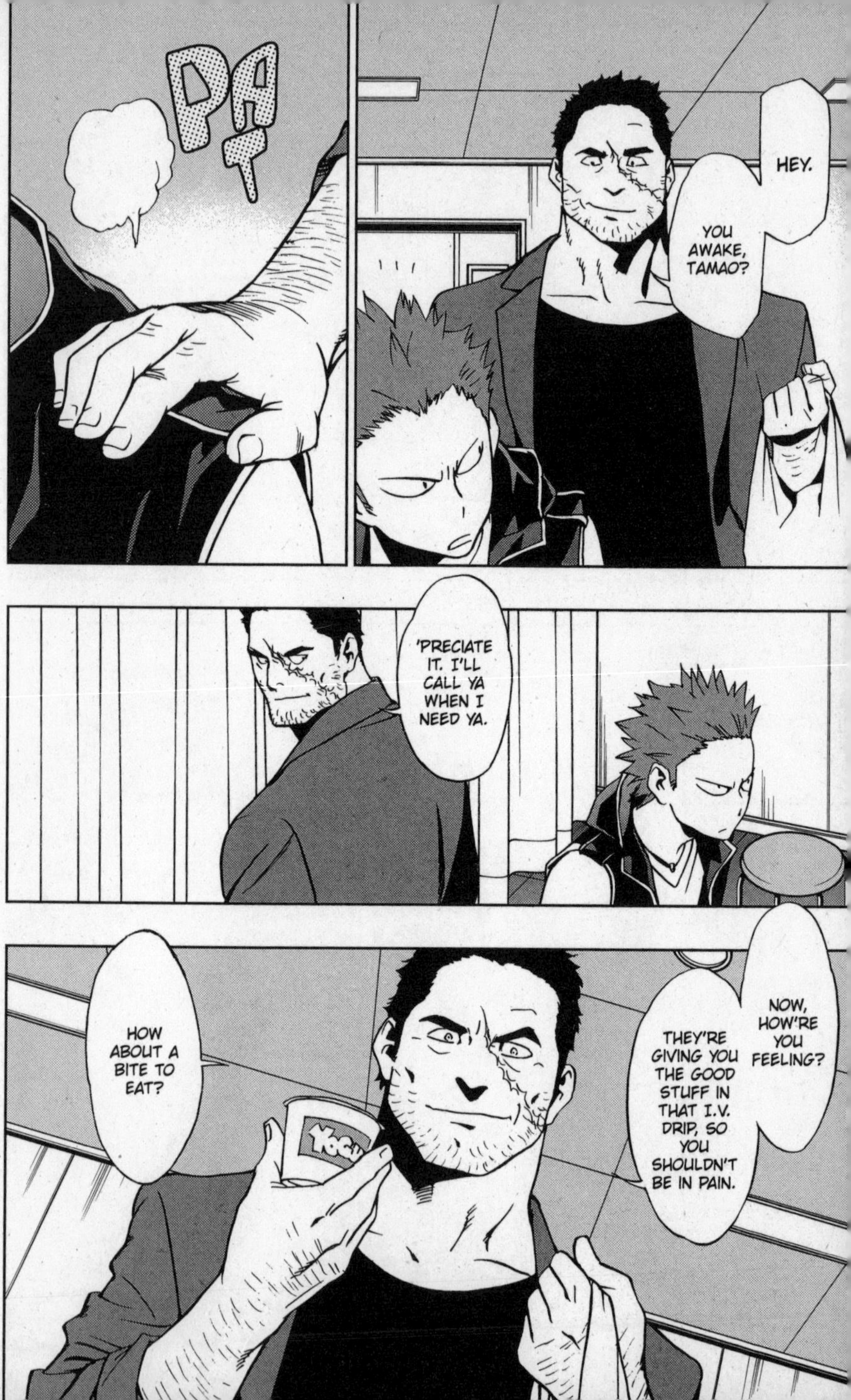
HEY.
YOU AWAKE, TAMAO?
PAT
'PRECIATE IT. I'LL CALL YA WHEN I NEED YA.
NOW, HOW'RE YOU FEELING?
THEY'RE GIVING YOU THE GOOD STUFF IN THAT I.V. DRIP, SO YOU SHOULDN'T BE IN PAIN.
HOW ABOUT A BITE TO EAT?

RUSTLE

YEAH. NOTHING MUCH WE CAN DO ABOUT THAT FOR NOW.

EXCEPT GIVE IT TIME.

MY HEAD HURTS.

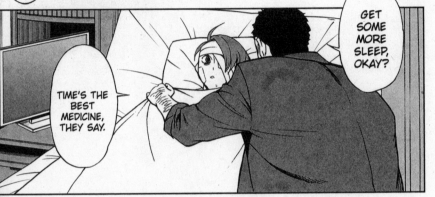

GET SOME MORE SLEEP, OKAY?

TIME'S THE BEST MEDICINE, THEY SAY.

WHERE'S MOM?

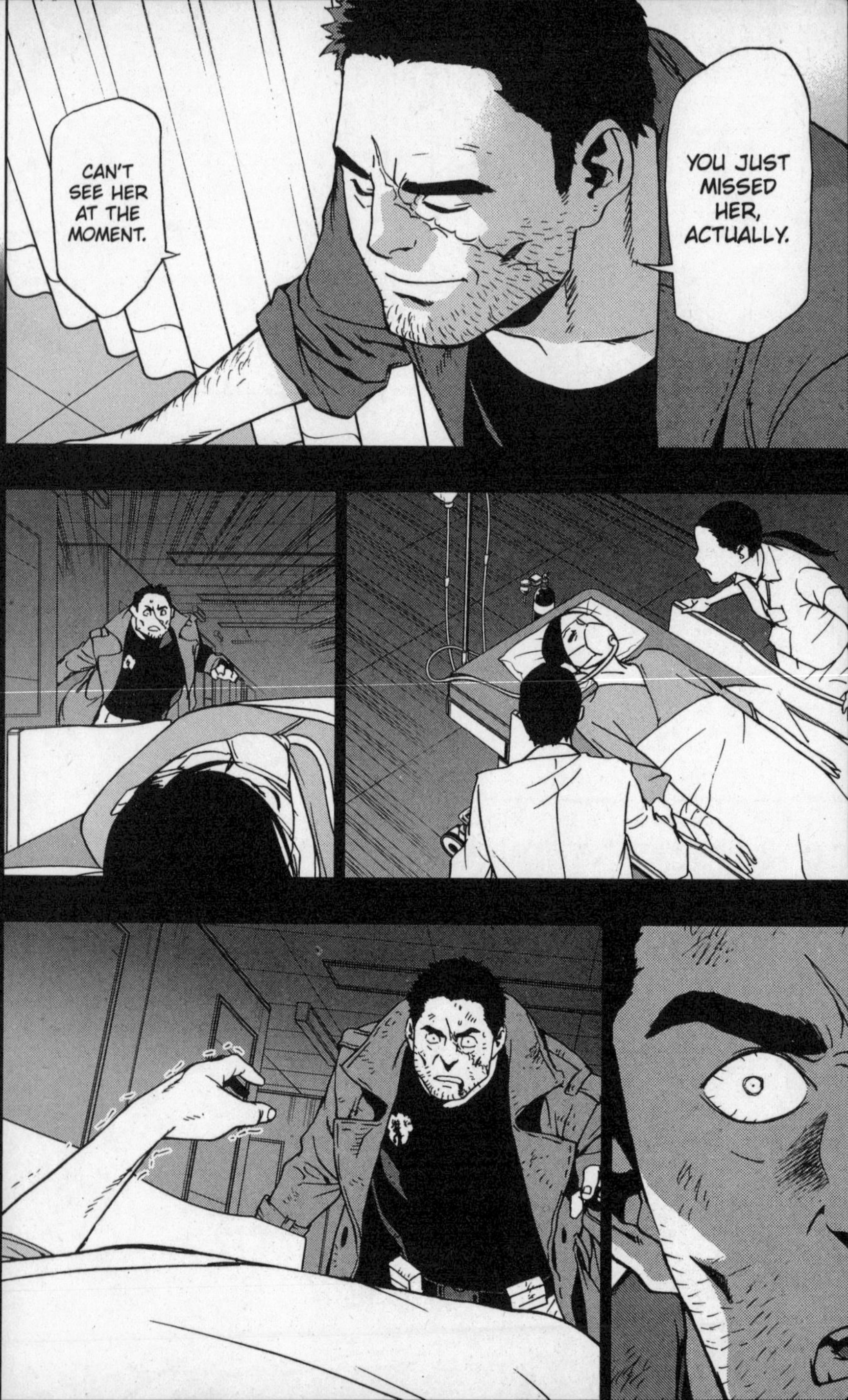
YOU JUST MISSED HER, ACTUALLY.
CAN'T SEE HER AT THE MOMENT.

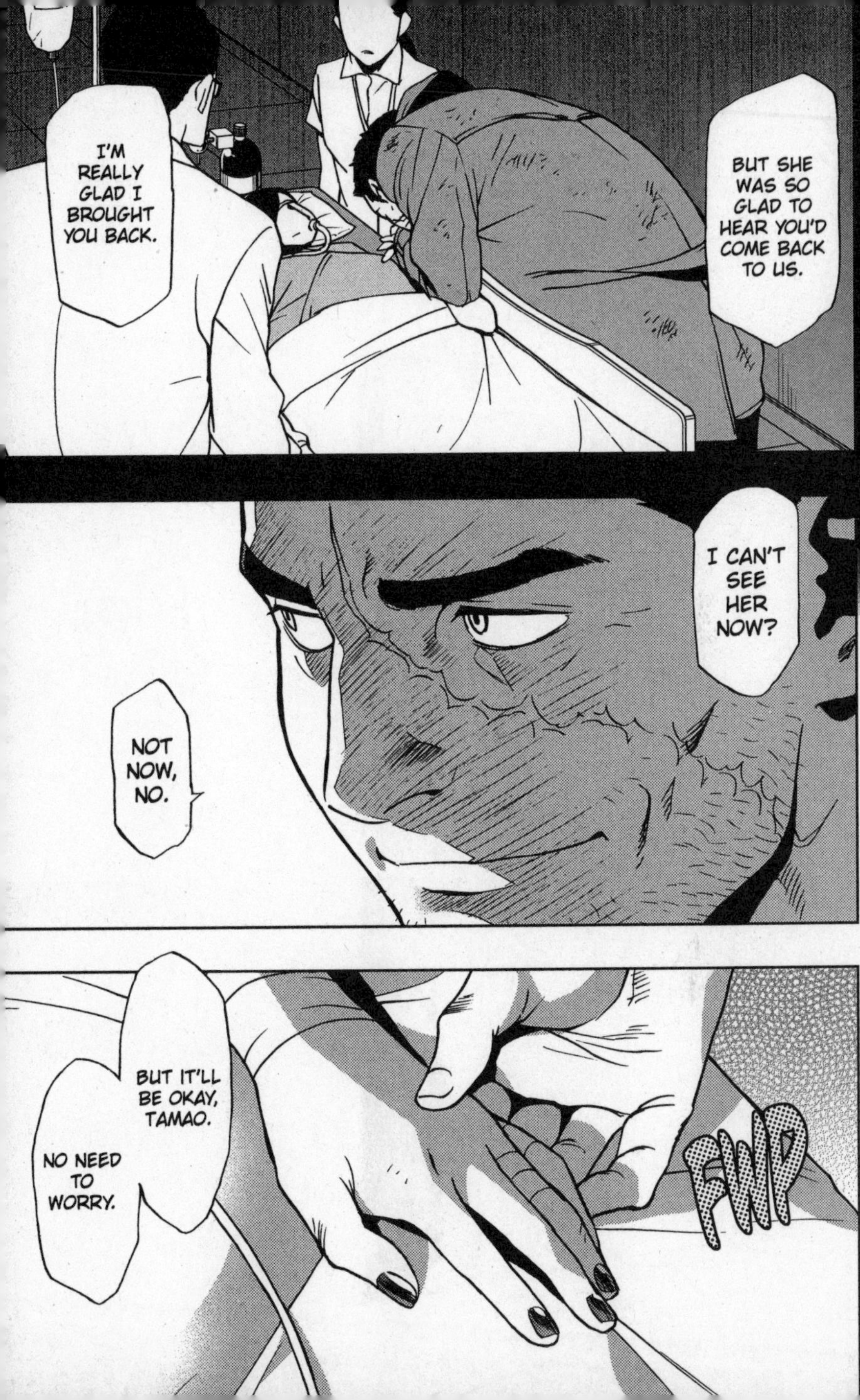
BUT SHE WAS SO GLAD TO HEAR YOU'D COME BACK TO US.
I'M REALLY GLAD I BROUGHT YOU BACK.
I CAN'T SEE HER NOW?
NOT NOW, NO.
FWP
BUT IT'LL BE OKAY, TAMAO.
NO NEED TO WORRY.

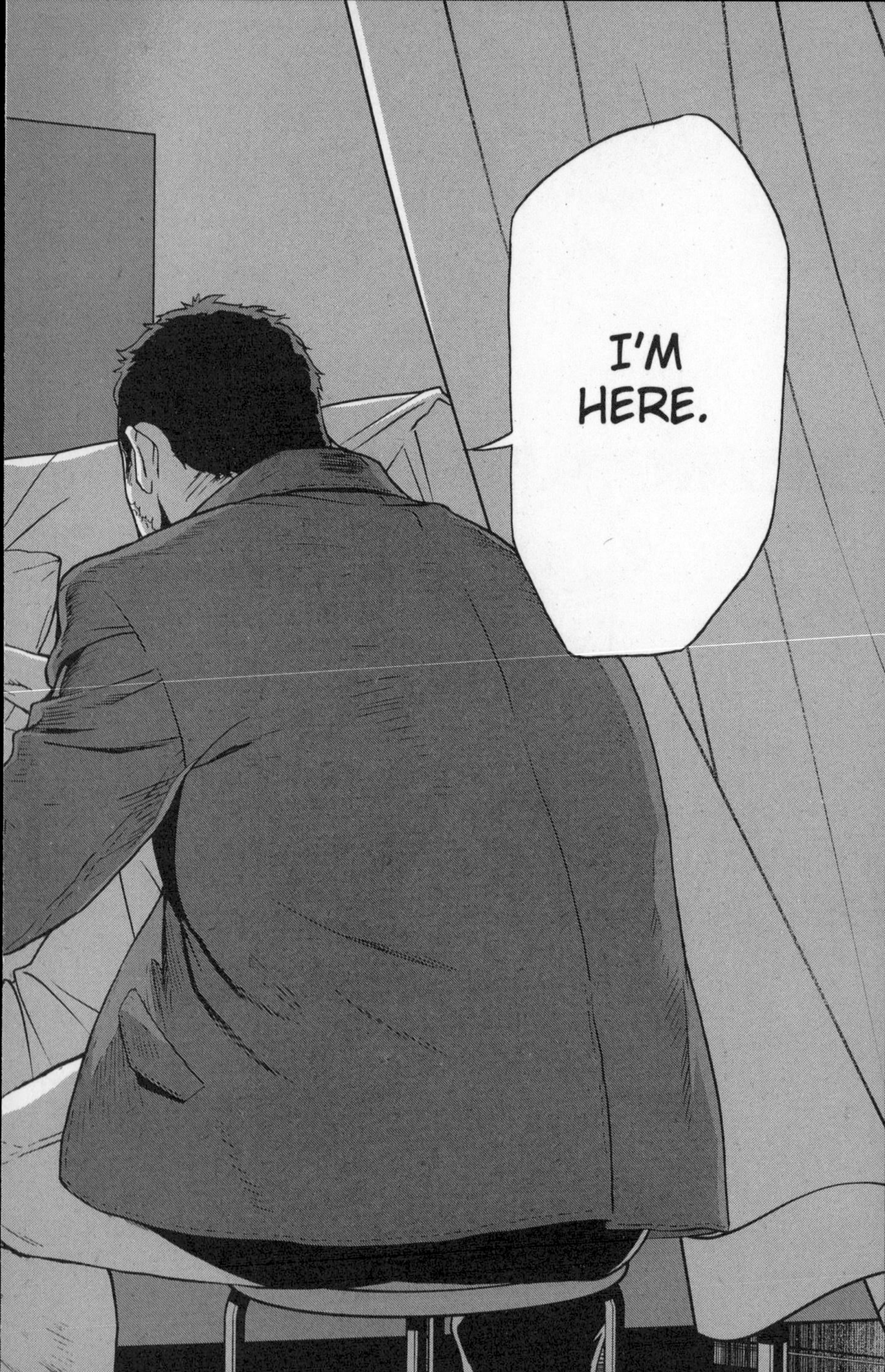
I'M HERE.

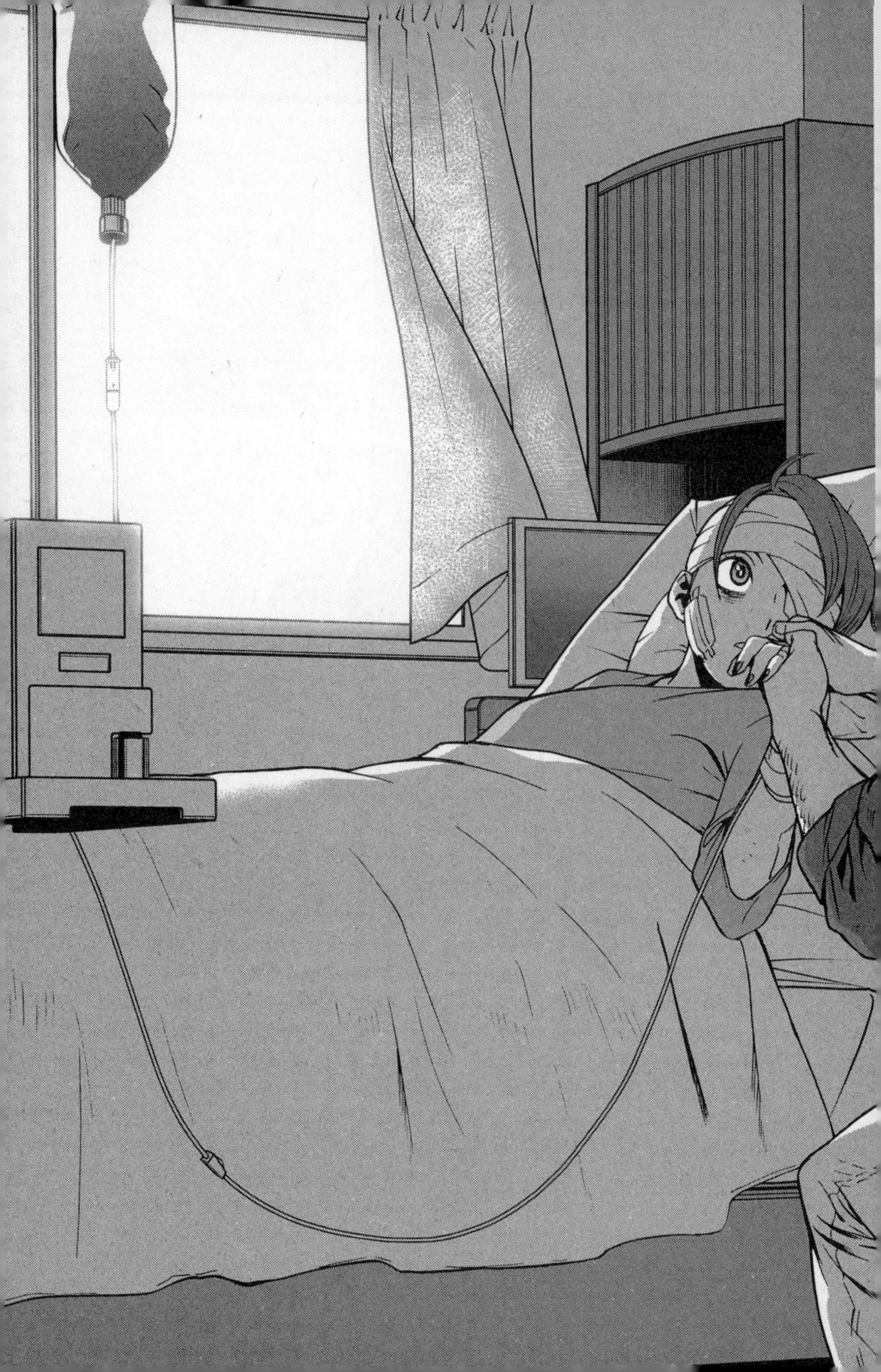

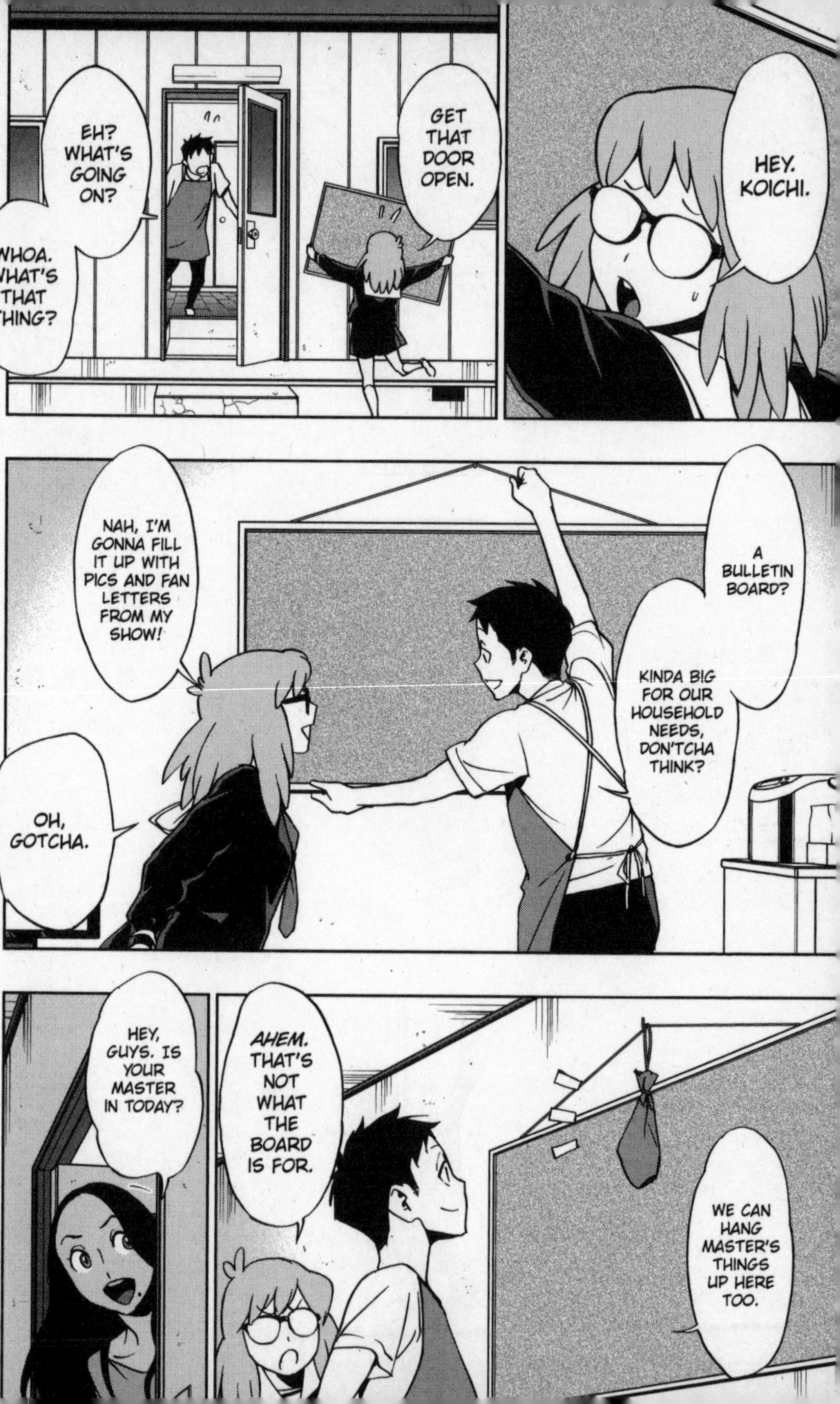
HEY. KOICHI.
GET THAT DOOR OPEN.
EH? WHAT'S GOING ON?
WHOA. WHAT'S THAT THING?
A BULLETIN BOARD?
KINDA BIG FOR OUR HOUSEHOLD NEEDS, DON'TCHA THINK?
NAH, I'M GONNA FILL IT UP WITH PICS AND FAN LETTERS FROM MY SHOW!
OH, GOTCHA.
WE CAN HANG MASTER'S THINGS UP HERE TOO.
AHEM. THAT'S NOT WHAT THE BOARD IS FOR.
HEY, GUYS. IS YOUR MASTER IN TODAY?

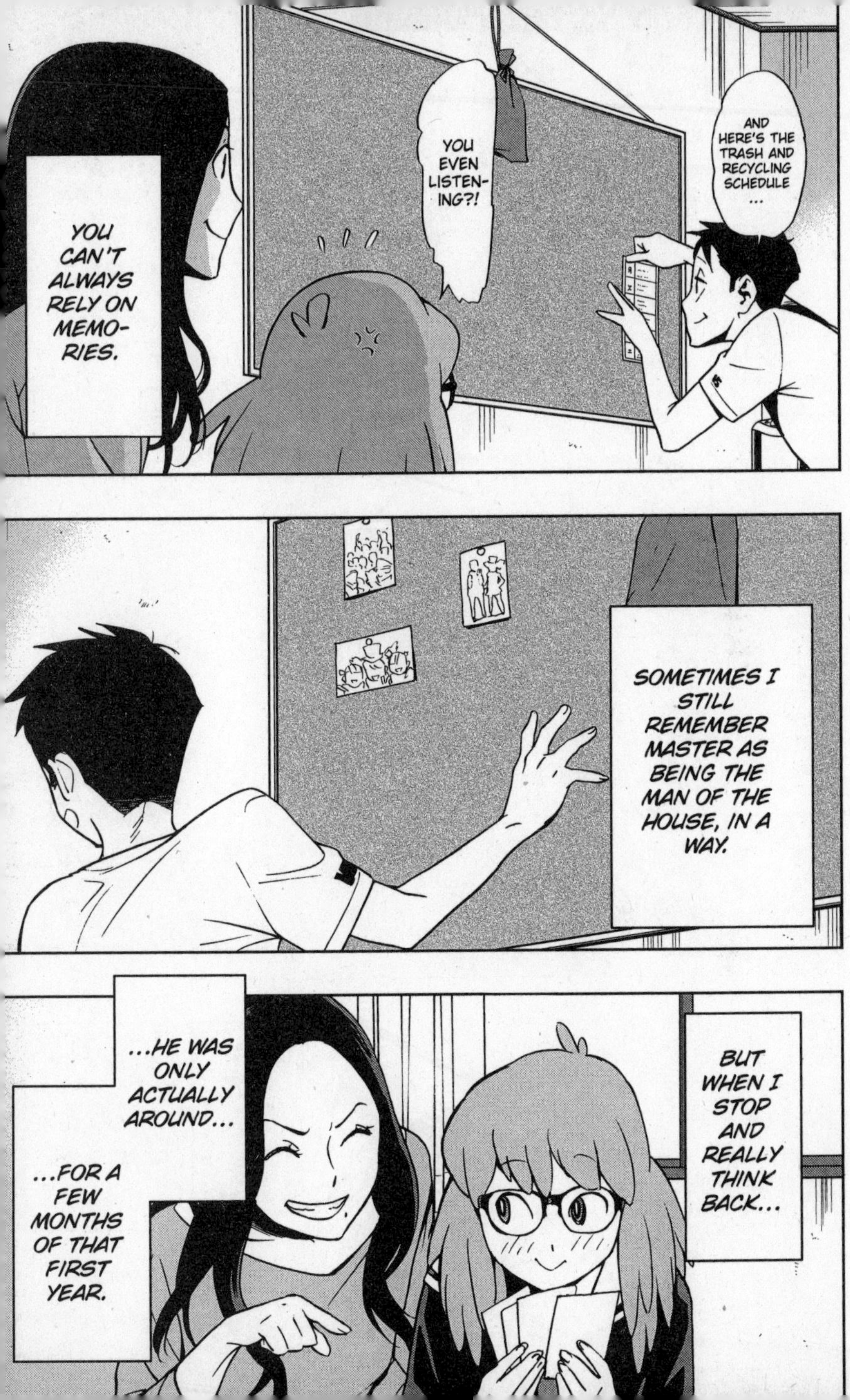
AND HERE'S THE TRASH AND RECYCLING SCHEDULE...
YOU EVEN LISTENING?!
YOU CAN'T ALWAYS RELY ON MEMORIES.
SOMETIMES I STILL REMEMBER MASTER AS BEING THE MAN OF THE HOUSE, IN A WAY.
BUT WHEN I STOP AND REALLY THINK BACK...
...HE WAS ONLY ACTUALLY AROUND...
...FOR A FEW MONTHS OF THAT FIRST YEAR.

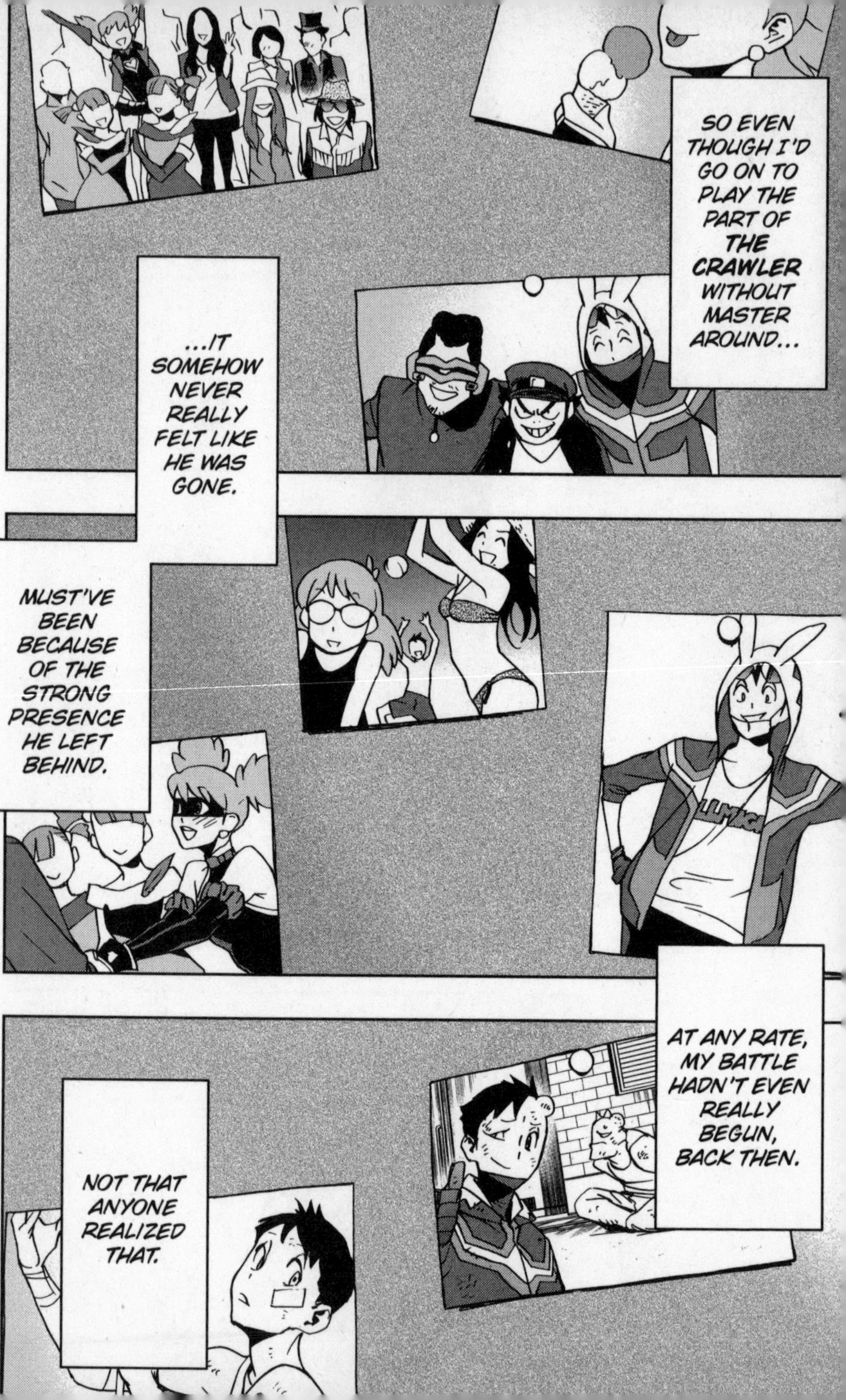
SO EVEN THOUGH I'D GO ON TO PLAY THE PART OF THE CRAWLER WITHOUT MASTER AROUND...
...IT SOMEHOW NEVER REALLY FELT LIKE HE WAS GONE.
MUST'VE BEEN BECAUSE OF THE STRONG PRESENCE HE LEFT BEHIND.
AT ANY RATE, MY BATTLE HADN'T EVEN REALLY BEGUN, BACK THEN.
NOT THAT ANYONE REALIZED THAT.

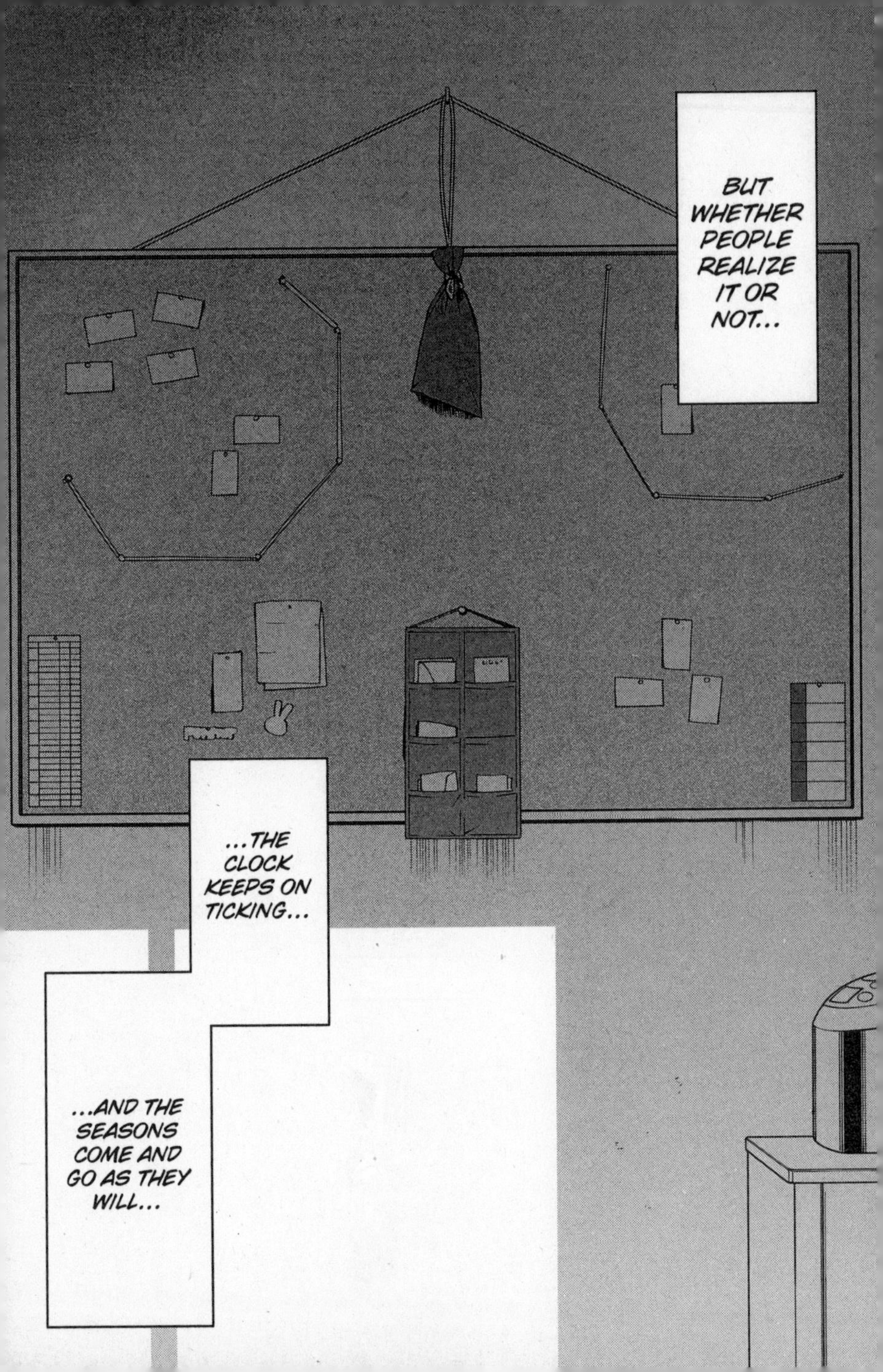
BUT WHETHER PEOPLE REALIZE IT OR NOT...
...THE CLOCK KEEPS ON TICKING...
...AND THE SEASONS COME AND GO AS THEY WILL...

THE COLUMN

MASTER'S PRIVATE SIDE

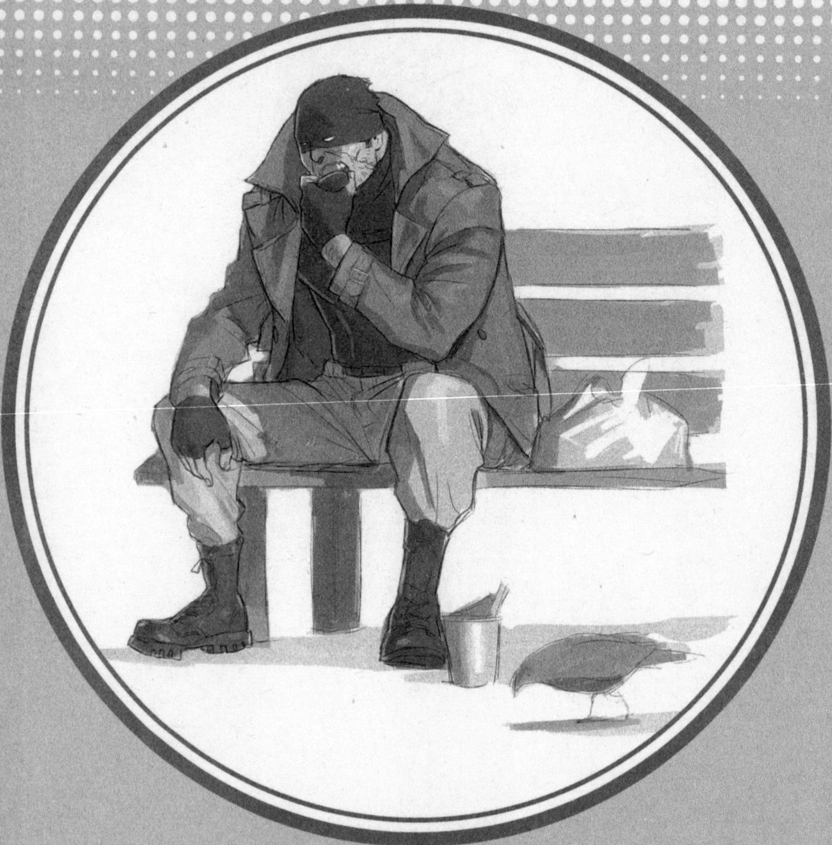

I posted this sketch of Master on Twitter. At the time, I didn't know much about his background, so this was the image I had of what he looked like, during his free time.

He seems kind of solitary. Solitary? Like the sad Keanu Reeves meme. (LOL)
Showing someone eating and drinking always feels like a glimpse of their private side.

Koichi's civilian clothes are the epitome of inoffensive. (LOL)

Pop doesn't exactly have bad style, but she's not sophisticated either. I struggle with her.

—Betten

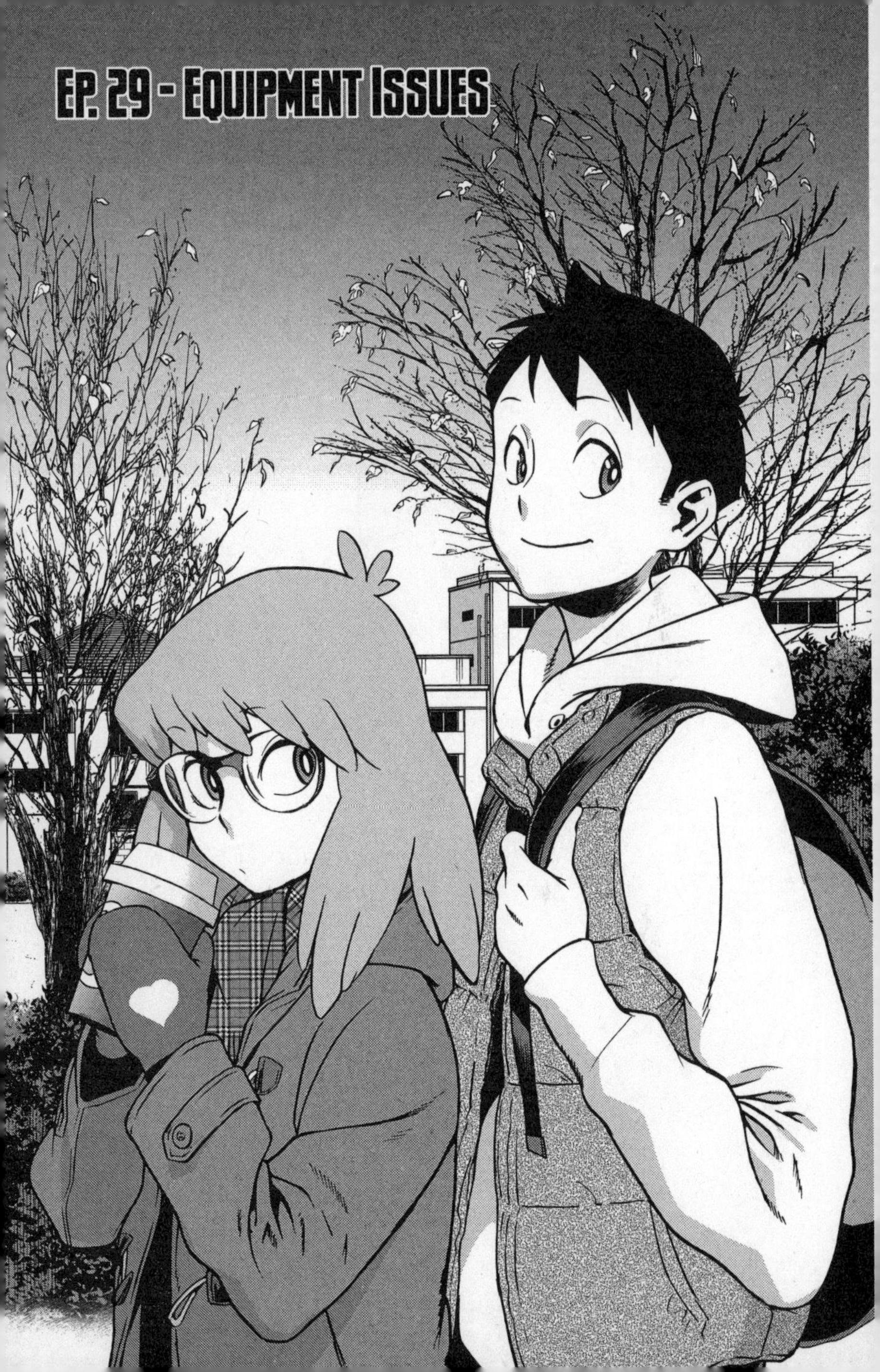
EP. 29 - EQUIPMENT ISSUES

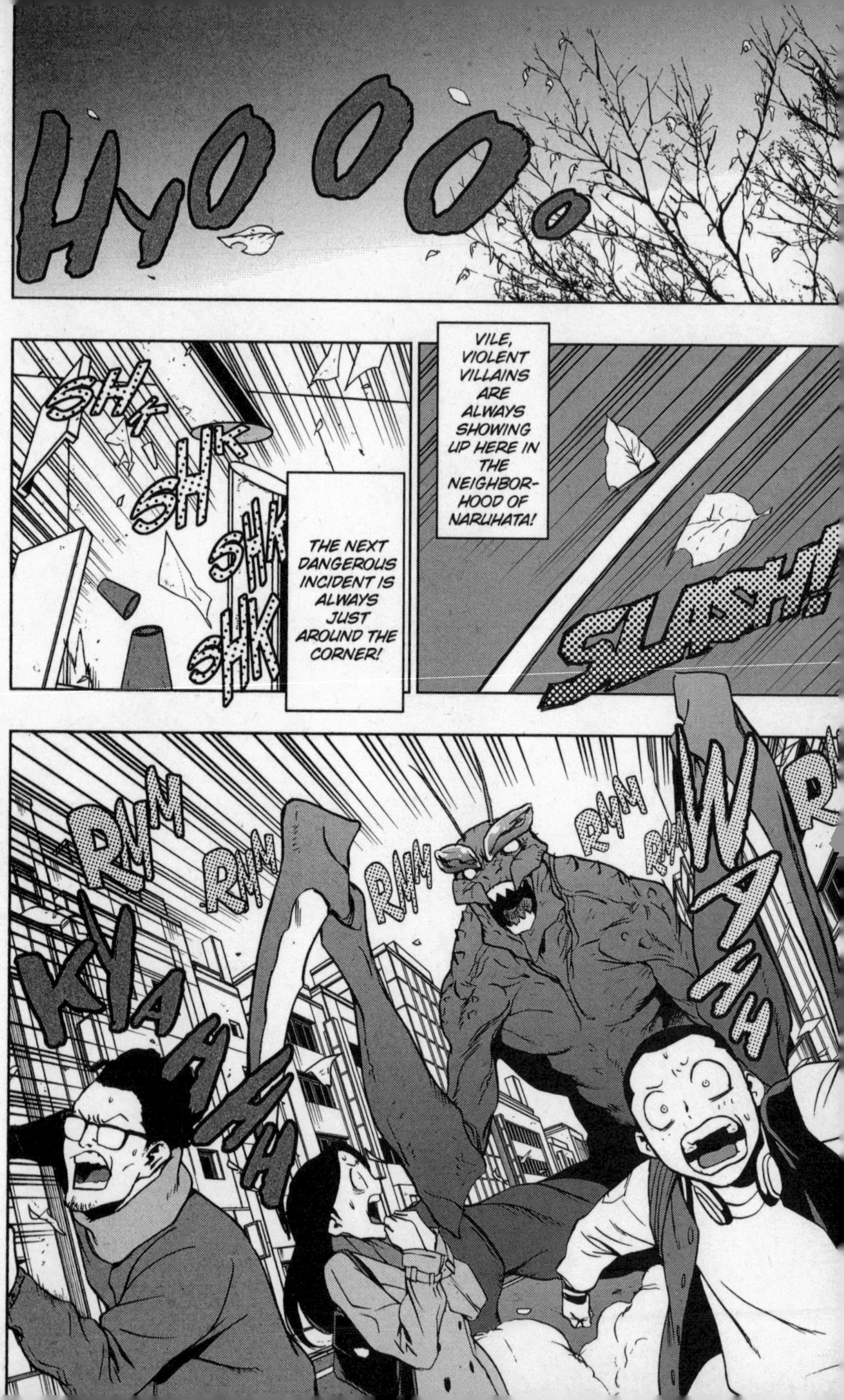
HYOOOo
VILE, VIOLENT VILLAINS ARE ALWAYS SHOWING UP HERE IN THE NEIGHBOR-HOOD OF NARUHATA!
SLASH!!
THE NEXT DANGEROUS INCIDENT IS ALWAYS JUST AROUND THE CORNER!
SHK
SHK
SHK
SHK
WAAHH
RMM
RMM
RMM
RMM
RMM
KYAAHHH

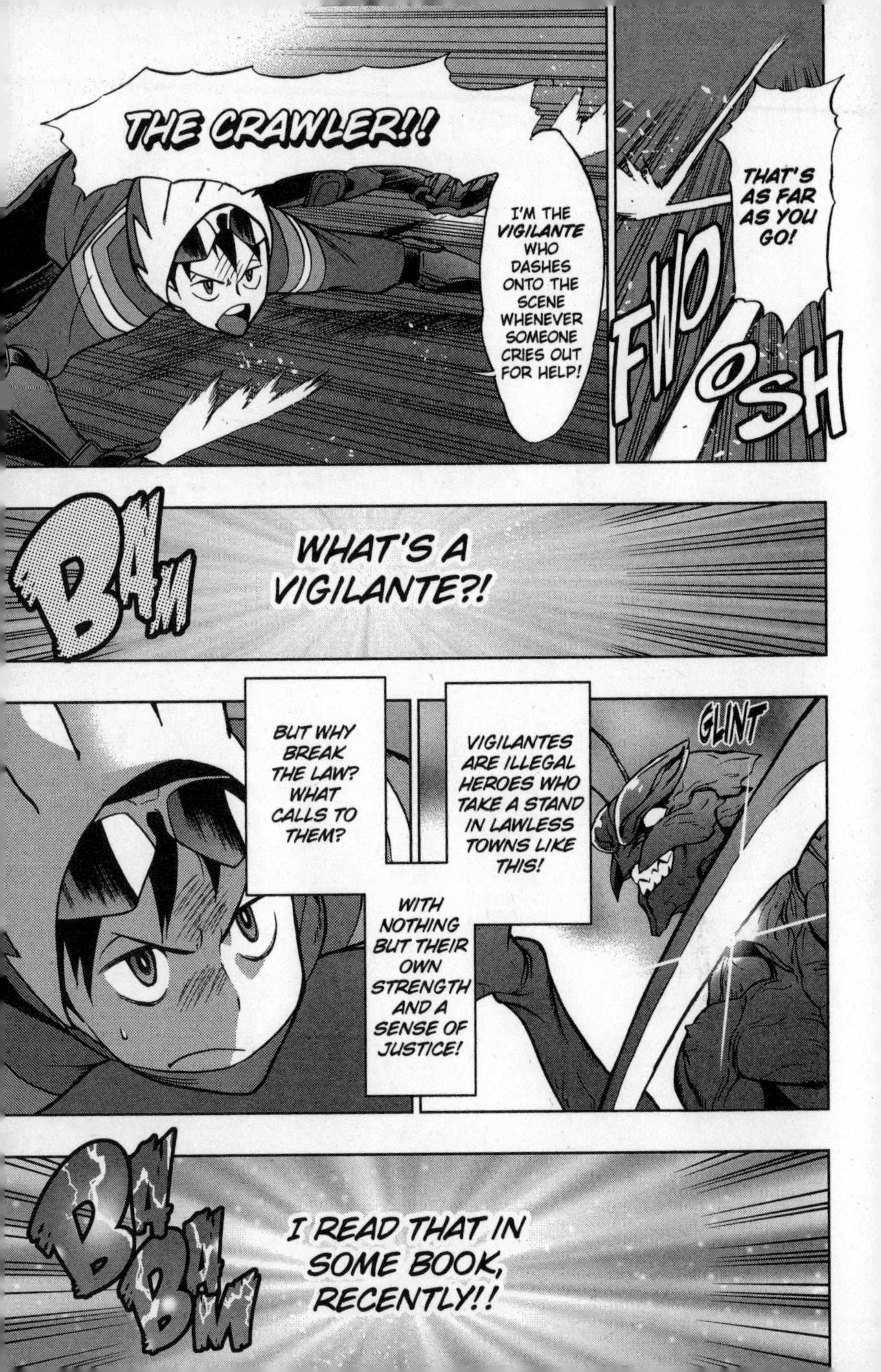
THAT'S AS FAR AS YOU GO!
FWOOSH
I'M THE VIGILANTE WHO DASHES ONTO THE SCENE WHENEVER SOMEONE CRIES OUT FOR HELP!
THE CRAWLER!!
BAM
WHAT'S A VIGILANTE?!
GLINT
VIGILANTES ARE ILLEGAL HEROES WHO TAKE A STAND IN LAWLESS TOWNS LIKE THIS!
WITH NOTHING BUT THEIR OWN STRENGTH AND A SENSE OF JUSTICE!
BUT WHY BREAK THE LAW? WHAT CALLS TO THEM?
I READ THAT IN SOME BOOK, RECENTLY!!

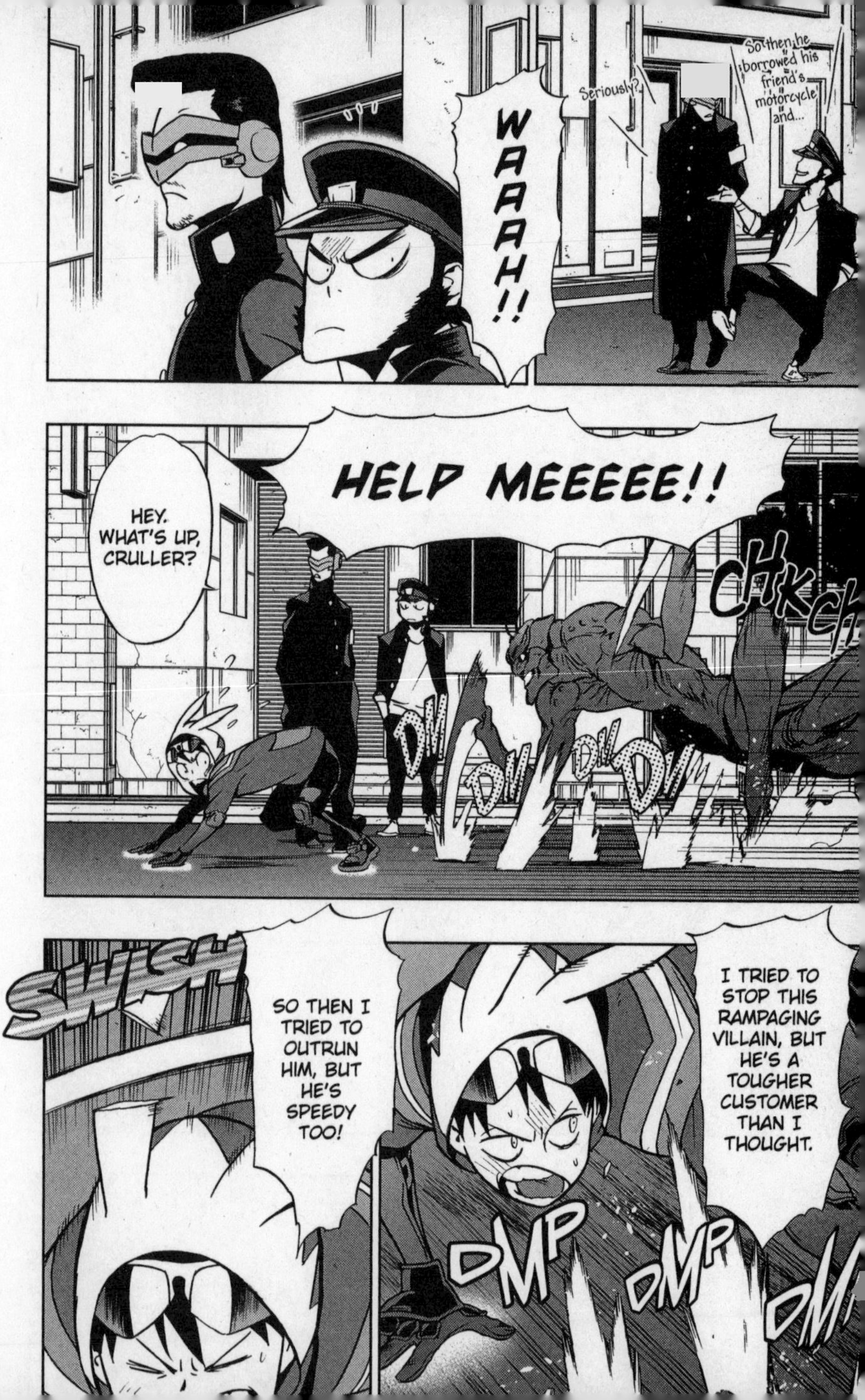
So then he borrowed his friend's motorcycle and...
Seriously?
WAAAH!!
HELP MEEEEE!!
HEY. WHAT'S UP, CRULLER?
CHKCH
DM DM DM DM
I TRIED TO STOP THIS RAMPAGING VILLAIN, BUT HE'S A TOUGHER CUSTOMER THAN I THOUGHT.
SO THEN I TRIED TO OUTRUN HIM, BUT HE'S SPEEDY TOO!
SWISH
DMP DMP DM

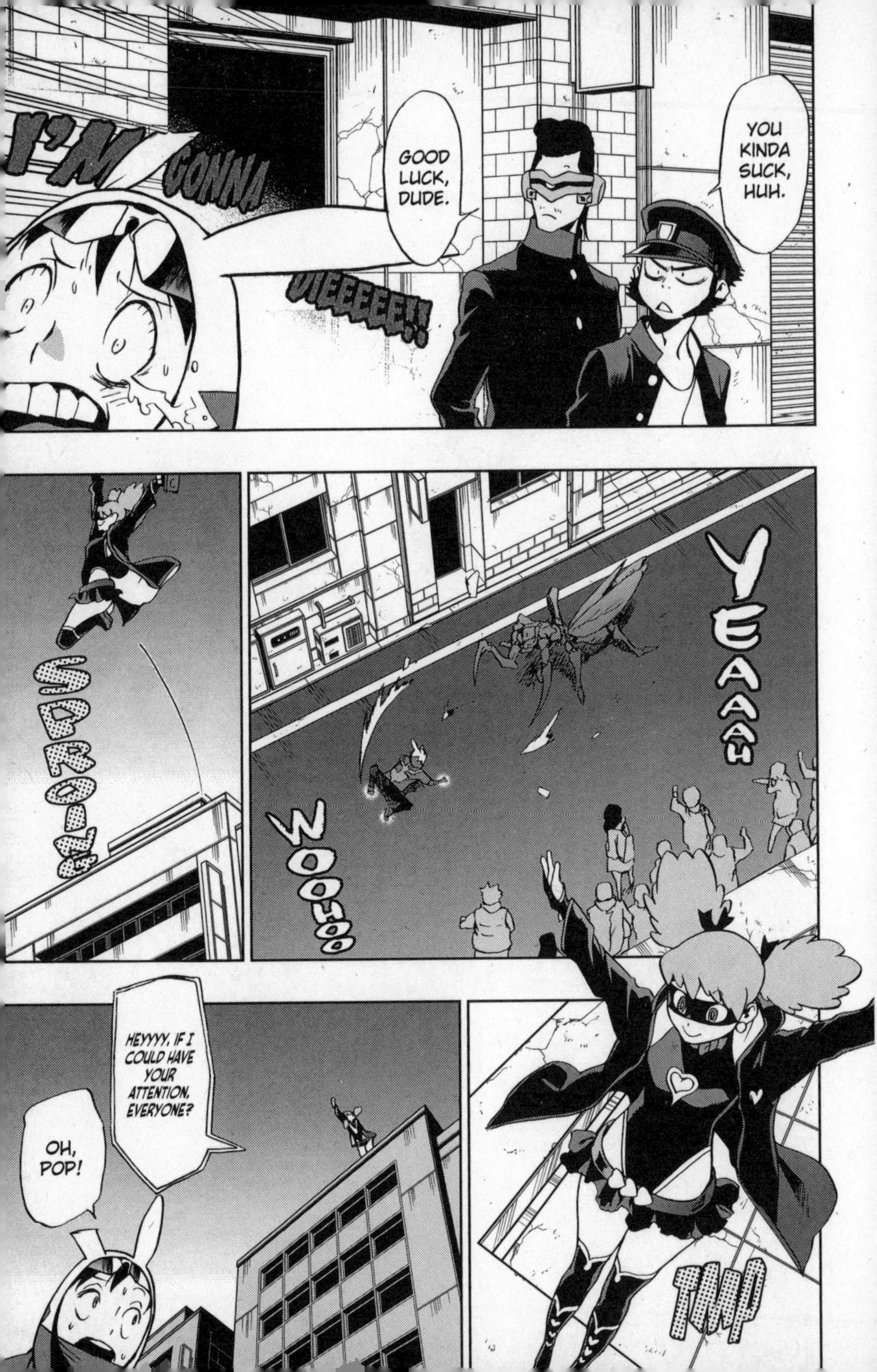
YOU KINDA SUCK, HUH.
GOOD LUCK, DUDE.
I'M GONNA DIEEEEEE!!
YEAAAAH
WOOHOO
SPROING
TMP
HEYYYY. IF I COULD HAVE YOUR ATTENTION, EVERYONE?
OH, POP!

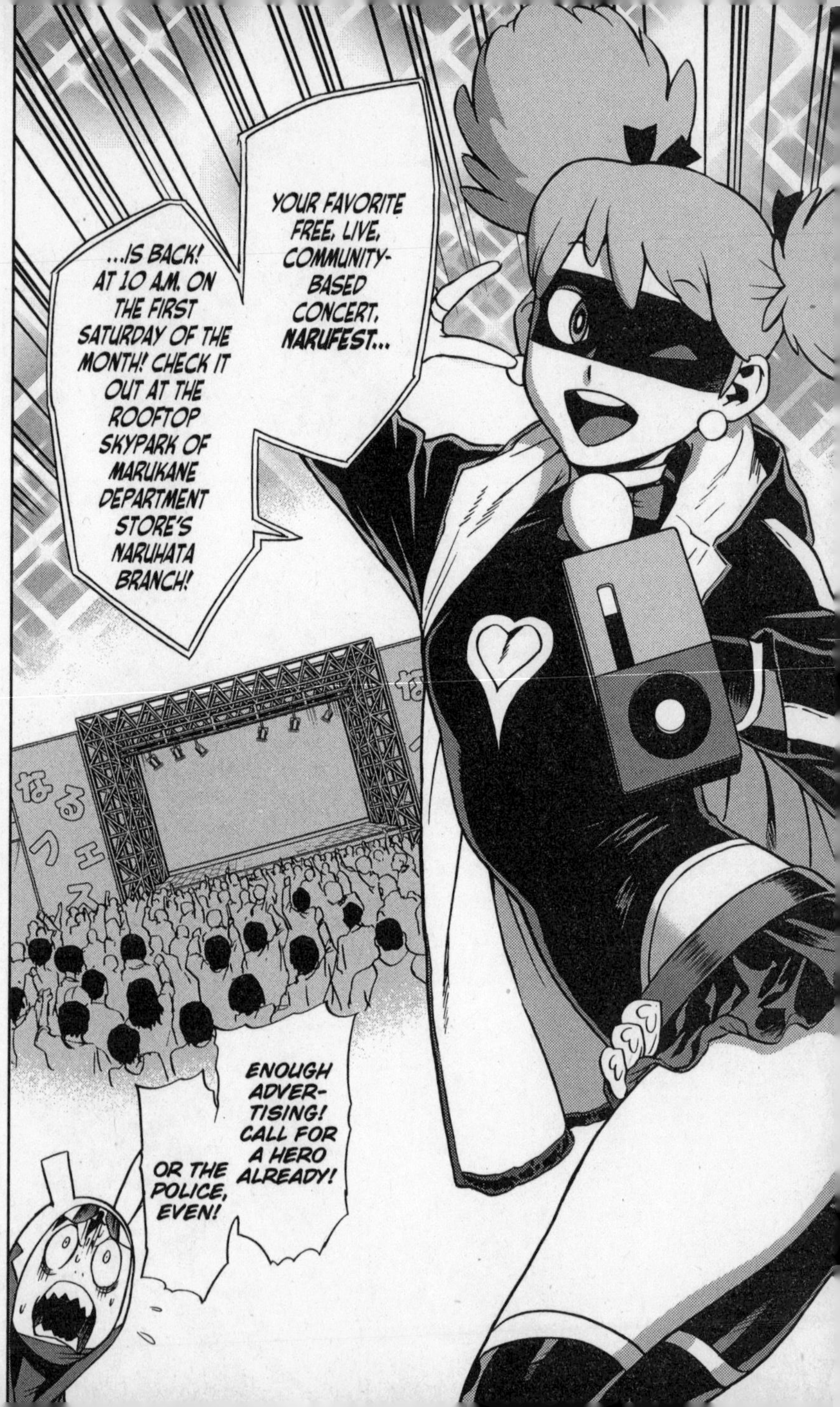
YOUR FAVORITE FREE, LIVE, COMMUNITY-BASED CONCERT, NARUFEST...
...IS BACK! AT 10 A.M. ON THE FIRST SATURDAY OF THE MONTH! CHECK IT OUT AT THE ROOFTOP SKYPARK OF MARUKANE DEPARTMENT STORE'S NARUHATA BRANCH!
なるフェス
ENOUGH ADVER-TISING! CALL FOR A HERO ALREADY!
OR THE POLICE, EVEN!

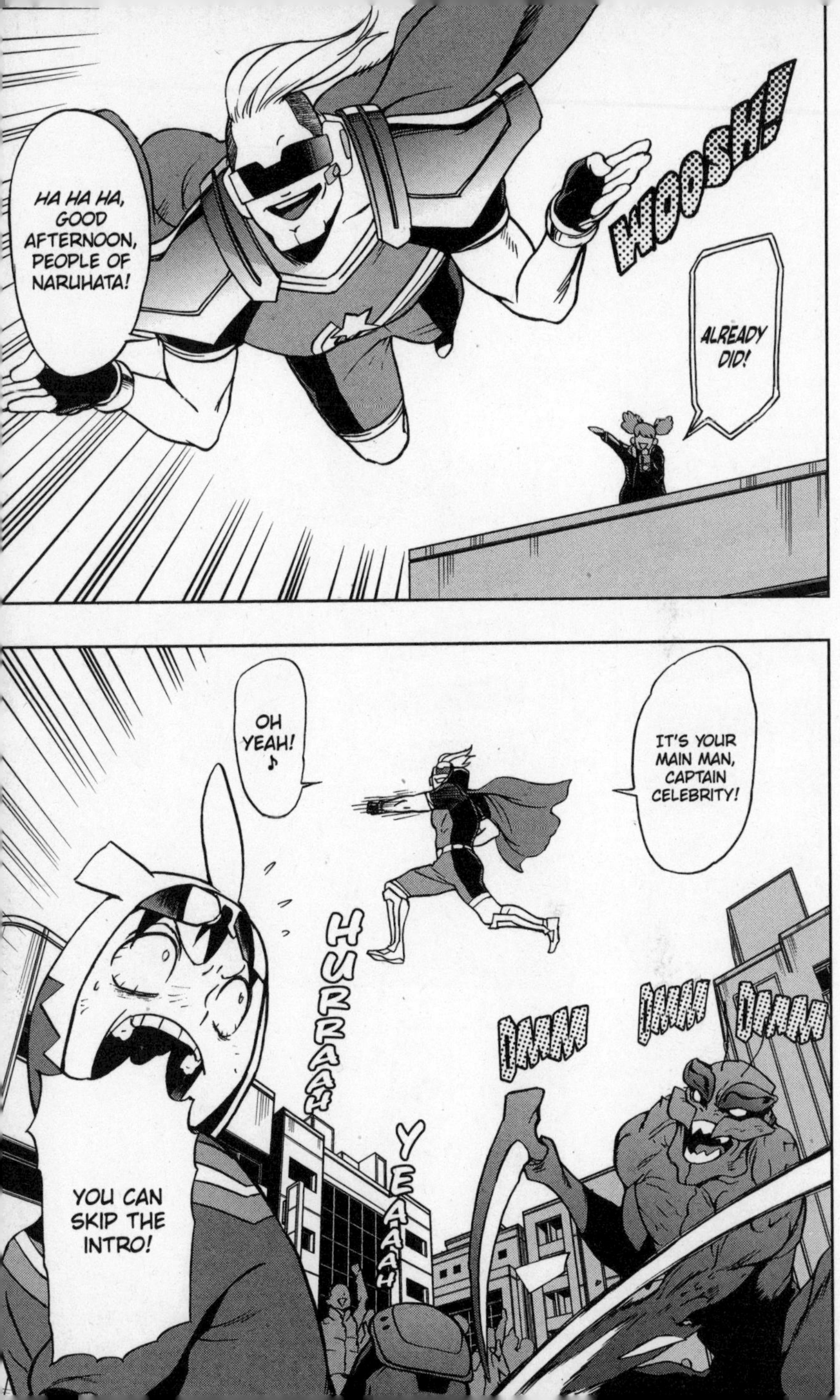
WOOSH!
ALREADY DID!
HA HA HA, GOOD AFTERNOON, PEOPLE OF NARUHATA!
IT'S YOUR MAIN MAN, CAPTAIN CELEBRITY!
OH YEAH! ♪
DMM DMM DMM
HURRAAAH
YEAAAAH
YOU CAN SKIP THE INTRO!

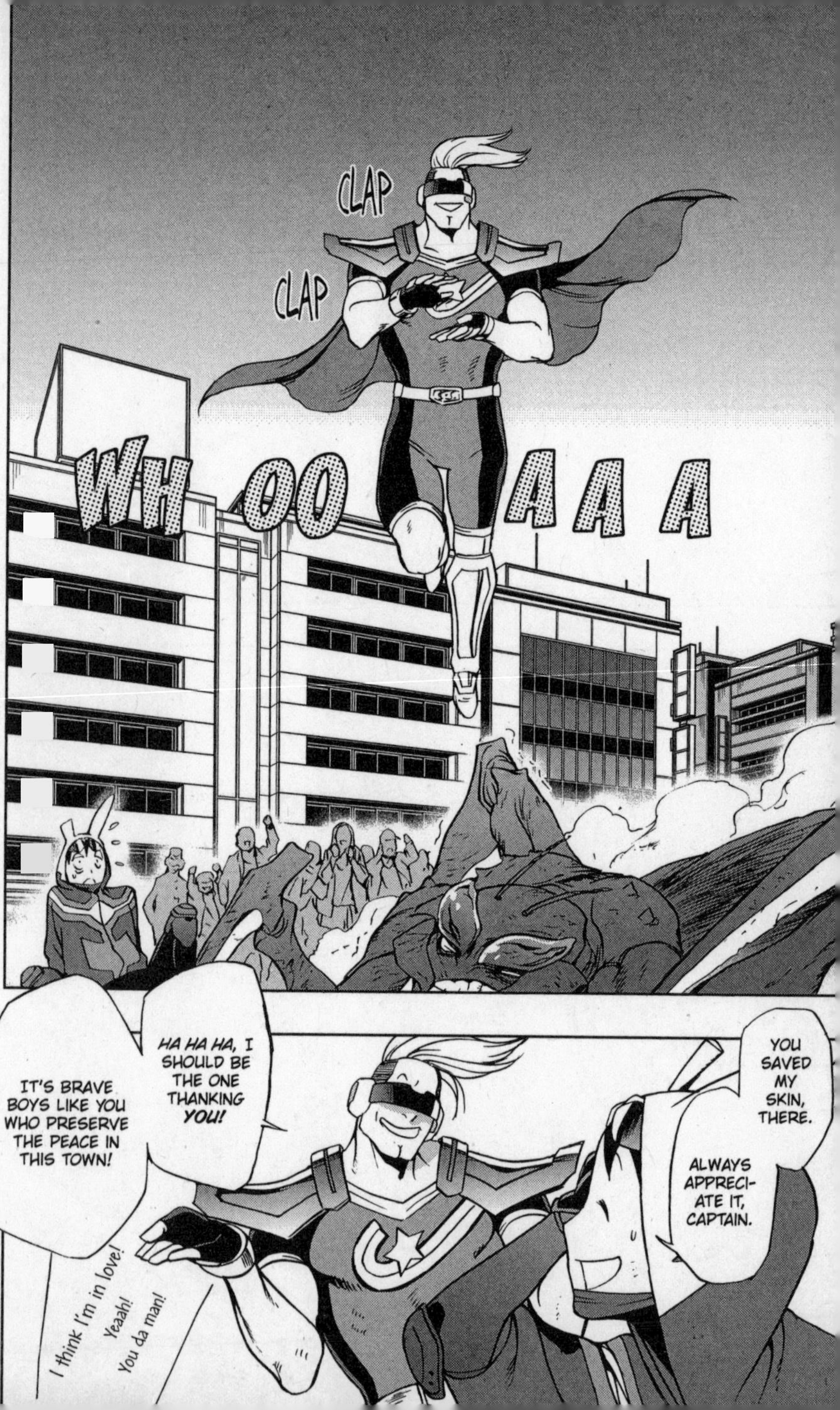
CLAP
CLAP
WHOOAAA
YOU SAVED MY SKIN, THERE.
ALWAYS APPRECIATE IT, CAPTAIN.
HA HA HA, I SHOULD BE THE ONE THANKING *YOU!*
IT'S BRAVE BOYS LIKE YOU WHO PRESERVE THE PEACE IN THIS TOWN!
I think I'm in love!
Yeaah!
You da man!

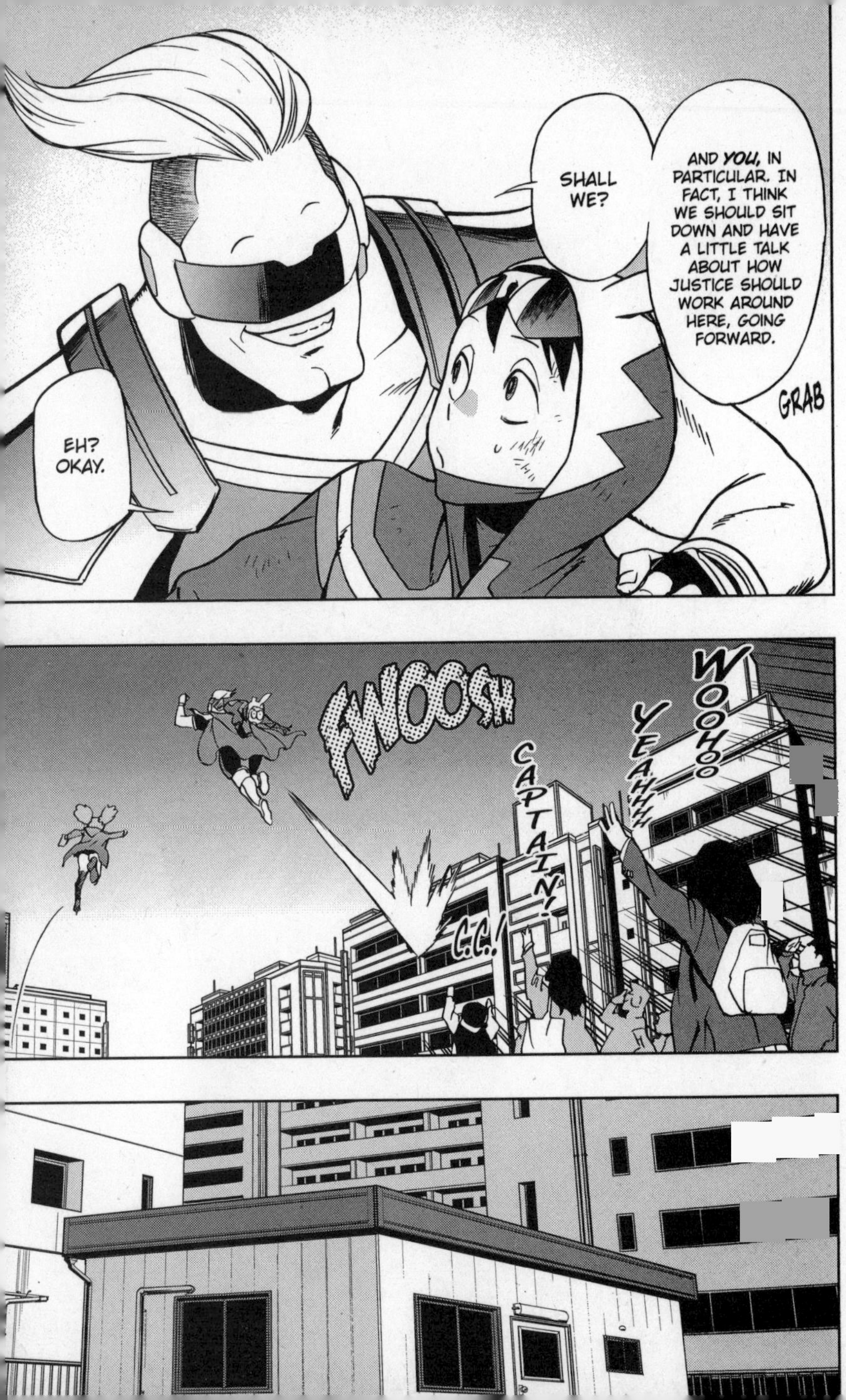
AND YOU, IN PARTICULAR. IN FACT, I THINK WE SHOULD SIT DOWN AND HAVE A LITTLE TALK ABOUT HOW JUSTICE SHOULD WORK AROUND HERE, GOING FORWARD.
SHALL WE?
GRAB
EH? OKAY.
WOOHOO
YEAHHH
CAPTAIN!
C.C.!
FWOOSH

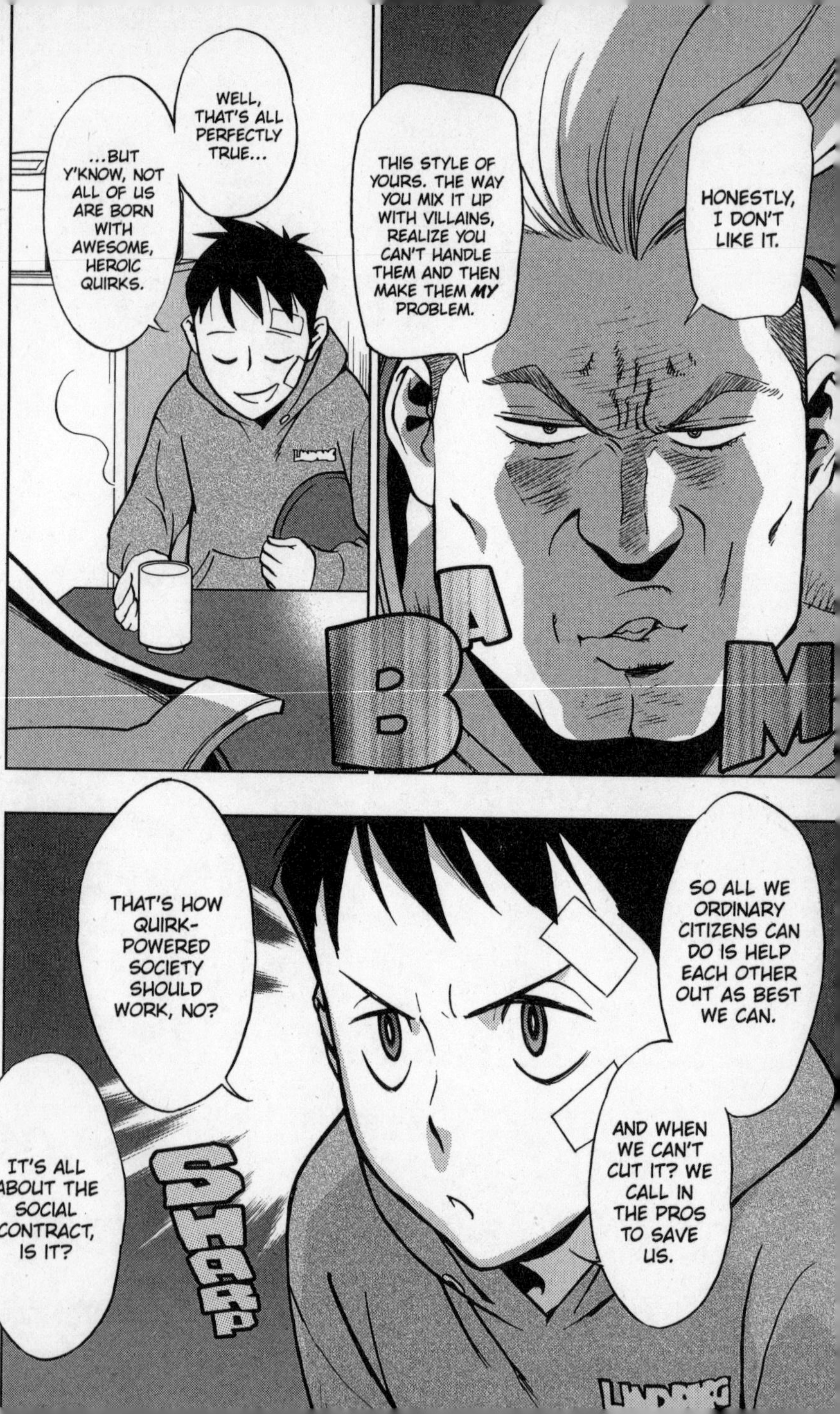
HONESTLY, I DON'T LIKE IT.
THIS STYLE OF YOURS. THE WAY YOU MIX IT UP WITH VILLAINS, REALIZE YOU CAN'T HANDLE THEM AND THEN MAKE THEM *MY* PROBLEM.
BAM
WELL, THAT'S ALL PERFECTLY TRUE...
...BUT Y'KNOW, NOT ALL OF US ARE BORN WITH AWESOME, HEROIC QUIRKS.
SO ALL WE ORDINARY CITIZENS CAN DO IS HELP EACH OTHER OUT AS BEST WE CAN.
THAT'S HOW QUIRK-POWERED SOCIETY SHOULD WORK, NO?
AND WHEN WE CAN'T CUT IT? WE CALL IN THE PROS TO SAVE US.
IT'S ALL ABOUT THE SOCIAL CONTRACT, IS IT?
SHARP

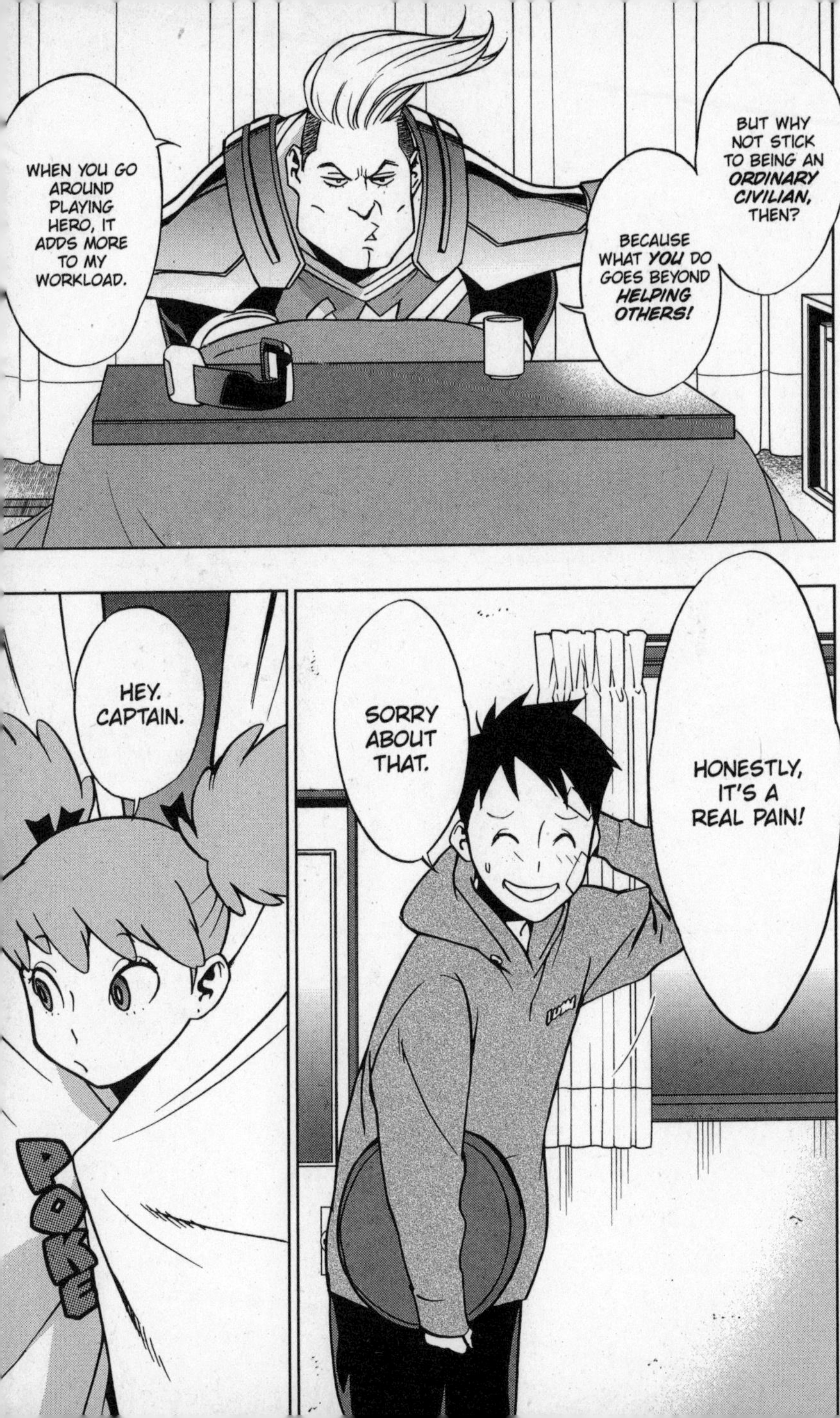
BUT WHY NOT STICK TO BEING AN ORDINARY CIVILIAN, THEN?
BECAUSE WHAT YOU DO GOES BEYOND HELPING OTHERS!
WHEN YOU GO AROUND PLAYING HERO, IT ADDS MORE TO MY WORKLOAD.
HONESTLY, IT'S A REAL PAIN!
SORRY ABOUT THAT.
HEY. CAPTAIN.
POKE

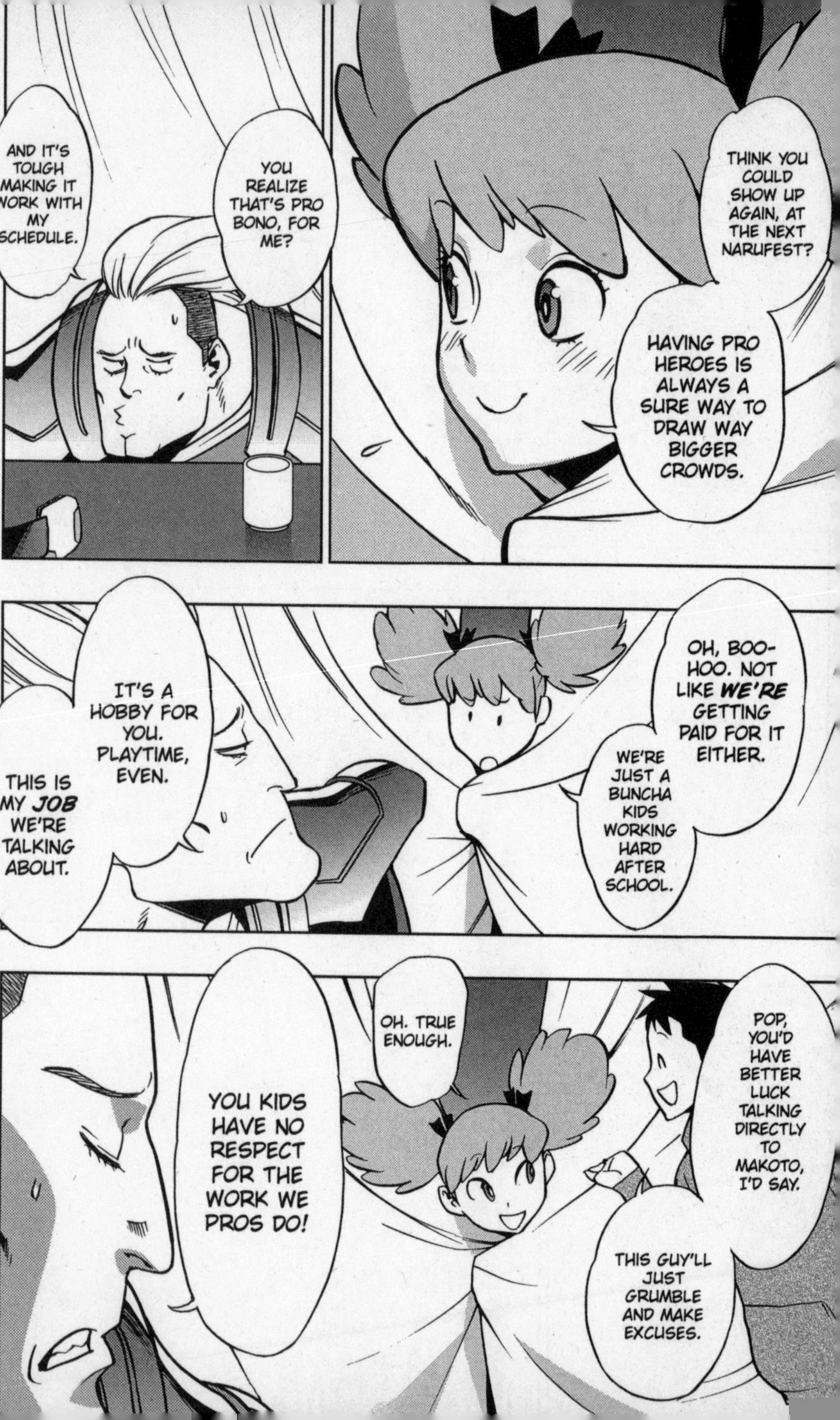
THINK YOU COULD SHOW UP AGAIN, AT THE NEXT NARUFEST?
HAVING PRO HEROES IS ALWAYS A SURE WAY TO DRAW WAY BIGGER CROWDS.
YOU REALIZE THAT'S PRO BONO, FOR ME?
AND IT'S TOUGH MAKING IT WORK WITH MY SCHEDULE.
OH, BOO-HOO. NOT LIKE *WE'RE* GETTING PAID FOR IT EITHER.
WE'RE JUST A BUNCHA KIDS WORKING HARD AFTER SCHOOL.
IT'S A HOBBY FOR YOU. PLAYTIME, EVEN.
THIS IS MY *JOB* WE'RE TALKING ABOUT.
POP, YOU'D HAVE BETTER LUCK TALKING DIRECTLY TO MAKOTO, I'D SAY.
THIS GUY'LL JUST GRUMBLE AND MAKE EXCUSES.
OH. TRUE ENOUGH.
YOU KIDS HAVE NO RESPECT FOR THE WORK WE PROS DO!

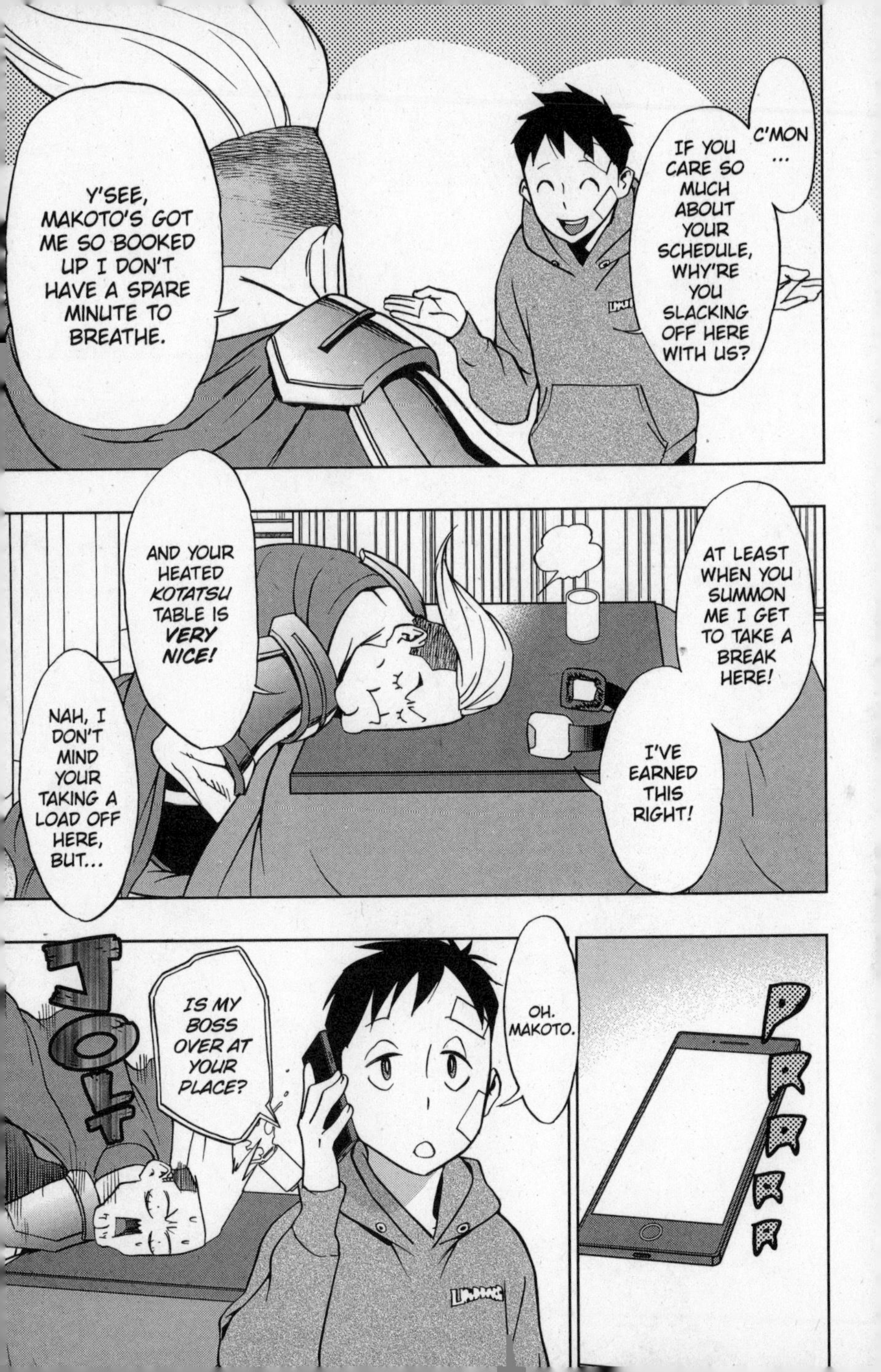
C'MON ...
IF YOU CARE SO MUCH ABOUT YOUR SCHEDULE, WHY'RE YOU SLACKING OFF HERE WITH US?
Y'SEE, MAKOTO'S GOT ME SO BOOKED UP I DON'T HAVE A SPARE MINUTE TO BREATHE.
AT LEAST WHEN YOU SUMMON ME I GET TO TAKE A BREAK HERE!
I'VE EARNED THIS RIGHT!
AND YOUR HEATED *KOTATSU* TABLE IS ***VERY NICE!***
NAH, I DON'T MIND YOUR TAKING A LOAD OFF HERE, BUT...
PRRRR
OH. MAKOTO.
IS MY BOSS OVER AT YOUR PLACE?
JOLT

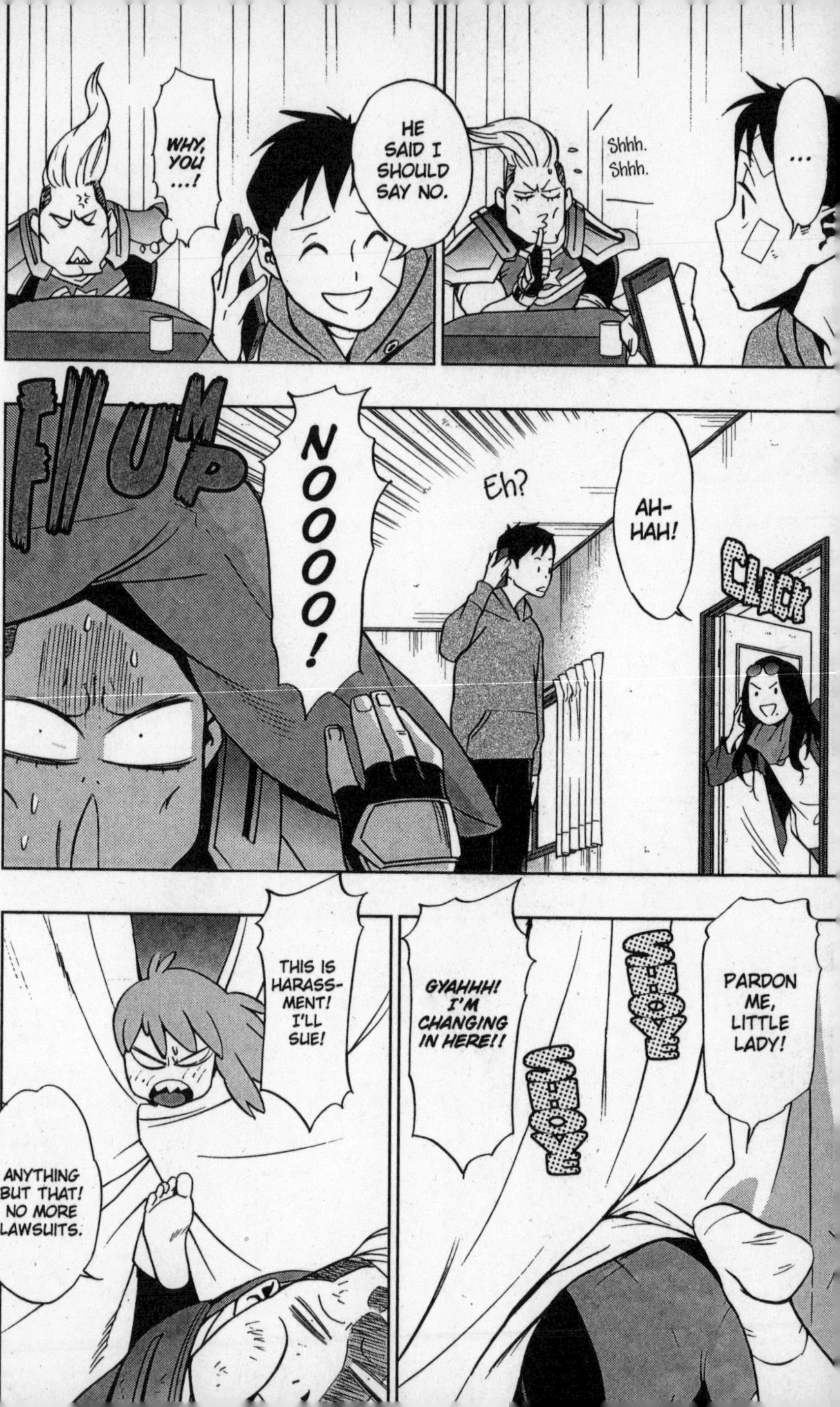
...
Shhh. Shhh.
HE SAID I SHOULD SAY NO.
WHY, YOU ...!
AH-HAH!
CLICK
Eh?
NOOOOO!
FWUMP
PARDON ME, LITTLE LADY!
GYAHHH! I'M CHANGING IN HERE!!
THIS IS HARASS-MENT! I'LL SUE!
ANYTHING BUT THAT! NO MORE LAWSUITS.

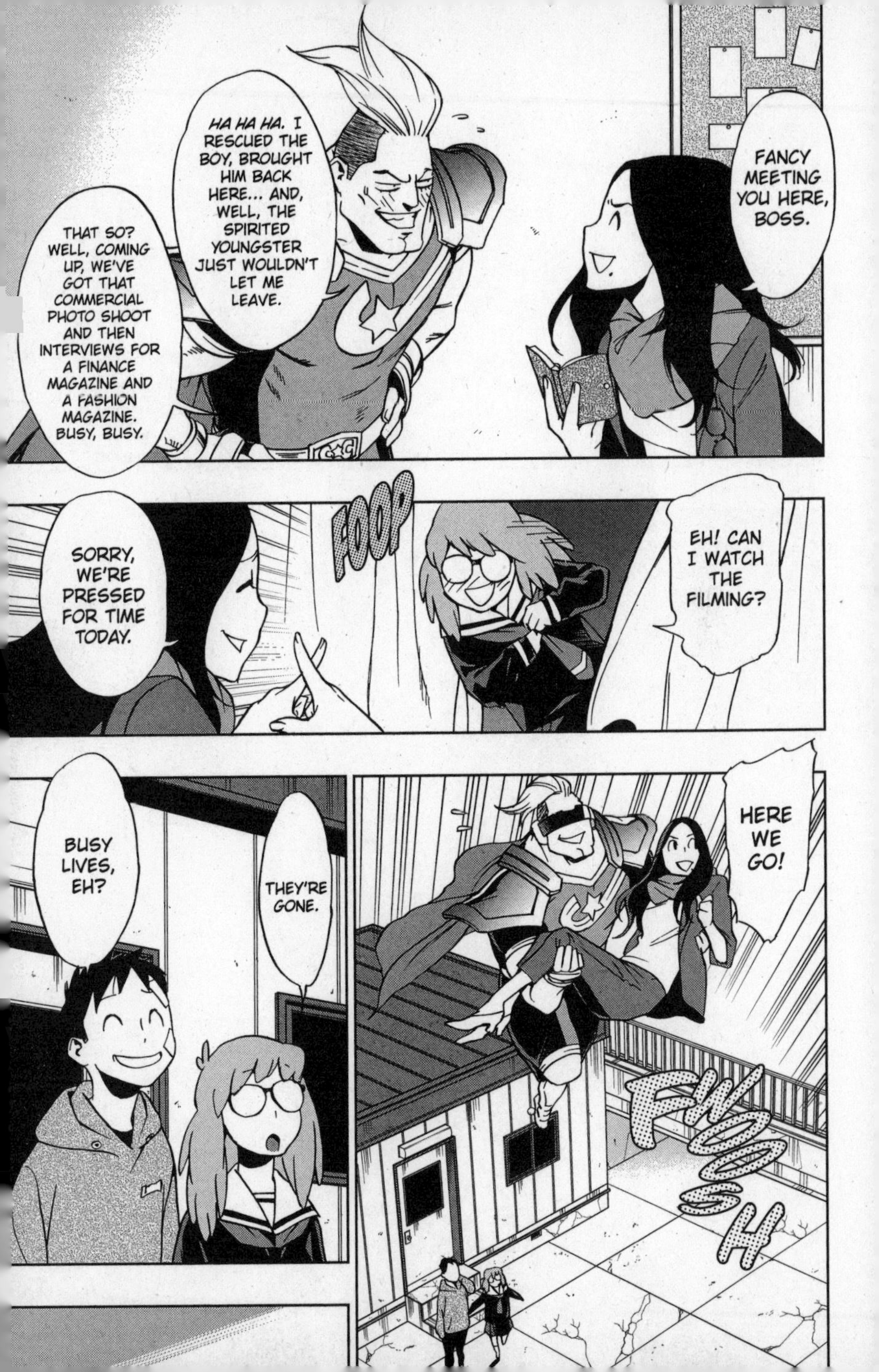
FANCY MEETING YOU HERE, BOSS.
HA HA HA. I RESCUED THE BOY, BROUGHT HIM BACK HERE... AND, WELL, THE SPIRITED YOUNGSTER JUST WOULDN'T LET ME LEAVE.
THAT SO? WELL, COMING UP, WE'VE GOT THAT COMMERCIAL PHOTO SHOOT AND THEN INTERVIEWS FOR A FINANCE MAGAZINE AND A FASHION MAGAZINE. BUSY, BUSY.
EH! CAN I WATCH THE FILMING?
FOOP
SORRY, WE'RE PRESSED FOR TIME TODAY.
HERE WE GO!
FWOOSH
THEY'RE GONE.
BUSY LIVES, EH?

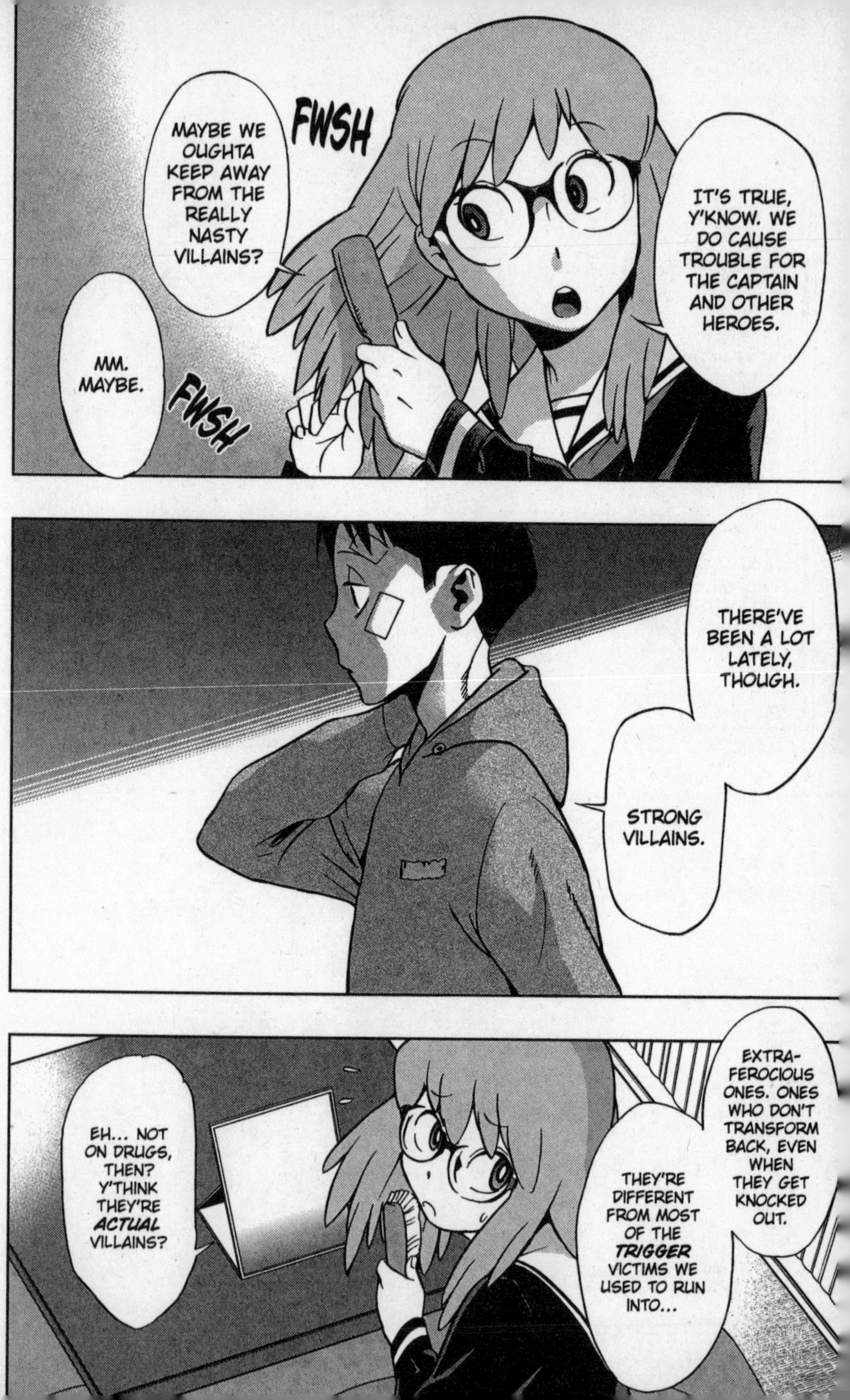
IT'S TRUE, Y'KNOW. WE DO CAUSE TROUBLE FOR THE CAPTAIN AND OTHER HEROES.
FWSH
MAYBE WE OUGHTA KEEP AWAY FROM THE REALLY NASTY VILLAINS?
FWSH
MM. MAYBE.
THERE'VE BEEN A LOT LATELY, THOUGH.
STRONG VILLAINS.
EXTRA-FEROCIOUS ONES. ONES WHO DON'T TRANSFORM BACK, EVEN WHEN THEY GET KNOCKED OUT.
THEY'RE DIFFERENT FROM MOST OF THE *TRIGGER* VICTIMS WE USED TO RUN INTO...
EH... NOT ON DRUGS, THEN? Y'THINK THEY'RE *ACTUAL* VILLAINS?

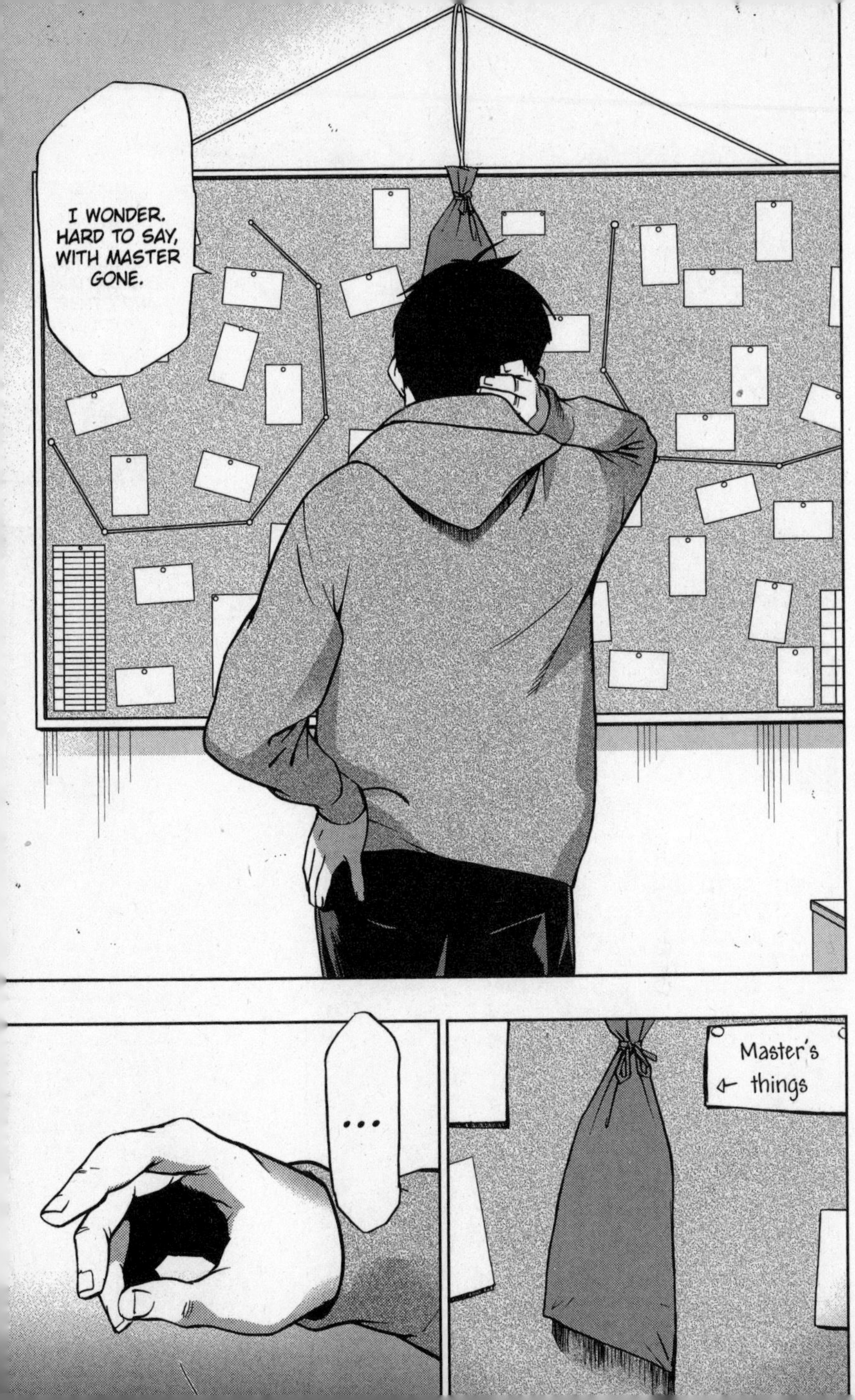
I WONDER. HARD TO SAY, WITH MASTER GONE.
Master's ← things
...

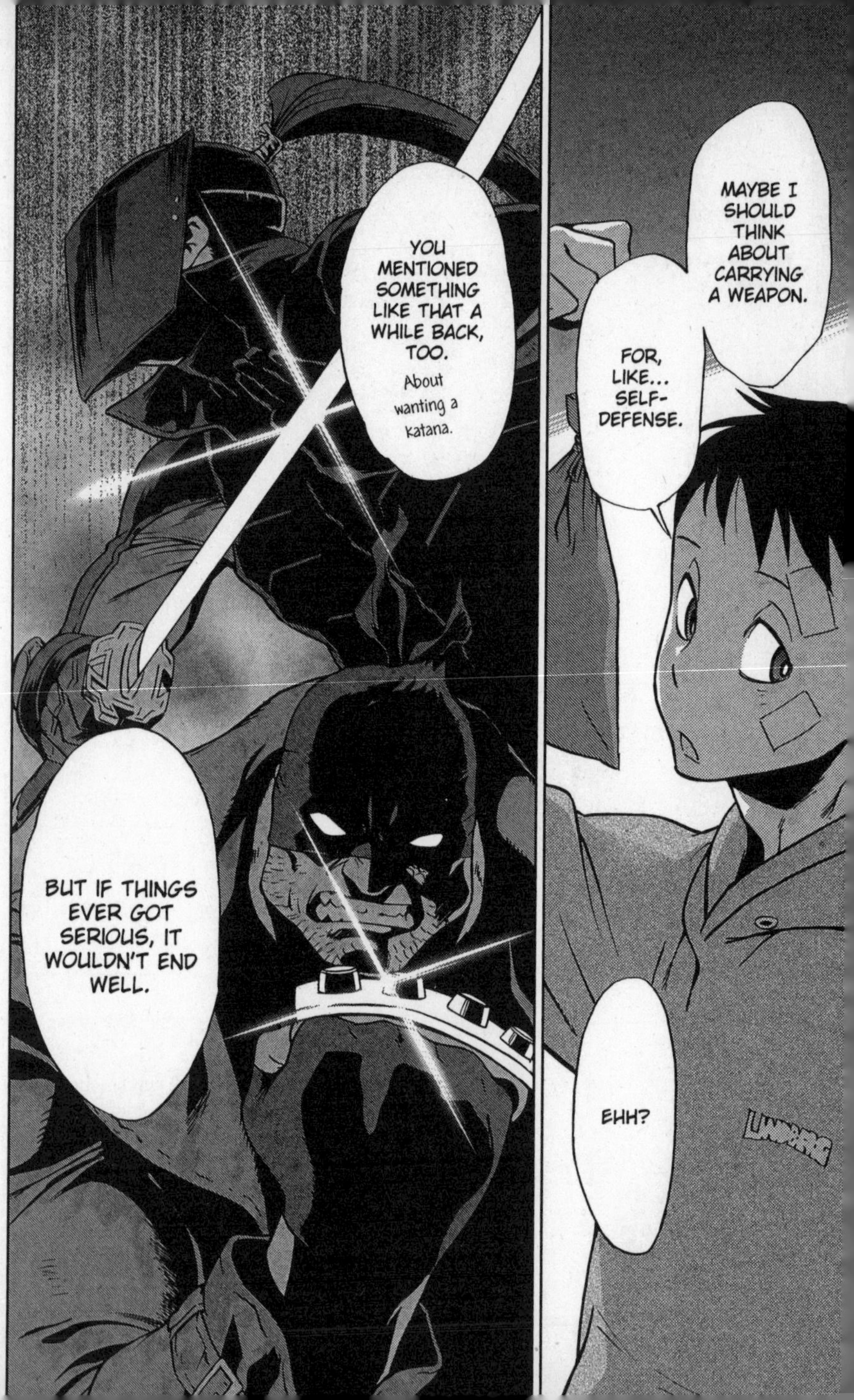
MAYBE I SHOULD THINK ABOUT CARRYING A WEAPON.
FOR, LIKE... SELF-DEFENSE.
EHH?
YOU MENTIONED SOMETHING LIKE THAT A WHILE BACK, TOO.
About wanting a katana.
BUT IF THINGS EVER GOT SERIOUS, IT WOULDN'T END WELL.

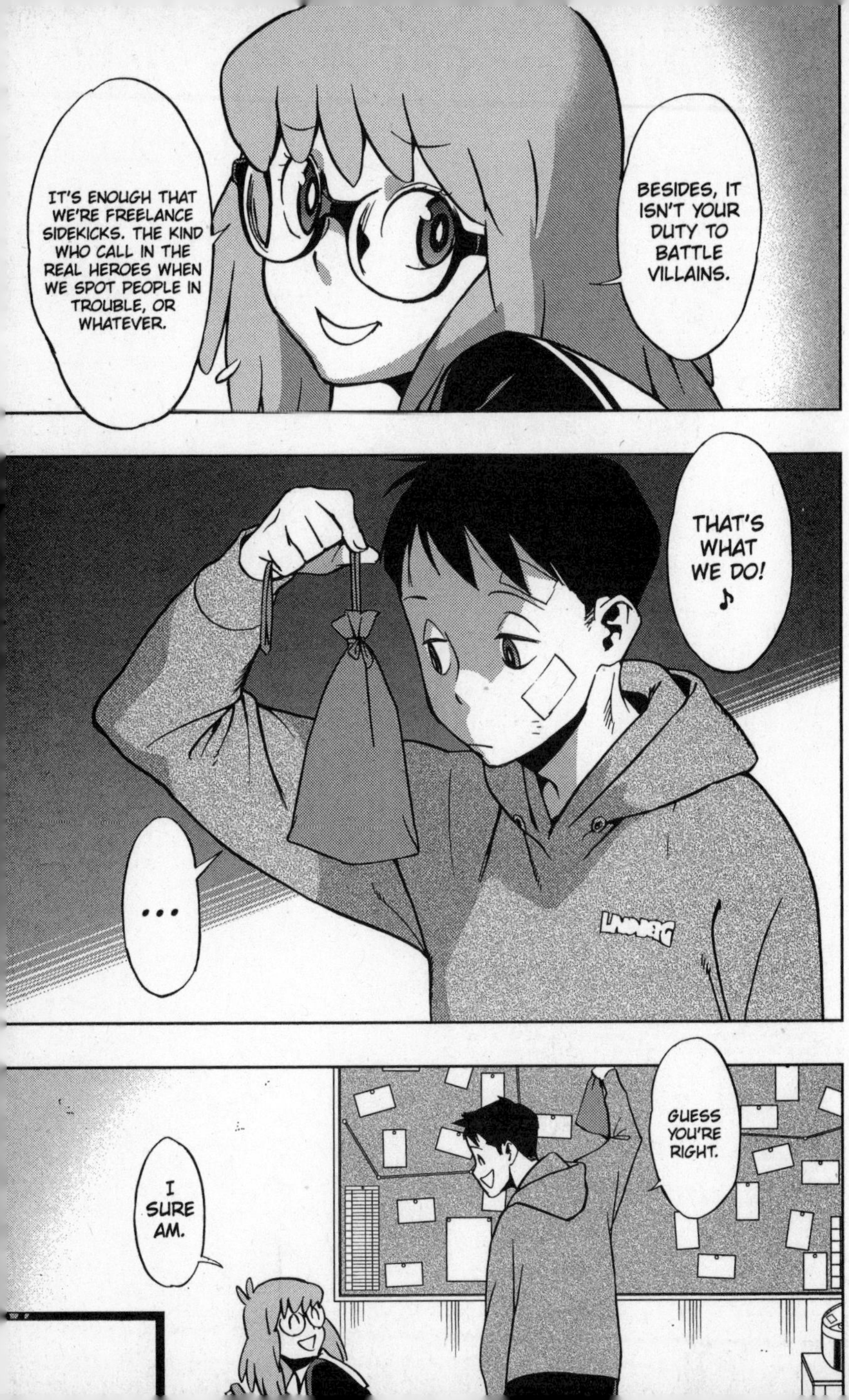
BESIDES, IT ISN'T YOUR DUTY TO BATTLE VILLAINS.
IT'S ENOUGH THAT WE'RE FREELANCE SIDEKICKS. THE KIND WHO CALL IN THE REAL HEROES WHEN WE SPOT PEOPLE IN TROUBLE, OR WHATEVER.
THAT'S WHAT WE DO! ♪
...
GUESS YOU'RE RIGHT.
I SURE AM.

PRAYING MANTIS VILLAIN

THE ROUGH DESIGN

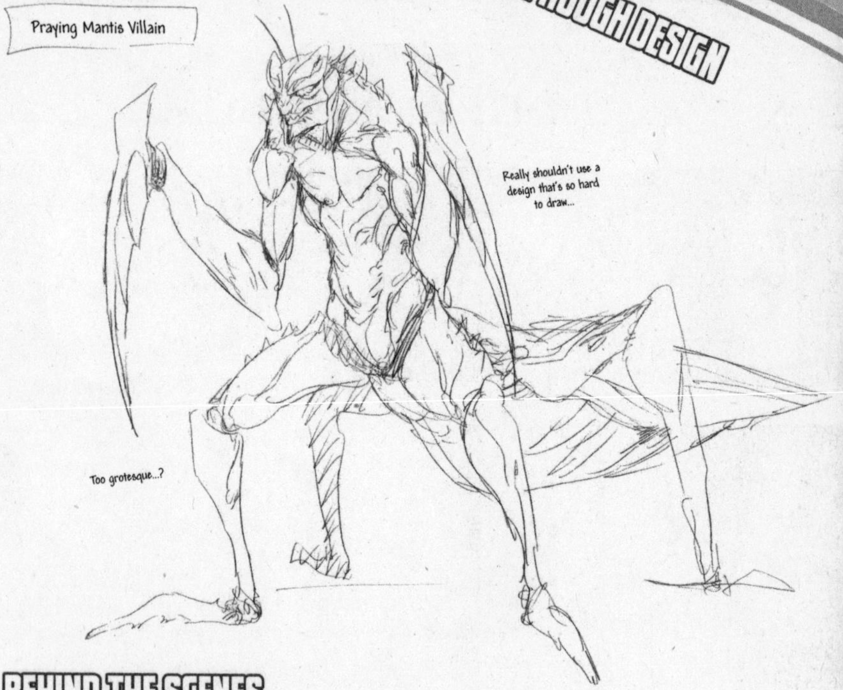
Praying Mantis Villain
Really shouldn't use a design that's so hard to draw...
Too grotesque...?

BEHIND THE SCENES

Another bioengineered villain, like Teruo the eel boy. The defining characteristics for this guy were "Extremely mutated," "Pretty big" and "Body is black because of the drugs coursing through him (when not on drugs, he's white)."

He's just convenient cannon fodder at first, but he turns out to be friends with the Hotta Brothers and gets some character development later.

—Furuhashi

The concept art felt a little lacking, so I added more details for his actual appearance in the story. Of course, adding details amounts to digging my own grave. Striking that balance is tough. (LOL)

—Betten

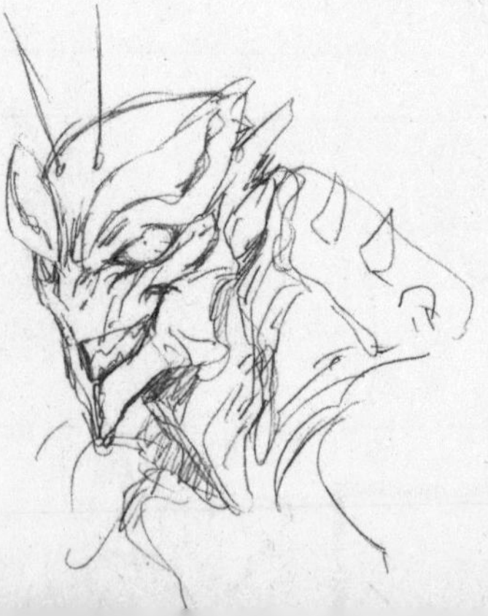

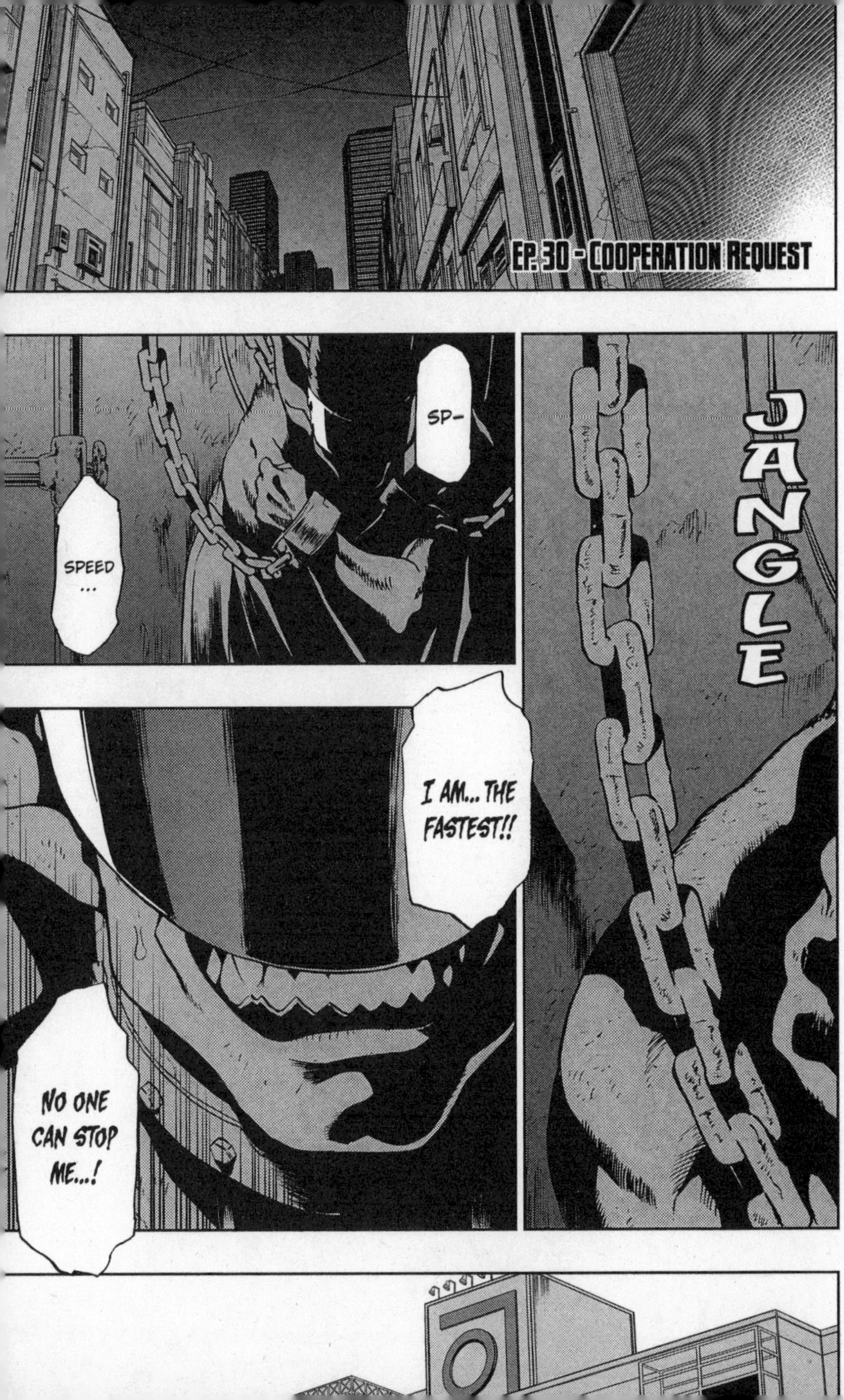
EP. 30 - COOPERATION REQUEST
JANGLE
SP-
SPEED ...
I AM... THE FASTEST!!
NO ONE CAN STOP ME...!

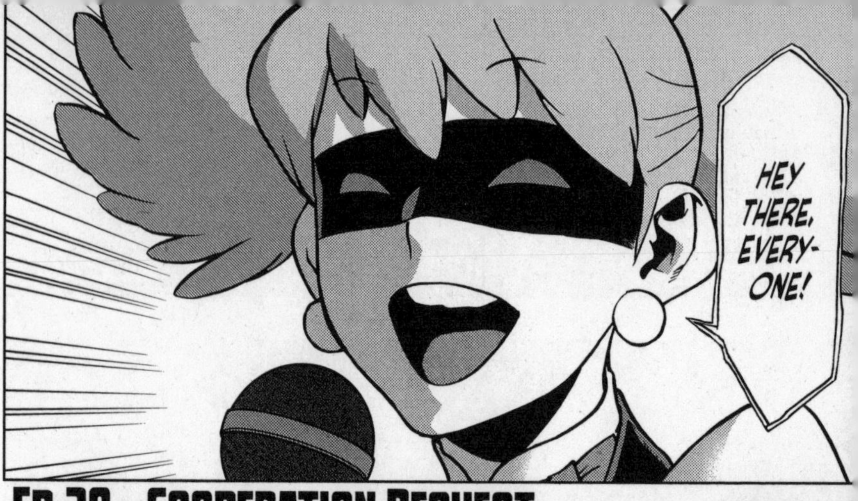
HEY THERE, EVERYONE!

EP. 30 - COOPERATION REQUEST

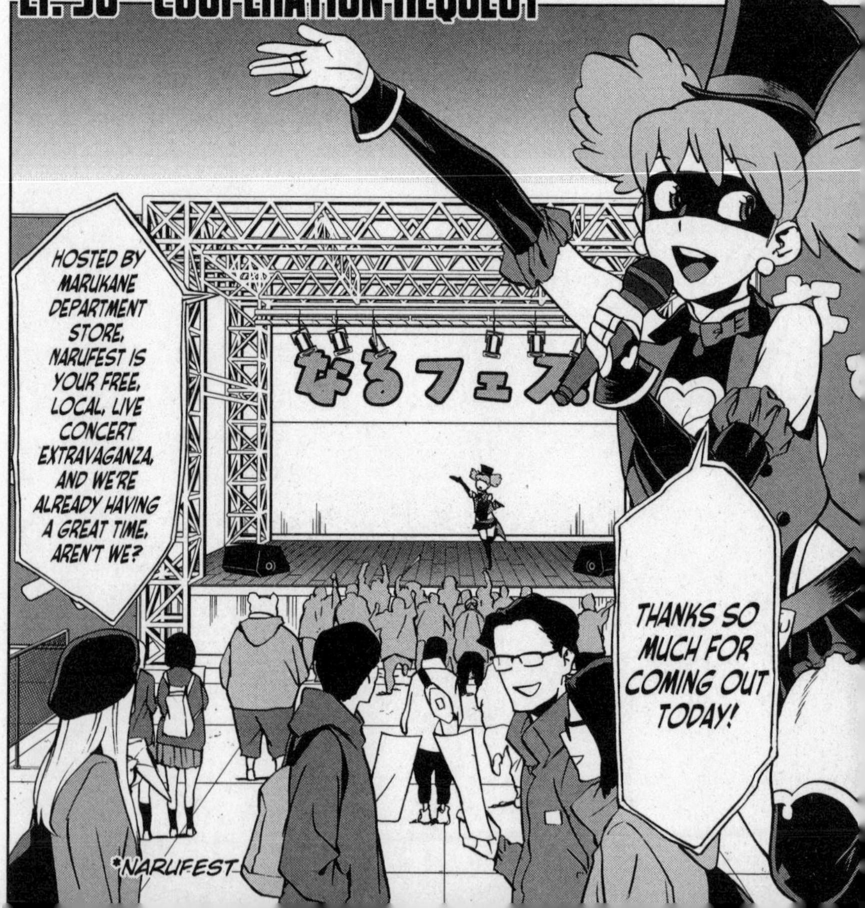
THANKS SO MUCH FOR COMING OUT TODAY!
HOSTED BY MARUKANE DEPARTMENT STORE, NARUFEST IS YOUR FREE, LOCAL, LIVE CONCERT EXTRAVAGANZA, AND WE'RE ALREADY HAVING A GREAT TIME, AREN'T WE?
なるフェス
*NARUFEST

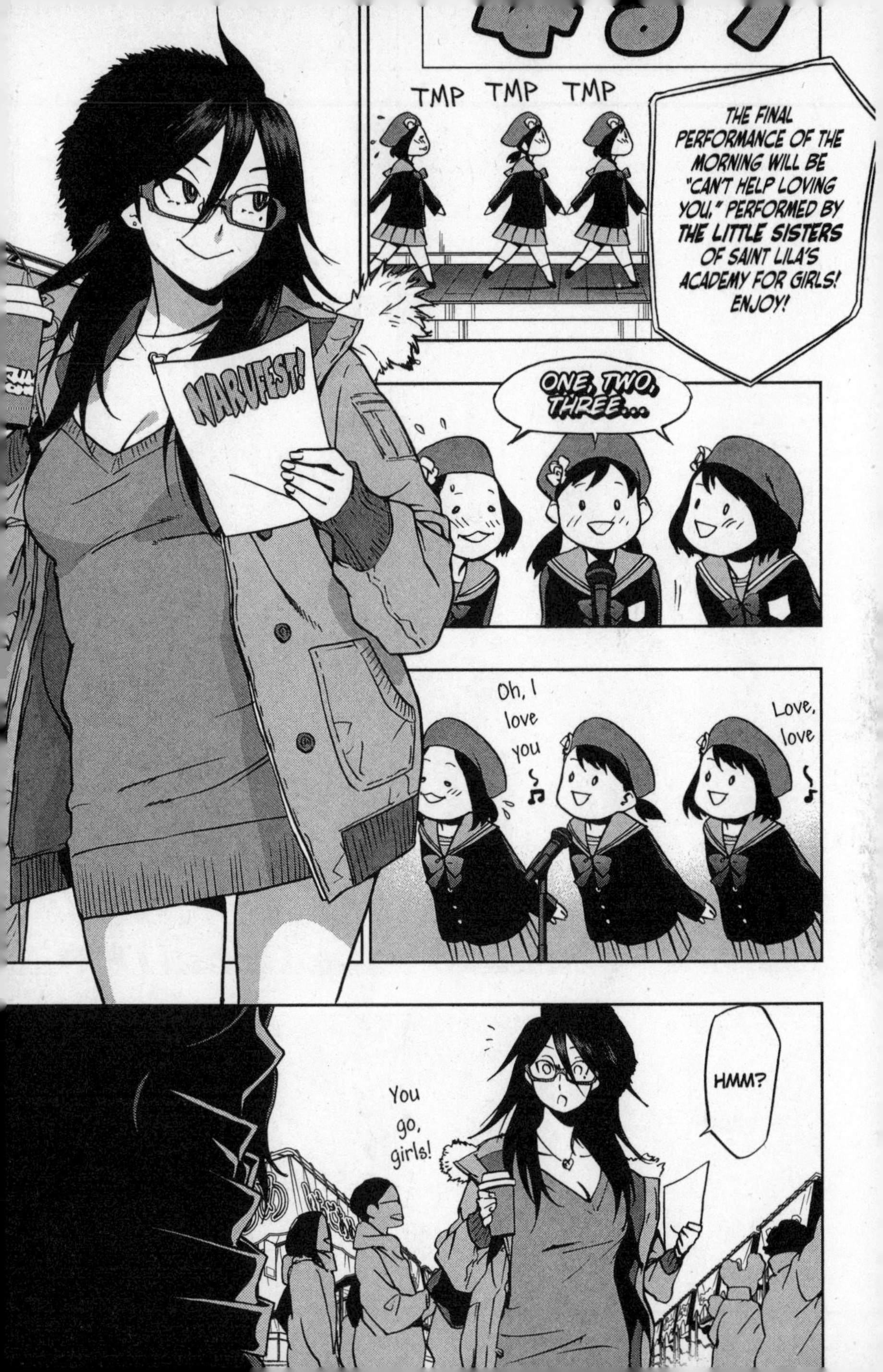
THE FINAL PERFORMANCE OF THE MORNING WILL BE "CAN'T HELP LOVING YOU," PERFORMED BY THE LITTLE SISTERS OF SAINT LILA'S ACADEMY FOR GIRLS! ENJOY!
TMP TMP TMP
ONE, TWO, THREE...
Love, love
Oh, I love you
NARUFEST!
HMM?
You go, girls!

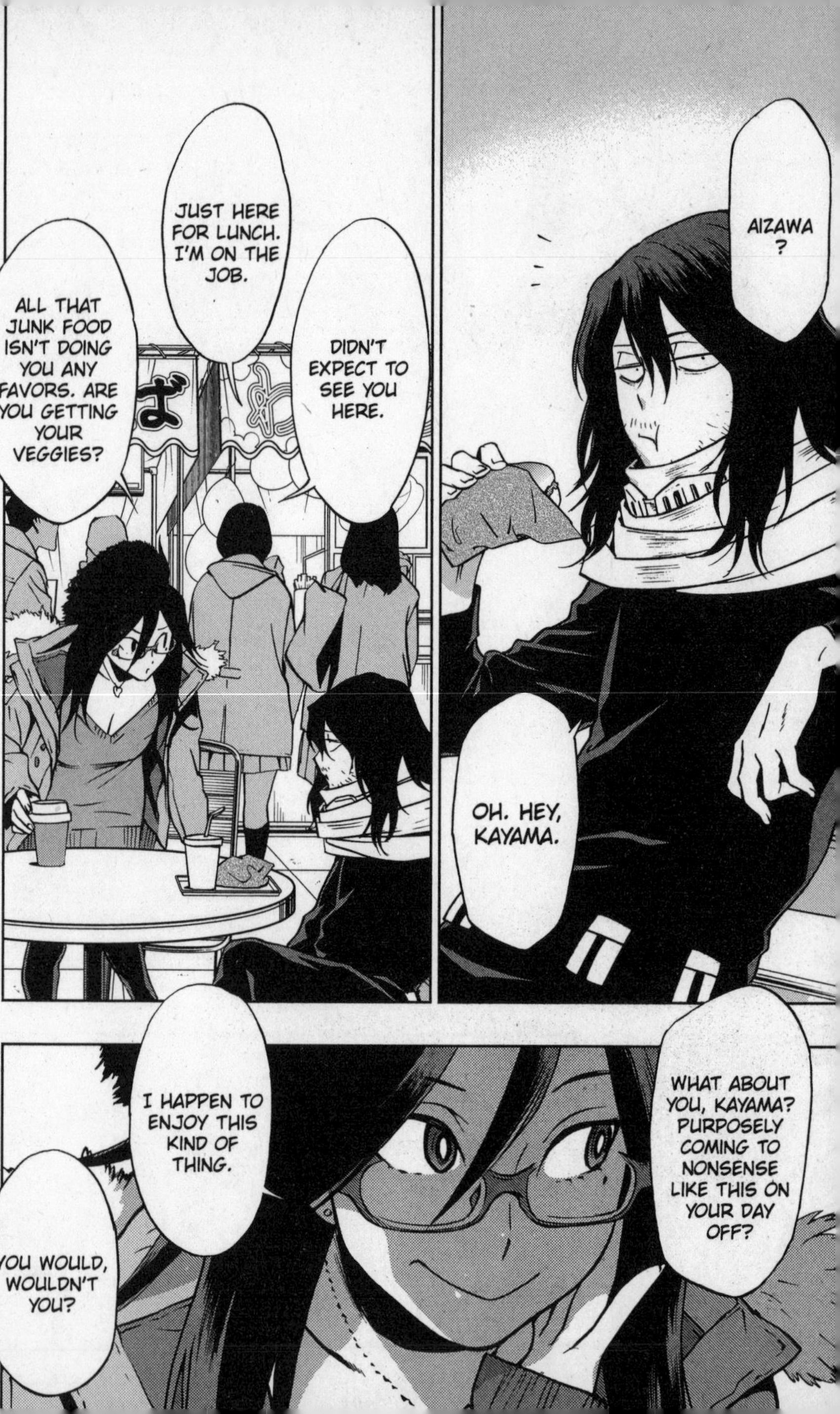
AIZAWA?
OH. HEY, KAYAMA.
DIDN'T EXPECT TO SEE YOU HERE.
JUST HERE FOR LUNCH. I'M ON THE JOB.
ALL THAT JUNK FOOD ISN'T DOING YOU ANY FAVORS. ARE YOU GETTING YOUR VEGGIES?
WHAT ABOUT YOU, KAYAMA? PURPOSELY COMING TO NONSENSE LIKE THIS ON YOUR DAY OFF?
I HAPPEN TO ENJOY THIS KIND OF THING.
YOU WOULD, WOULDN'T YOU?

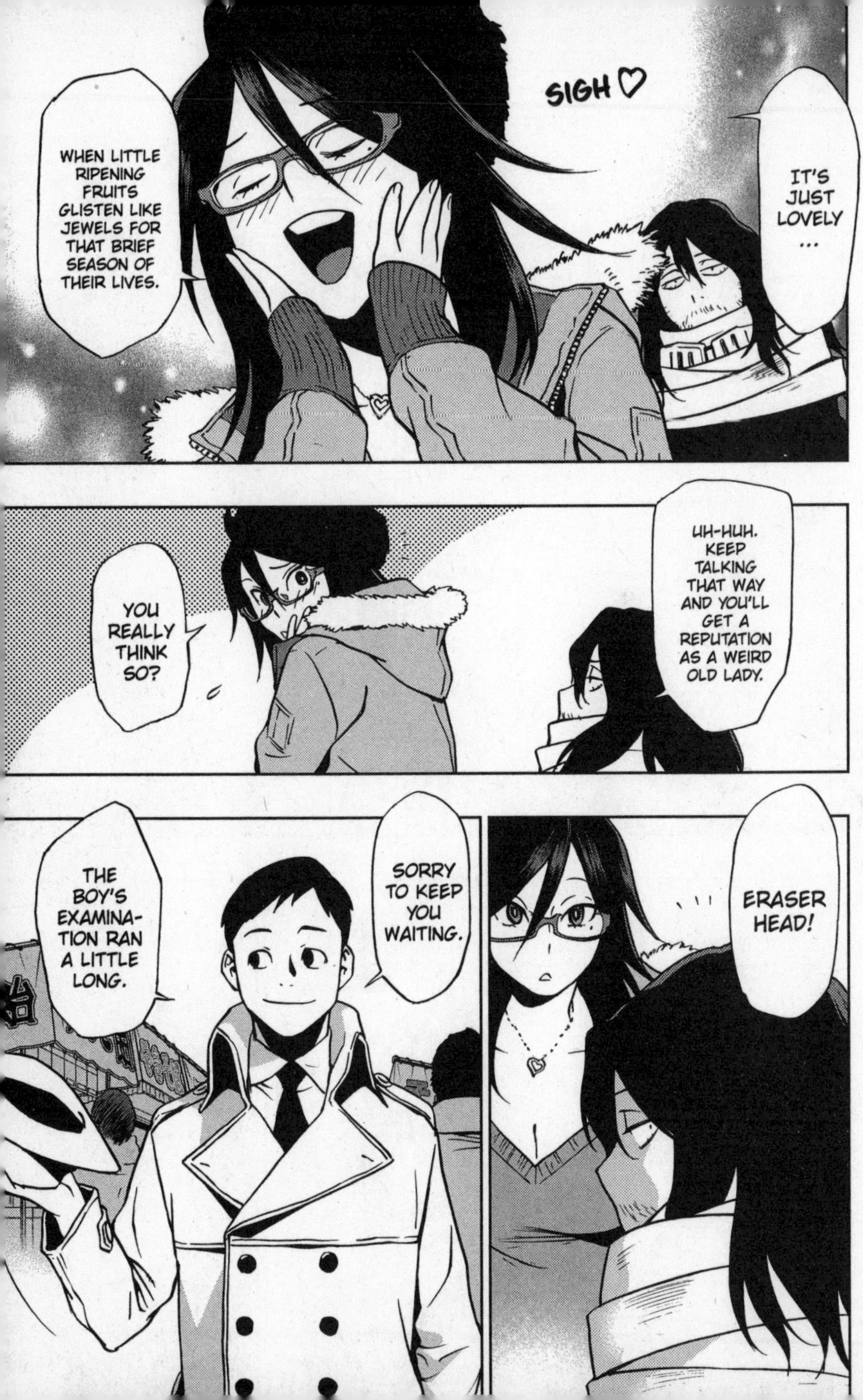
IT'S JUST LOVELY ...
SIGH ♡
WHEN LITTLE RIPENING FRUITS GLISTEN LIKE JEWELS FOR THAT BRIEF SEASON OF THEIR LIVES.
UH-HUH. KEEP TALKING THAT WAY AND YOU'LL GET A REPUTATION AS A WEIRD OLD LADY.
YOU REALLY THINK SO?
ERASER HEAD!
SORRY TO KEEP YOU WAITING.
THE BOY'S EXAMINATION RAN A LITTLE LONG.

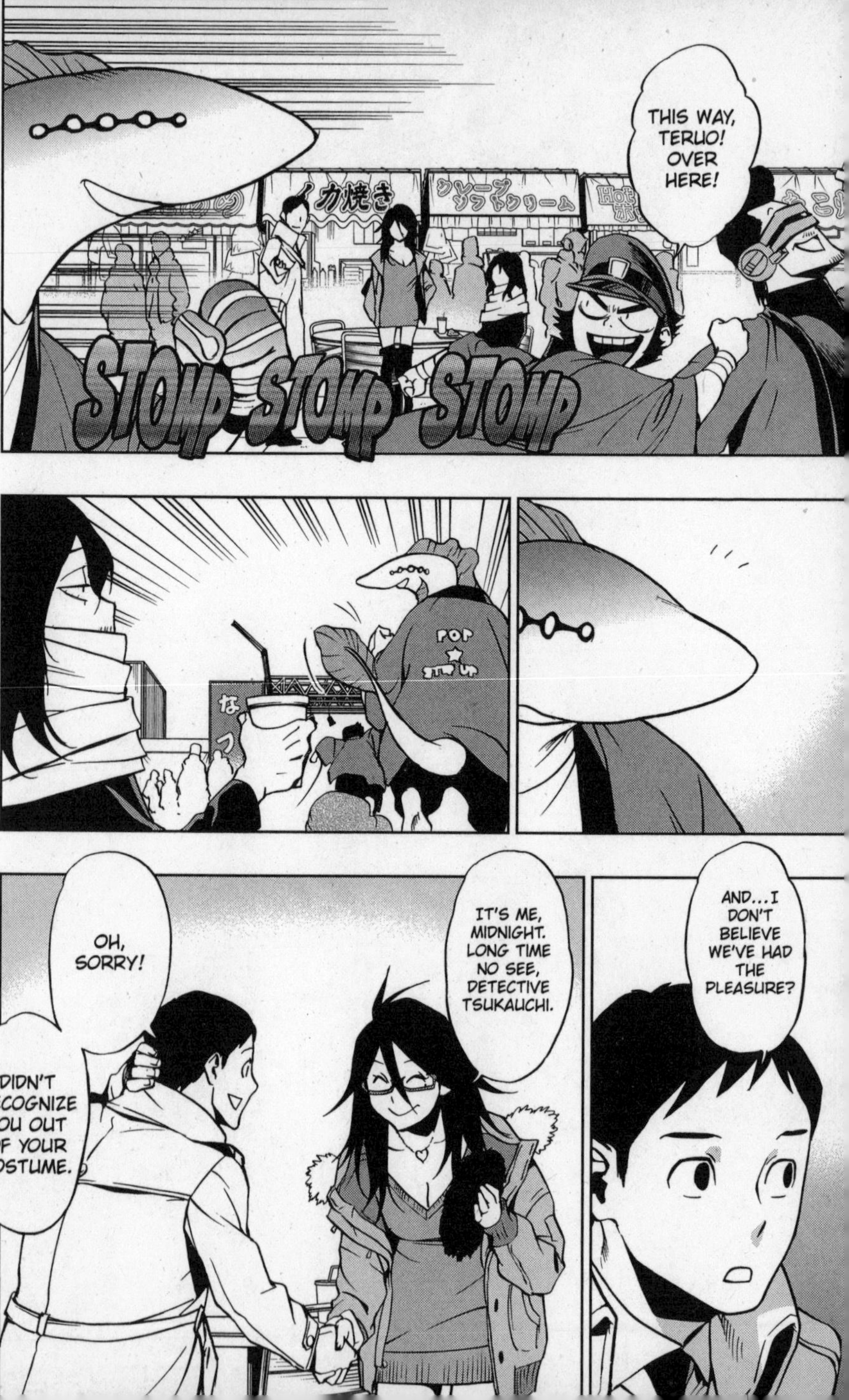
THIS WAY, TERUO! OVER HERE!
クレープ ソフトクリーム
イカ焼き
STOMP STOMP STOMP
AND...I DON'T BELIEVE WE'VE HAD THE PLEASURE?
IT'S ME, MIDNIGHT. LONG TIME NO SEE, DETECTIVE TSUKAUCHI.
OH, SORRY!
DIDN'T RECOGNIZE YOU OUT OF YOUR COSTUME.

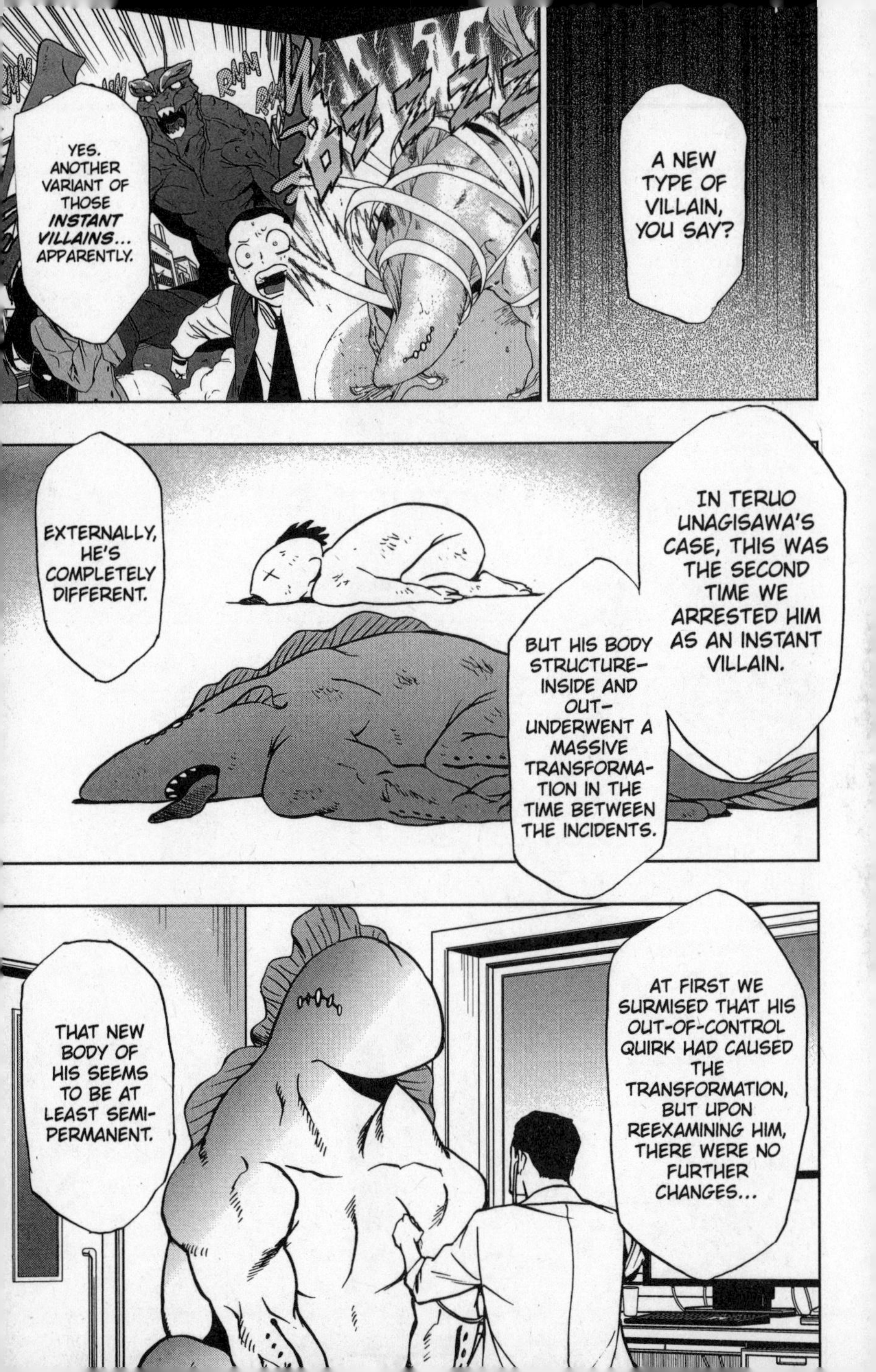
A NEW TYPE OF VILLAIN, YOU SAY?
YES. ANOTHER VARIANT OF THOSE ***INSTANT VILLAINS***... APPARENTLY.
IN TERUO UNAGISAWA'S CASE, THIS WAS THE SECOND TIME WE ARRESTED HIM AS AN INSTANT VILLAIN.
EXTERNALLY, HE'S COMPLETELY DIFFERENT.
BUT HIS BODY STRUCTURE—INSIDE AND OUT—UNDERWENT A MASSIVE TRANSFORMATION IN THE TIME BETWEEN THE INCIDENTS.
AT FIRST WE SURMISED THAT HIS OUT-OF-CONTROL QUIRK HAD CAUSED THE TRANSFORMATION, BUT UPON REEXAMINING HIM, THERE WERE NO FURTHER CHANGES...
THAT NEW BODY OF HIS SEEMS TO BE AT LEAST SEMI-PERMANENT.

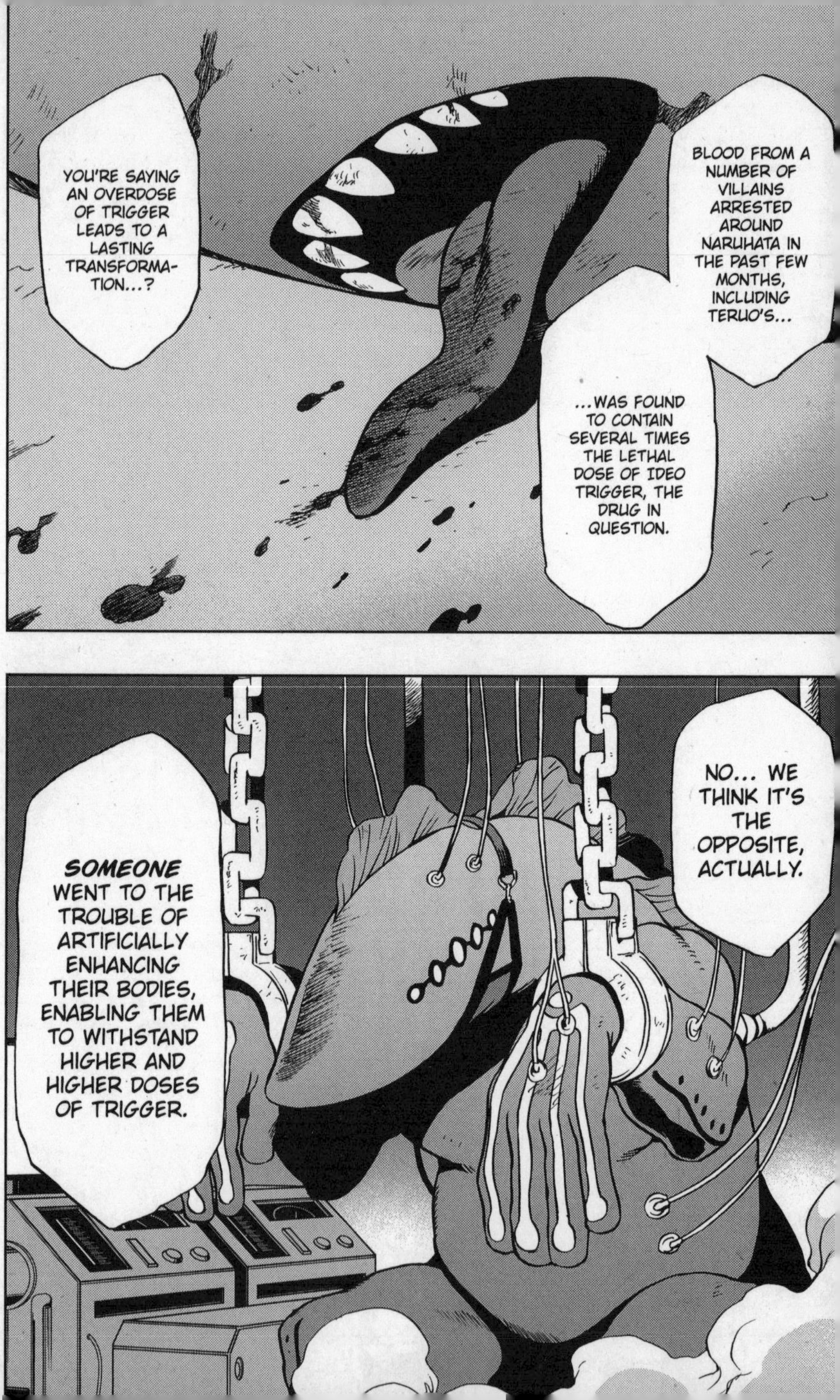
BLOOD FROM A NUMBER OF VILLAINS ARRESTED AROUND NARUHATA IN THE PAST FEW MONTHS, INCLUDING TERUO'S...
...WAS FOUND TO CONTAIN SEVERAL TIMES THE LETHAL DOSE OF IDEO TRIGGER, THE DRUG IN QUESTION.
YOU'RE SAYING AN OVERDOSE OF TRIGGER LEADS TO A LASTING TRANSFORMATION...?
NO... WE THINK IT'S THE OPPOSITE, ACTUALLY.
SOMEONE WENT TO THE TROUBLE OF ARTIFICIALLY ENHANCING THEIR BODIES, ENABLING THEM TO WITHSTAND HIGHER AND HIGHER DOSES OF TRIGGER.

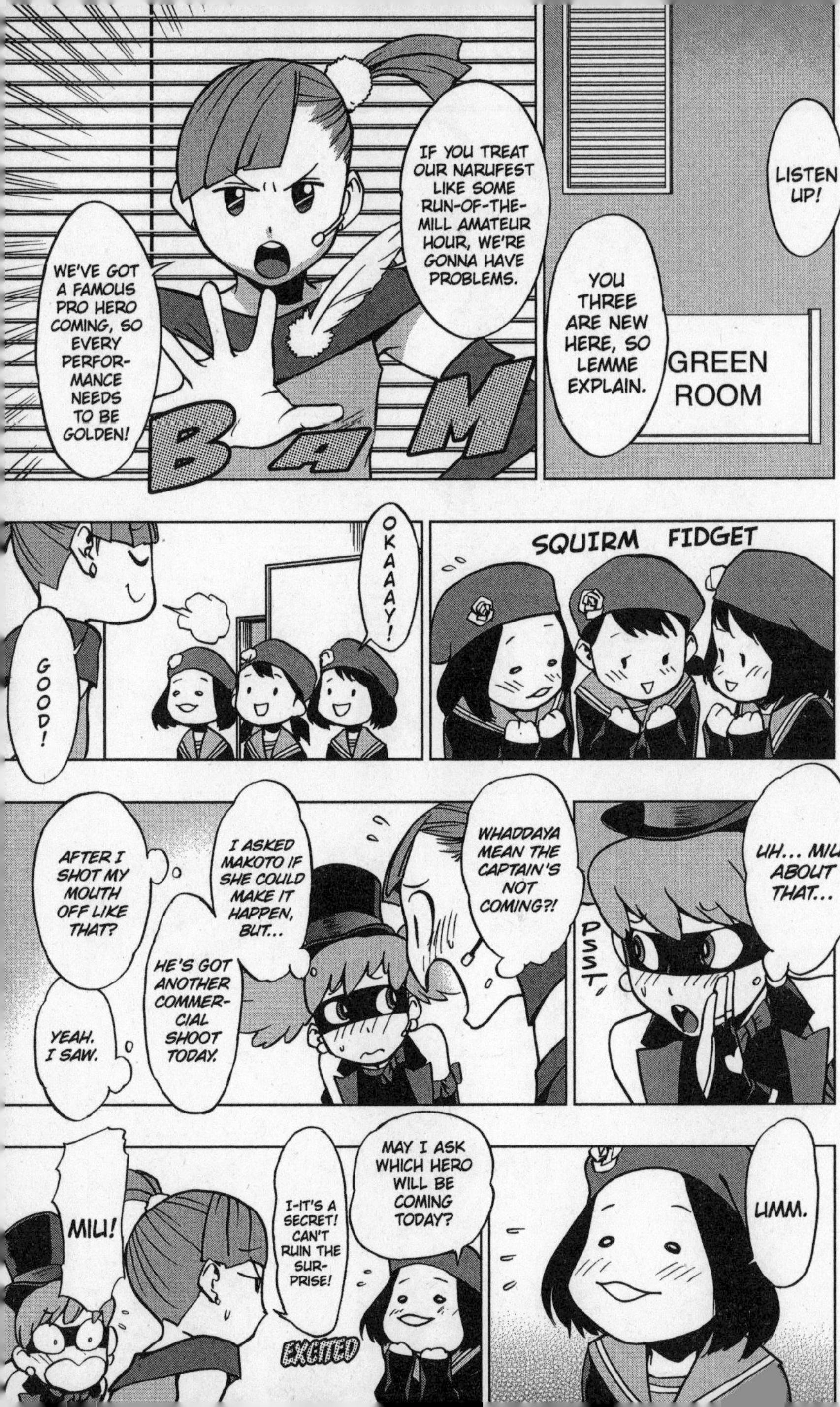
LISTEN UP!
YOU THREE ARE NEW HERE, SO LEMME EXPLAIN.
GREEN ROOM
IF YOU TREAT OUR NARUFEST LIKE SOME RUN-OF-THE-MILL AMATEUR HOUR, WE'RE GONNA HAVE PROBLEMS.
WE'VE GOT A FAMOUS PRO HERO COMING, SO EVERY PERFORMANCE NEEDS TO BE GOLDEN!
BAM
SQUIRM FIDGET
OKAAAY!
GOOD!
PSST
UH... MIU. ABOUT THAT...
WHADDAYA MEAN THE CAPTAIN'S NOT COMING?!
I ASKED MAKOTO IF SHE COULD MAKE IT HAPPEN, BUT...
HE'S GOT ANOTHER COMMERCIAL SHOOT TODAY.
AFTER I SHOT MY MOUTH OFF LIKE THAT?
YEAH. I SAW.
UMM.
MAY I ASK WHICH HERO WILL BE COMING TODAY?
I-IT'S A SECRET! CAN'T RUIN THE SURPRISE!
EXCITED
MIU!

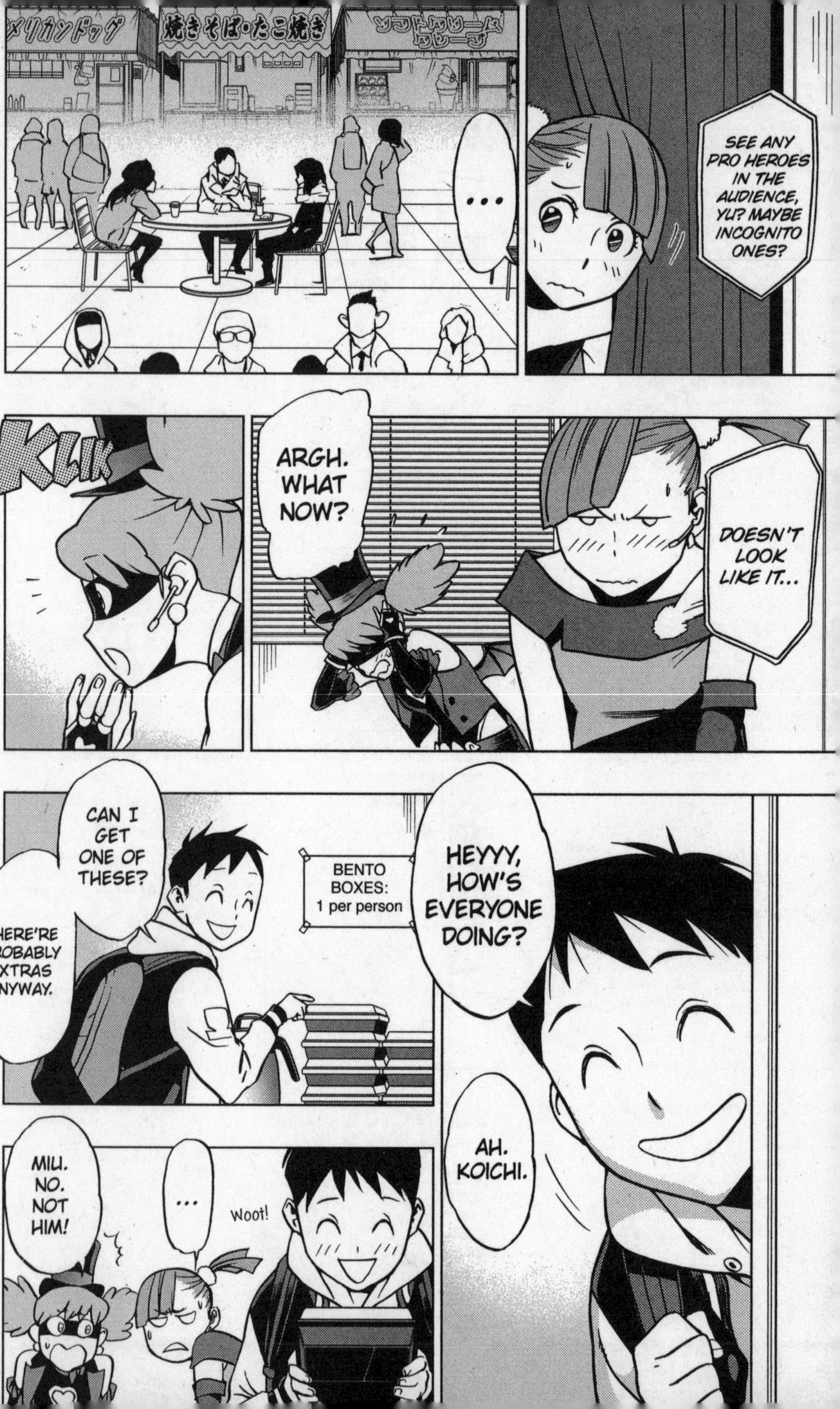
SEE ANY PRO HEROES IN THE AUDIENCE, YU? MAYBE INCOGNITO ONES?
メリカンドッグ
焼きそば・たこ焼き
...
DOESN'T LOOK LIKE IT...
ARGH. WHAT NOW?
KLIK
HEYYY, HOW'S EVERYONE DOING?
AH. KOICHI.
CAN I GET ONE OF THESE?
BENTO BOXES: 1 per person
THERE'RE PROBABLY EXTRAS ANYWAY.
Woot!
...
MIU. NO. NOT HIM!

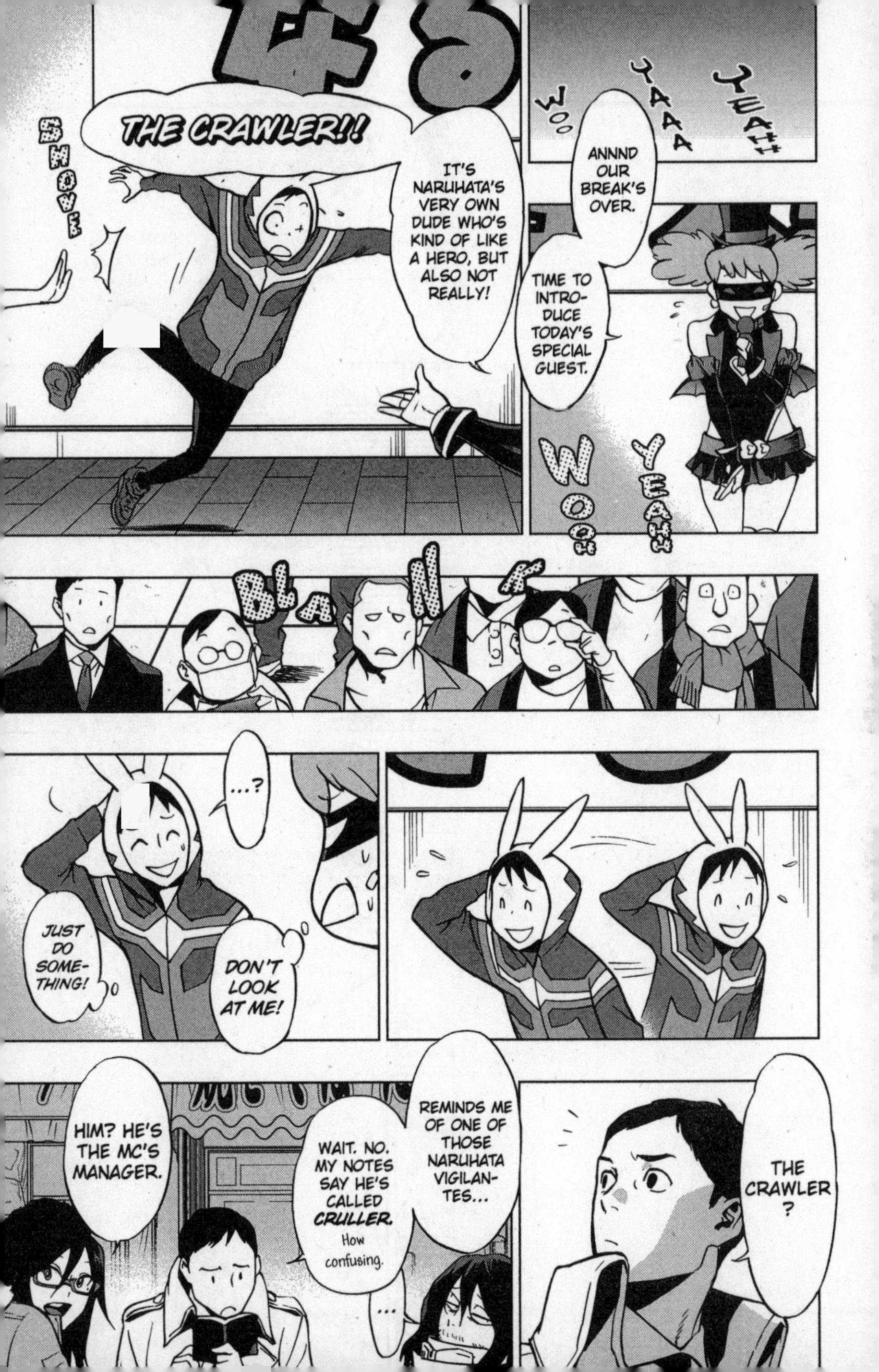
YEAHH
YAAAA
WOO
ANNND OUR BREAK'S OVER.
TIME TO INTRO-DUCE TODAY'S SPECIAL GUEST.
YEAHH
WOO!
IT'S NARUHATA'S VERY OWN DUDE WHO'S KIND OF LIKE A HERO, BUT ALSO NOT REALLY!
THE CRAWLER!!
SHOVE
BLANK
...?
JUST DO SOME-THING!
DON'T LOOK AT ME!
THE CRAWLER?
REMINDS ME OF ONE OF THOSE NARUHATA VIGILAN-TES...
WAIT. NO. MY NOTES SAY HE'S CALLED CRULLER.
How confusing.
HIM? HE'S THE MC'S MANAGER.
...

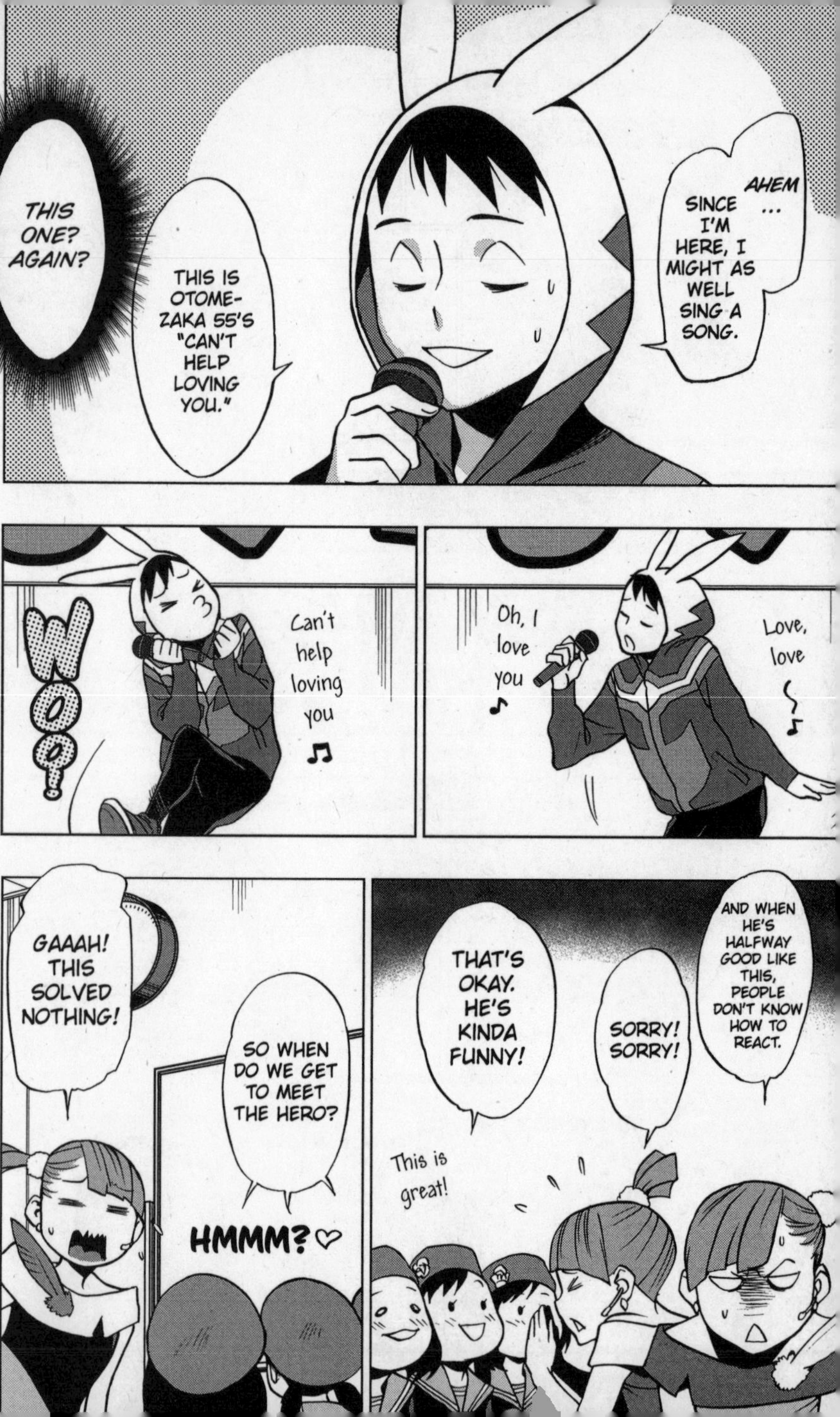
AHEM ...
SINCE I'M HERE, I MIGHT AS WELL SING A SONG.
THIS IS OTOMEZAKA 55'S "CAN'T HELP LOVING YOU."
THIS ONE? AGAIN?
Love, love ♪
Oh, I love you ♪
Can't help loving you ♫
WOO!
AND WHEN HE'S HALFWAY GOOD LIKE THIS, PEOPLE DON'T KNOW HOW TO REACT.
SORRY! SORRY!
THAT'S OKAY. HE'S KINDA FUNNY!
This is great!
GAAAH! THIS SOLVED NOTHING!
SO WHEN DO WE GET TO MEET THE HERO?
HMMM?♡

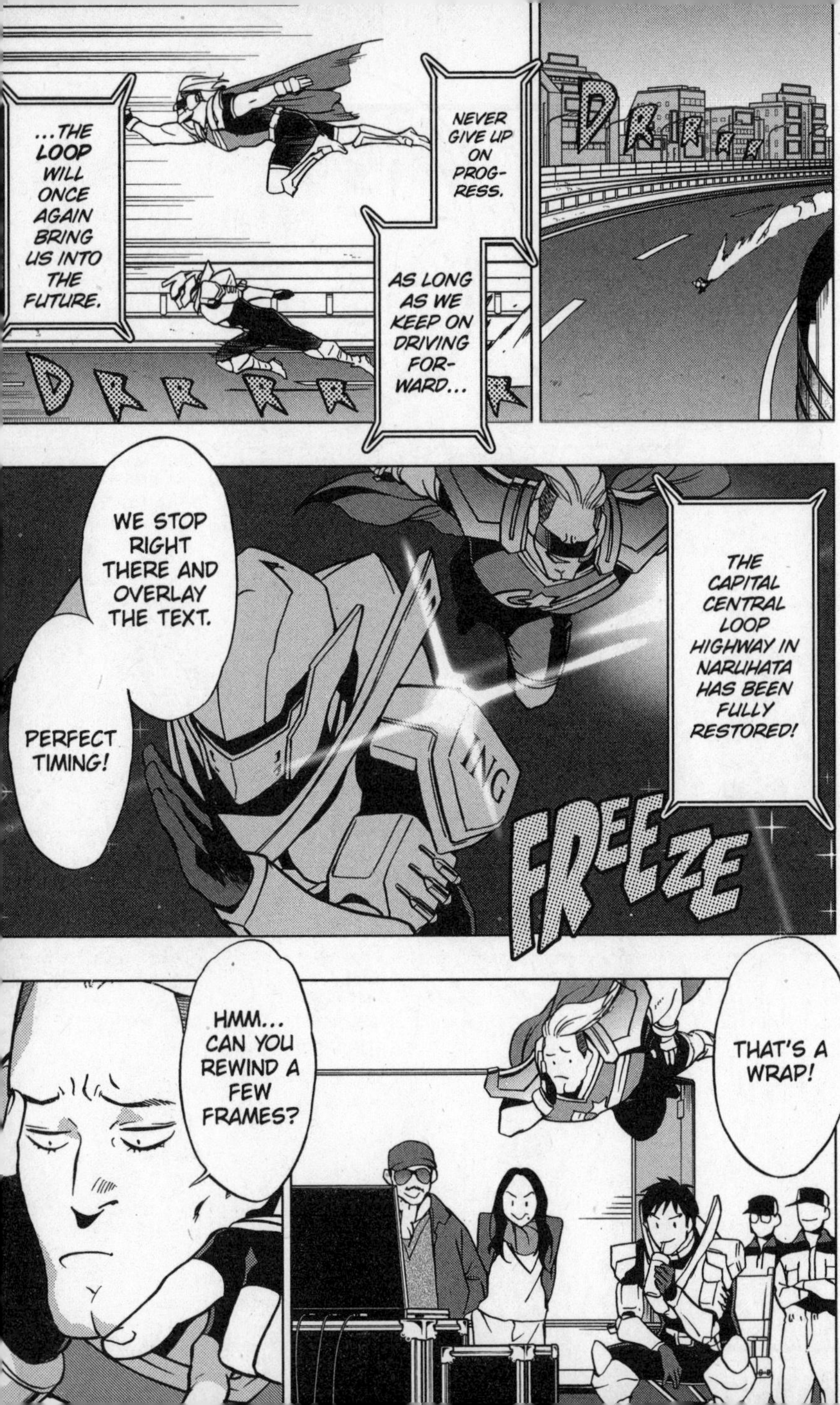
DRRR
NEVER GIVE UP ON PROGRESS.
AS LONG AS WE KEEP ON DRIVING FORWARD...
...THE LOOP WILL ONCE AGAIN BRING US INTO THE FUTURE.
DRRRRR
THE CAPITAL CENTRAL LOOP HIGHWAY IN NARUHATA HAS BEEN FULLY RESTORED!
FREEZE
WE STOP RIGHT THERE AND OVERLAY THE TEXT.
PERFECT TIMING!
THAT'S A WRAP!
HMM... CAN YOU REWIND A FEW FRAMES?

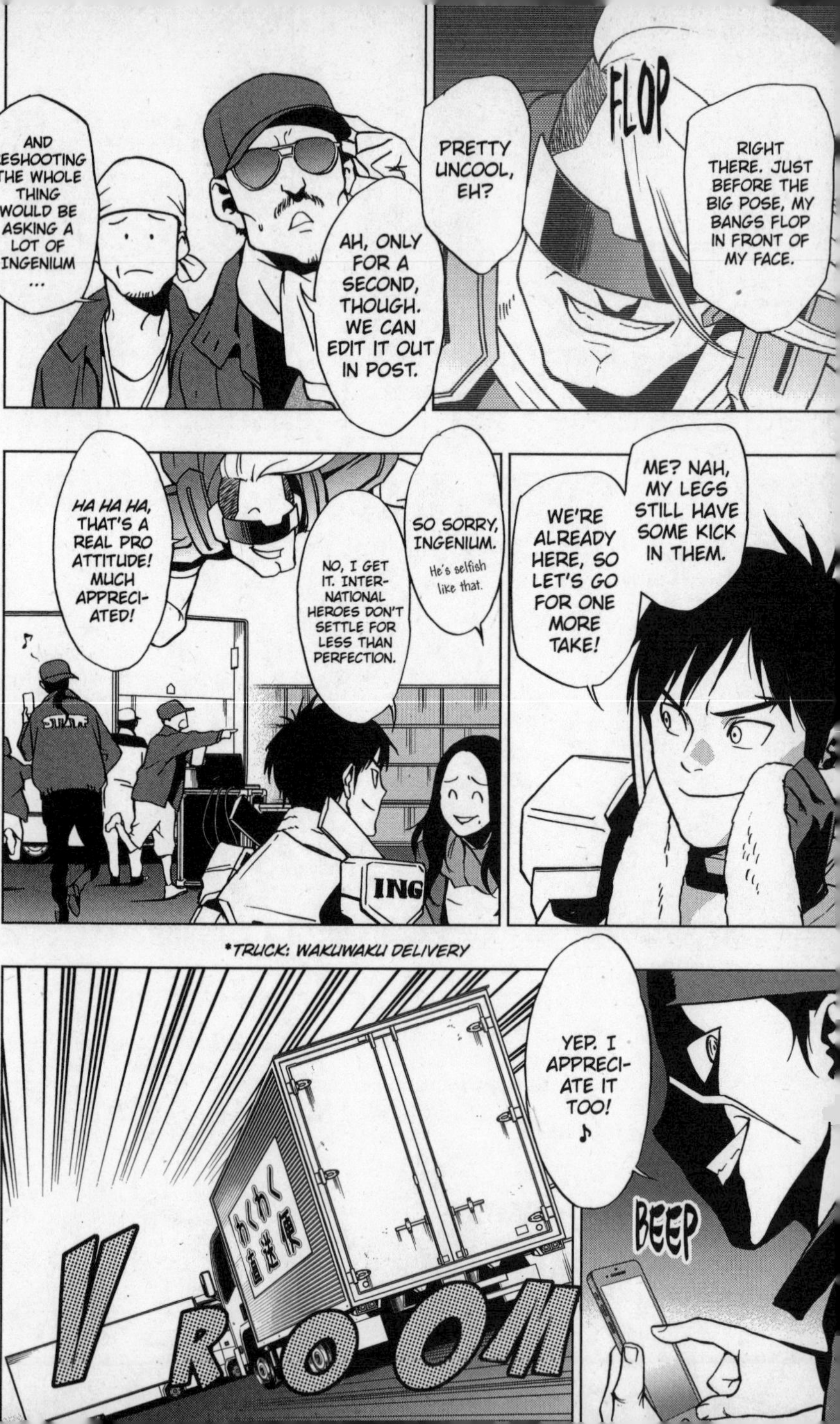
RIGHT THERE. JUST BEFORE THE BIG POSE, MY BANGS FLOP IN FRONT OF MY FACE.
FLOP
PRETTY UNCOOL, EH?
AH, ONLY FOR A SECOND, THOUGH. WE CAN EDIT IT OUT IN POST.
AND RESHOOTING THE WHOLE THING WOULD BE ASKING A LOT OF INGENIUM ...
ME? NAH, MY LEGS STILL HAVE SOME KICK IN THEM.
WE'RE ALREADY HERE, SO LET'S GO FOR ONE MORE TAKE!
SO SORRY, INGENIUM.
He's selfish like that.
NO, I GET IT. INTER-NATIONAL HEROES DON'T SETTLE FOR LESS THAN PERFECTION.
HA HA HA, THAT'S A REAL PRO ATTITUDE! MUCH APPRECI-ATED!
ING
*TRUCK: WAKUWAKU DELIVERY
YEP. I APPRECI-ATE IT TOO! ♪
BEEP
わくわく直送便
VROOM

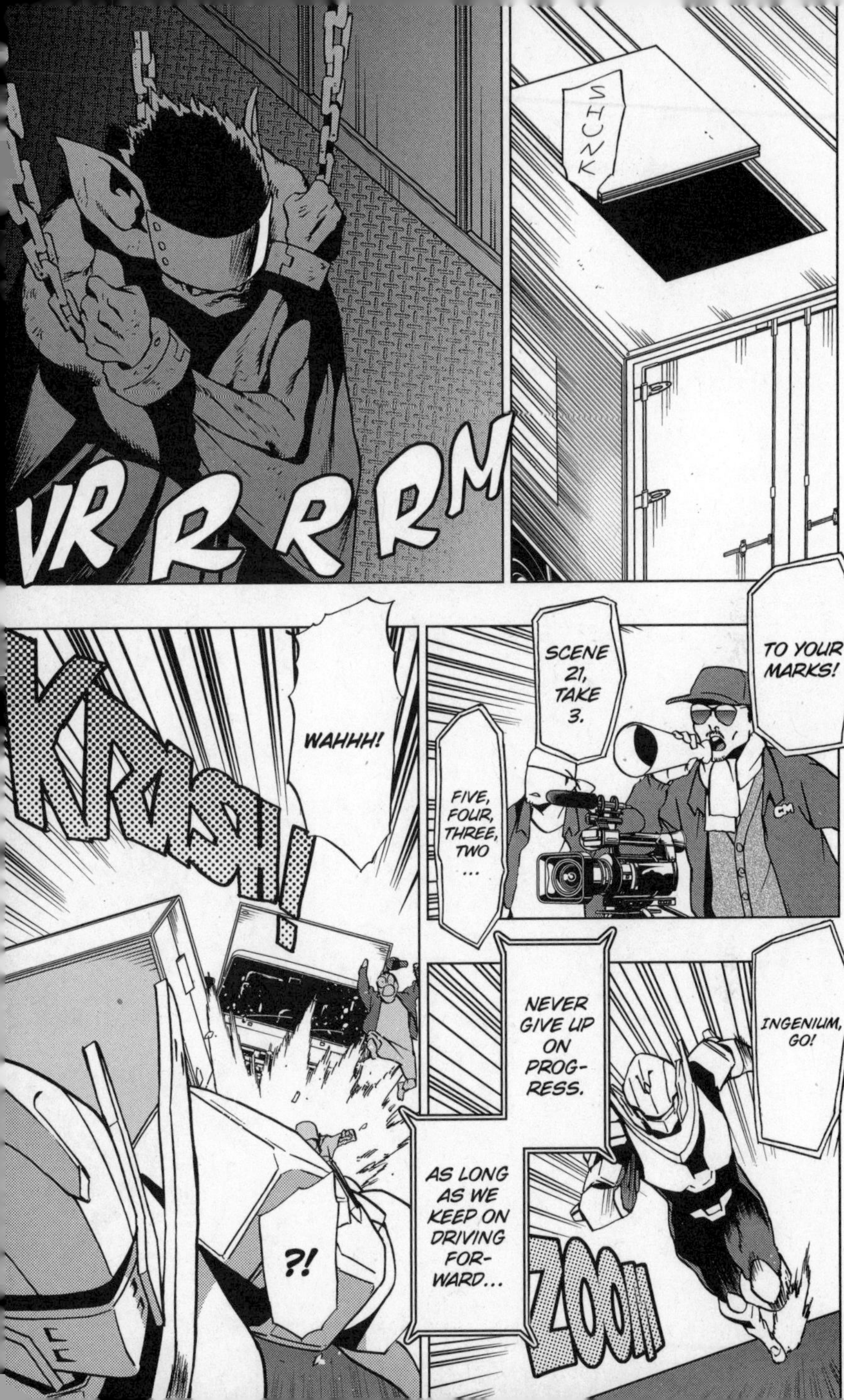
SHUNK
VRRRRM
TO YOUR MARKS!
SCENE 21, TAKE 3.
FIVE, FOUR, THREE, TWO ...
INGENIUM, GO!
NEVER GIVE UP ON PROG-RESS.
AS LONG AS WE KEEP ON DRIVING FOR-WARD...
ZOOM
KRASH!!
WAHHH!
?!

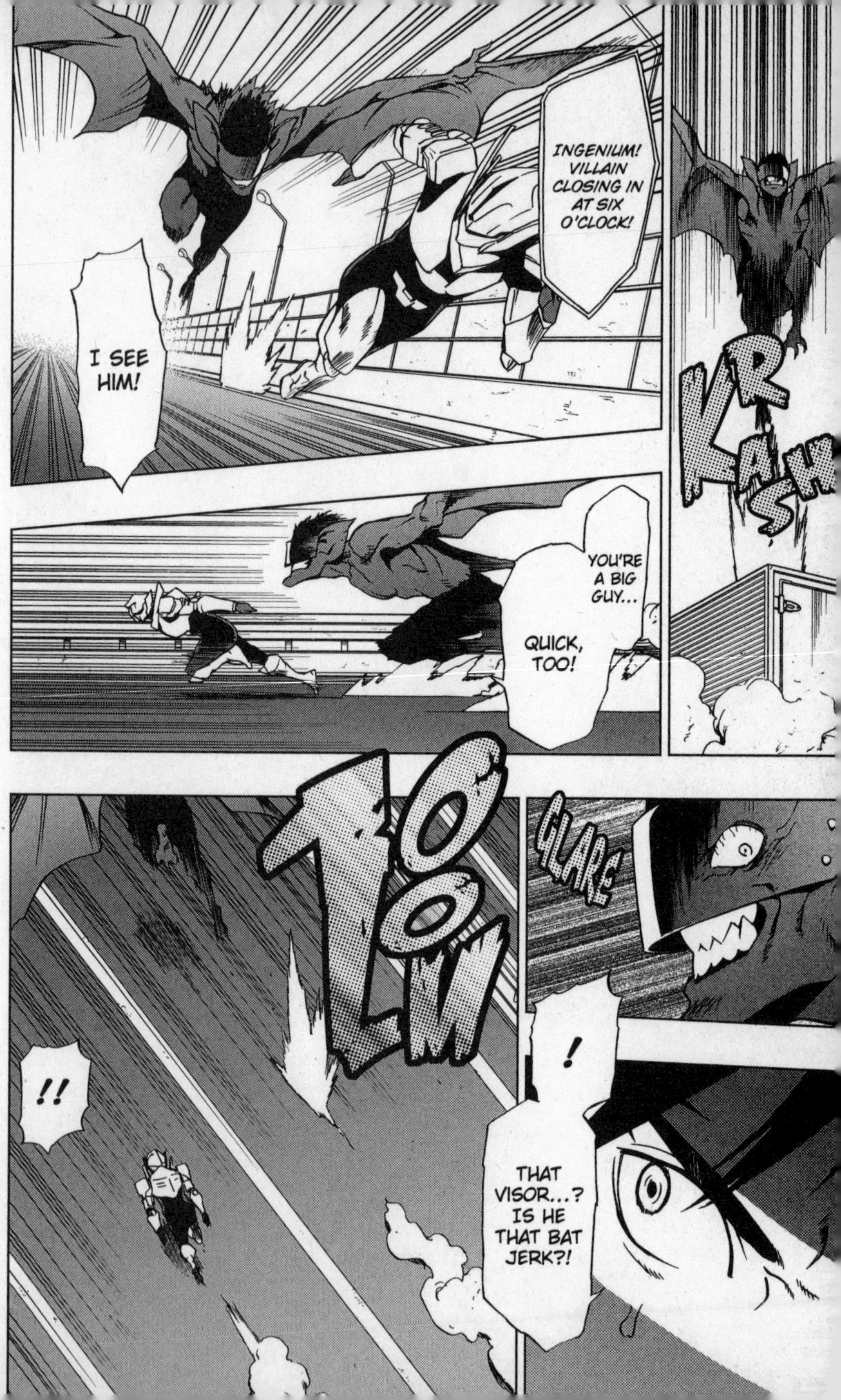
KRASH
INGENIUM! VILLAIN CLOSING IN AT SIX O'CLOCK!
I SEE HIM!
YOU'RE A BIG GUY...
QUICK, TOO!
GLARE
!
THAT VISOR...? IS HE THAT BAT JERK?!
!!

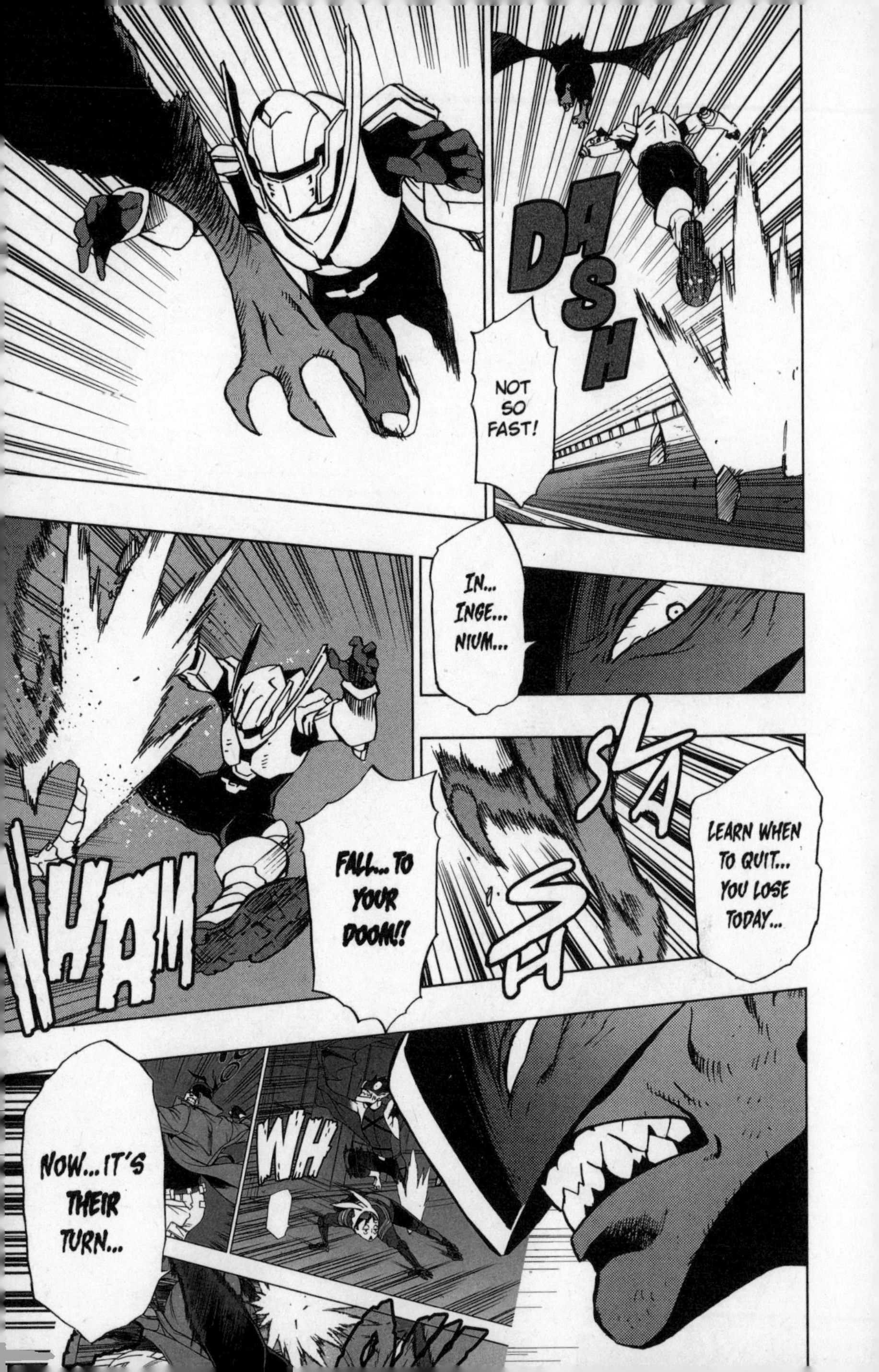
DASH
NOT SO FAST!
IN... INGE... NIUM...
SLASH
LEARN WHEN TO QUIT... YOU LOSE TODAY...
FALL... TO YOUR DOOM!!
WHAM
WH
NOW... IT'S THEIR TURN...

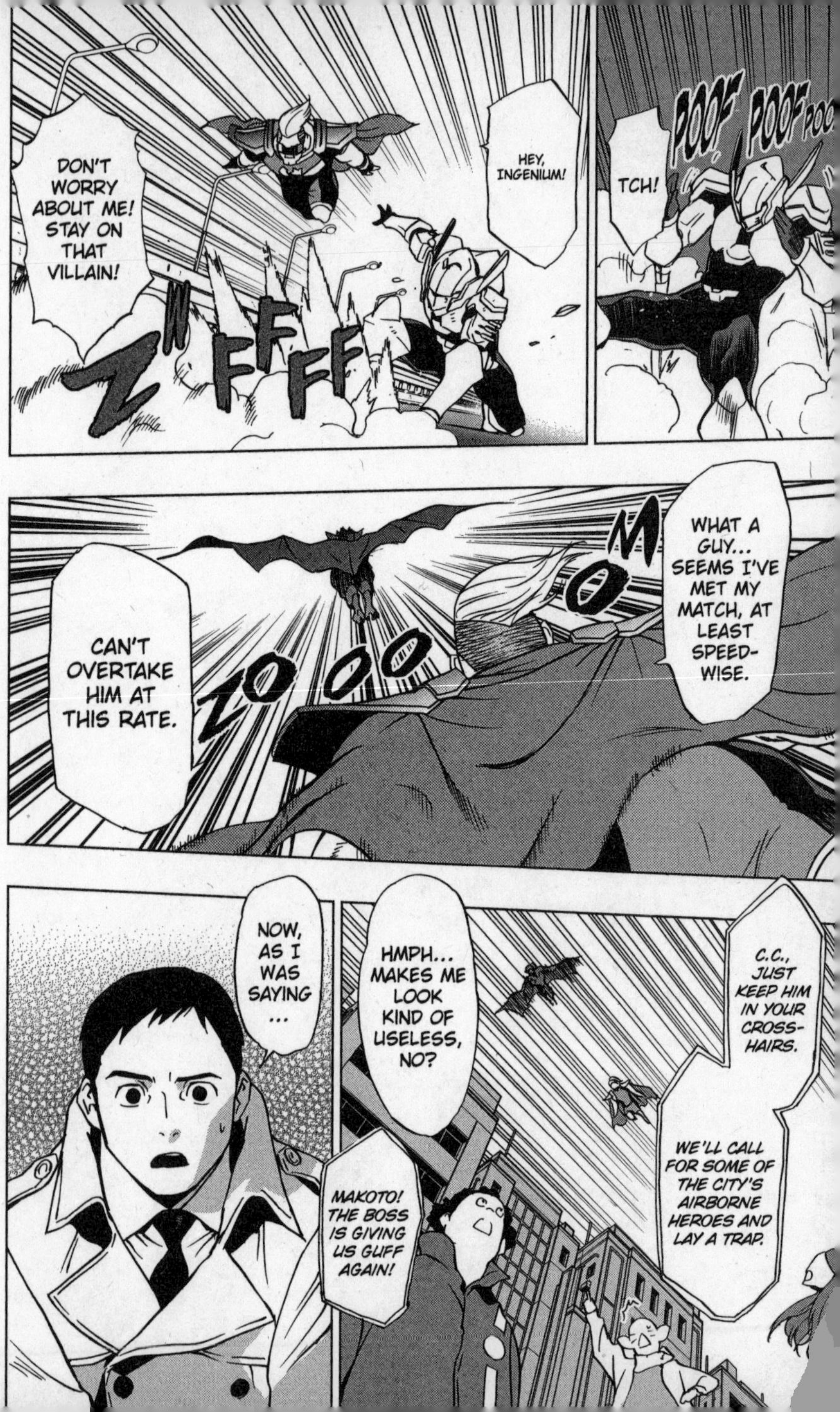
POOF POOF POO
TCH!
HEY, INGENIUM!
DON'T WORRY ABOUT ME! STAY ON THAT VILLAIN!
ZWFFFF
WHAT A GUY... SEEMS I'VE MET MY MATCH, AT LEAST SPEED-WISE.
ZOOOOOM
CAN'T OVERTAKE HIM AT THIS RATE.
C.C., JUST KEEP HIM IN YOUR CROSS-HAIRS.
WE'LL CALL FOR SOME OF THE CITY'S AIRBORNE HEROES AND LAY A TRAP.
HMPH... MAKES ME LOOK KIND OF USELESS, NO?
MAKOTO! THE BOSS IS GIVING US GUFF AGAIN!
NOW, AS I WAS SAYING ...

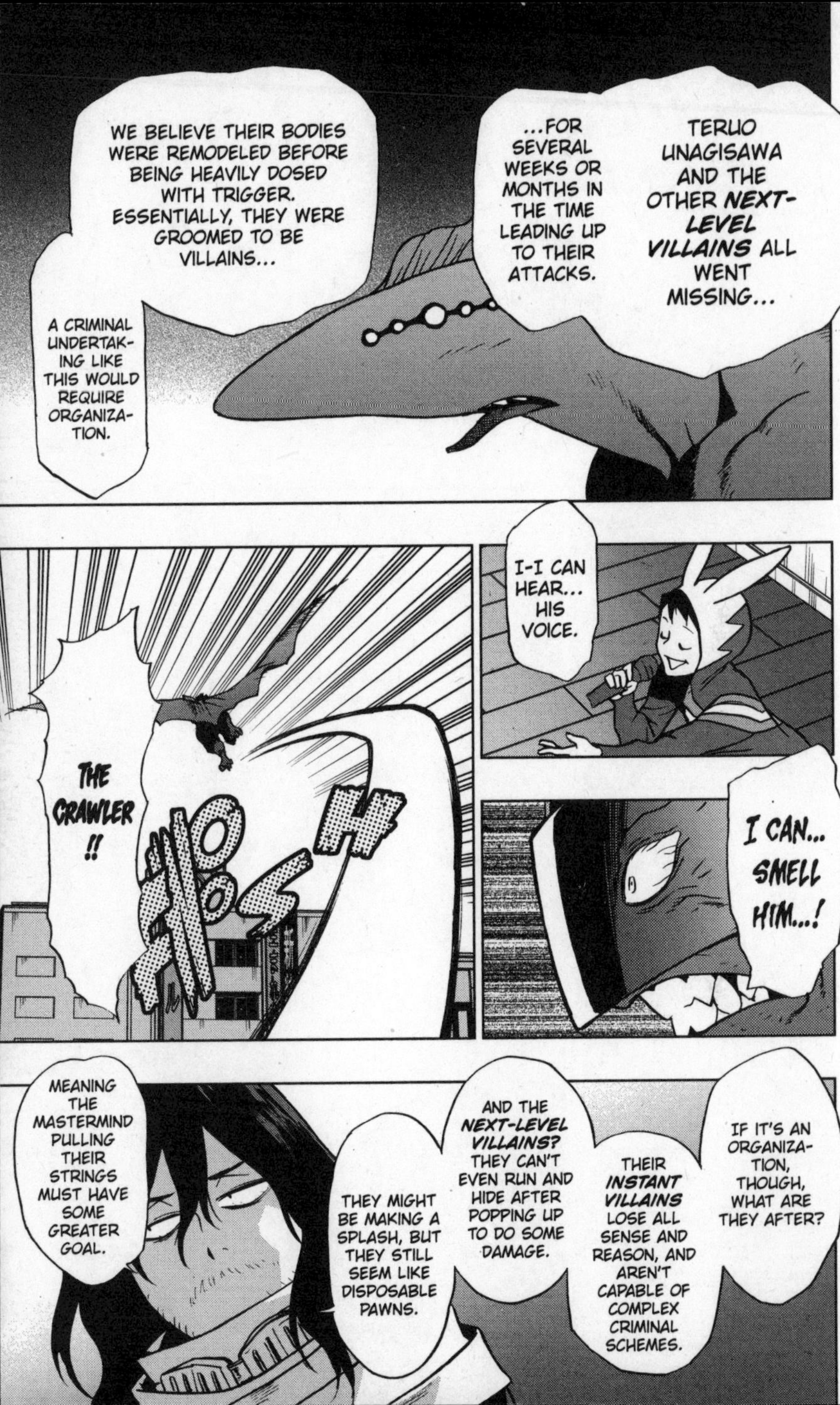
TERUO UNAGISAWA AND THE OTHER NEXT-LEVEL VILLAINS ALL WENT MISSING...
...FOR SEVERAL WEEKS OR MONTHS IN THE TIME LEADING UP TO THEIR ATTACKS.
WE BELIEVE THEIR BODIES WERE REMODELED BEFORE BEING HEAVILY DOSED WITH TRIGGER. ESSENTIALLY, THEY WERE GROOMED TO BE VILLAINS...
A CRIMINAL UNDERTAKING LIKE THIS WOULD REQUIRE ORGANIZATION.
I-I CAN HEAR... HIS VOICE.
I CAN... SMELL HIM...!
THE CRAWLER !!
WHOOSH
IF IT'S AN ORGANIZATION, THOUGH, WHAT ARE THEY AFTER?
THEIR INSTANT VILLAINS LOSE ALL SENSE AND REASON, AND AREN'T CAPABLE OF COMPLEX CRIMINAL SCHEMES.
AND THE NEXT-LEVEL VILLAINS? THEY CAN'T EVEN RUN AND HIDE AFTER POPPING UP TO DO SOME DAMAGE.
THEY MIGHT BE MAKING A SPLASH, BUT THEY STILL SEEM LIKE DISPOSABLE PAWNS.
MEANING THE MASTERMIND PULLING THEIR STRINGS MUST HAVE SOME GREATER GOAL.

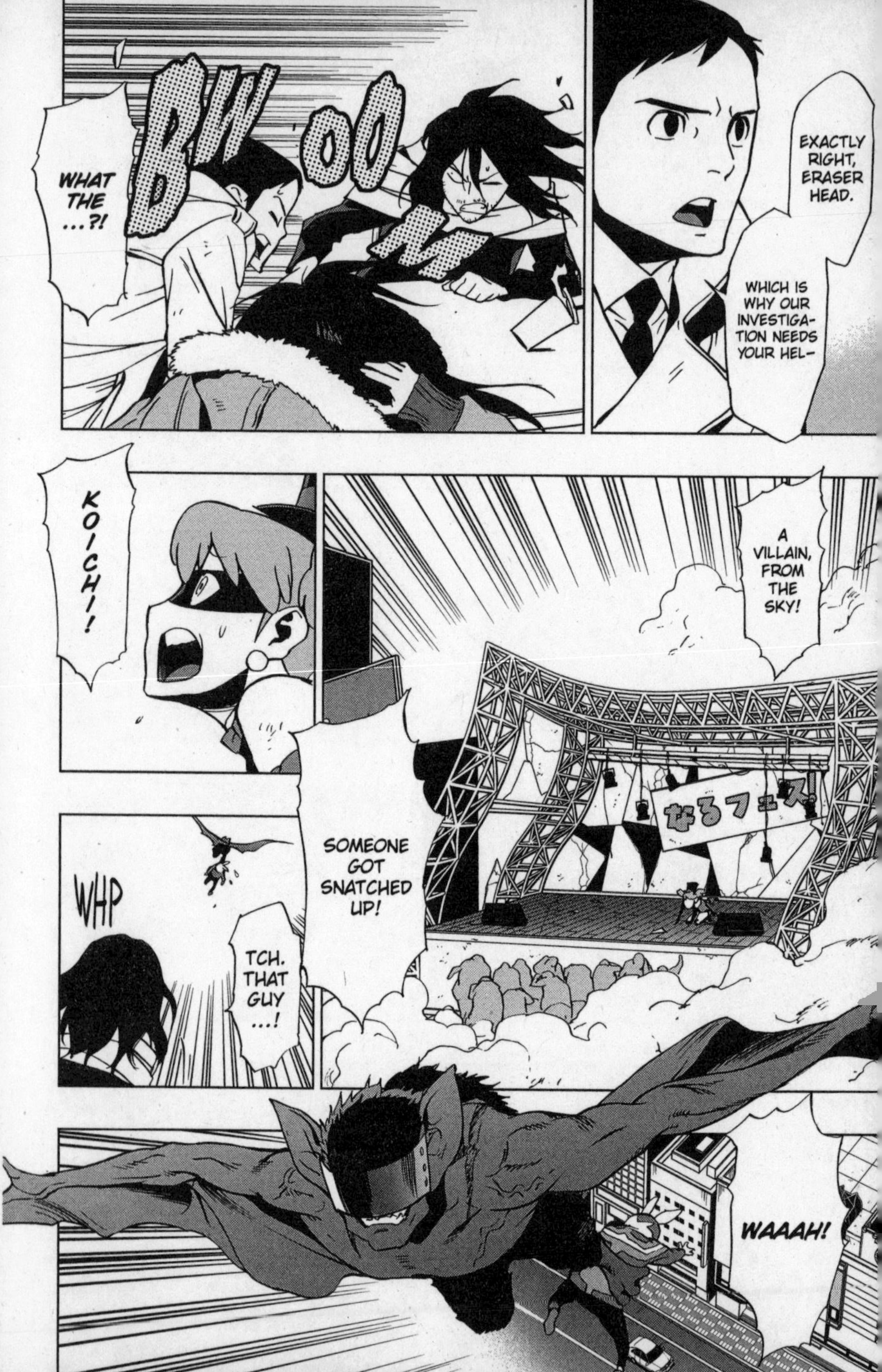
EXACTLY RIGHT, ERASER HEAD.
WHICH IS WHY OUR INVESTIGATION NEEDS YOUR HEL-
BWOOM
WHAT THE ...?!
A VILLAIN, FROM THE SKY!
なるフェス!
SOMEONE GOT SNATCHED UP!
KOICHI!
WHP
TCH. THAT GUY ...!
WAAAH!

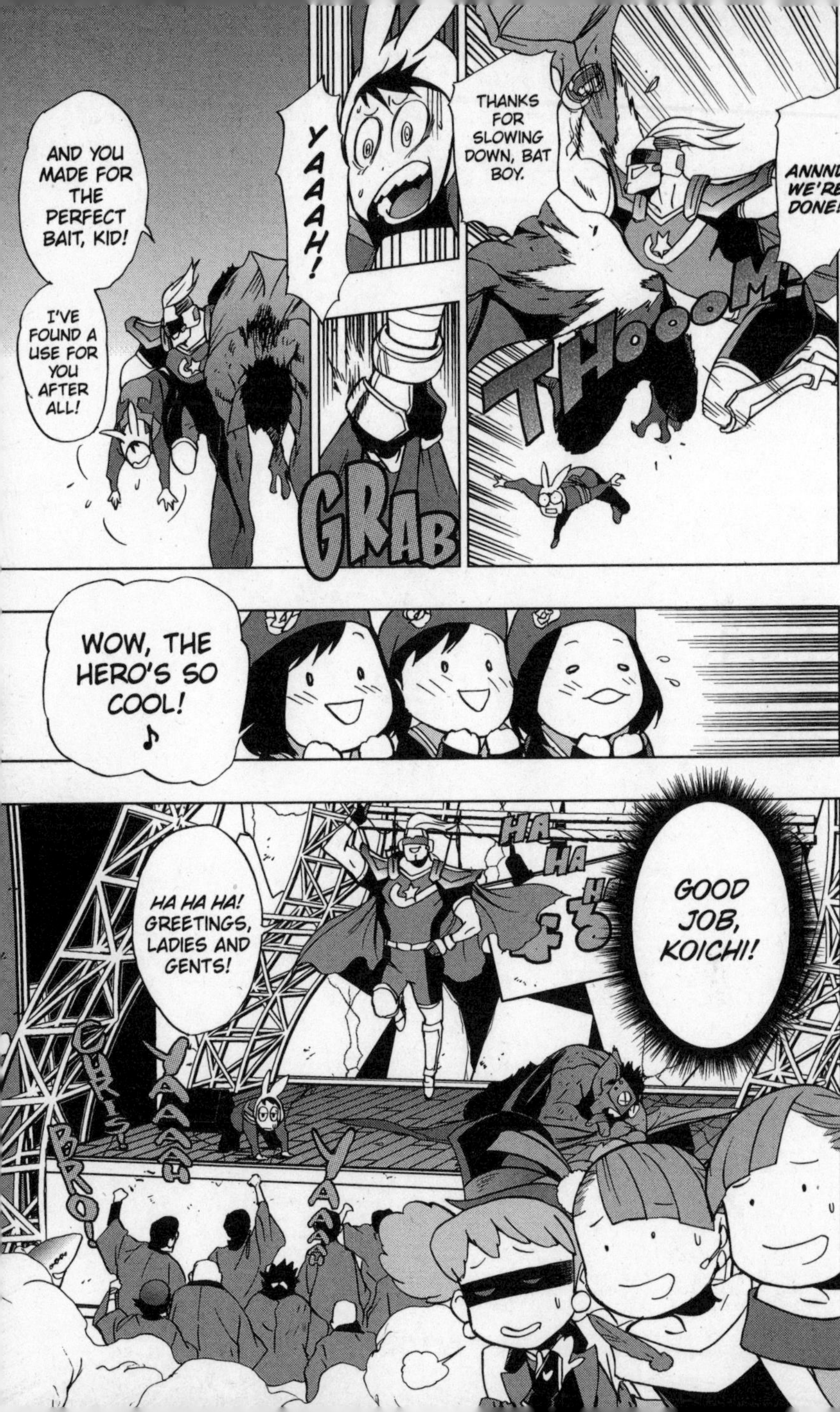
ANNND WE'RE DONE!
THANKS FOR SLOWING DOWN, BAT BOY.
THOOOM!
YAAAAH!
GRAB
AND YOU MADE FOR THE PERFECT BAIT, KID!
I'VE FOUND A USE FOR YOU AFTER ALL!
WOW, THE HERO'S SO COOL! ♪
GOOD JOB, KOICHI!
HA HA
HA HA HA! GREETINGS, LADIES AND GENTS!

CASUAL MIDNIGHT & THE LITTLE SISTERS

THE ROUGH DESIGN

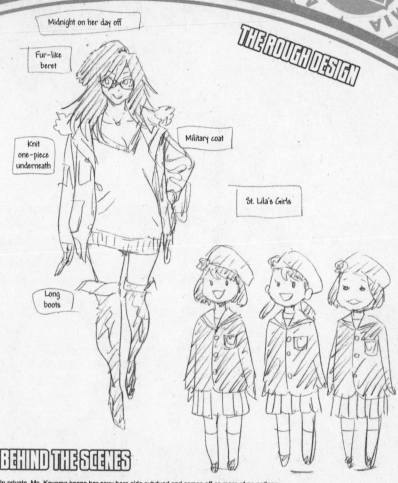

Midnight on her day off
Fur-like beret
Knit one-piece underneath
Military coat
St. Lila's Girls
Long boots

BEHIND THE SCENES

In private, Ms. Kayama keeps her sexy hero side subdued and comes off as more of an ordinary woman. Almost motherly even.

The three little girls are cute and inoffensive, making them easy additions to any scene. By the way—they're in middle school, making them teenagers, just like Pop and the twins.

—Furuhashi

For Midnight's casual look, I referenced her "house clothes" profile page from the main series. I'm a big fan of the knit one-piece and boots, but sadly there weren't any really good angles of the boots in the story. (LOL)

In Furuhashi's rough draft, all three of the girls had the same face, but I decided to make one out of the three a *little* off, just like with the Sturm und Drang perv brothers. It's becoming a trend.

—Betten

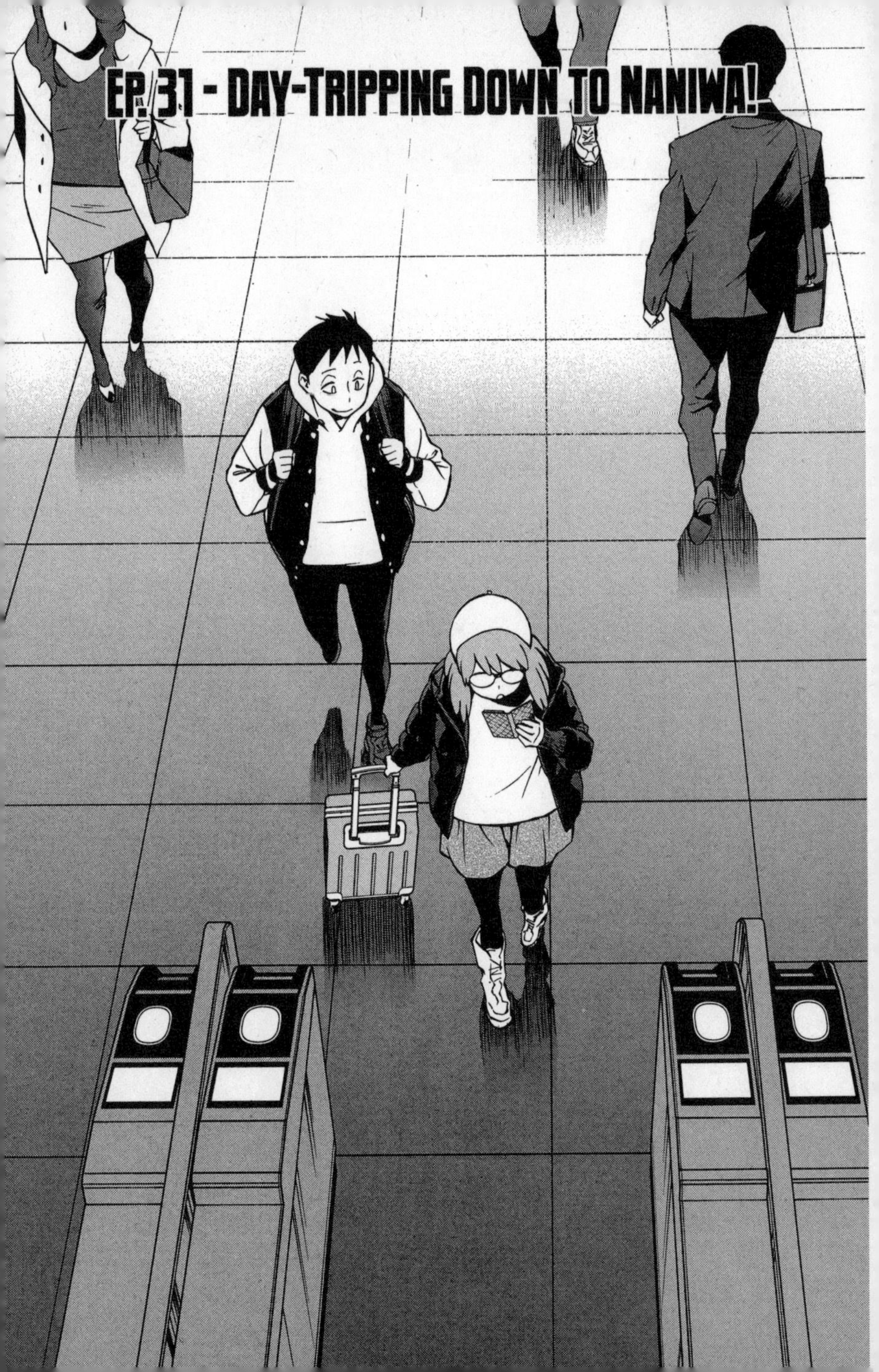
Ep. 31 - Day-Tripping Down to Naniwa!

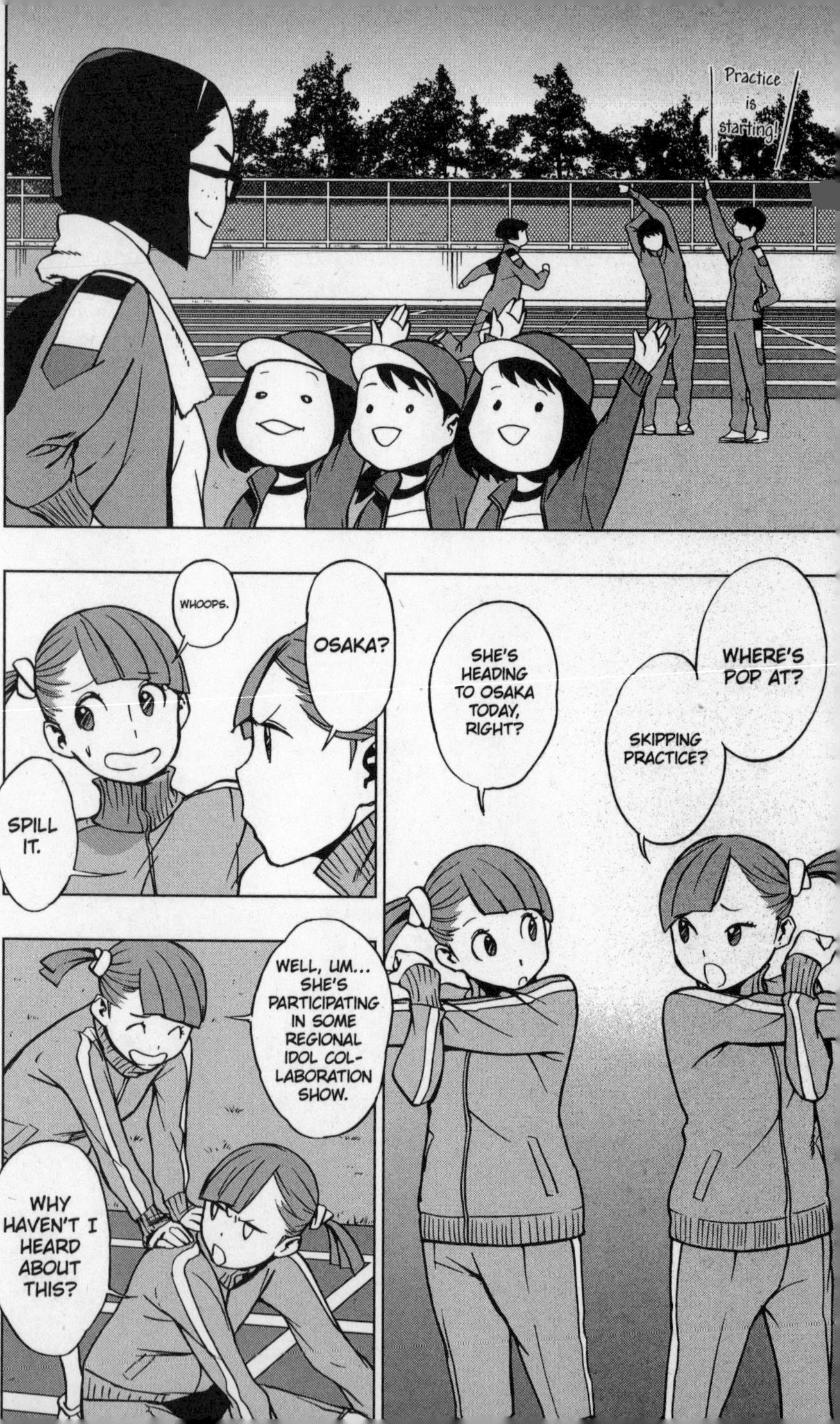
Practice is starting!
WHERE'S POP AT?
SKIPPING PRACTICE?
SHE'S HEADING TO OSAKA TODAY, RIGHT?
OSAKA?
WHOOPS.
SPILL IT.
WELL, UM... SHE'S PARTICIPATING IN SOME REGIONAL IDOL COL-LABORATION SHOW.
WHY HAVEN'T I HEARD ABOUT THIS?

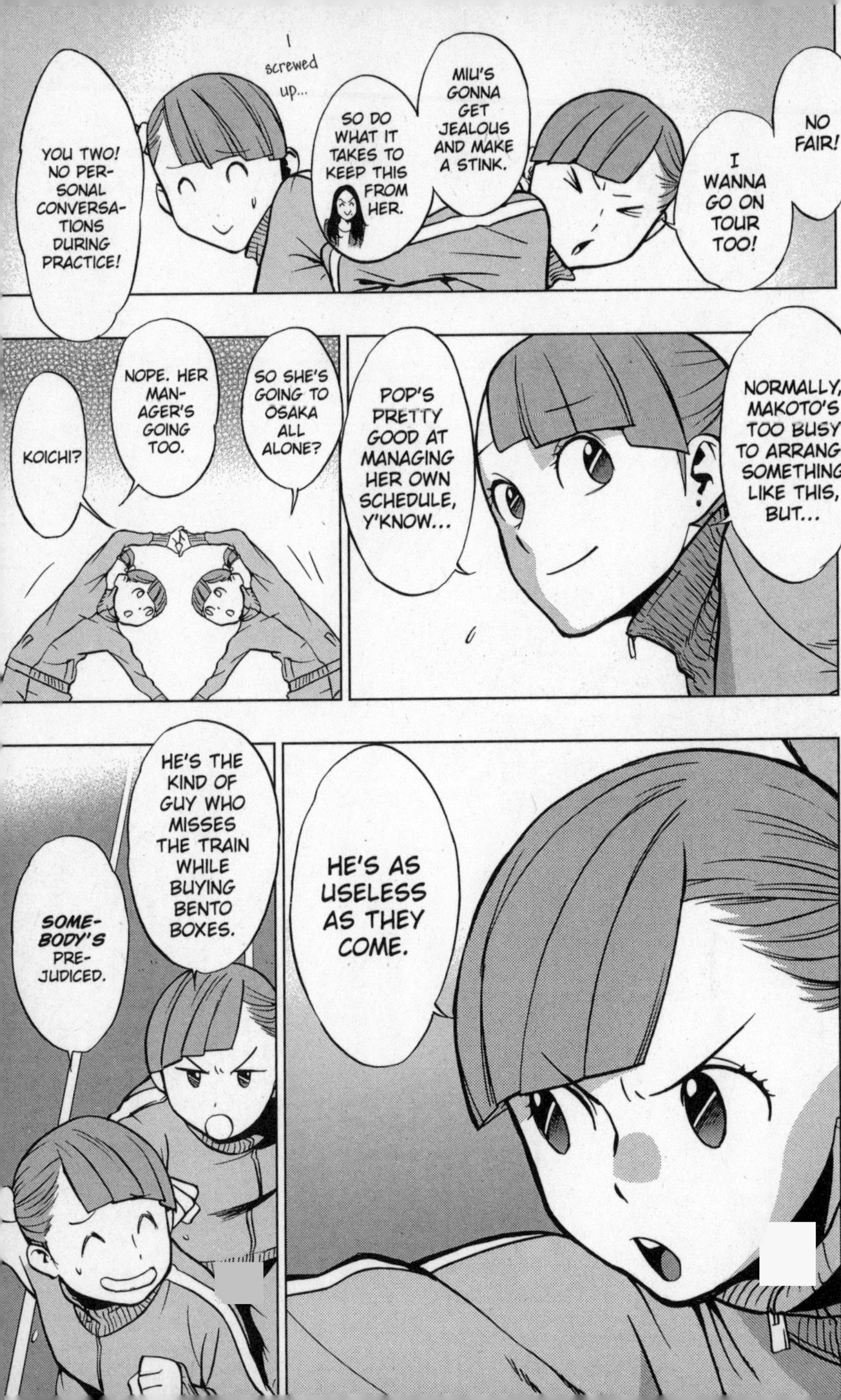
NO FAIR!
I WANNA GO ON TOUR TOO!
MIU'S GONNA GET JEALOUS AND MAKE A STINK.
SO DO WHAT IT TAKES TO KEEP THIS FROM HER.
I screwed up...
YOU TWO! NO PERSONAL CONVERSATIONS DURING PRACTICE!
NORMALLY, MAKOTO'S TOO BUSY TO ARRANGE SOMETHING LIKE THIS, BUT...
POP'S PRETTY GOOD AT MANAGING HER OWN SCHEDULE, Y'KNOW...
SO SHE'S GOING TO OSAKA ALL ALONE?
NOPE. HER MANAGER'S GOING TOO.
KOICHI?
HE'S AS USELESS AS THEY COME.
HE'S THE KIND OF GUY WHO MISSES THE TRAIN WHILE BUYING BENTO BOXES.
SOMEBODY'S PREJUDICED.

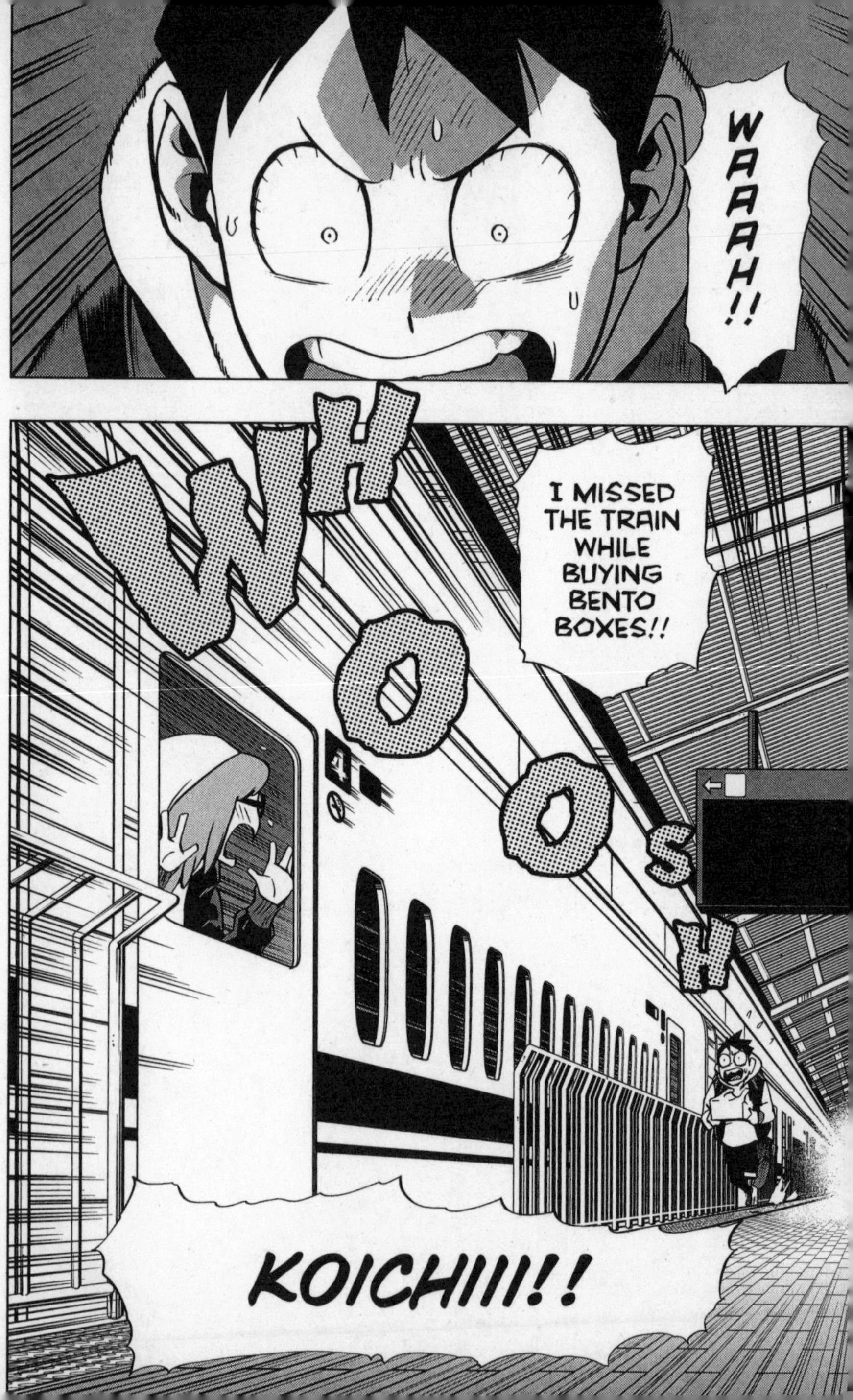
WAAAH!!
I MISSED THE TRAIN WHILE BUYING BENTO BOXES!!
WHOOSH
KOICHIII!!

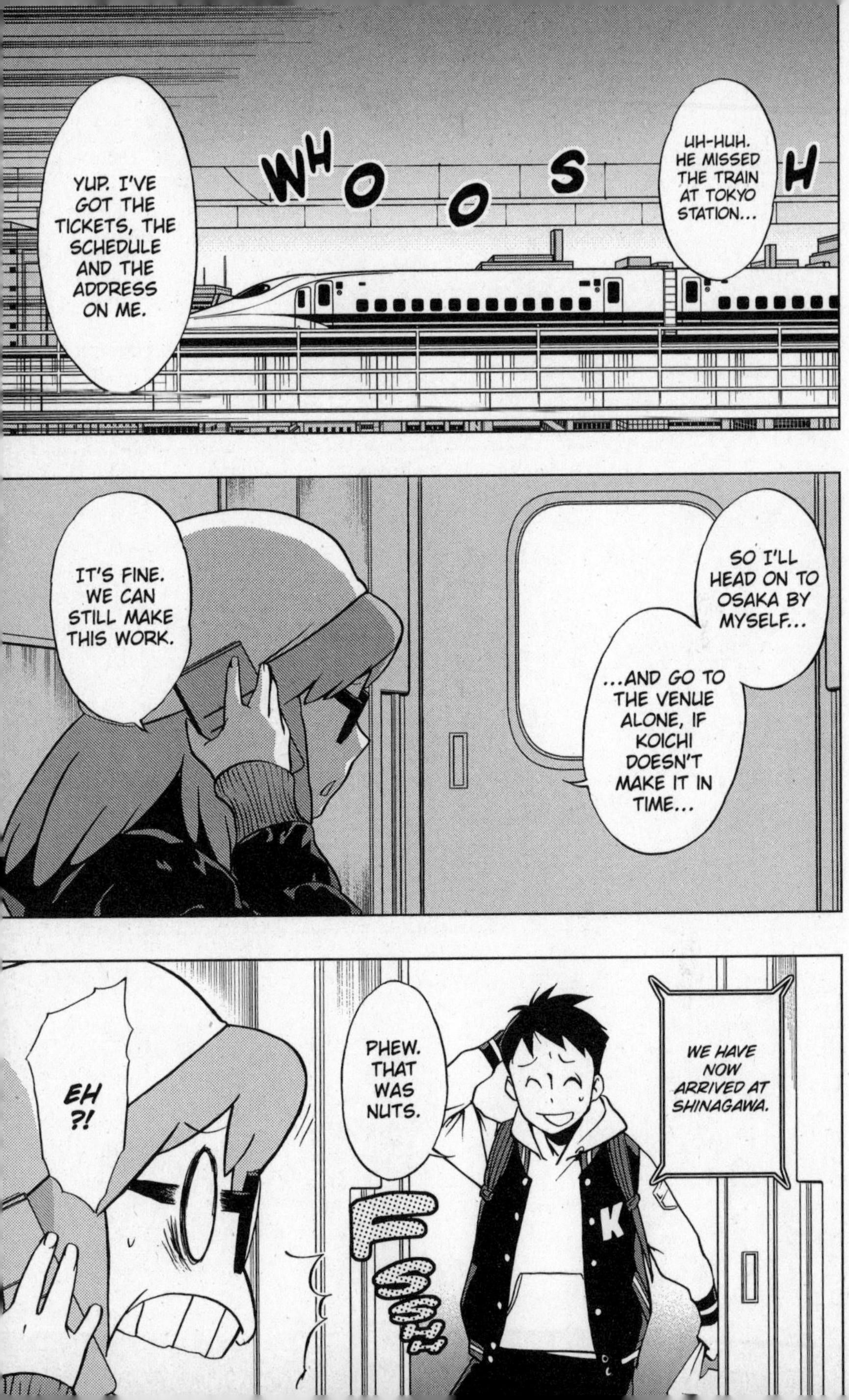
UH-HUH. HE MISSED THE TRAIN AT TOKYO STATION...
WHOOSH
YUP. I'VE GOT THE TICKETS, THE SCHEDULE AND THE ADDRESS ON ME.
SO I'LL HEAD ON TO OSAKA BY MYSELF...
...AND GO TO THE VENUE ALONE, IF KOICHI DOESN'T MAKE IT IN TIME...
IT'S FINE. WE CAN STILL MAKE THIS WORK.
WE HAVE NOW ARRIVED AT SHINAGAWA.
PHEW. THAT WAS NUTS.
EH ?!

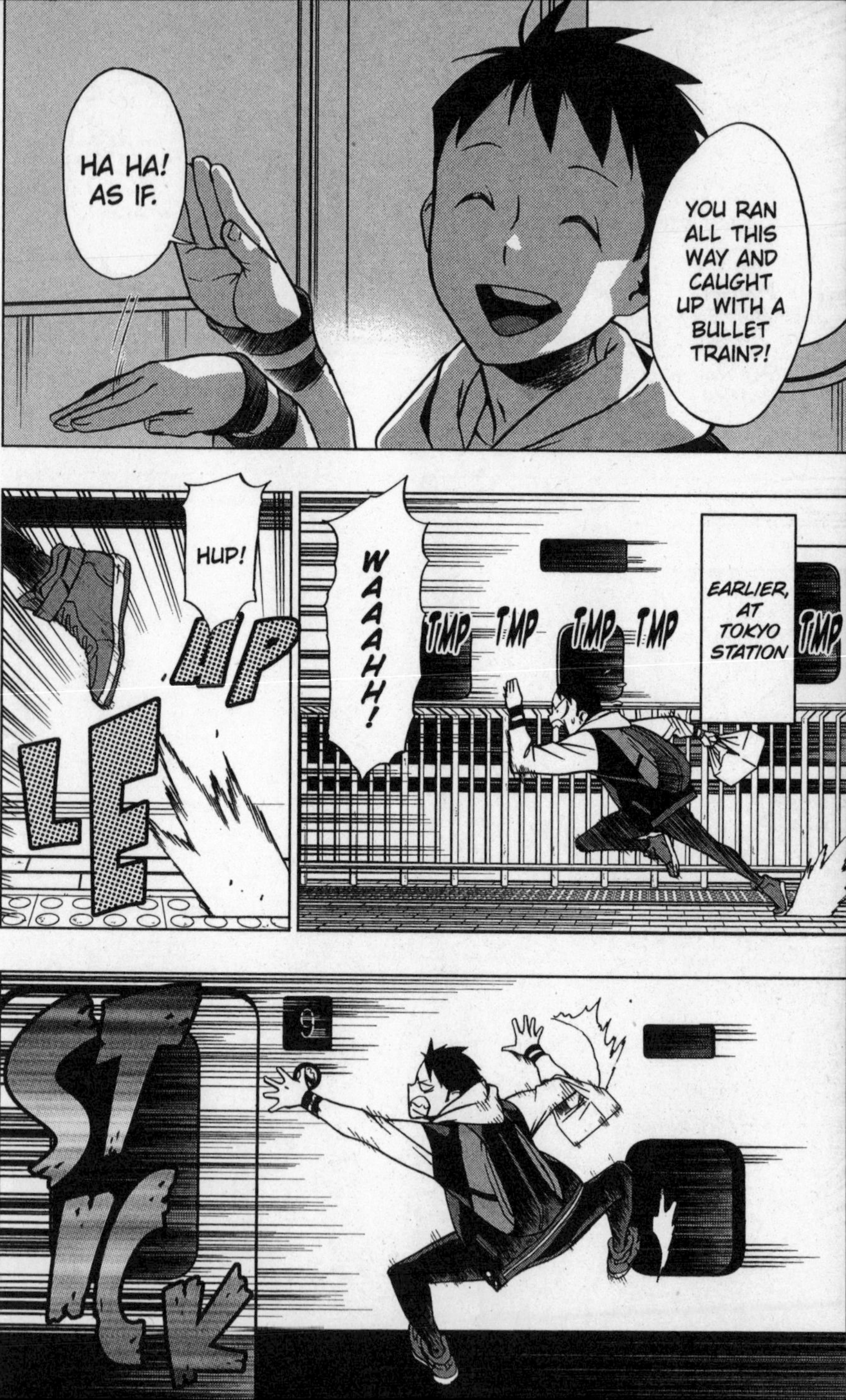
YOU RAN ALL THIS WAY AND CAUGHT UP WITH A BULLET TRAIN?!
HA HA! AS IF.
EARLIER, AT TOKYO STATION
TMP TMP TMP TMP TMP
WAAAAHH!
HUP!
LEAP
STICK

WHOA, GONNA FALL, GONNA FALL!

ACK!

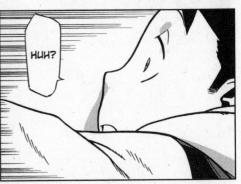

HUH?

YOU STUCK TO IT?

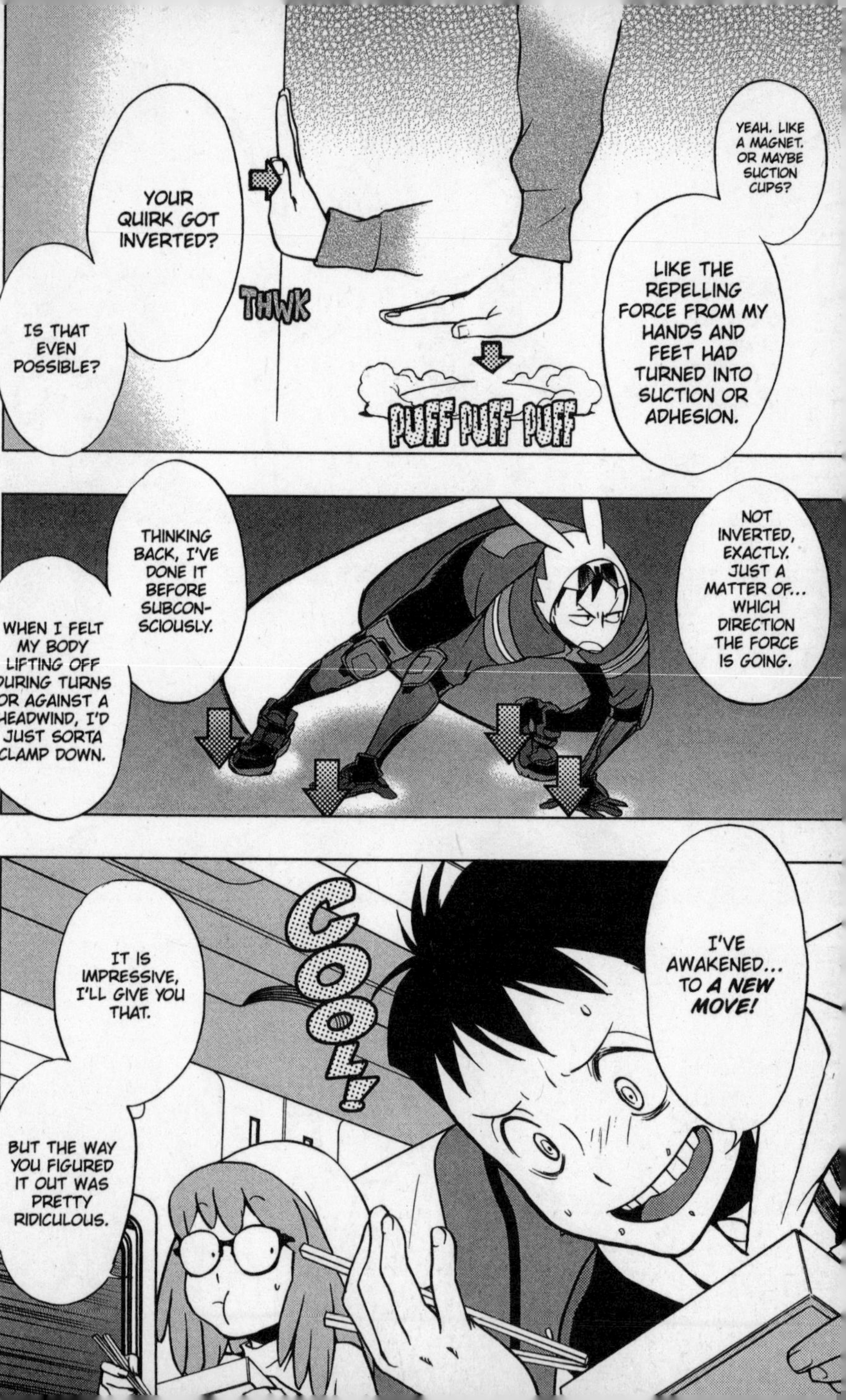
YEAH. LIKE A MAGNET. OR MAYBE SUCTION CUPS?
LIKE THE REPELLING FORCE FROM MY HANDS AND FEET HAD TURNED INTO SUCTION OR ADHESION.
THWK
PUFF PUFF PUFF
YOUR QUIRK GOT INVERTED?
IS THAT EVEN POSSIBLE?
NOT INVERTED, EXACTLY. JUST A MATTER OF... WHICH DIRECTION THE FORCE IS GOING.
THINKING BACK, I'VE DONE IT BEFORE SUBCON-SCIOUSLY.
WHEN I FELT MY BODY LIFTING OFF DURING TURNS OR AGAINST A HEADWIND, I'D JUST SORTA CLAMP DOWN.
I'VE AWAKENED... TO ***A NEW MOVE!***
COOL!
IT IS IMPRESSIVE, I'LL GIVE YOU THAT.
BUT THE WAY YOU FIGURED IT OUT WAS PRETTY RIDICULOUS.

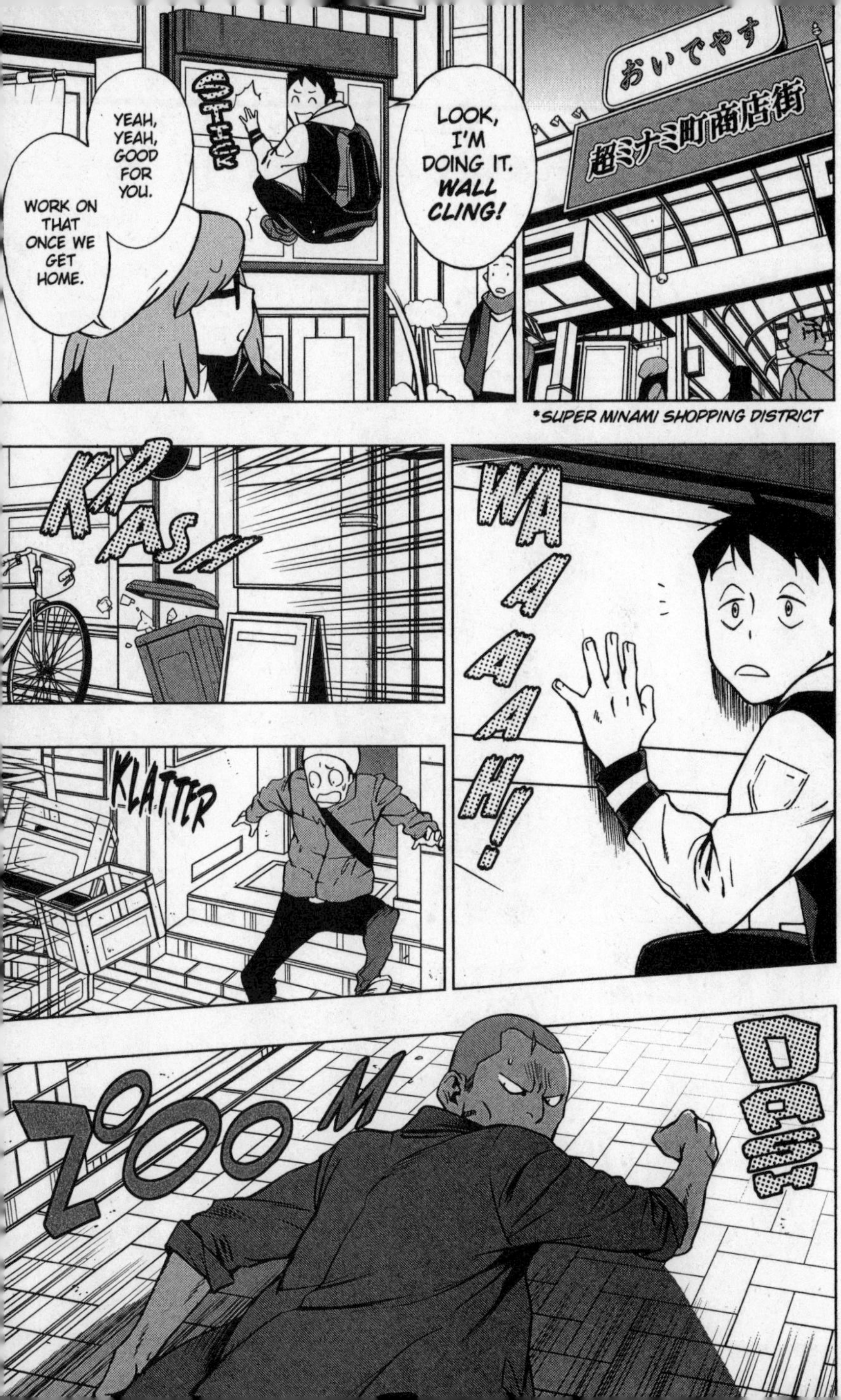

おいでやす
超ミナミ町商店街
*SUPER MINAMI SHOPPING DISTRICT
LOOK, I'M DOING IT. WALL CLING!
STICK
YEAH, YEAH, GOOD FOR YOU.
WORK ON THAT ONCE WE GET HOME.
WAAAAAH!
KRASH
KLATTER
DASH
ZOOOM

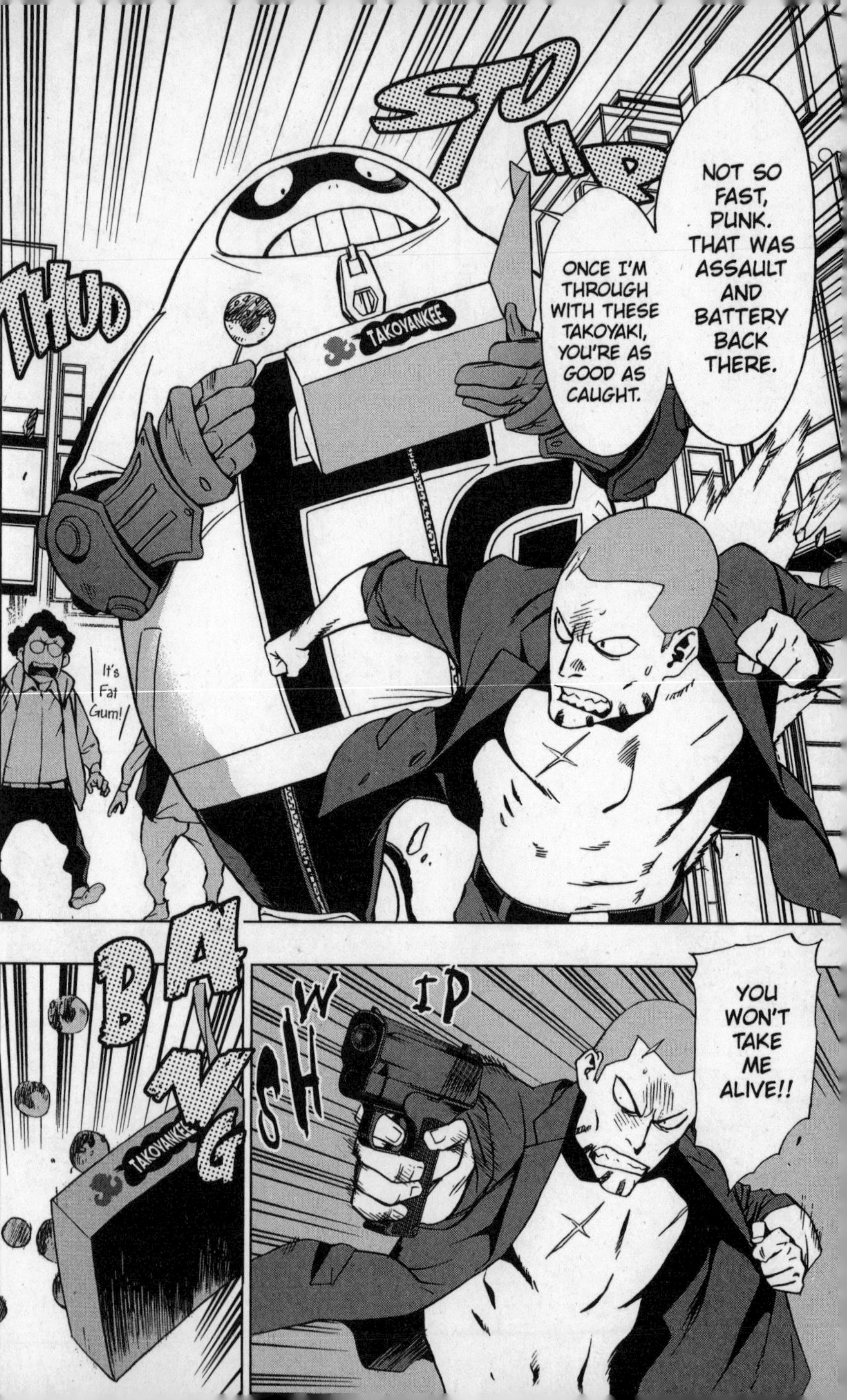
NOT SO FAST, PUNK. THAT WAS ASSAULT AND BATTERY BACK THERE.
ONCE I'M THROUGH WITH THESE TAKOYAKI, YOU'RE AS GOOD AS CAUGHT.
STOMP
TAKOYANKEE
THUD
It's Fat Gum!
YOU WON'T TAKE ME ALIVE!!
BANG
TAKOYANKEE

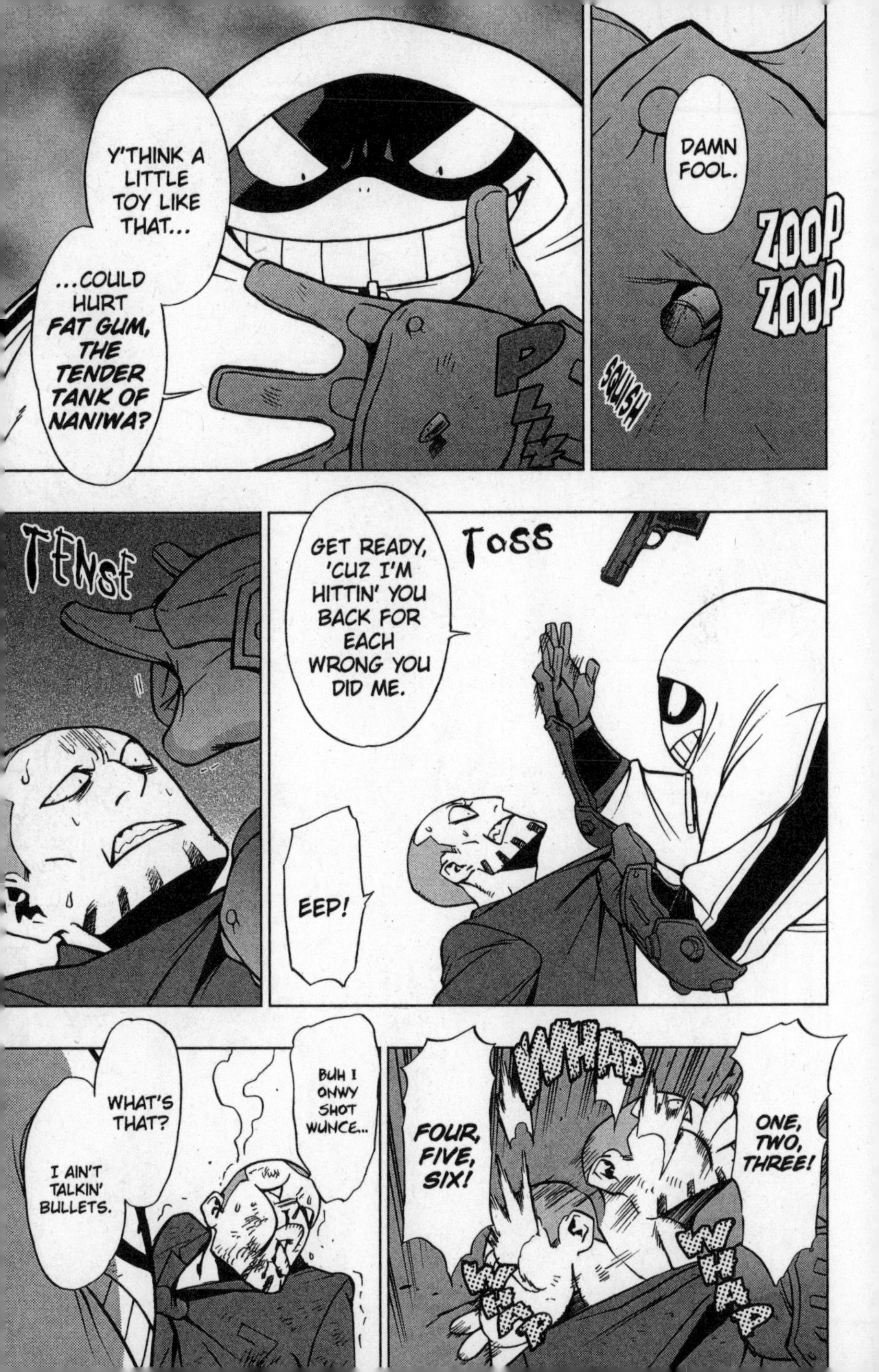
DAMN FOOL.
ZOOP ZOOP
SQUISH
Y'THINK A LITTLE TOY LIKE THAT...
...COULD HURT FAT GUM, THE TENDER TANK OF NANIWA?
Toss
GET READY, 'CUZ I'M HITTIN' YOU BACK FOR EACH WRONG YOU DID ME.
EEP!
TENSE
WHAP
ONE, TWO, THREE!
FOUR, FIVE, SIX!
WHAP
WHAP
BUH I ONWY SHOT WUNCE...
WHAT'S THAT?
I AIN'T TALKIN' BULLETS.

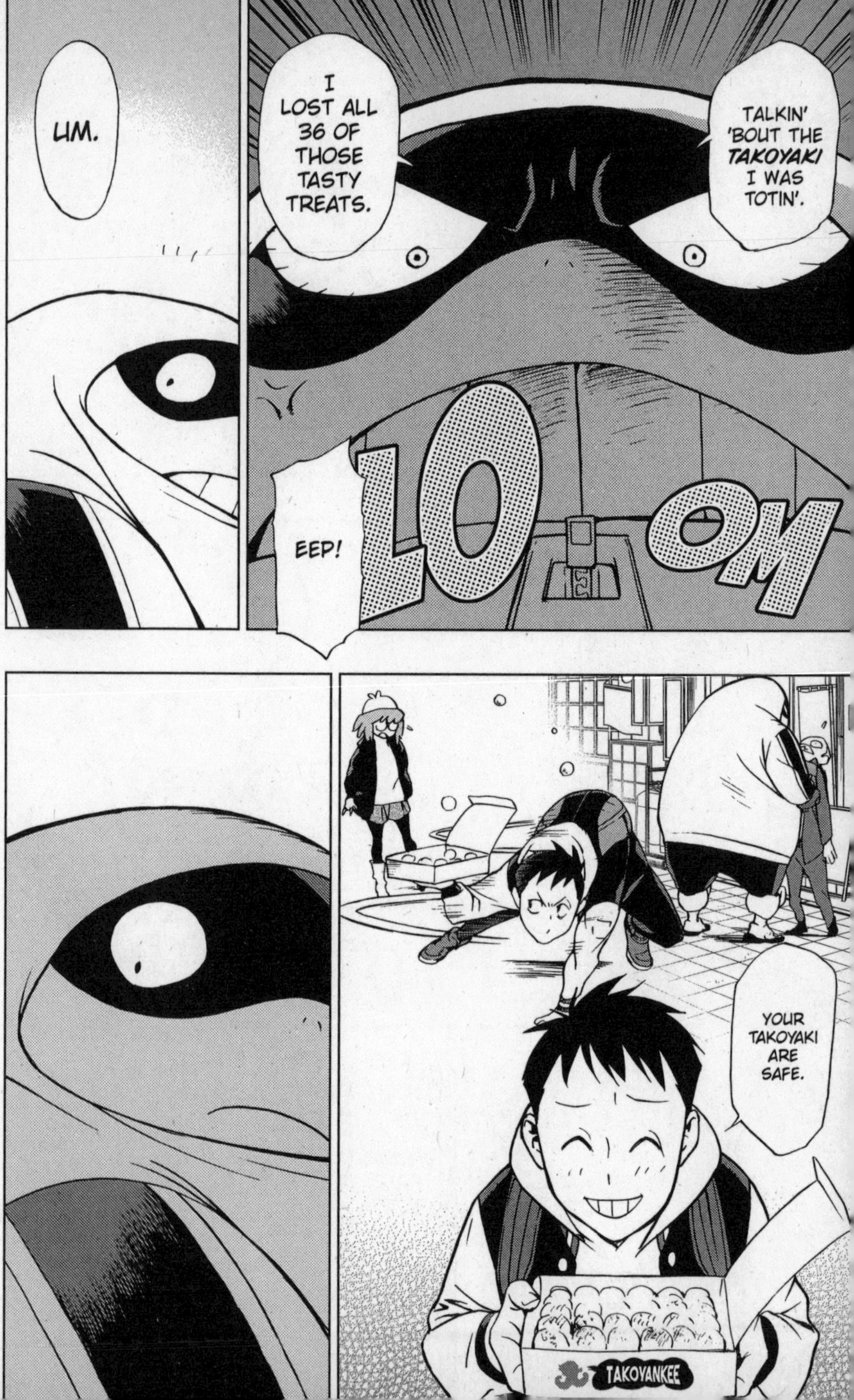
TALKIN' 'BOUT THE TAKOYAKI I WAS TOTIN'.
I LOST ALL 36 OF THOSE TASTY TREATS.
LOOM
EEP!
UM.
YOUR TAKOYAKI ARE SAFE.
TAKOYANKEE

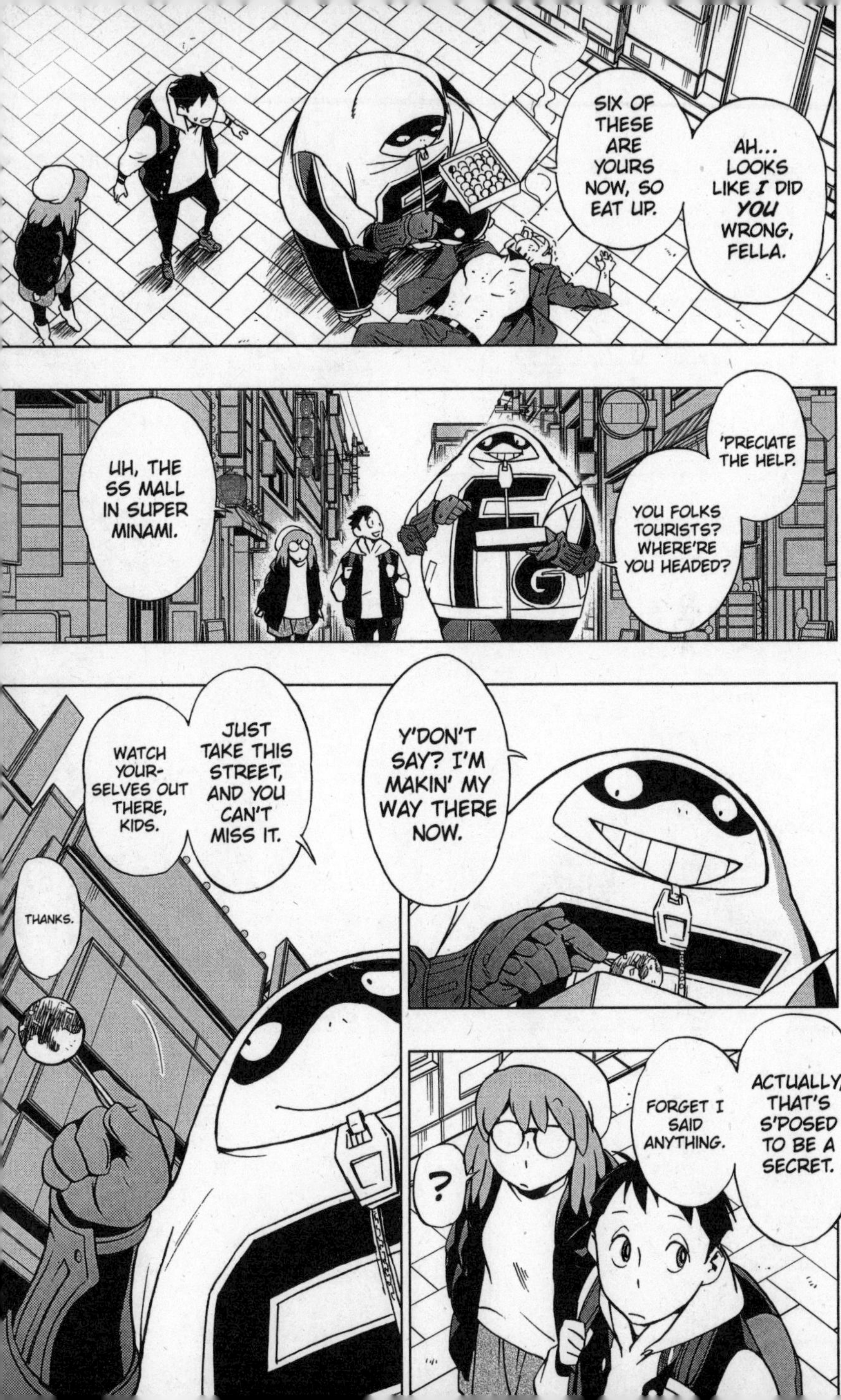
AH... LOOKS LIKE *I* DID *YOU* WRONG, FELLA.
SIX OF THESE ARE YOURS NOW, SO EAT UP.
'PRECIATE THE HELP.
YOU FOLKS TOURISTS? WHERE'RE YOU HEADED?
UH, THE SS MALL IN SUPER MINAMI.
Y'DON'T SAY? I'M MAKIN' MY WAY THERE NOW.
ACTUALLY, THAT'S S'POSED TO BE A SECRET.
FORGET I SAID ANYTHING.
?
JUST TAKE THIS STREET, AND YOU CAN'T MISS IT.
WATCH YOUR-SELVES OUT THERE, KIDS.
THANKS.

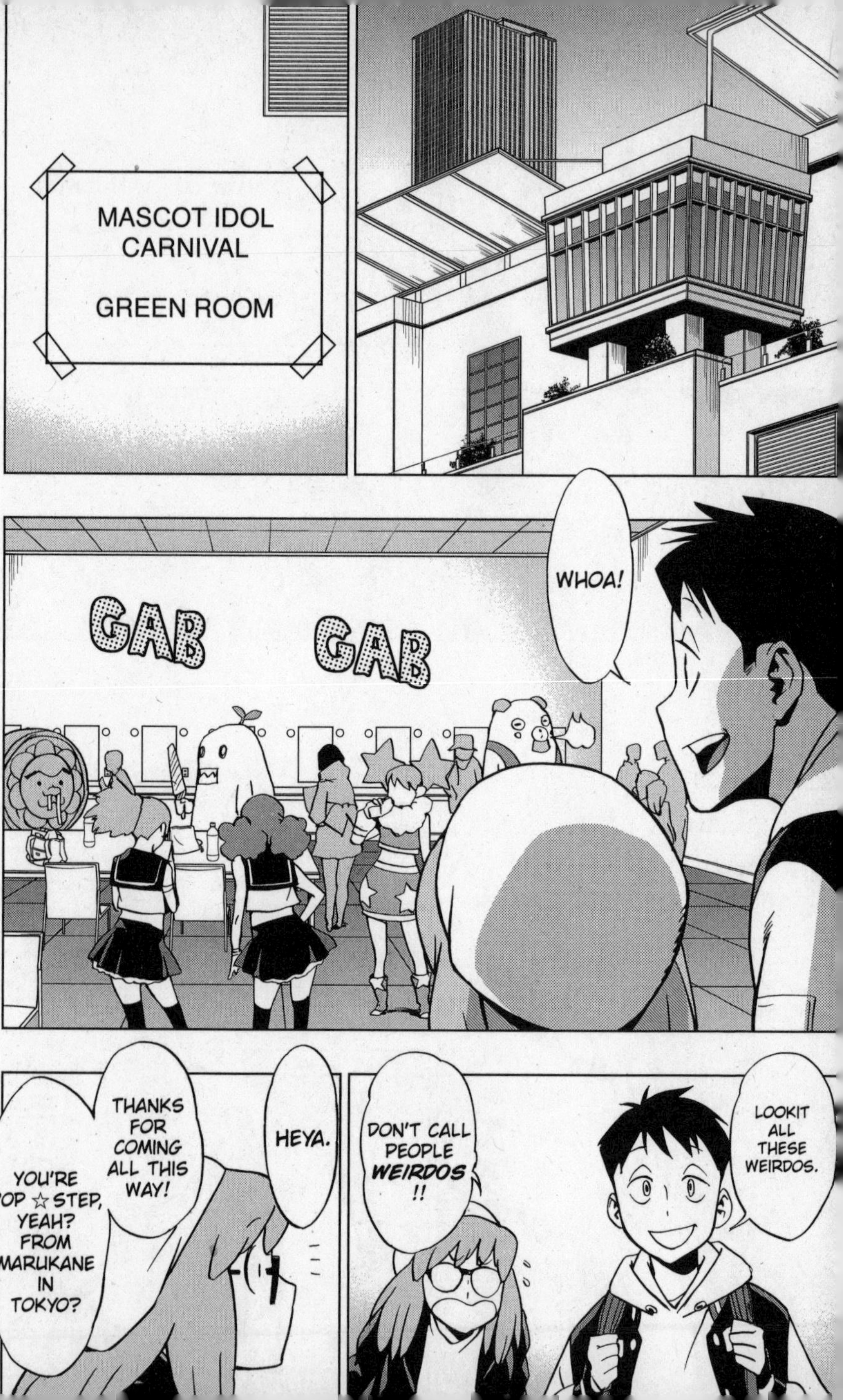
MASCOT IDOL CARNIVAL
GREEN ROOM
WHOA!
GAB GAB
LOOKIT ALL THESE WEIRDOS.
DON'T CALL PEOPLE *WEIRDOS* !!
HEYA.
THANKS FOR COMING ALL THIS WAY!
YOU'RE POP☆STEP, YEAH? FROM MARUKANE IN TOKYO?

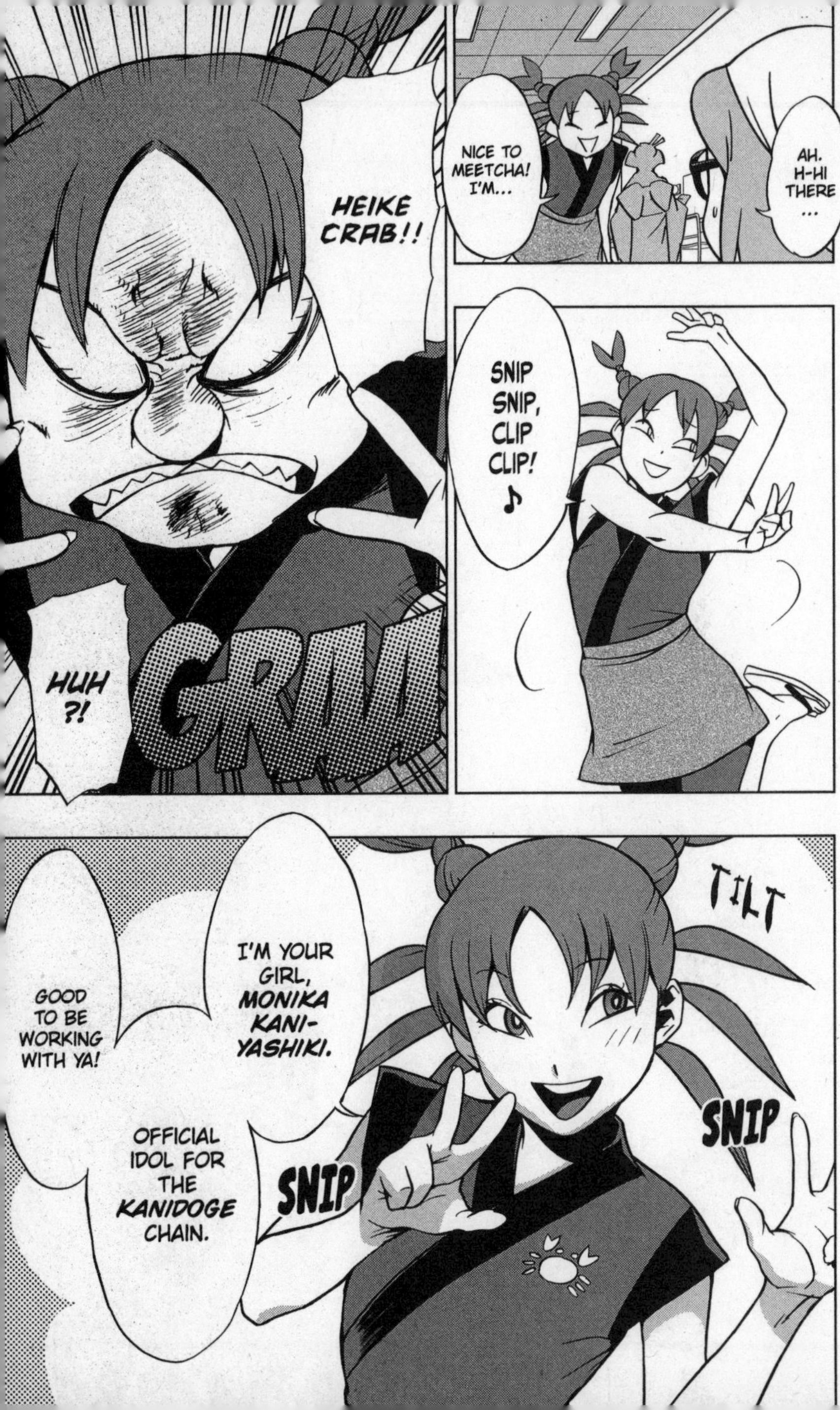
AH. H-HI THERE ...
NICE TO MEETCHA! I'M...
SNIP SNIP, CLIP CLIP! ♪
HEIKE CRAB!!
GRAM
HUH ?!
TILT
I'M YOUR GIRL, MONIKA KANI-YASHIKI.
SNIP
GOOD TO BE WORKING WITH YA!
OFFICIAL IDOL FOR THE KANIDOGE CHAIN.
SNIP

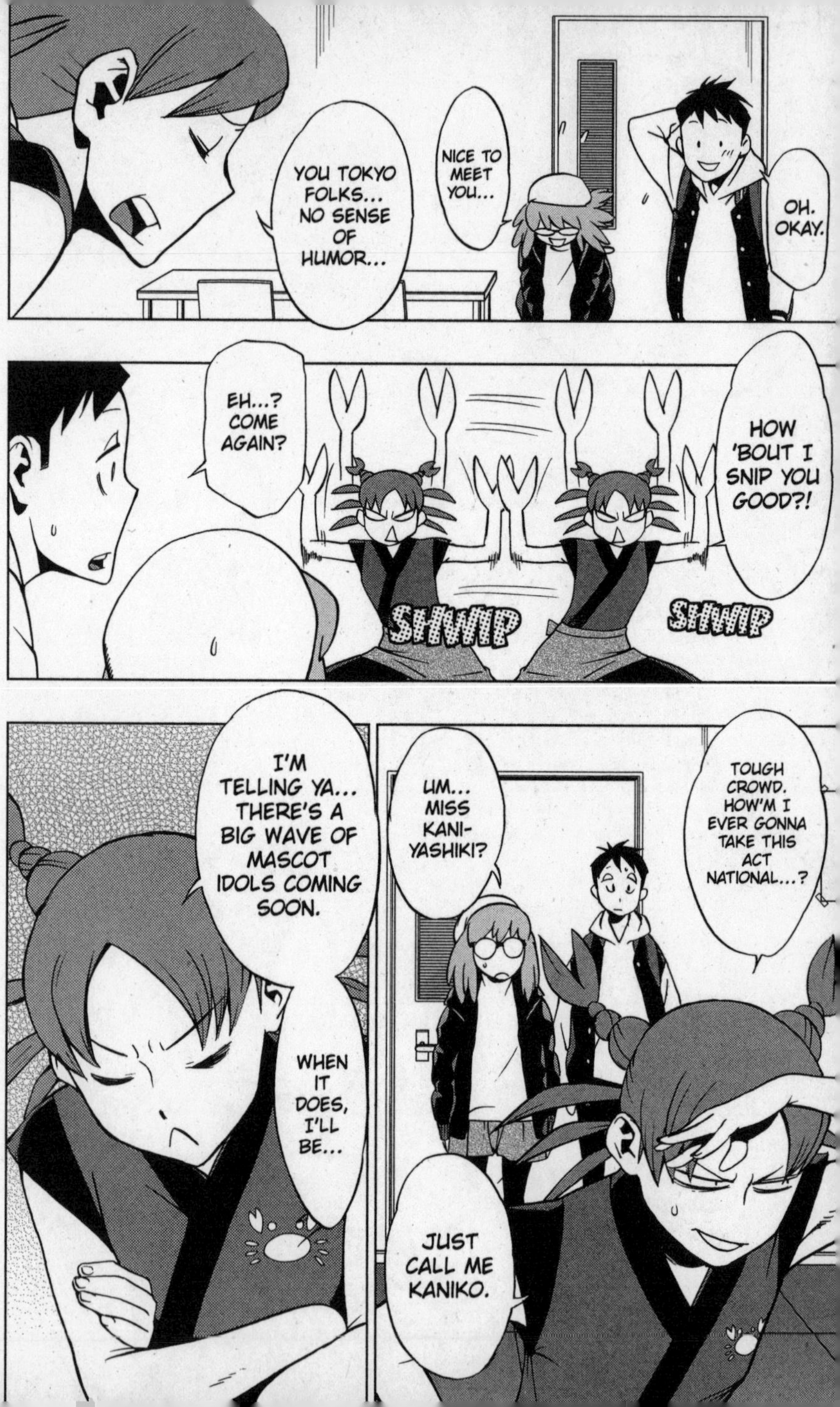
OH. OKAY.
NICE TO MEET YOU...
YOU TOKYO FOLKS... NO SENSE OF HUMOR...
HOW 'BOUT I SNIP YOU GOOD?!
SHWIP
SHWIP
EH...? COME AGAIN?
TOUGH CROWD. HOW'M I EVER GONNA TAKE THIS ACT NATIONAL...?
UM... MISS KANI-YASHIKI?
JUST CALL ME KANIKO.
I'M TELLING YA... THERE'S A BIG WAVE OF MASCOT IDOLS COMING SOON.
WHEN IT DOES, I'LL BE...

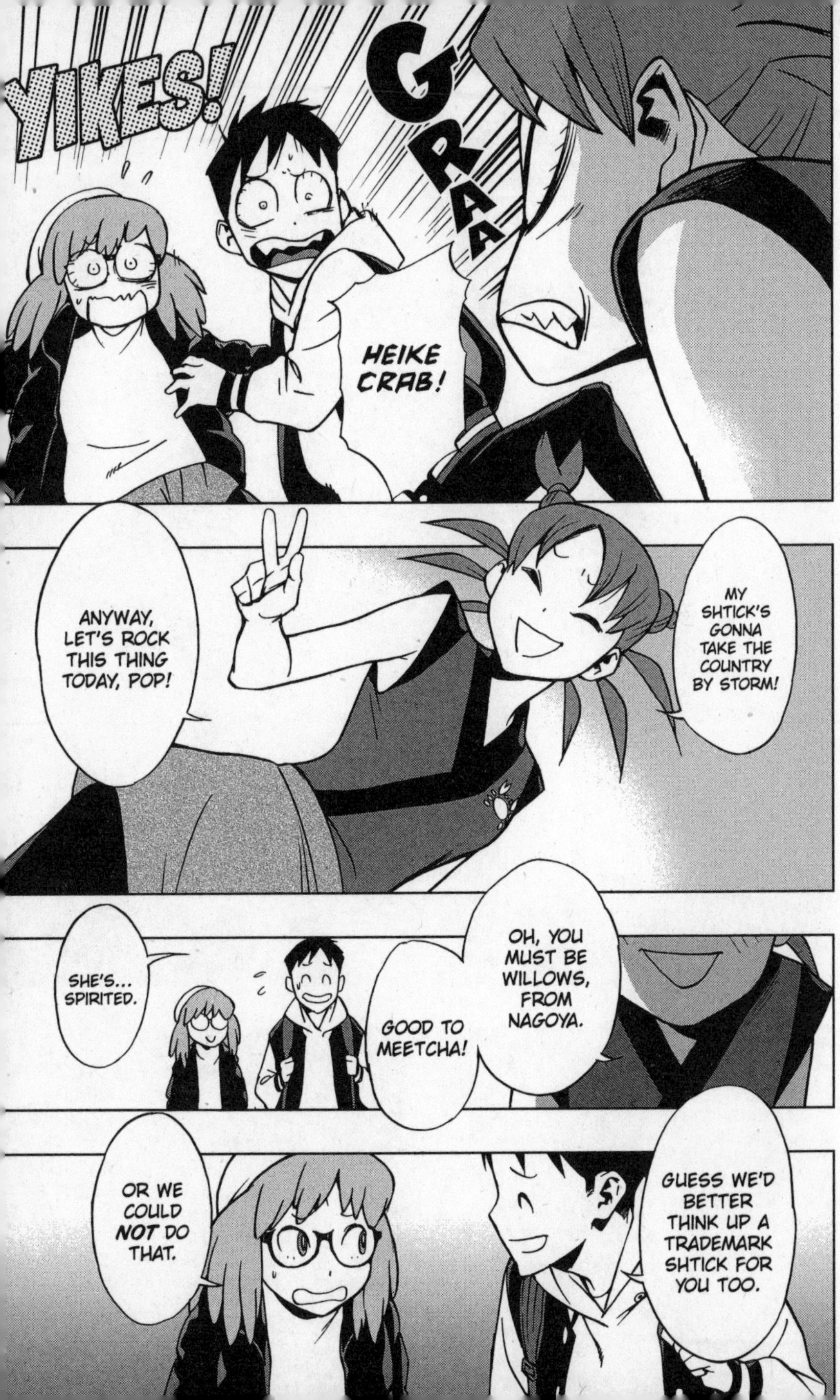
GRAA
YIKES!
HEIKE CRAB!
MY SHTICK'S GONNA TAKE THE COUNTRY BY STORM!
ANYWAY, LET'S ROCK THIS THING TODAY, POP!
OH, YOU MUST BE WILLOWS, FROM NAGOYA.
GOOD TO MEETCHA!
SHE'S... SPIRITED.
GUESS WE'D BETTER THINK UP A TRADEMARK SHTICK FOR YOU TOO.
OR WE COULD *NOT* DO THAT.

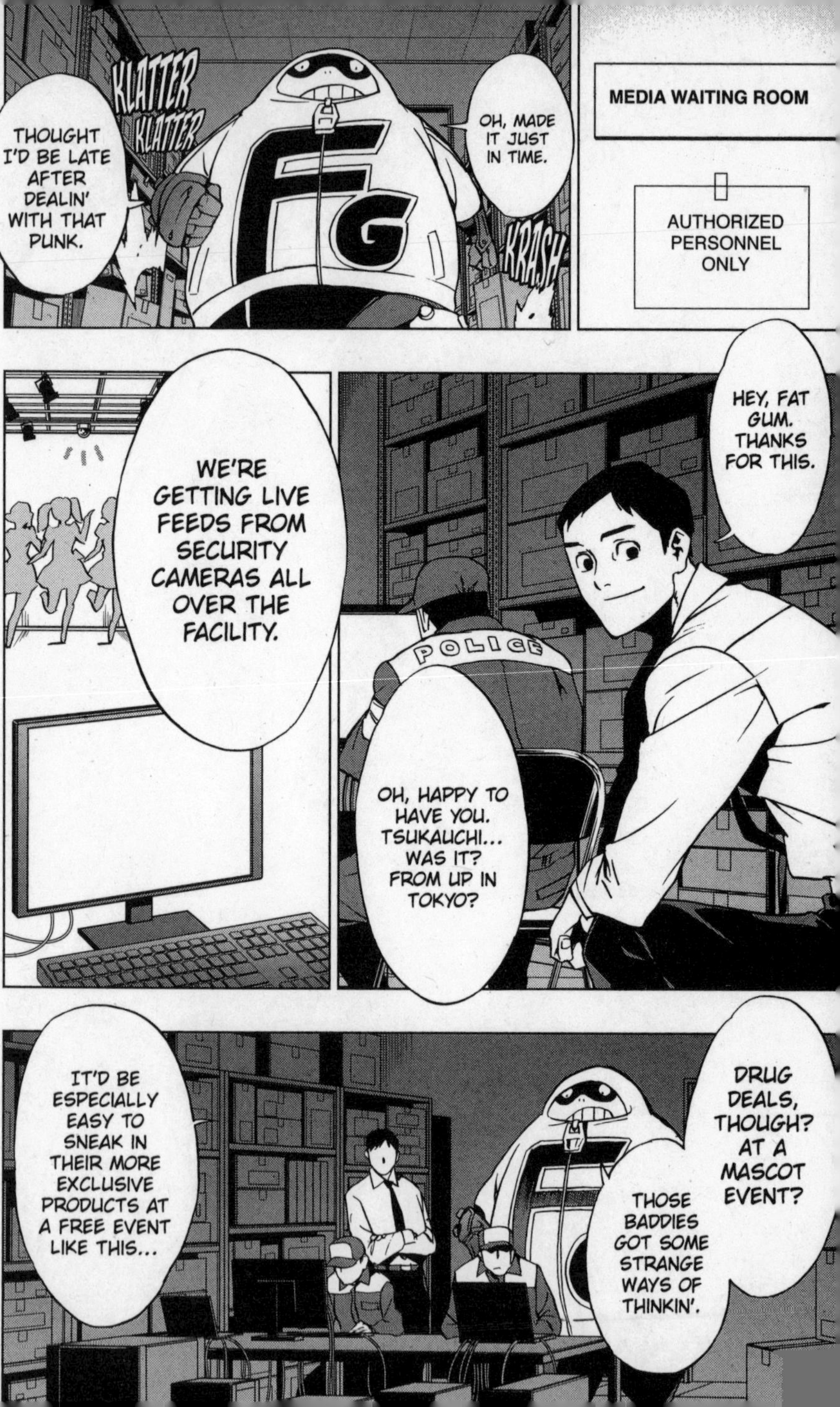
MEDIA WAITING ROOM
AUTHORIZED PERSONNEL ONLY
OH, MADE IT JUST IN TIME.
KLATTER KLATTER
KRASH
THOUGHT I'D BE LATE AFTER DEALIN' WITH THAT PUNK.
HEY, FAT GUM. THANKS FOR THIS.
POLICE
OH, HAPPY TO HAVE YOU. TSUKAUCHI... WAS IT? FROM UP IN TOKYO?
WE'RE GETTING LIVE FEEDS FROM SECURITY CAMERAS ALL OVER THE FACILITY.
DRUG DEALS, THOUGH? AT A MASCOT EVENT?
THOSE BADDIES GOT SOME STRANGE WAYS OF THINKIN'.
IT'D BE ESPECIALLY EASY TO SNEAK IN THEIR MORE EXCLUSIVE PRODUCTS AT A FREE EVENT LIKE THIS...

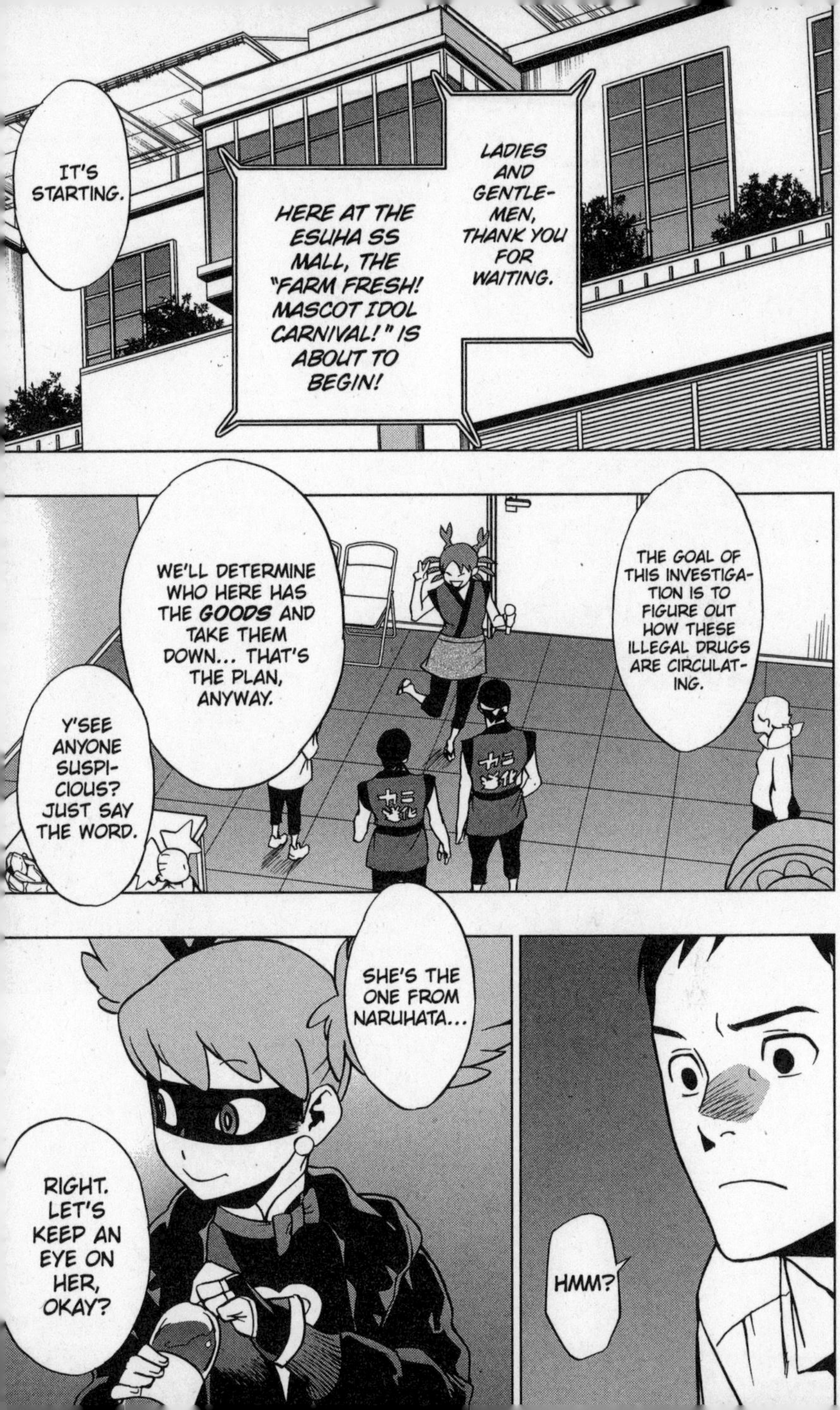
LADIES AND GENTLE-MEN, THANK YOU FOR WAITING.
HERE AT THE ESUHA SS MALL, THE "FARM FRESH! MASCOT IDOL CARNIVAL!" IS ABOUT TO BEGIN!
IT'S STARTING.
THE GOAL OF THIS INVESTIGA-TION IS TO FIGURE OUT HOW THESE ILLEGAL DRUGS ARE CIRCULAT-ING.
WE'LL DETERMINE WHO HERE HAS THE GOODS AND TAKE THEM DOWN... THAT'S THE PLAN, ANYWAY.
Y'SEE ANYONE SUSPI-CIOUS? JUST SAY THE WORD.
HMM?
SHE'S THE ONE FROM NARUHATA...
RIGHT. LET'S KEEP AN EYE ON HER, OKAY?

FAT GUM

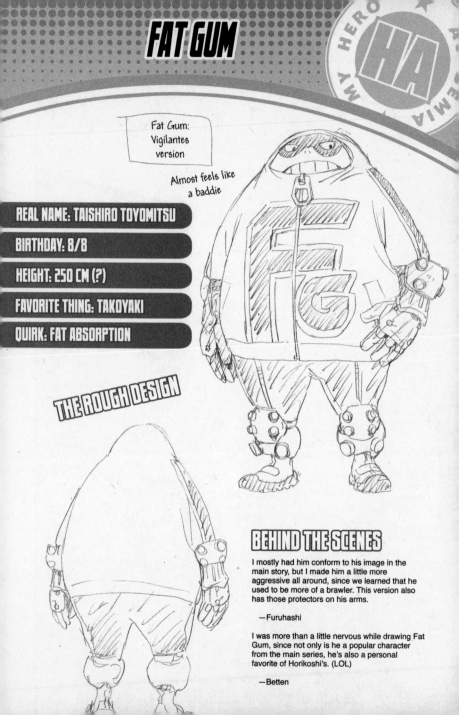

Fat Gum:
Vigilantes
version

Almost feels like
a baddie

REAL NAME: TAISHIRO TOYOMITSU

BIRTHDAY: 8/8

HEIGHT: 250 CM (?)

FAVORITE THING: TAKOYAKI

QUIRK: FAT ABSORPTION

THE ROUGH DESIGN

BEHIND THE SCENES

I mostly had him conform to his image in the main story, but I made him a little more aggressive all around, since we learned that he used to be more of a brawler. This version also has those protectors on his arms.

—Furuhashi

I was more than a little nervous while drawing Fat Gum, since not only is he a popular character from the main series, he's also a personal favorite of Horikoshi's. (LOL)

—Betten

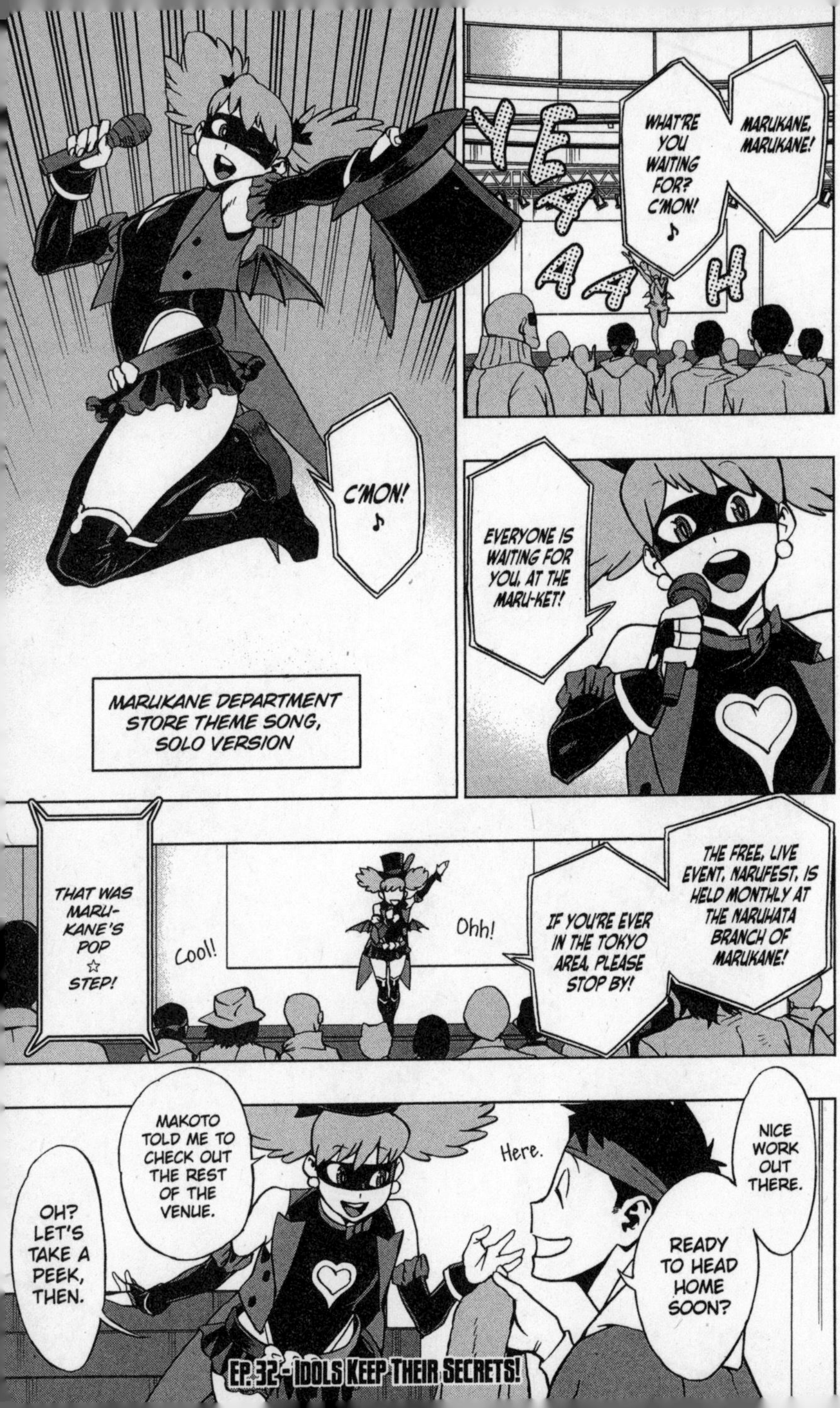
MARUKANE, MARUKANE!
WHAT'RE YOU WAITING FOR? C'MON! ♪
YEAAAH
EVERYONE IS WAITING FOR YOU, AT THE MARU-KET!
C'MON! ♪
MARUKANE DEPARTMENT STORE THEME SONG, SOLO VERSION
THE FREE, LIVE EVENT, NARUFEST, IS HELD MONTHLY AT THE NARUHATA BRANCH OF MARUKANE!
IF YOU'RE EVER IN THE TOKYO AREA, PLEASE STOP BY!
Ohh!
Cool!
THAT WAS MARU-KANE'S POP ☆ STEP!
NICE WORK OUT THERE.
READY TO HEAD HOME SOON?
Here.
MAKOTO TOLD ME TO CHECK OUT THE REST OF THE VENUE.
OH? LET'S TAKE A PEEK, THEN.
EP. 32 - IDOLS KEEP THEIR SECRETS!

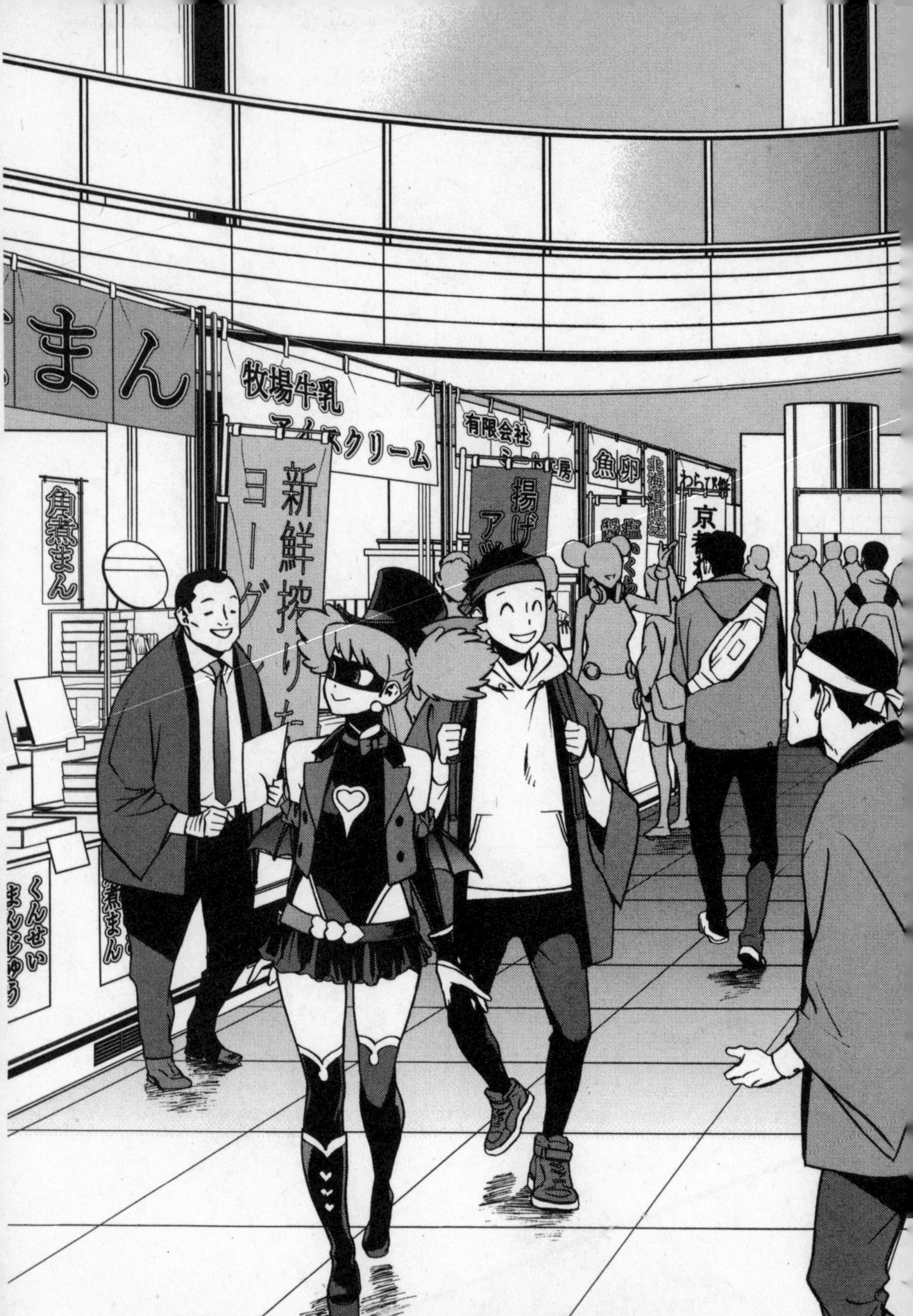
まん
牧場牛乳
有限会社
魚卵
北海道直送
角煮まん
揚げ
くんせい
まんじゅう

EP. 32 - IDOLS KEEP THEIR SECRETS!

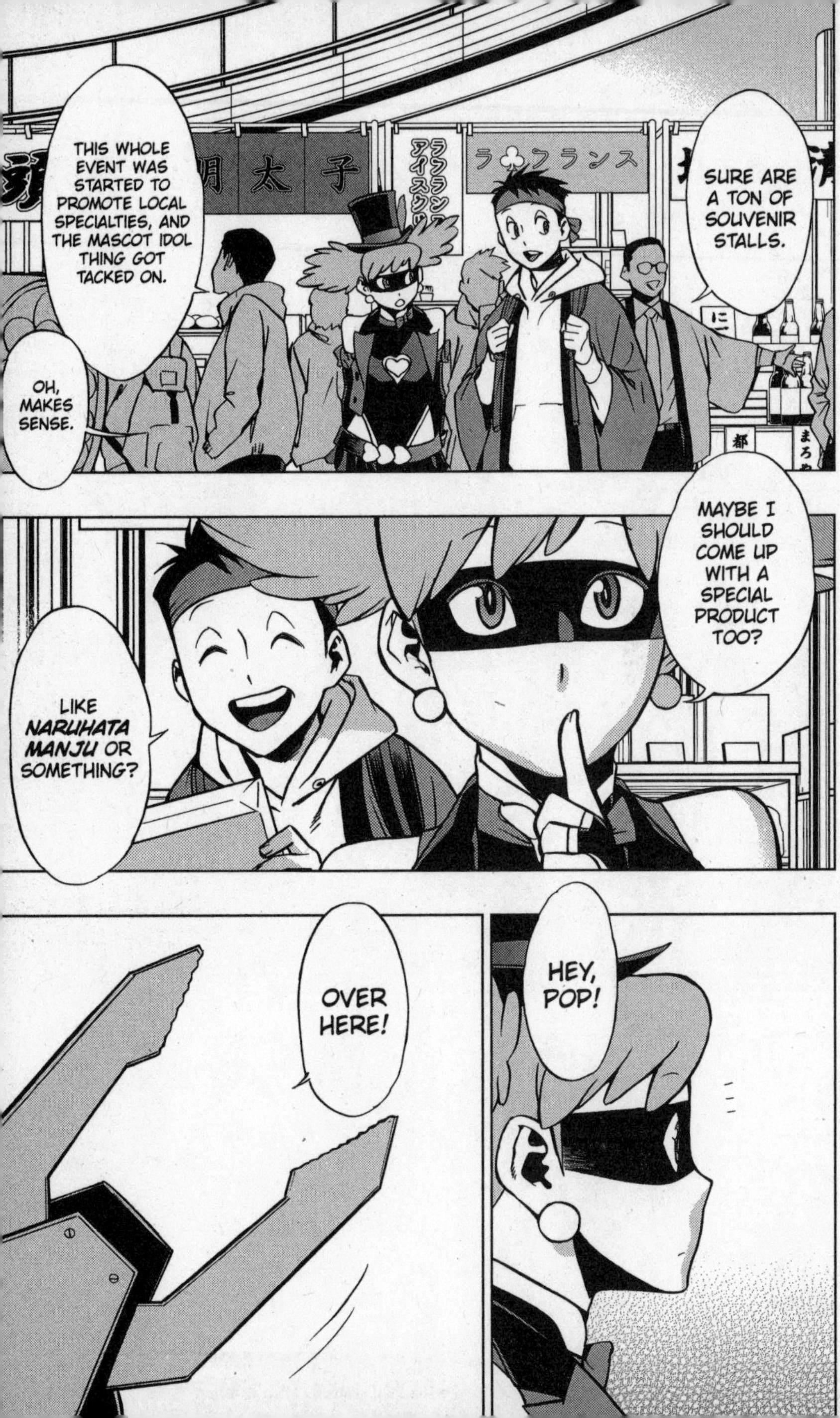
SURE ARE A TON OF SOUVENIR STALLS.
THIS WHOLE EVENT WAS STARTED TO PROMOTE LOCAL SPECIALTIES, AND THE MASCOT IDOL THING GOT TACKED ON.
OH, MAKES SENSE.
MAYBE I SHOULD COME UP WITH A SPECIAL PRODUCT TOO?
LIKE *NARUHATA MANJU* OR SOMETHING?
HEY, POP!
OVER HERE!

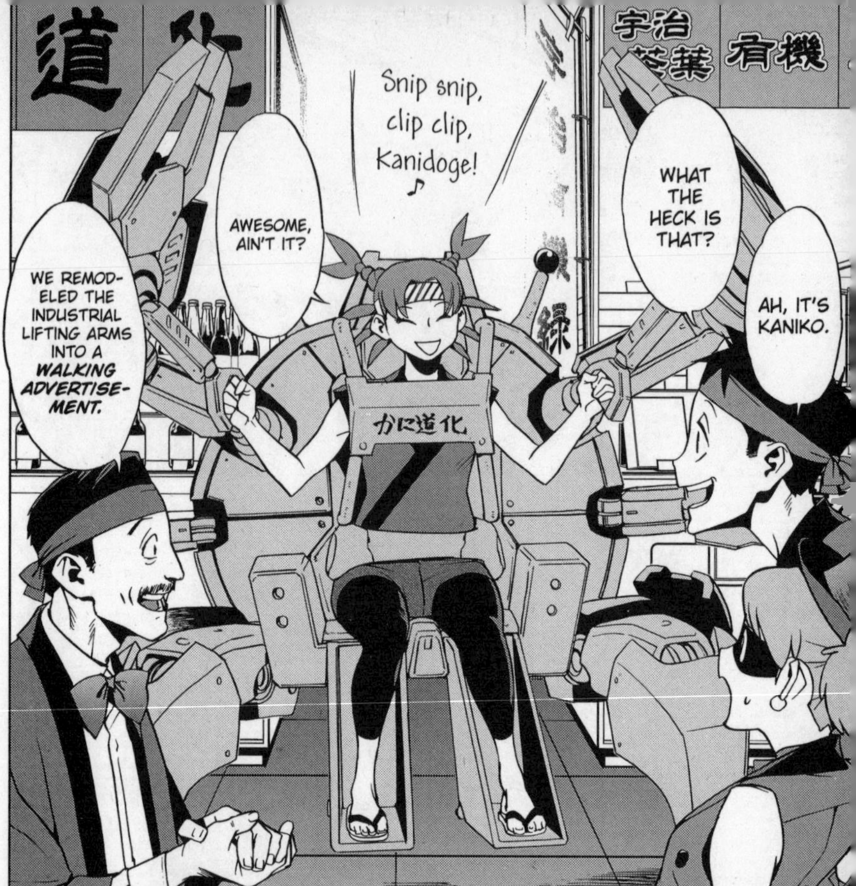
WHAT THE HECK IS THAT?
AH, IT'S KANIKO.
Snip snip, clip clip, Kanidoge! ♪
AWESOME, AIN'T IT?
WE REMODELED THE INDUSTRIAL LIFTING ARMS INTO A ***WALKING ADVERTISEMENT.***
かに道化
道化

*KANIDOGE

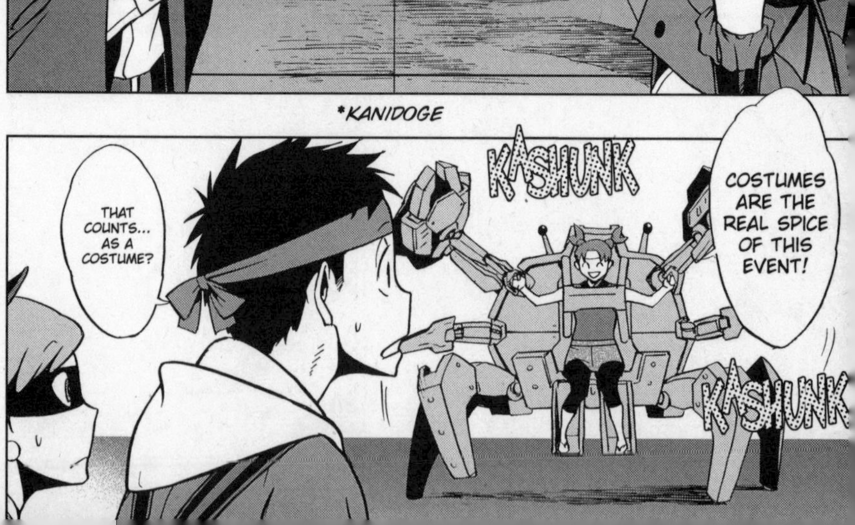
COSTUMES ARE THE REAL SPICE OF THIS EVENT!
KASHUNK
KASHUNK
THAT COUNTS... AS A COSTUME?

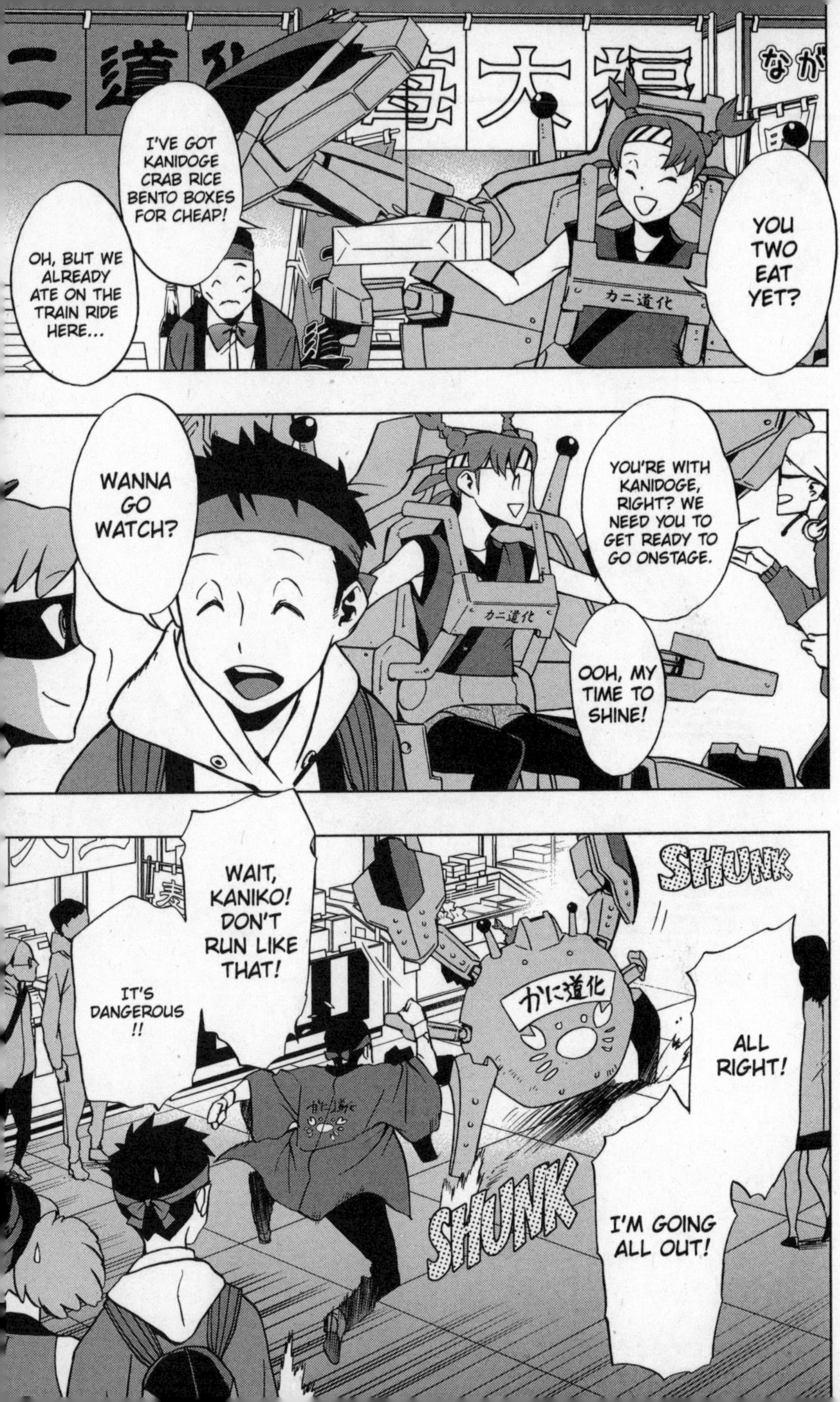
YOU TWO EAT YET?
カニ道化
I'VE GOT KANIDOGE CRAB RICE BENTO BOXES FOR CHEAP!
OH, BUT WE ALREADY ATE ON THE TRAIN RIDE HERE...
YOU'RE WITH KANIDOGE, RIGHT? WE NEED YOU TO GET READY TO GO ONSTAGE.
OOH, MY TIME TO SHINE!
カニ道化
WANNA GO WATCH?
SHUNK
ALL RIGHT!
I'M GOING ALL OUT!
かに道化
SHUNK
WAIT, KANIKO! DON'T RUN LIKE THAT!
IT'S DANGEROUS!!

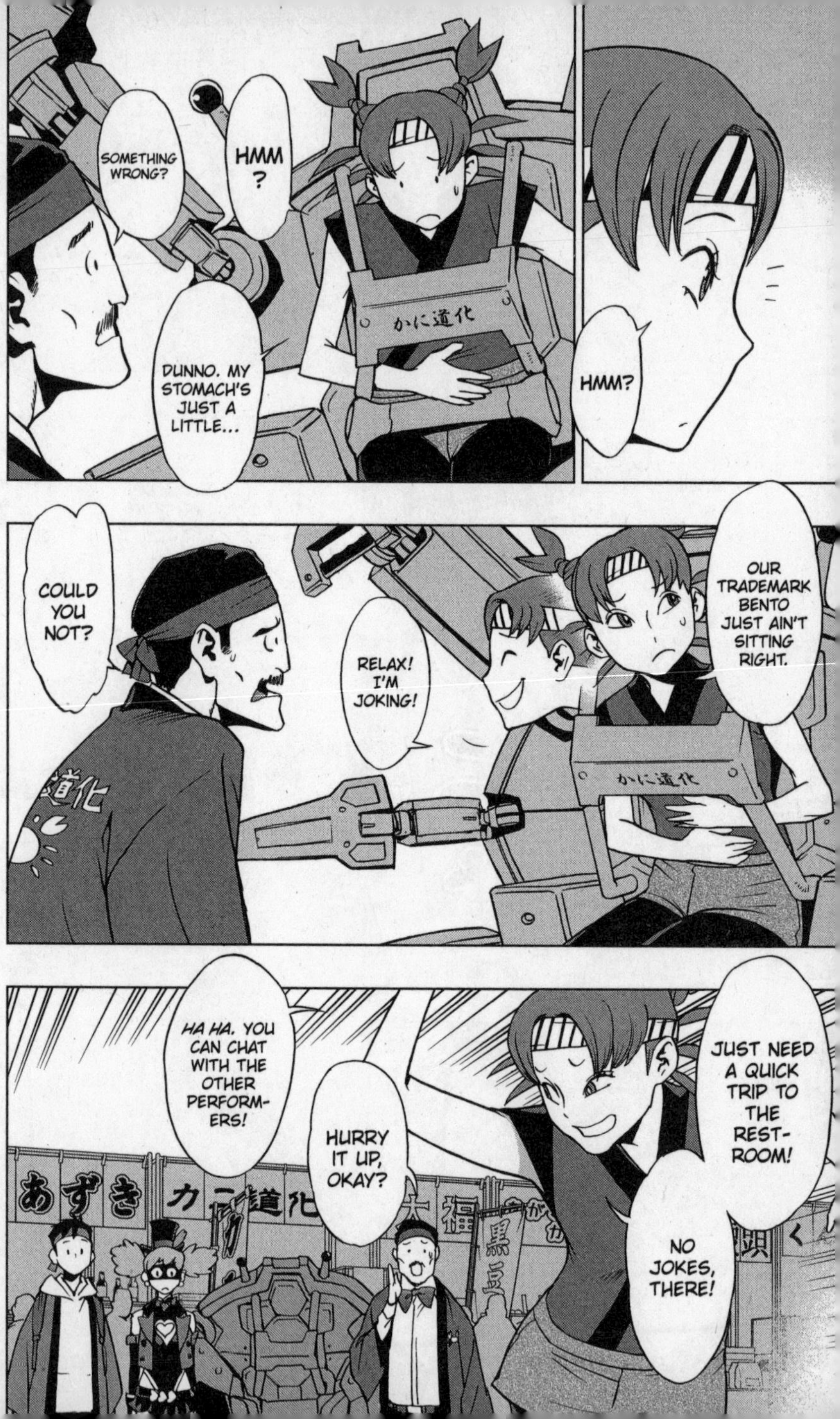
HMM?
HMM ?
SOMETHING WRONG?
かに道化
DUNNO. MY STOMACH'S JUST A LITTLE...
OUR TRADEMARK BENTO JUST AIN'T SITTING RIGHT.
COULD YOU NOT?
RELAX! I'M JOKING!
かに道化
JUST NEED A QUICK TRIP TO THE REST-ROOM!
NO JOKES, THERE!
HA HA. YOU CAN CHAT WITH THE OTHER PERFORM-ERS!
HURRY IT UP, OKAY?
あずき
カニ道化

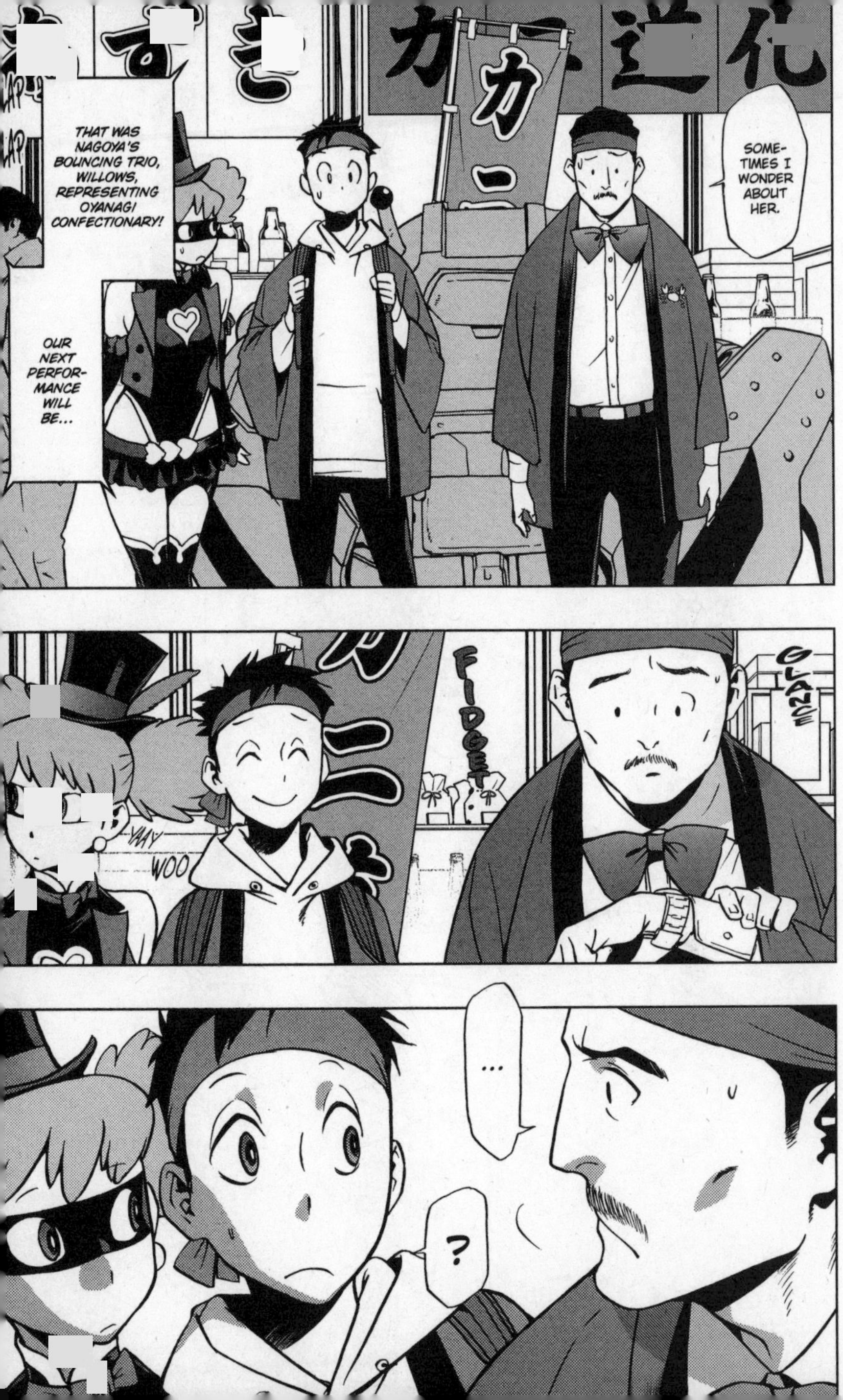

SOME-TIMES I WONDER ABOUT HER.
THAT WAS NAGOYA'S BOUNCING TRIO, WILLOWS, REPRESENTING OYANAGI CONFECTIONARY!
OUR NEXT PERFOR-MANCE WILL BE...
GLANCE
FIDGET
YAAY
WOO
...
?

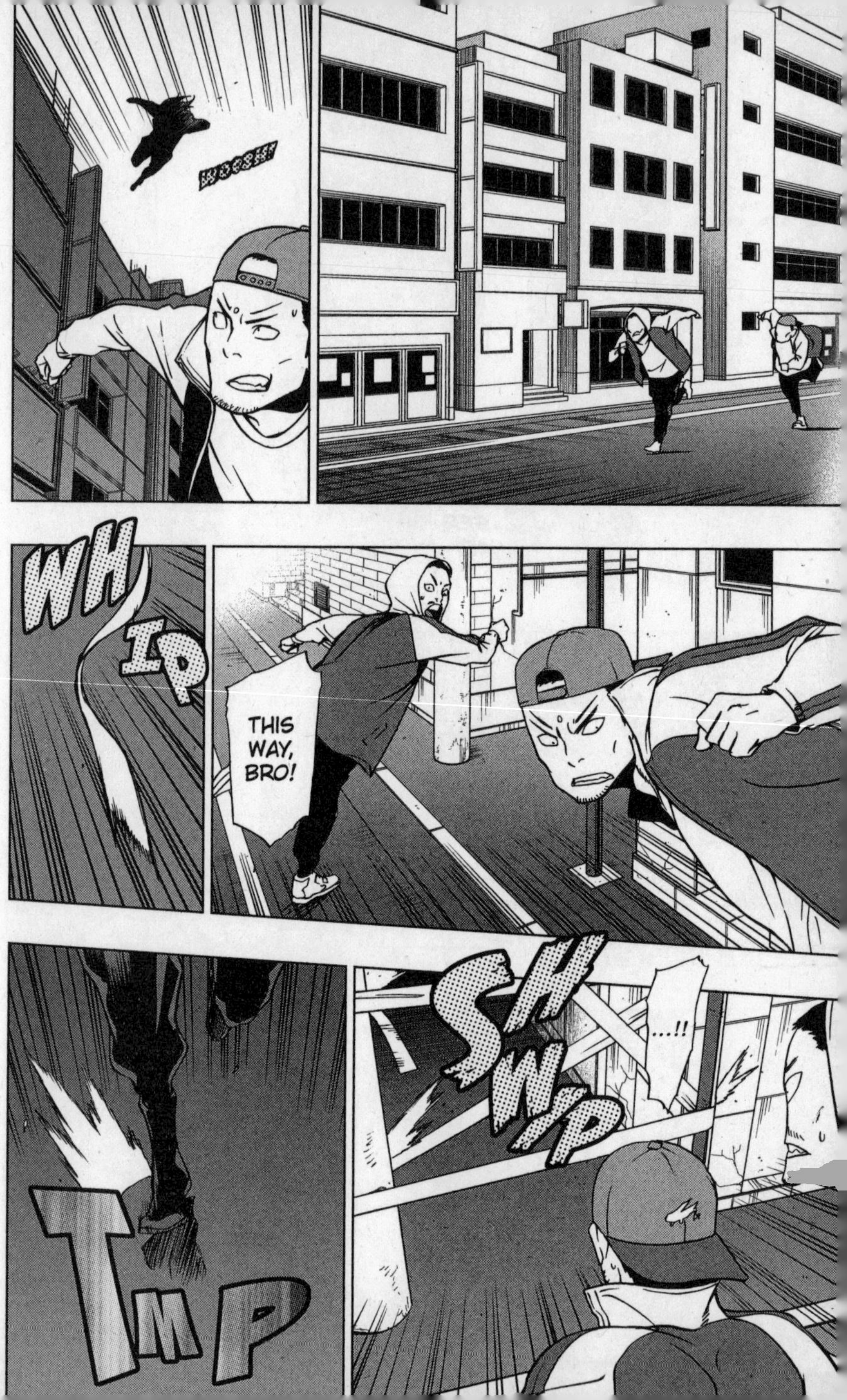
WOOSH!
THIS WAY, BRO!
WHIP
SHWP
...!!
TMP

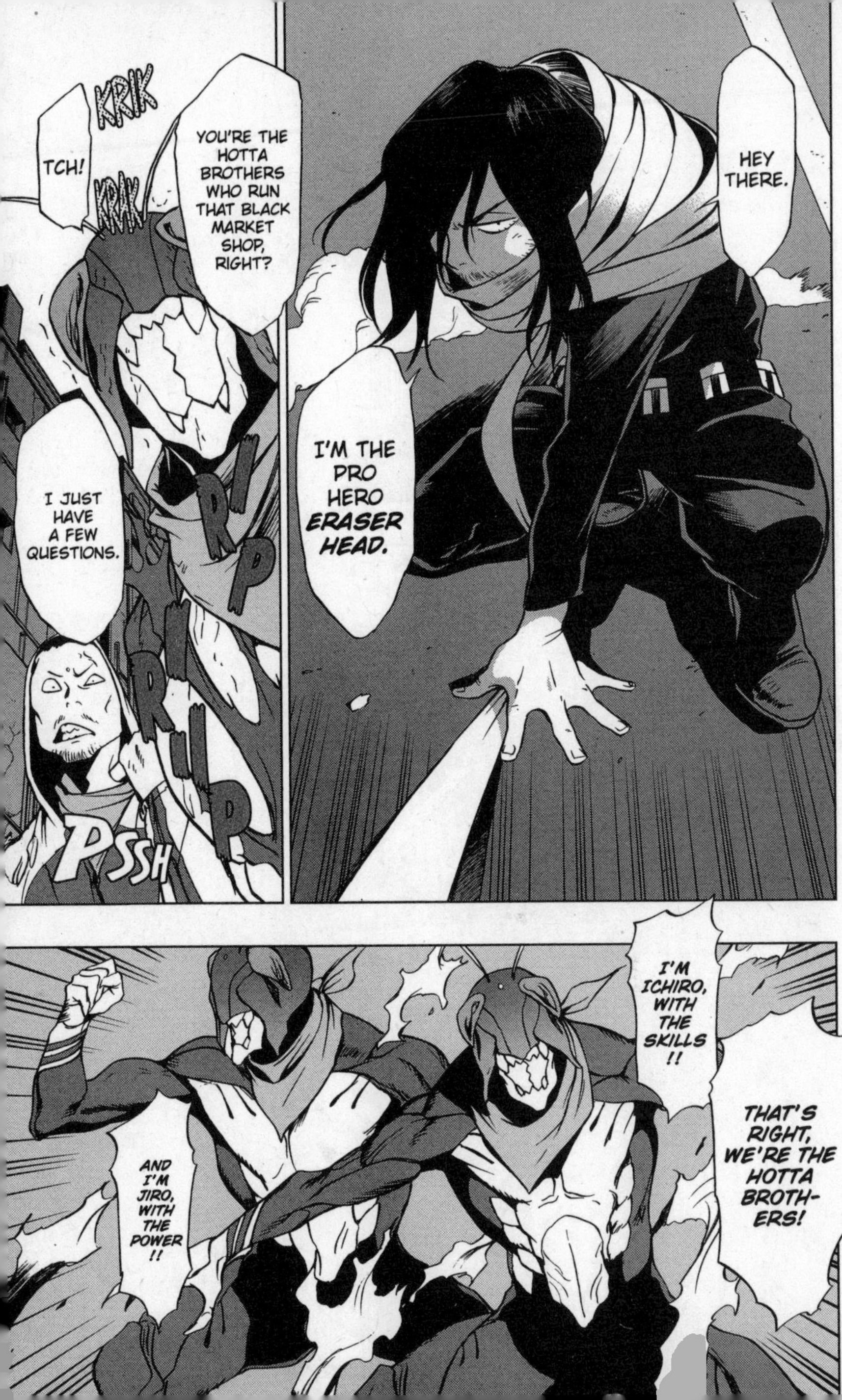
HEY THERE.
I'M THE PRO HERO ERASER HEAD.
YOU'RE THE HOTTA BROTHERS WHO RUN THAT BLACK MARKET SHOP, RIGHT?
KRIK
TCH!
KRIK
I JUST HAVE A FEW QUESTIONS.
RIP
RIP
PSSH
I'M ICHIRO, WITH THE SKILLS!!
THAT'S RIGHT, WE'RE THE HOTTA BROTH-ERS!
AND I'M JIRO, WITH THE POWER!!

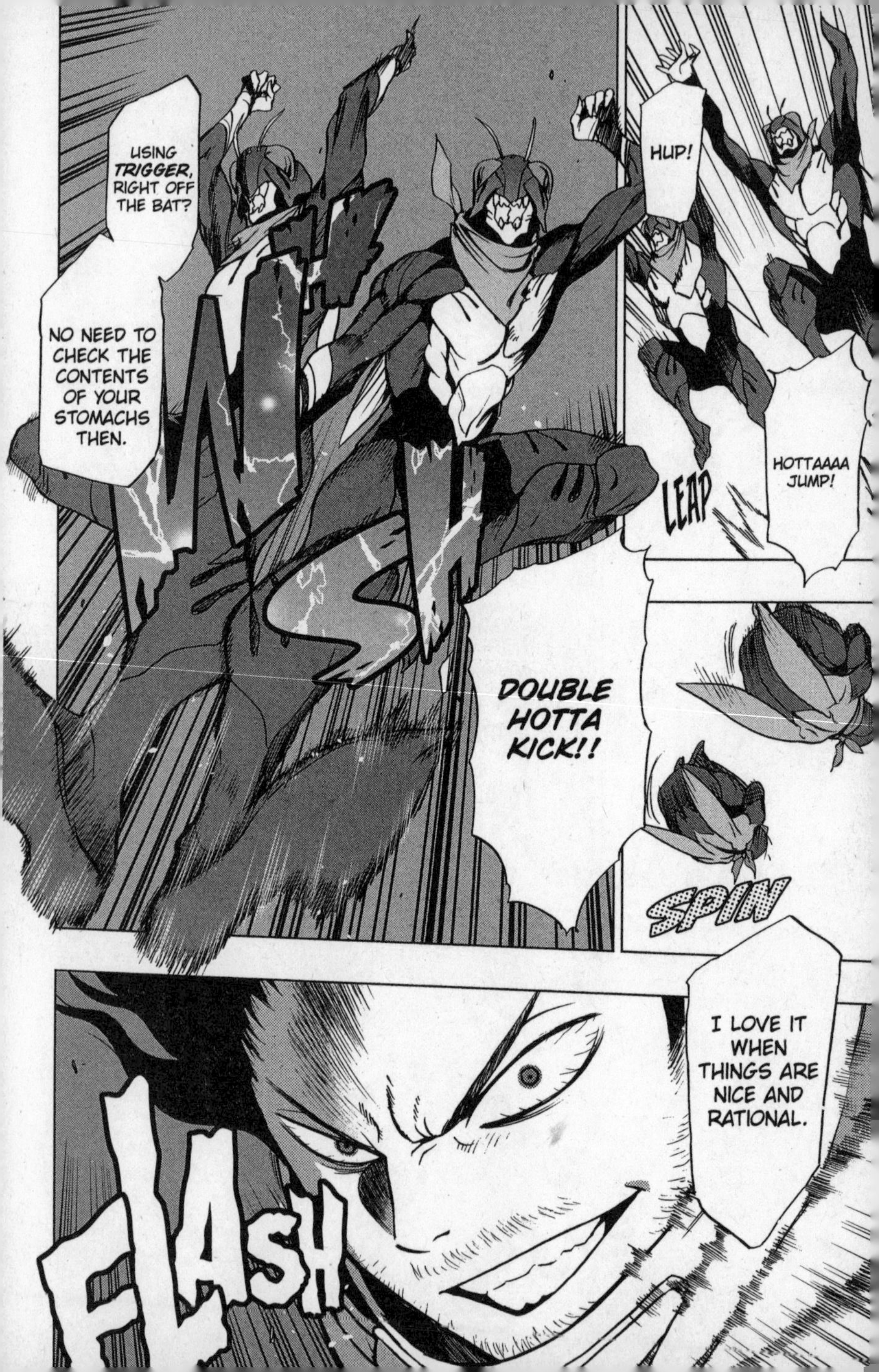
HUP!
LEAP
HOTTAAAA JUMP!
SPIN
DOUBLE HOTTA KICK!!
USING *TRIGGER*, RIGHT OFF THE BAT?
NO NEED TO CHECK THE CONTENTS OF YOUR STOMACHS THEN.
I LOVE IT WHEN THINGS ARE NICE AND RATIONAL.
FLASH

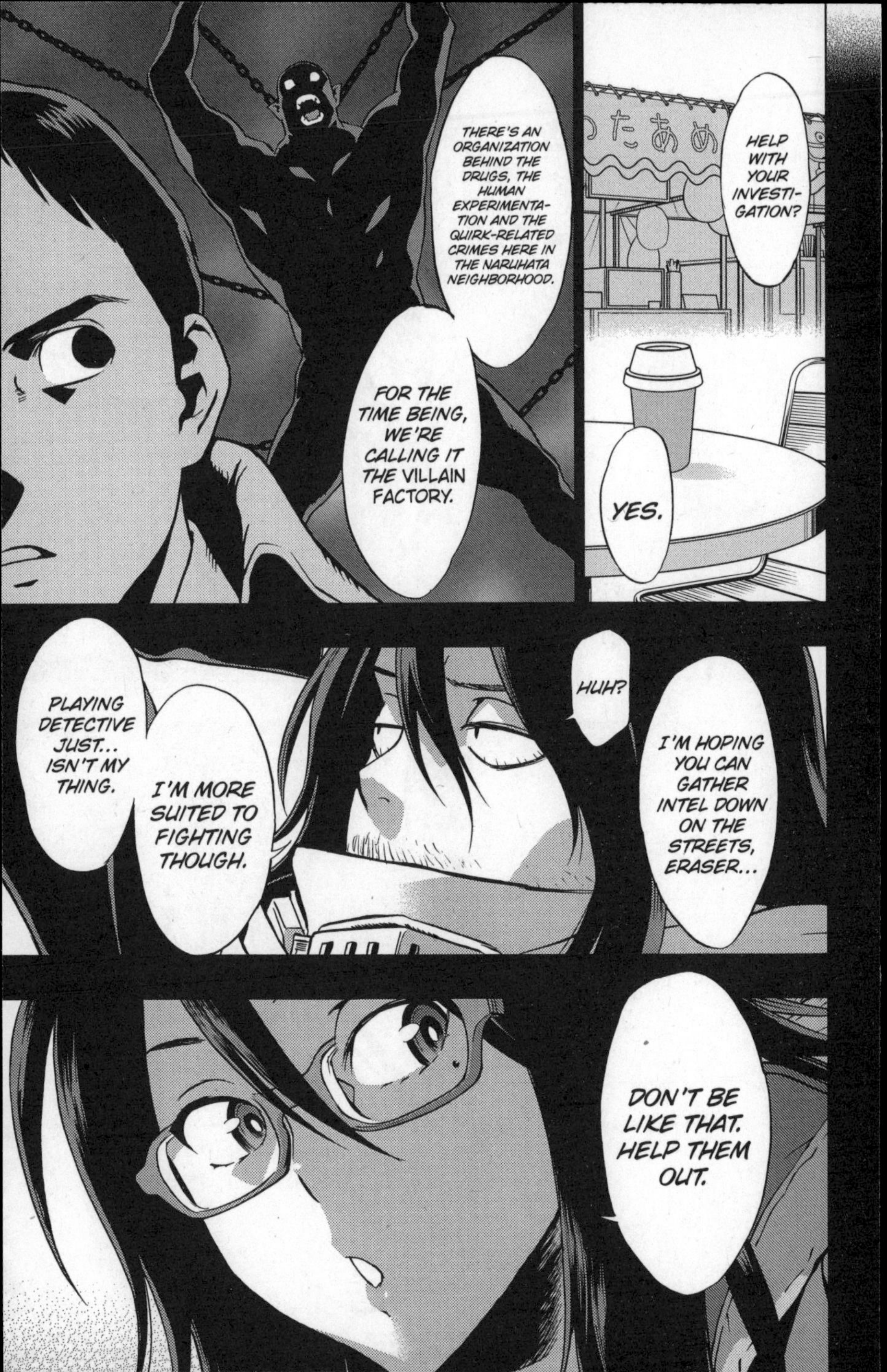
HELP WITH YOUR INVESTIGATION?
YES.
THERE'S AN ORGANIZATION BEHIND THE DRUGS, THE HUMAN EXPERIMENTATION AND THE QUIRK-RELATED CRIMES HERE IN THE NARUHATA NEIGHBORHOOD.
FOR THE TIME BEING, WE'RE CALLING IT THE VILLAIN FACTORY.
HUH?
I'M HOPING YOU CAN GATHER INTEL DOWN ON THE STREETS, ERASER...
PLAYING DETECTIVE JUST... ISN'T MY THING.
I'M MORE SUITED TO FIGHTING THOUGH.
DON'T BE LIKE THAT. HELP THEM OUT.

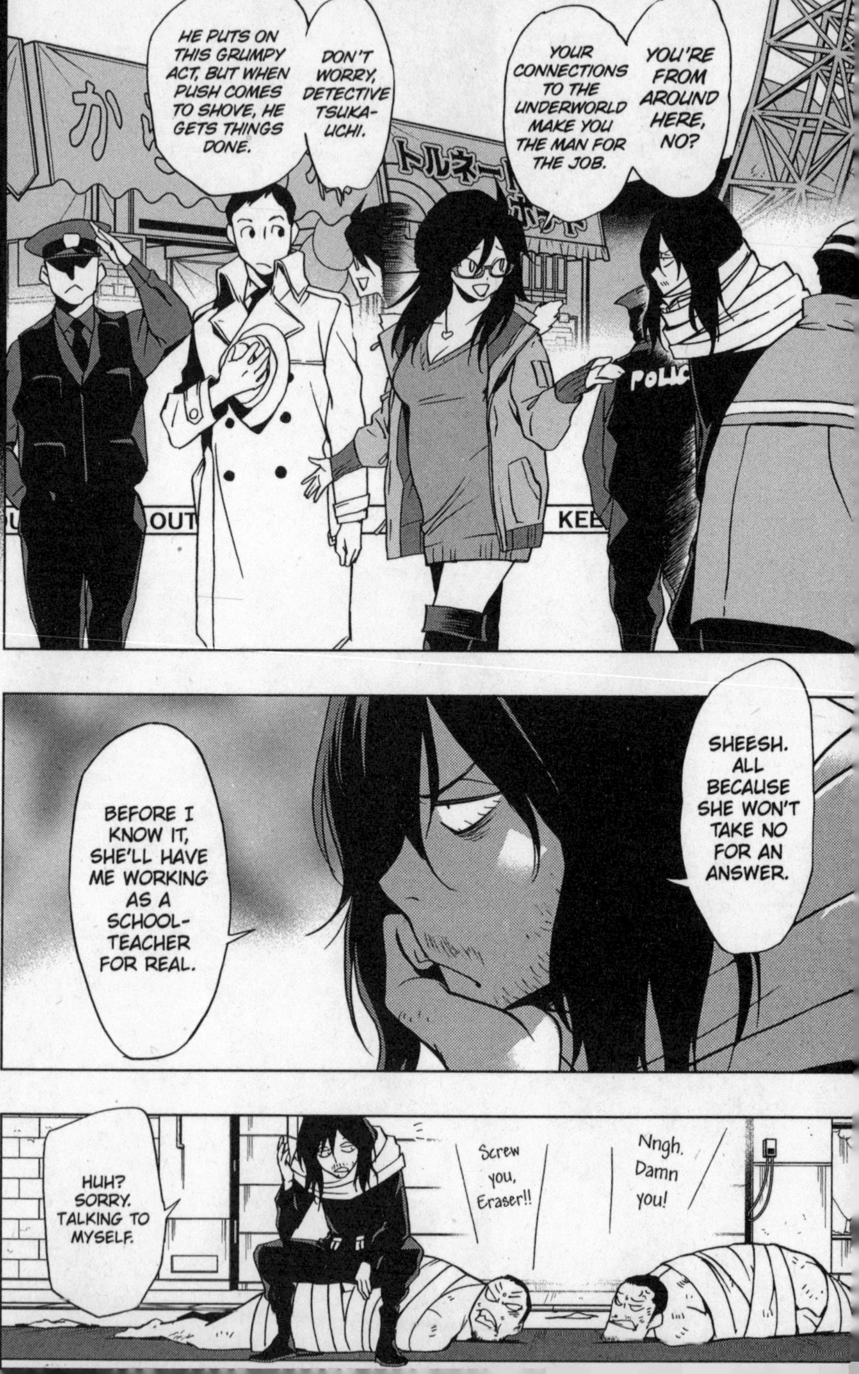
YOU'RE FROM AROUND HERE, NO?
YOUR CONNECTIONS TO THE UNDERWORLD MAKE YOU THE MAN FOR THE JOB.
DON'T WORRY, DETECTIVE TSUKA-UCHI.
HE PUTS ON THIS GRUMPY ACT, BUT WHEN PUSH COMES TO SHOVE, HE GETS THINGS DONE.
SHEESH. ALL BECAUSE SHE WON'T TAKE NO FOR AN ANSWER.
BEFORE I KNOW IT, SHE'LL HAVE ME WORKING AS A SCHOOL-TEACHER FOR REAL.
Nngh. Damn you!
Screw you, Eraser!!
HUH? SORRY. TALKING TO MYSELF.

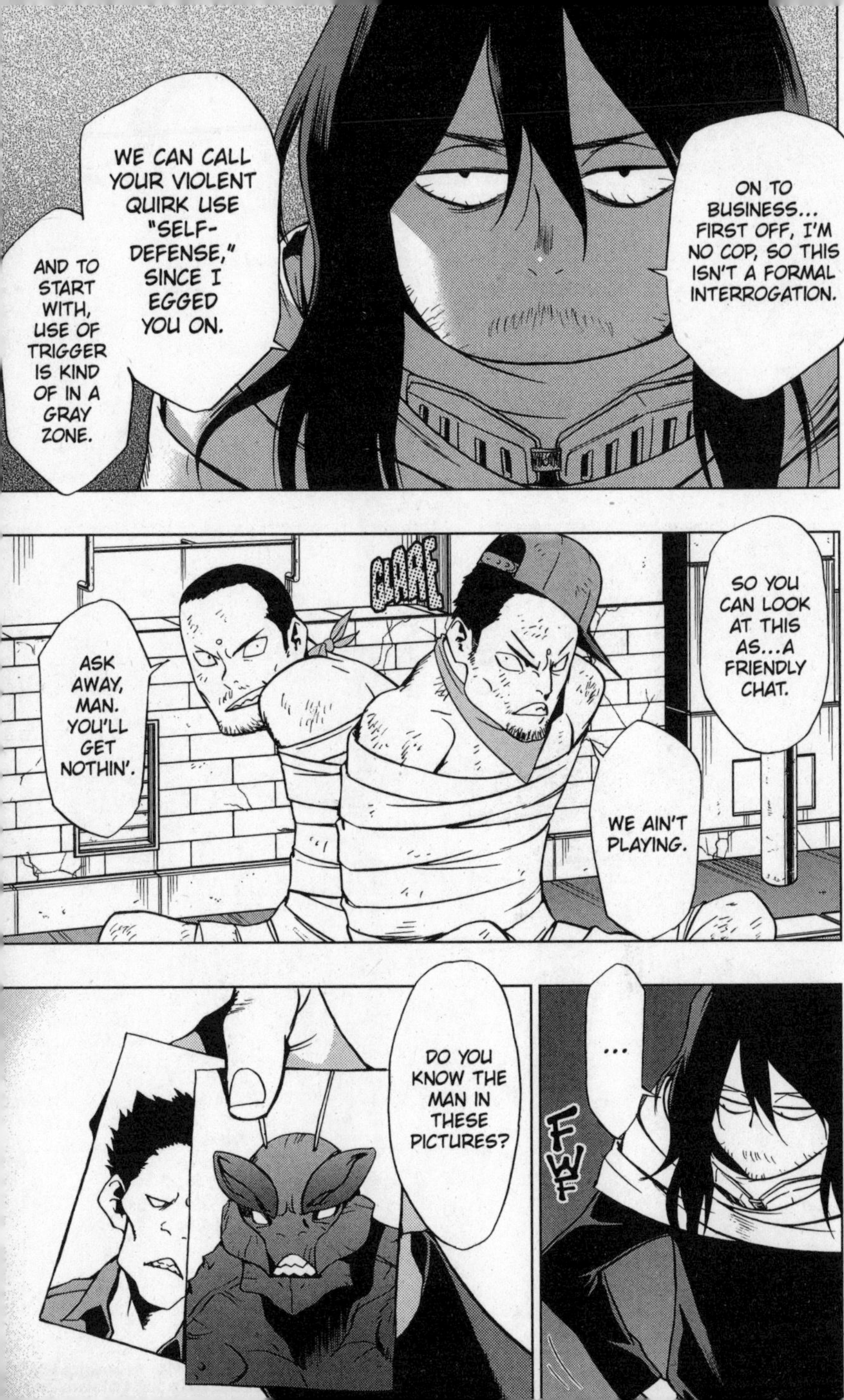
ON TO BUSINESS... FIRST OFF, I'M NO COP, SO THIS ISN'T A FORMAL INTERROGATION.
WE CAN CALL YOUR VIOLENT QUIRK USE "SELF-DEFENSE," SINCE I EGGED YOU ON.
AND TO START WITH, USE OF TRIGGER IS KIND OF IN A GRAY ZONE.
SO YOU CAN LOOK AT THIS AS...A FRIENDLY CHAT.
WE AIN'T PLAYING.
GLARE
ASK AWAY, MAN. YOU'LL GET NOTHIN'.
...
FWF
DO YOU KNOW THE MAN IN THESE PICTURES?

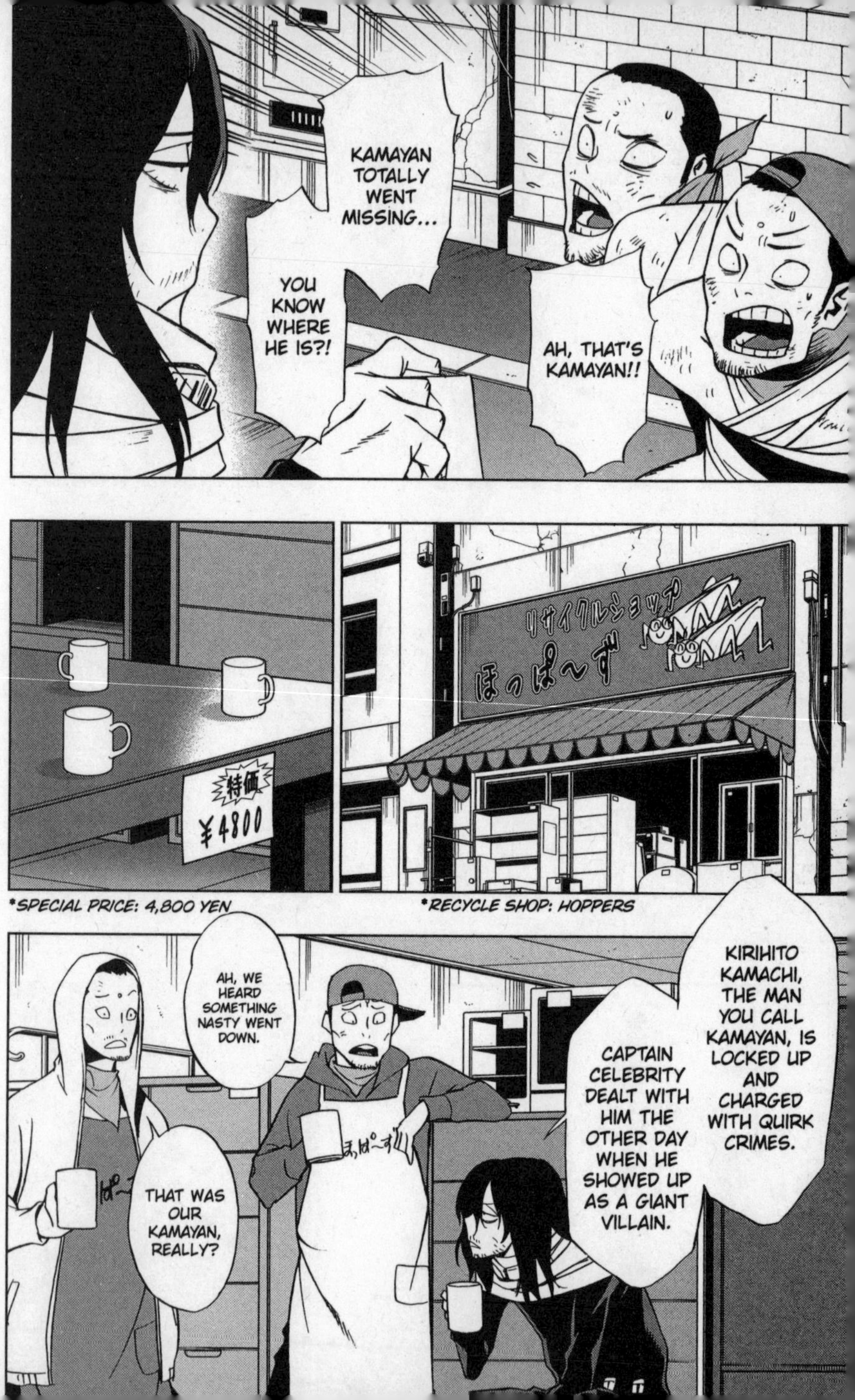
AH, THAT'S KAMAYAN!!
KAMAYAN TOTALLY WENT MISSING...
YOU KNOW WHERE HE IS?!
リサイクルショップ
ほっぱ〜ず
*RECYCLE SHOP: HOPPERS
特価
¥4800
*SPECIAL PRICE: 4,800 YEN
KIRIHITO KAMACHI, THE MAN YOU CALL KAMAYAN, IS LOCKED UP AND CHARGED WITH QUIRK CRIMES.
CAPTAIN CELEBRITY DEALT WITH HIM THE OTHER DAY WHEN HE SHOWED UP AS A GIANT VILLAIN.
AH, WE HEARD SOMETHING NASTY WENT DOWN.
THAT WAS OUR KAMAYAN, REALLY?

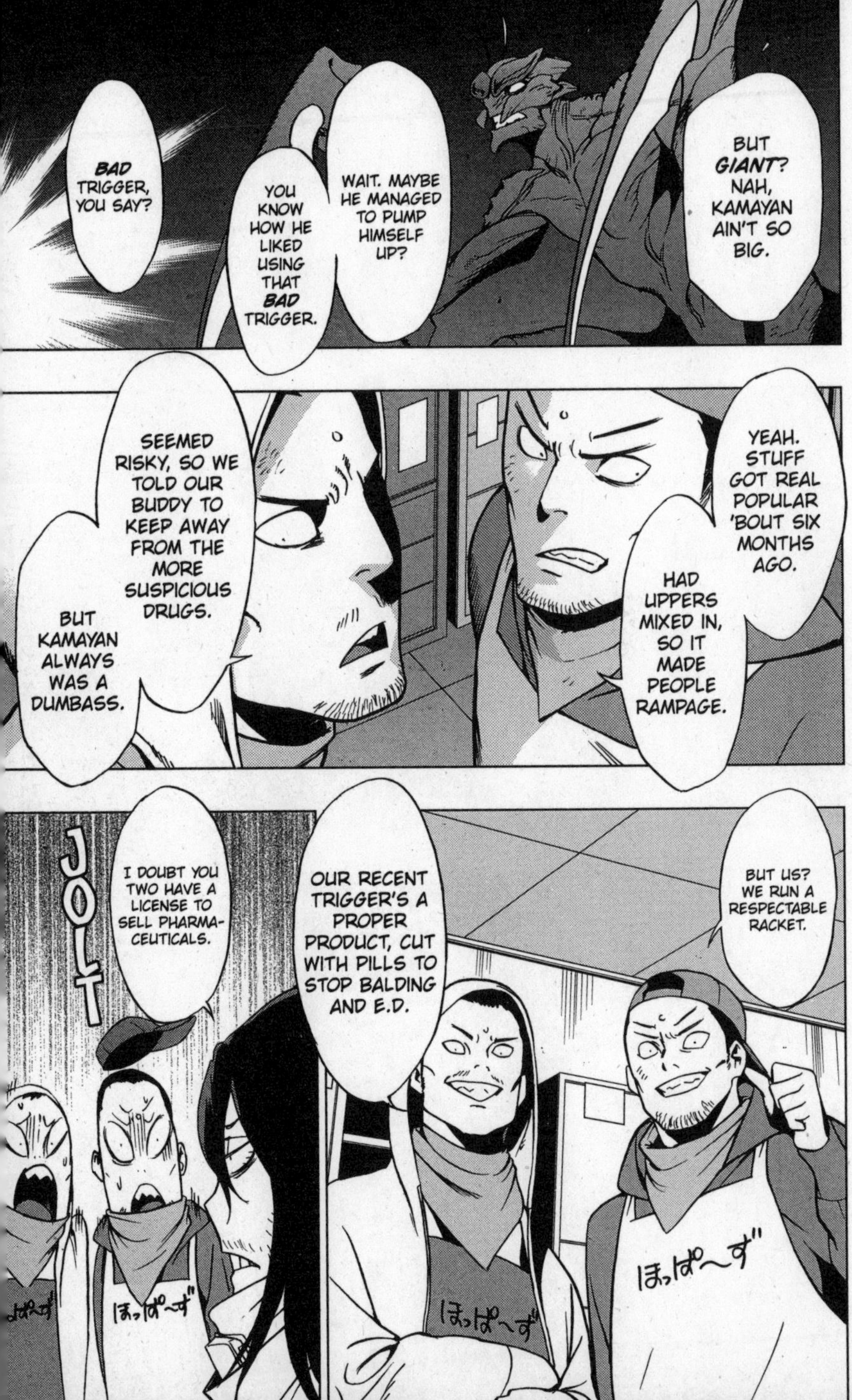
BUT GIANT? NAH, KAMAYAN AIN'T SO BIG.
WAIT. MAYBE HE MANAGED TO PUMP HIMSELF UP?
YOU KNOW HOW HE LIKED USING THAT BAD TRIGGER.
BAD TRIGGER, YOU SAY?
YEAH. STUFF GOT REAL POPULAR 'BOUT SIX MONTHS AGO.
HAD UPPERS MIXED IN, SO IT MADE PEOPLE RAMPAGE.
SEEMED RISKY, SO WE TOLD OUR BUDDY TO KEEP AWAY FROM THE MORE SUSPICIOUS DRUGS.
BUT KAMAYAN ALWAYS WAS A DUMBASS.
BUT US? WE RUN A RESPECTABLE RACKET.
ほっぱ〜ず
OUR RECENT TRIGGER'S A PROPER PRODUCT, CUT WITH PILLS TO STOP BALDING AND E.D.
ほっぱ〜ず
JOLT
I DOUBT YOU TWO HAVE A LICENSE TO SELL PHARMA-CEUTICALS.
ほっぱ〜ず

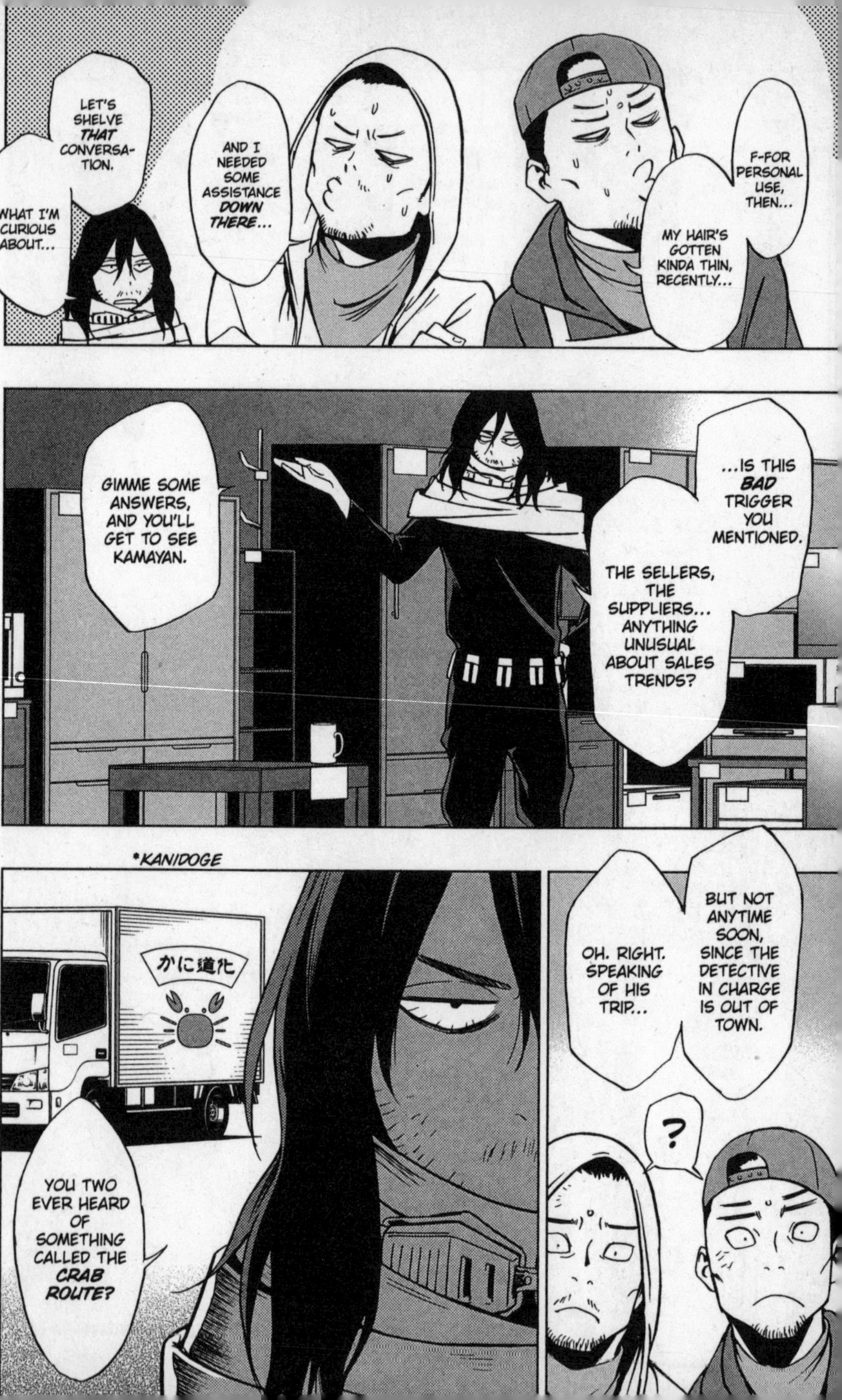
F-FOR PERSONAL USE, THEN...
MY HAIR'S GOTTEN KINDA THIN, RECENTLY...
AND I NEEDED SOME ASSISTANCE *DOWN THERE*...
LET'S SHELVE *THAT* CONVERSATION.
WHAT I'M CURIOUS ABOUT...
...IS THIS *BAD* TRIGGER YOU MENTIONED.
THE SELLERS, THE SUPPLIERS... ANYTHING UNUSUAL ABOUT SALES TRENDS?
GIMME SOME ANSWERS, AND YOU'LL GET TO SEE KAMAYAN.
BUT NOT ANYTIME SOON, SINCE THE DETECTIVE IN CHARGE IS OUT OF TOWN.
OH. RIGHT. SPEAKING OF HIS TRIP...
?
*KANIDOGE
かに道化
YOU TWO EVER HEARD OF SOMETHING CALLED THE *CRAB ROUTE*?

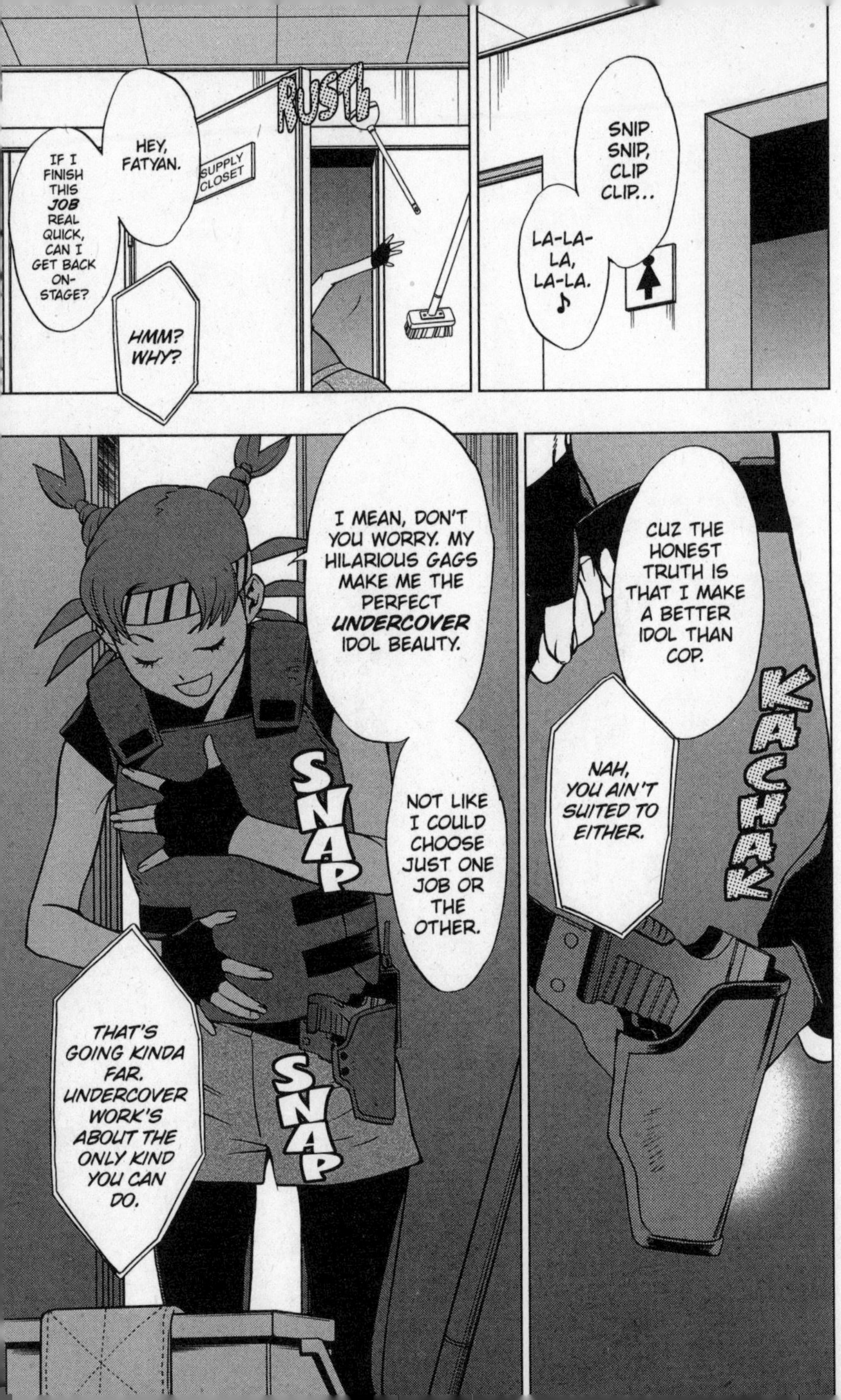
SNIP SNIP, CLIP CLIP...
LA-LA-LA, LA-LA. ♪
RUSTL
SUPPLY CLOSET
HEY, FATYAN.
IF I FINISH THIS JOB REAL QUICK, CAN I GET BACK ON-STAGE?
HMM? WHY?
CUZ THE HONEST TRUTH IS THAT I MAKE A BETTER IDOL THAN COP.
KACHAK
NAH, YOU AIN'T SUITED TO EITHER.
I MEAN, DON'T YOU WORRY. MY HILARIOUS GAGS MAKE ME THE PERFECT UNDERCOVER IDOL BEAUTY.
NOT LIKE I COULD CHOOSE JUST ONE JOB OR THE OTHER.
SNAP
SNAP
THAT'S GOING KINDA FAR. UNDERCOVER WORK'S ABOUT THE ONLY KIND YOU CAN DO.

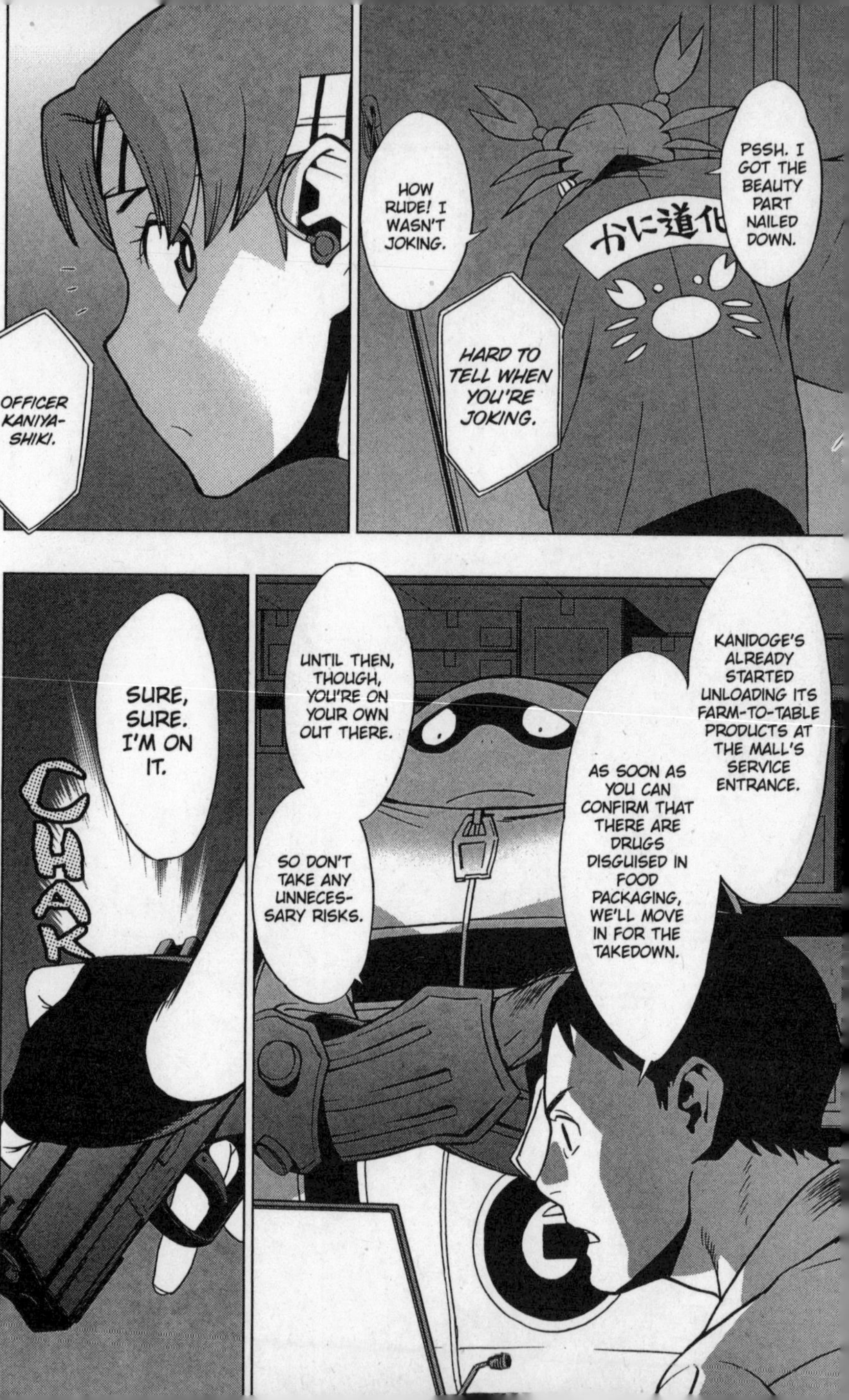
PSSH. I GOT THE BEAUTY PART NAILED DOWN.
かに道化
HOW RUDE! I WASN'T JOKING.
HARD TO TELL WHEN YOU'RE JOKING.
OFFICER KANIYA-SHIKI.
KANIDOGE'S ALREADY STARTED UNLOADING ITS FARM-TO-TABLE PRODUCTS AT THE MALL'S SERVICE ENTRANCE.
AS SOON AS YOU CAN CONFIRM THAT THERE ARE DRUGS DISGUISED IN FOOD PACKAGING, WE'LL MOVE IN FOR THE TAKEDOWN.
UNTIL THEN, THOUGH, YOU'RE ON YOUR OWN OUT THERE.
SO DON'T TAKE ANY UNNECES-SARY RISKS.
SURE, SURE. I'M ON IT.
CHAK

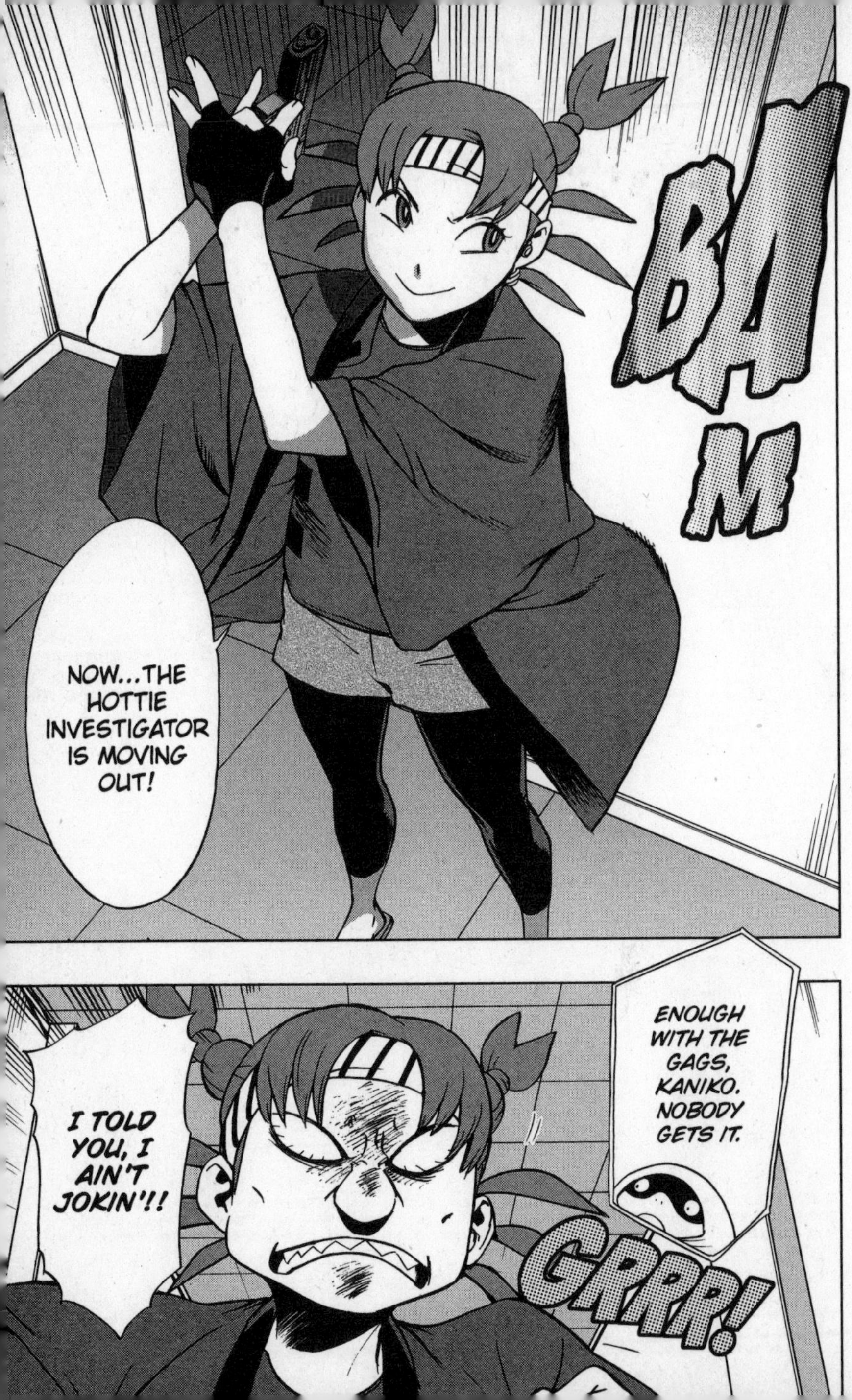
BAM
NOW...THE HOTTIE INVESTIGATOR IS MOVING OUT!
ENOUGH WITH THE GAGS, KANIKO. NOBODY GETS IT.
I TOLD YOU, I AIN'T JOKIN'!!
GRRR!

KANIKO & CRAB MECH

THE ROUGH DESIGN

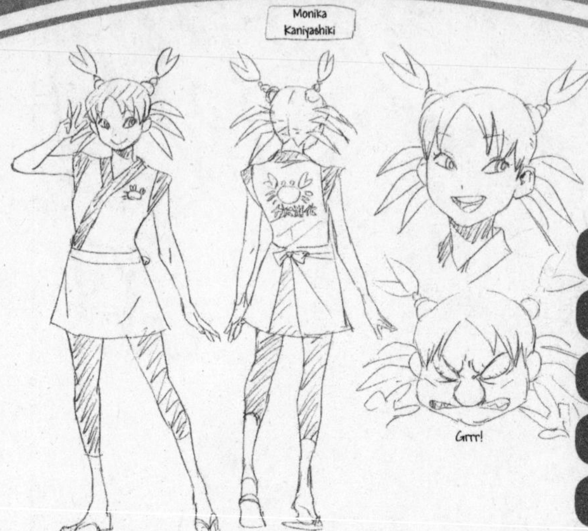
Monika Kaniyashiki
Grrr!

REAL NAME: MONIKA KANIYASHIKI

BIRTHDAY: 6/22

HEIGHT: 160 CM

FAVORITE THING: KANI MISO

QUIRK: SCISSORS

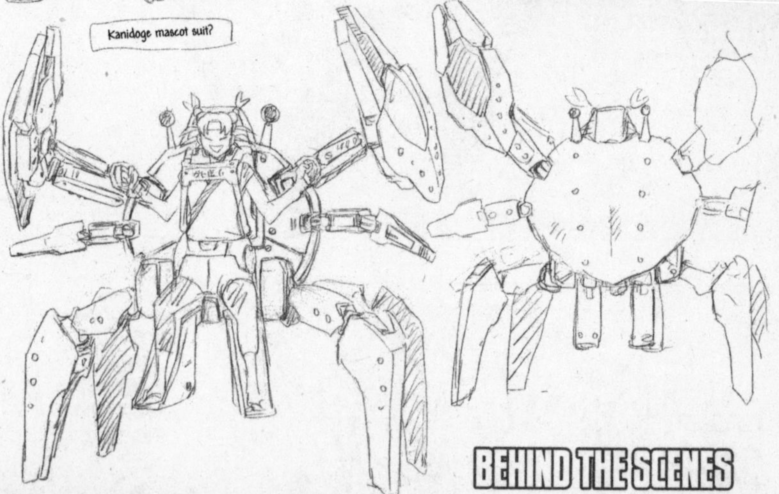
Kanidoge mascot suit?

BEHIND THE SCENES

The Osaka arc needed a native Osakan, another idol to interact with Pop and a law enforcement type working with Fat Gum. All those elements combined into this single character. She's a little absurd, but she really helped move the story along. Design-wise, she straddles the line between hammy variety act and cute girl, which is quite the delicate balance. Also, the mech suit! Can't forget that crab mech!

—Furuhashi

When I saw Kaniko in Furuhashi's rough draft, I thought, "How'm I supposed to make *her* look cute…?" I was really concerned at first, but as I started drawing (and reading her dialogue), she began to exude this mysterious charm. She may look like *that* on the outside, but there's something deliciously savory about her on the inside. Just like a crab. (LOL)

—Betten

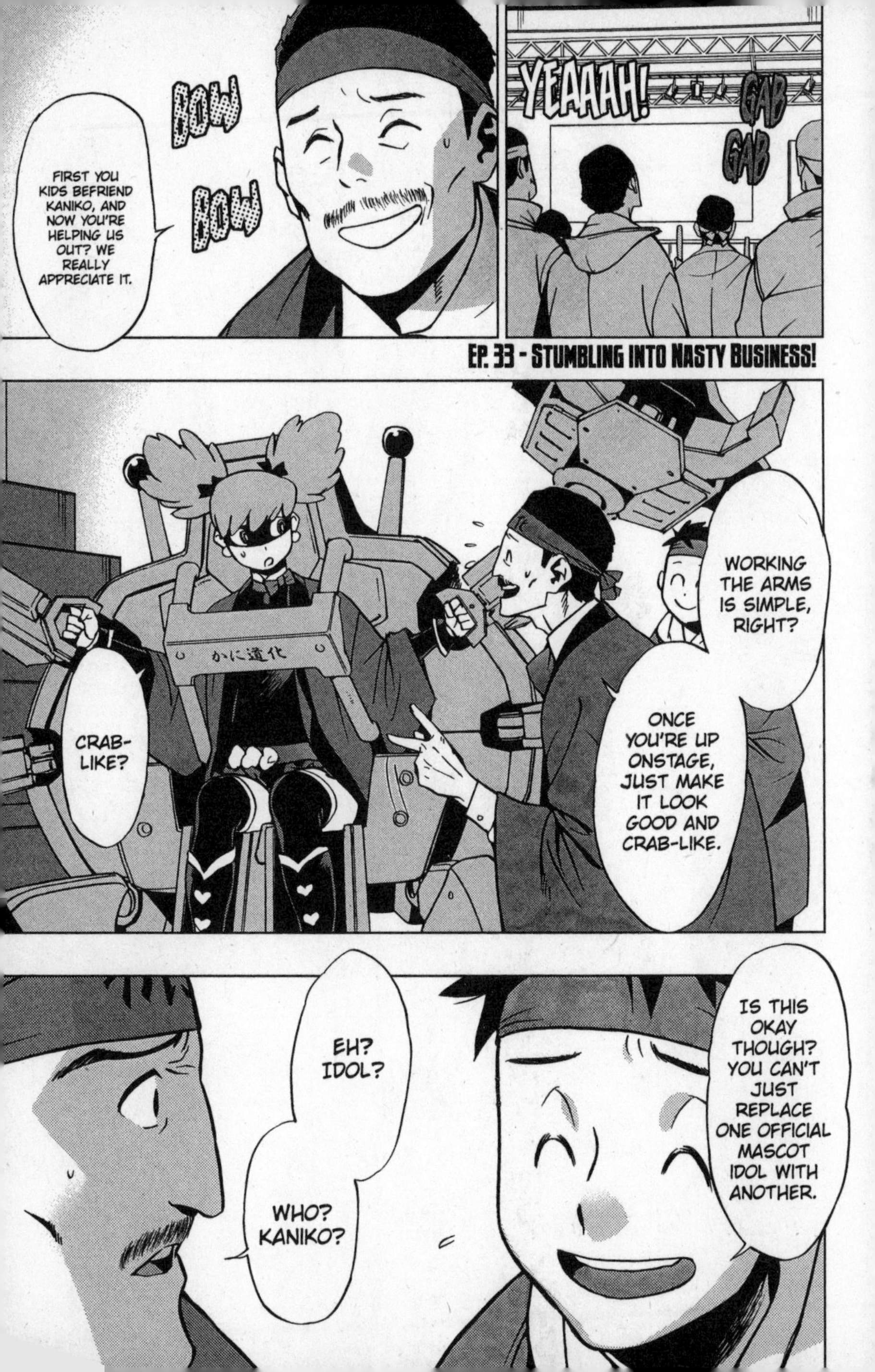
YEAAAH!
GAB GAB
BOW BOW
FIRST YOU KIDS BEFRIEND KANIKO, AND NOW YOU'RE HELPING US OUT? WE REALLY APPRECIATE IT.
EP. 33 - STUMBLING INTO NASTY BUSINESS!
WORKING THE ARMS IS SIMPLE, RIGHT?
ONCE YOU'RE UP ONSTAGE, JUST MAKE IT LOOK GOOD AND CRAB-LIKE.
かに道化
CRAB-LIKE?
IS THIS OKAY THOUGH? YOU CAN'T JUST REPLACE ONE OFFICIAL MASCOT IDOL WITH ANOTHER.
EH? IDOL?
WHO? KANIKO?

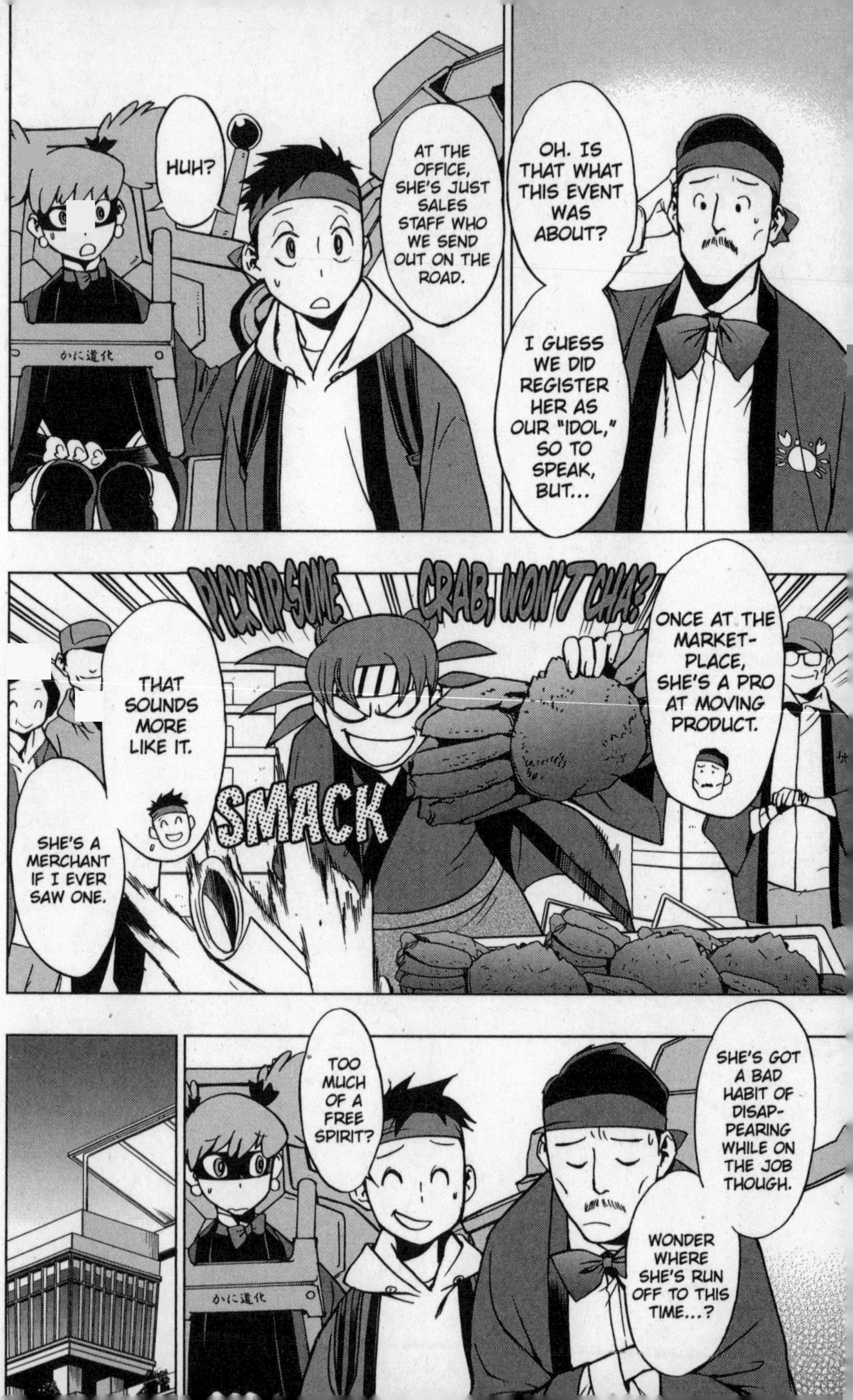
OH. IS THAT WHAT THIS EVENT WAS ABOUT?
I GUESS WE DID REGISTER HER AS OUR "IDOL," SO TO SPEAK, BUT...
AT THE OFFICE, SHE'S JUST SALES STAFF WHO WE SEND OUT ON THE ROAD.
HUH?
かに道化
ONCE AT THE MARKET-PLACE, SHE'S A PRO AT MOVING PRODUCT.
PICK UP SOME CRAB, WON'T CHA?
SMACK
THAT SOUNDS MORE LIKE IT.
SHE'S A MERCHANT IF I EVER SAW ONE.
SHE'S GOT A BAD HABIT OF DISAP-PEARING WHILE ON THE JOB THOUGH.
WONDER WHERE SHE'S RUN OFF TO THIS TIME...?
TOO MUCH OF A FREE SPIRIT?
かに道化

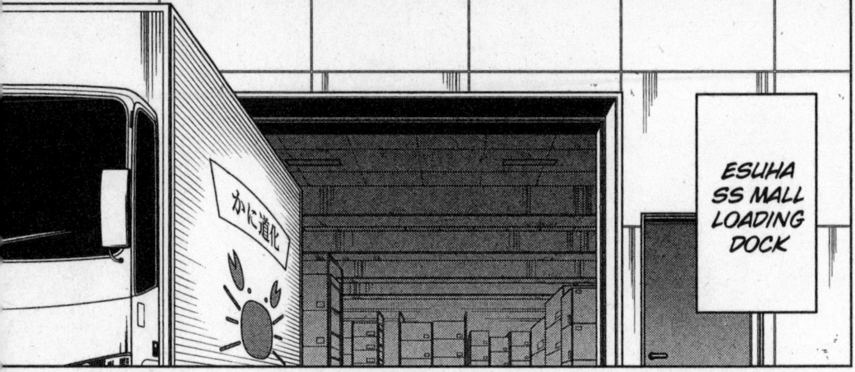
ESUHA SS MALL LOADING DOCK
かに道化

Ep. 33 - Stumbling into Nasty Business!

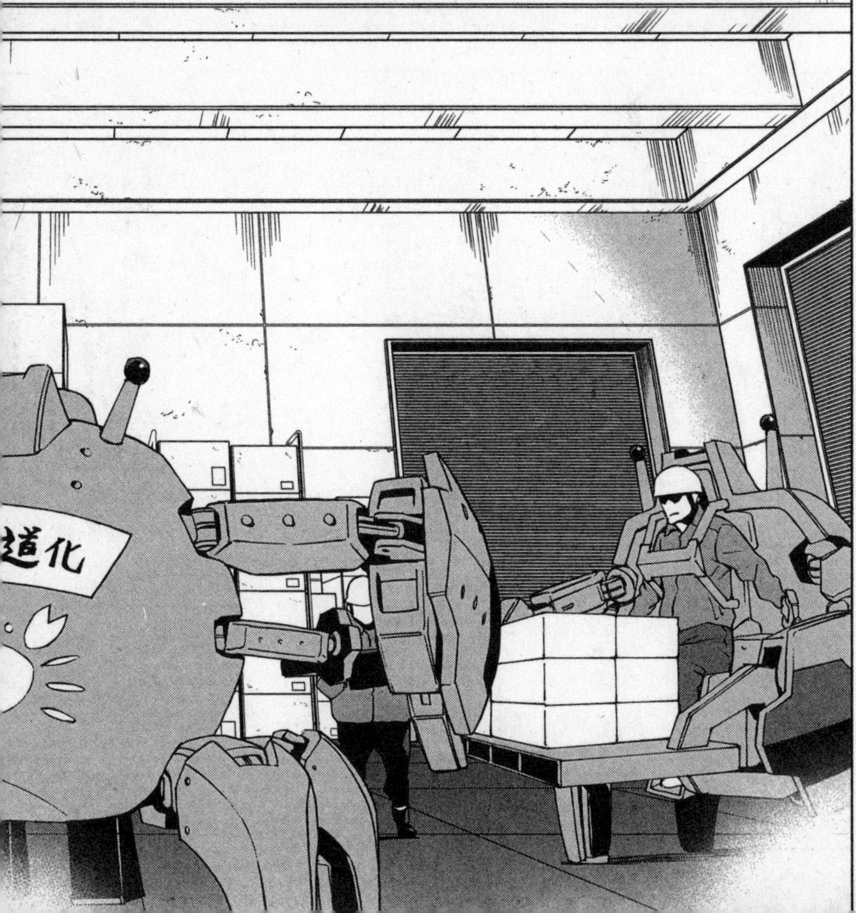
道化

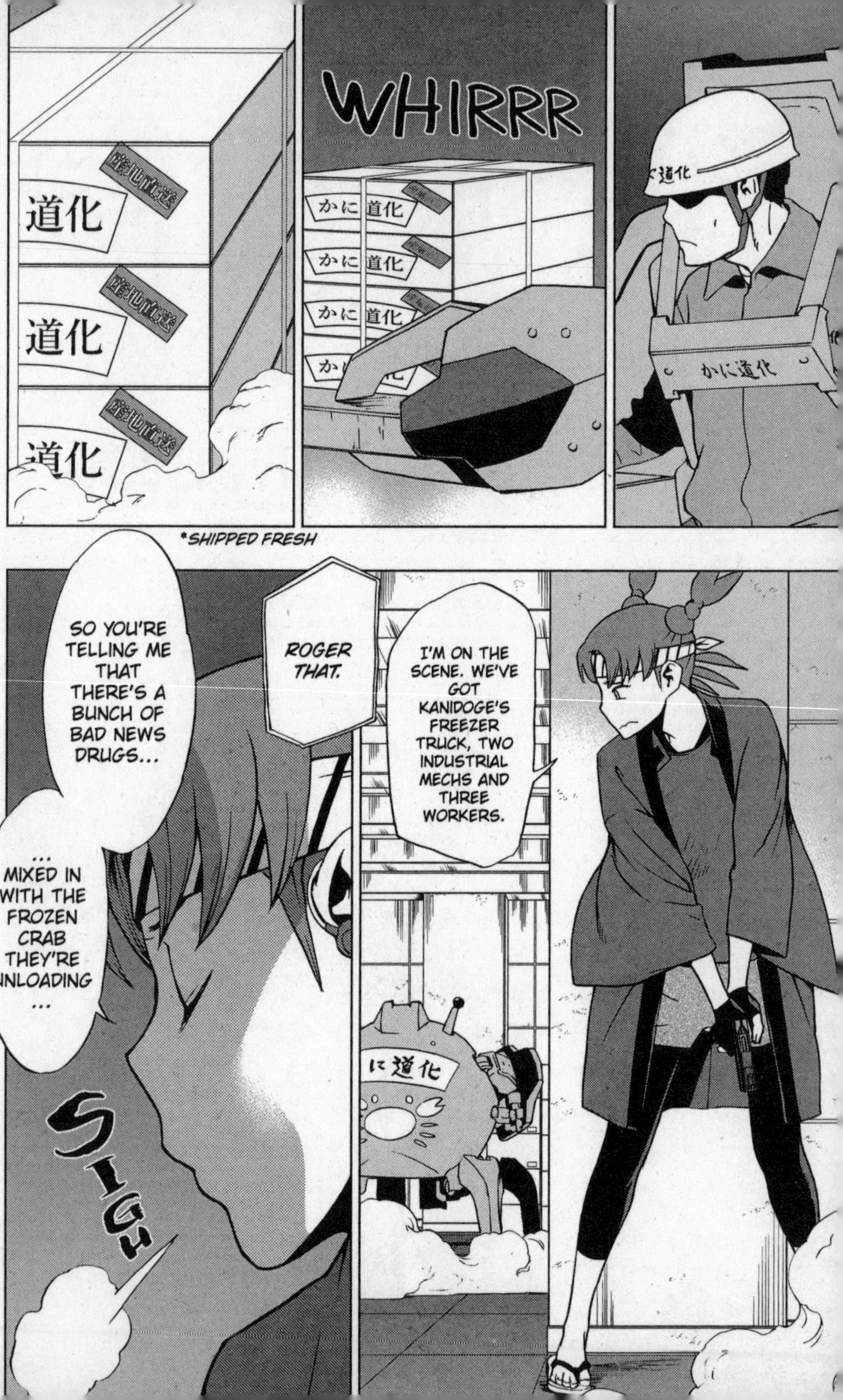
かに道化
WHIRRR
かに道化
産地直送
道化
*SHIPPED FRESH
I'M ON THE SCENE. WE'VE GOT KANIDOGE'S FREEZER TRUCK, TWO INDUSTRIAL MECHS AND THREE WORKERS.
ROGER THAT.
SO YOU'RE TELLING ME THAT THERE'S A BUNCH OF BAD NEWS DRUGS...
...MIXED IN WITH THE FROZEN CRAB THEY'RE UNLOADING...
に道化
SIGH

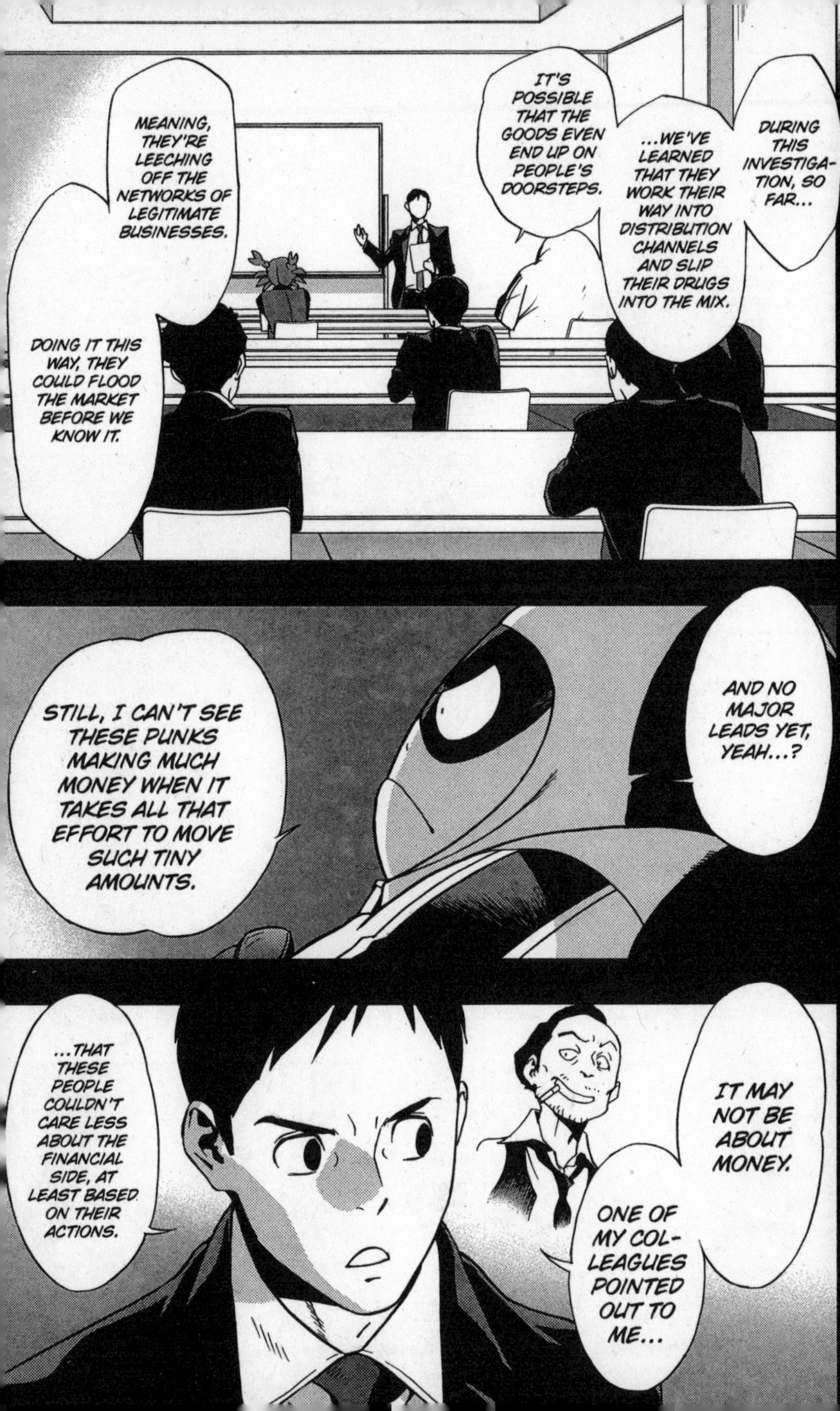
DURING THIS INVESTIGATION, SO FAR...
...WE'VE LEARNED THAT THEY WORK THEIR WAY INTO DISTRIBUTION CHANNELS AND SLIP THEIR DRUGS INTO THE MIX.
IT'S POSSIBLE THAT THE GOODS EVEN END UP ON PEOPLE'S DOORSTEPS.
MEANING, THEY'RE LEECHING OFF THE NETWORKS OF LEGITIMATE BUSINESSES.
DOING IT THIS WAY, THEY COULD FLOOD THE MARKET BEFORE WE KNOW IT.
AND NO MAJOR LEADS YET, YEAH...?
STILL, I CAN'T SEE THESE PUNKS MAKING MUCH MONEY WHEN IT TAKES ALL THAT EFFORT TO MOVE SUCH TINY AMOUNTS.
IT MAY NOT BE ABOUT MONEY.
ONE OF MY COLLEAGUES POINTED OUT TO ME...
...THAT THESE PEOPLE COULDN'T CARE LESS ABOUT THE FINANCIAL SIDE, AT LEAST BASED ON THEIR ACTIONS.

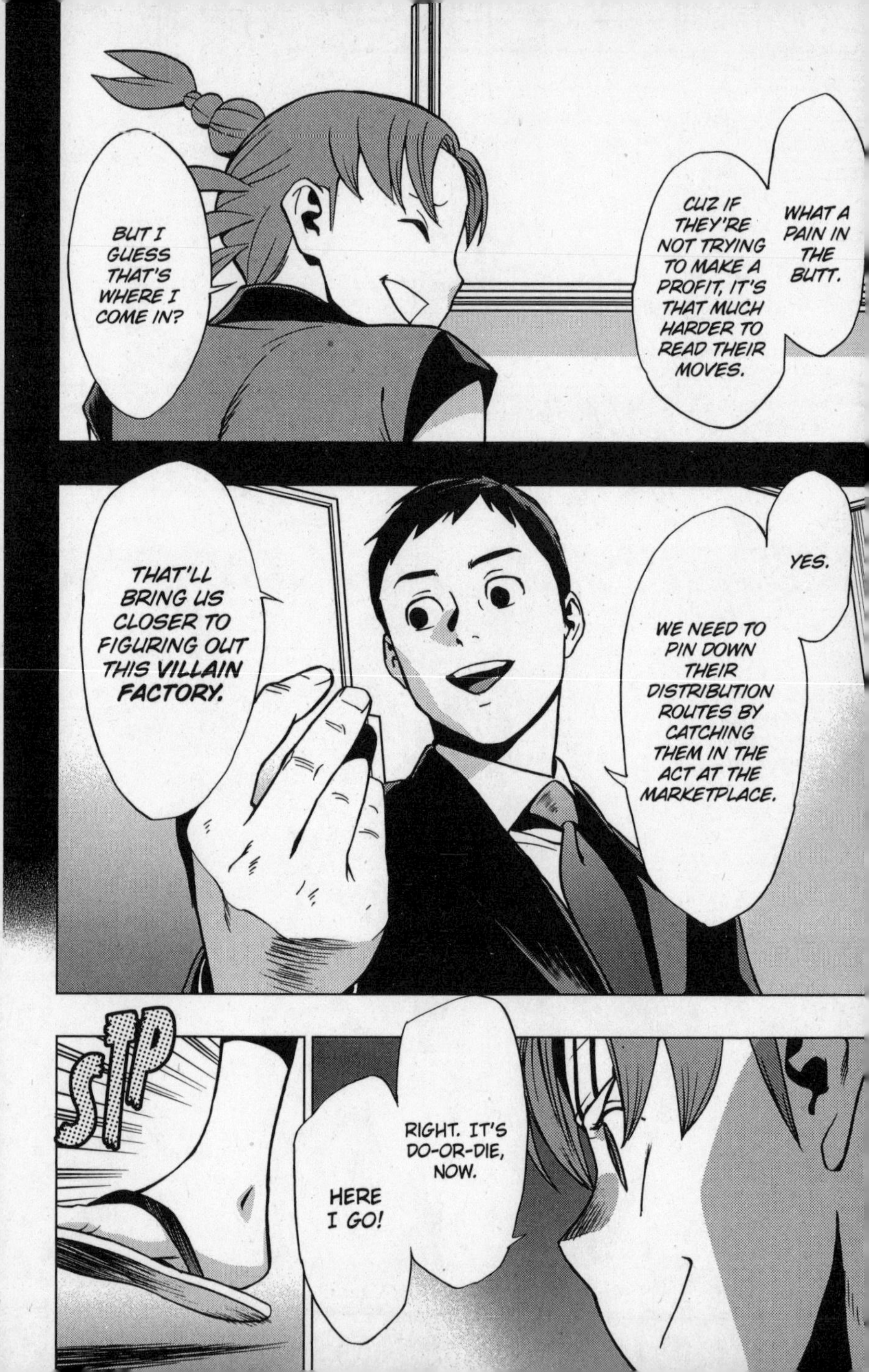
WHAT A PAIN IN THE BUTT.
CUZ IF THEY'RE NOT TRYING TO MAKE A PROFIT, IT'S THAT MUCH HARDER TO READ THEIR MOVES.
BUT I GUESS THAT'S WHERE I COME IN?
YES.
WE NEED TO PIN DOWN THEIR DISTRIBUTION ROUTES BY CATCHING THEM IN THE ACT AT THE MARKETPLACE.
THAT'LL BRING US CLOSER TO FIGURING OUT THIS VILLAIN FACTORY.
RIGHT. IT'S DO-OR-DIE, NOW.
HERE I GO!
STP

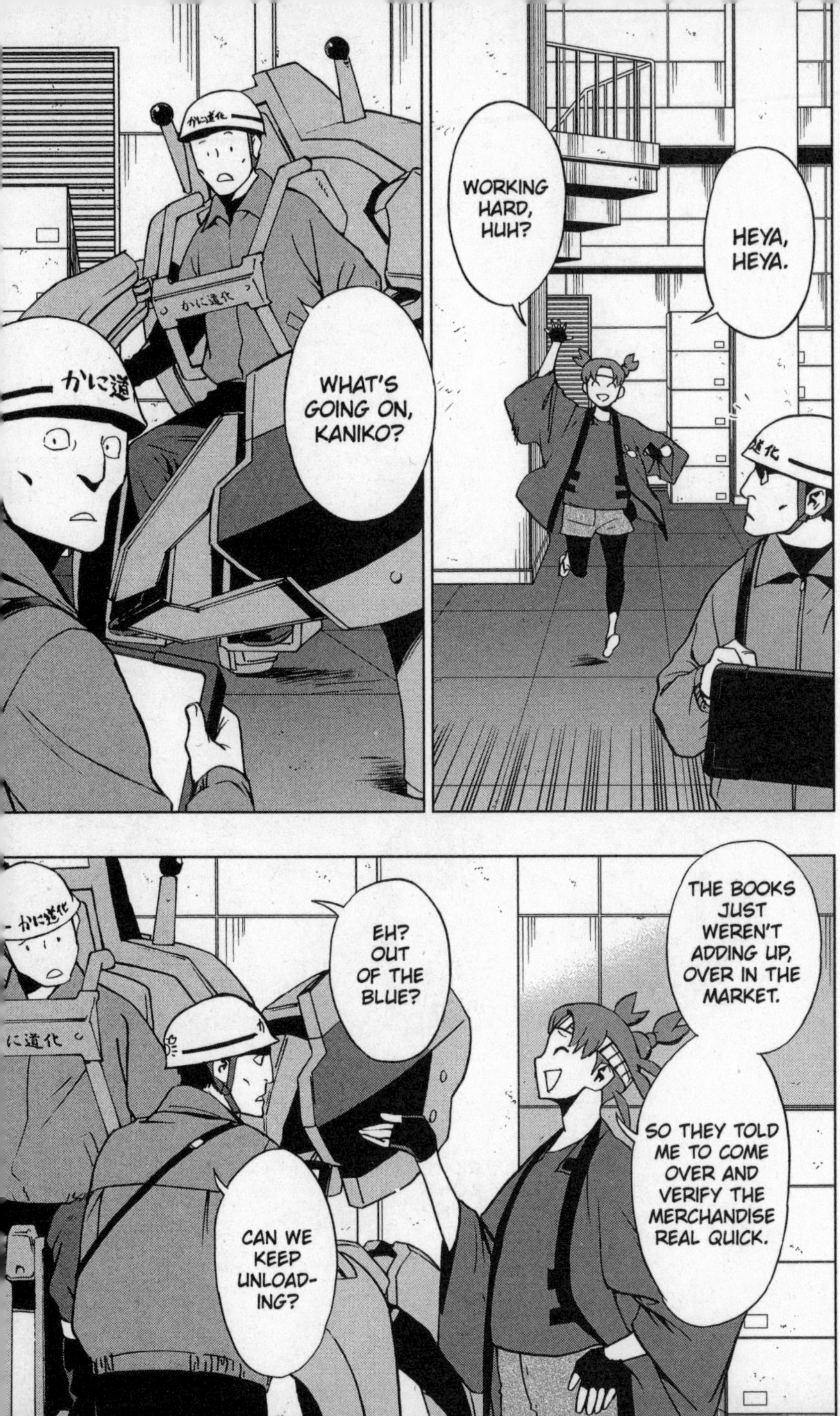
HEYA, HEYA.
WORKING HARD, HUH?
WHAT'S GOING ON, KANIKO?
THE BOOKS JUST WEREN'T ADDING UP, OVER IN THE MARKET.
EH? OUT OF THE BLUE?
SO THEY TOLD ME TO COME OVER AND VERIFY THE MERCHANDISE REAL QUICK.
CAN WE KEEP UNLOADING?

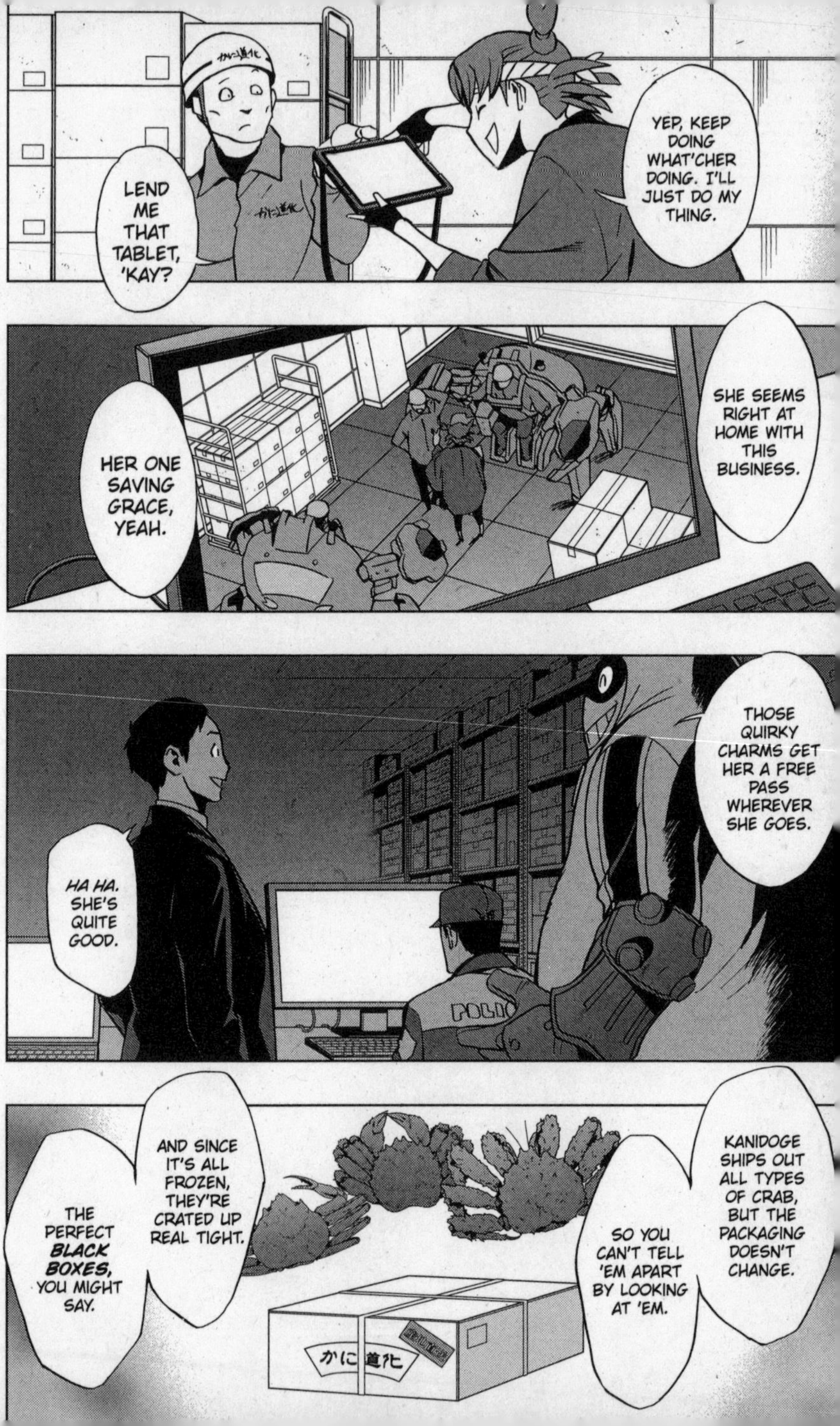
YEP, KEEP DOING WHAT'CHER DOING. I'LL JUST DO MY THING.
LEND ME THAT TABLET, 'KAY?
SHE SEEMS RIGHT AT HOME WITH THIS BUSINESS.
HER ONE SAVING GRACE, YEAH.
THOSE QUIRKY CHARMS GET HER A FREE PASS WHEREVER SHE GOES.
HA HA. SHE'S QUITE GOOD.
KANIDOGE SHIPS OUT ALL TYPES OF CRAB, BUT THE PACKAGING DOESN'T CHANGE.
SO YOU CAN'T TELL 'EM APART BY LOOKING AT 'EM.
AND SINCE IT'S ALL FROZEN, THEY'RE CRATED UP REAL TIGHT.
THE PERFECT ***BLACK BOXES,*** YOU MIGHT SAY.
かに道化

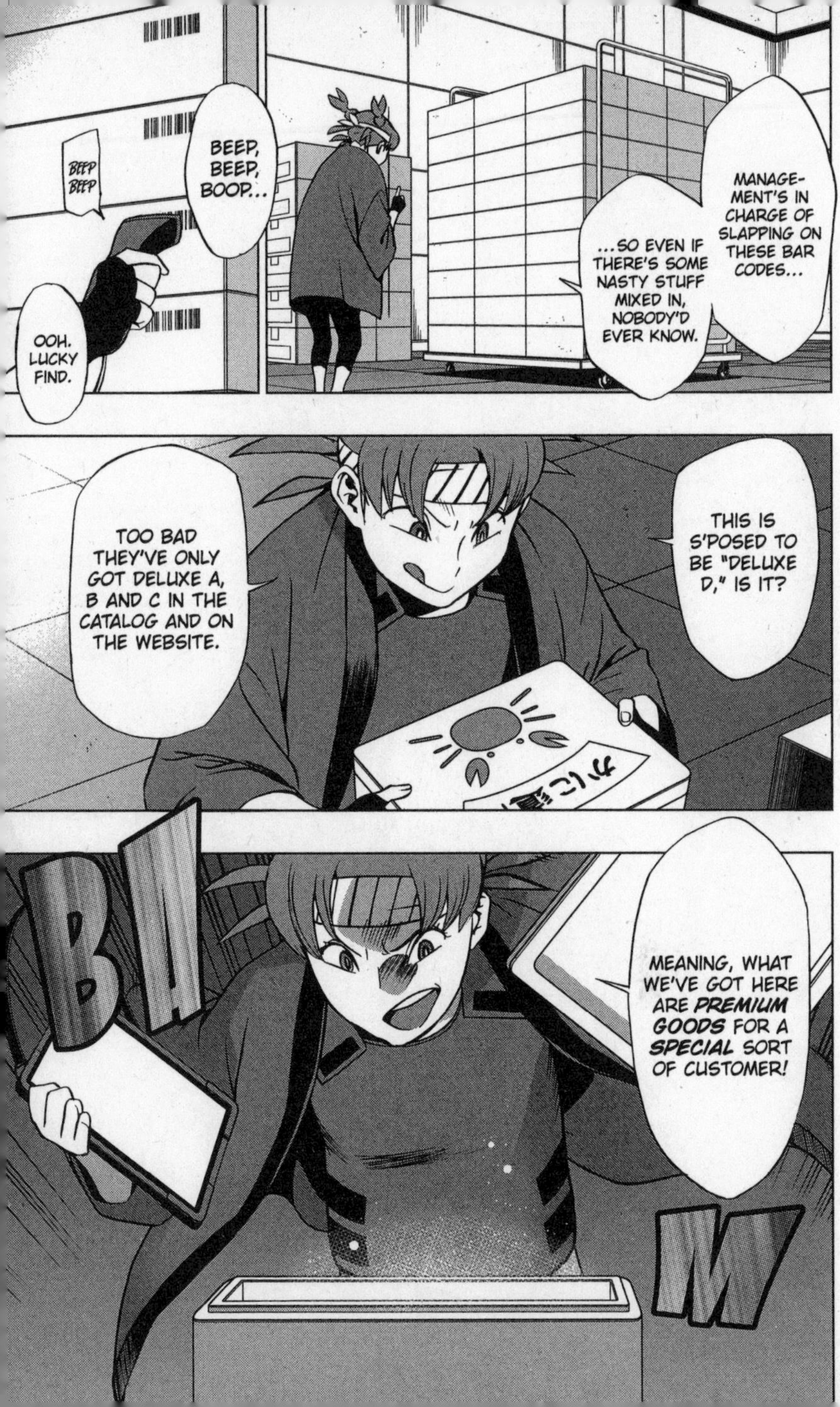
MANAGEMENT'S IN CHARGE OF SLAPPING ON THESE BAR CODES...
...SO EVEN IF THERE'S SOME NASTY STUFF MIXED IN, NOBODY'D EVER KNOW.
BEEP, BEEP, BOOP...
BEEP BEEP
OOH. LUCKY FIND.
THIS IS S'POSED TO BE "DELUXE D," IS IT?
TOO BAD THEY'VE ONLY GOT DELUXE A, B AND C IN THE CATALOG AND ON THE WEBSITE.
MEANING, WHAT WE'VE GOT HERE ARE PREMIUM GOODS FOR A SPECIAL SORT OF CUSTOMER!
BAM

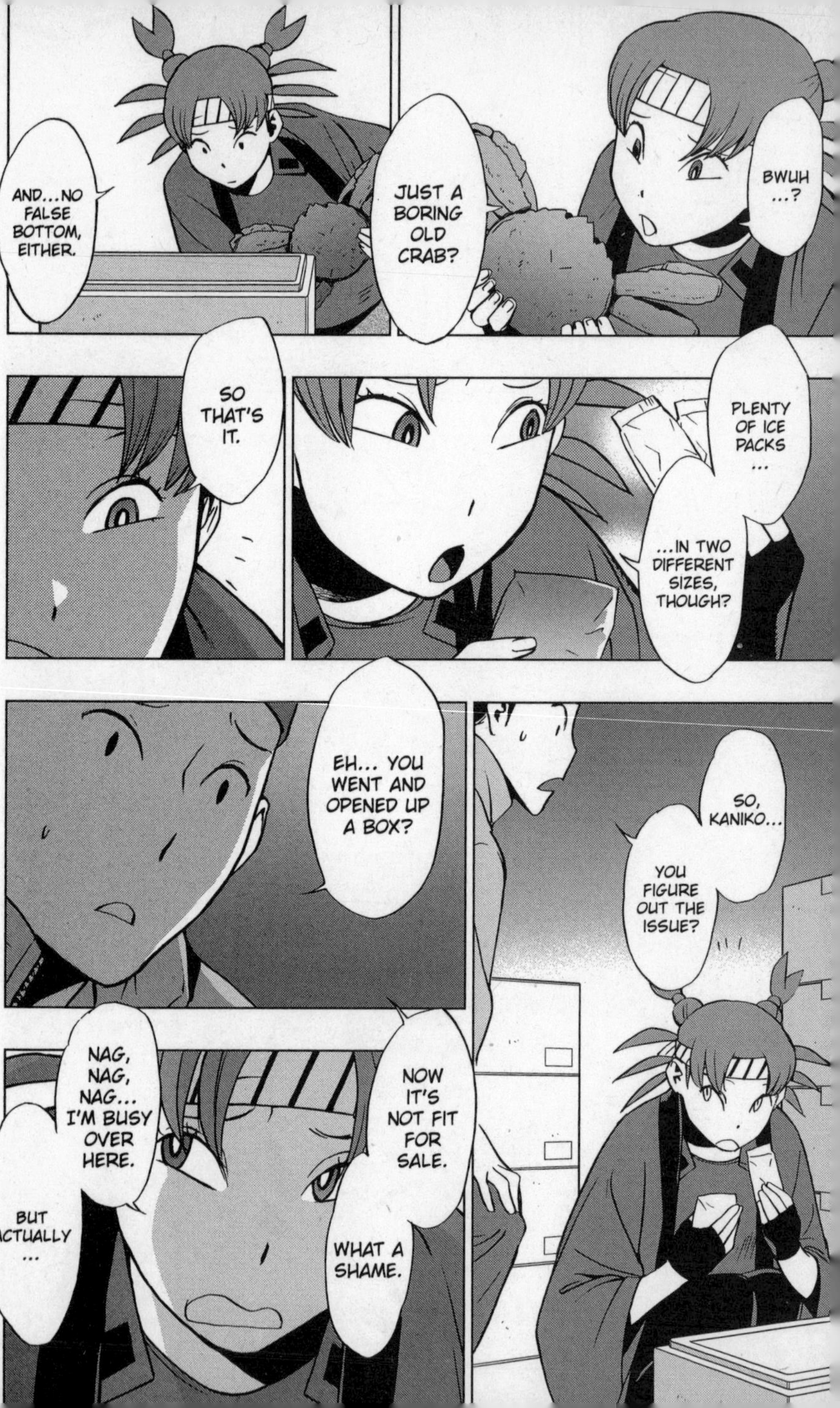
BWUH ...?
JUST A BORING OLD CRAB?
AND...NO FALSE BOTTOM, EITHER.
PLENTY OF ICE PACKS ...
...IN TWO DIFFERENT SIZES, THOUGH?
SO THAT'S IT.
SO, KANIKO...
YOU FIGURE OUT THE ISSUE?
EH... YOU WENT AND OPENED UP A BOX?
NOW IT'S NOT FIT FOR SALE.
WHAT A SHAME.
NAG, NAG, NAG... I'M BUSY OVER HERE.
BUT ACTUALLY ...

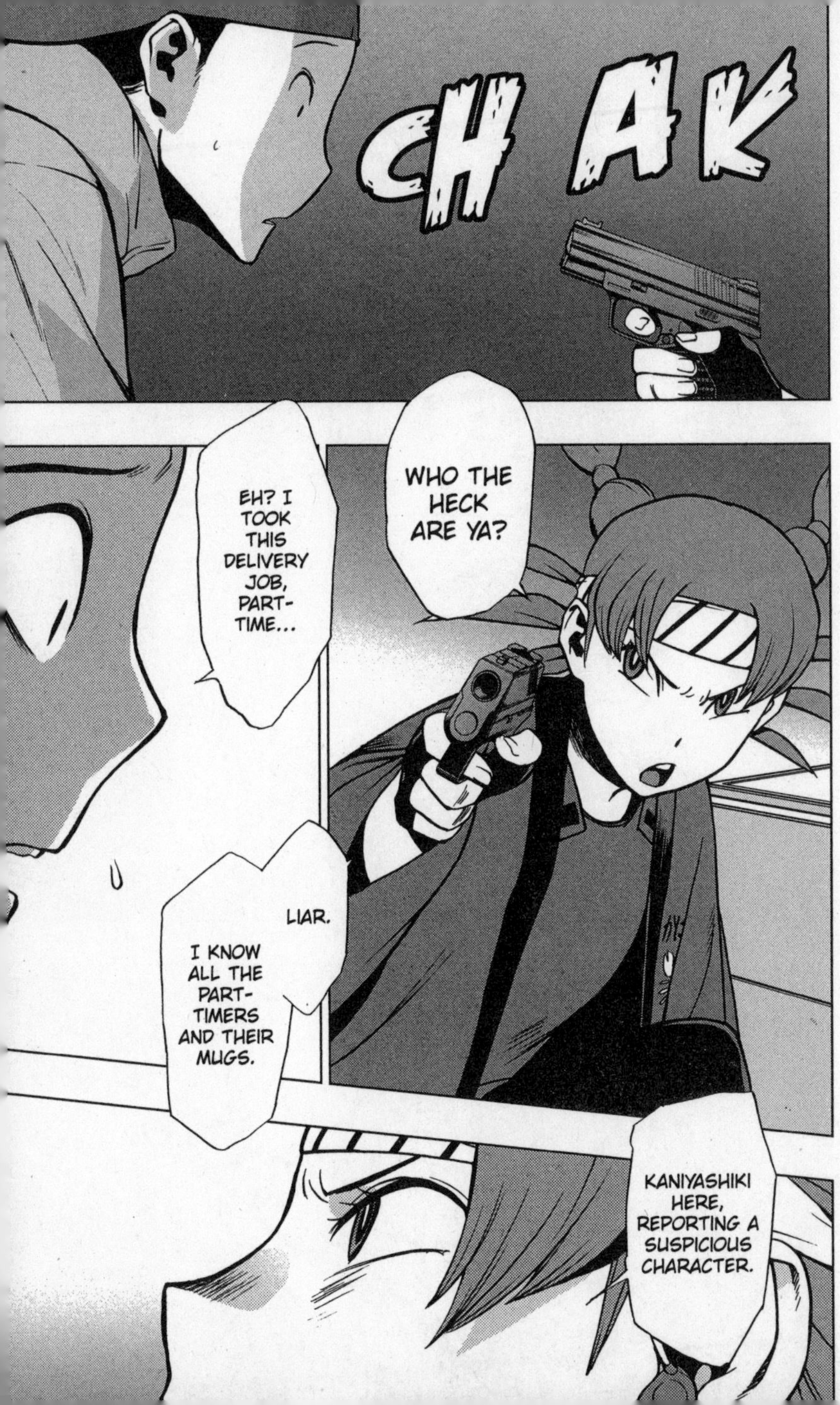
CHAK
WHO THE HECK ARE YA?
EH? I TOOK THIS DELIVERY JOB, PART-TIME...
LIAR.
I KNOW ALL THE PART-TIMERS AND THEIR MUGS.
KANIYASHIKI HERE, REPORTING A SUSPICIOUS CHARACTER.

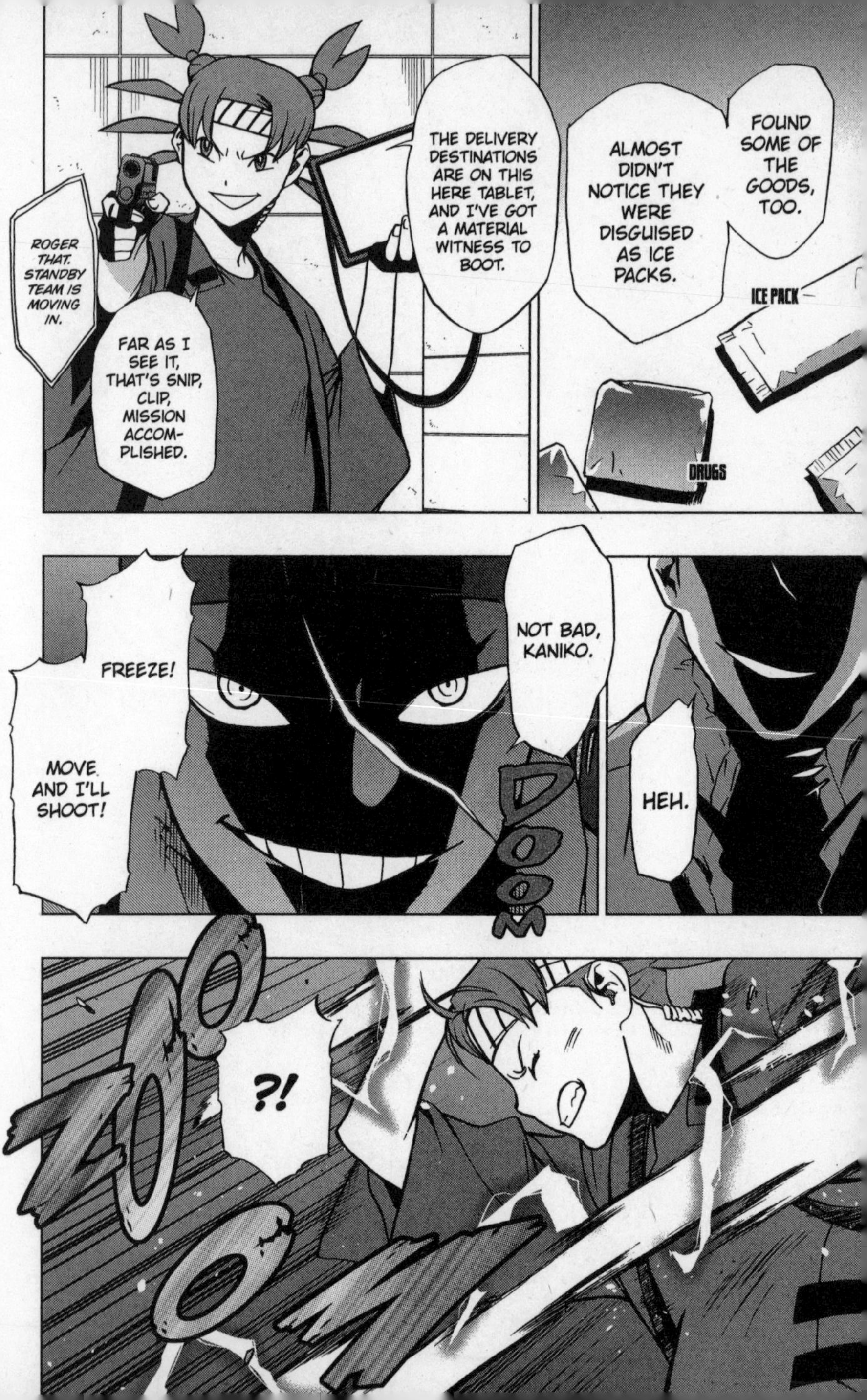
FOUND SOME OF THE GOODS, TOO.
ALMOST DIDN'T NOTICE THEY WERE DISGUISED AS ICE PACKS.
ICE PACK
DRUGS
THE DELIVERY DESTINATIONS ARE ON THIS HERE TABLET, AND I'VE GOT A MATERIAL WITNESS TO BOOT.
ROGER THAT. STANDBY TEAM IS MOVING IN.
FAR AS I SEE IT, THAT'S SNIP, CLIP, MISSION ACCOM-PLISHED.
NOT BAD, KANIKO.
HEH.
FREEZE!
MOVE AND I'LL SHOOT!
DOOOM
?!

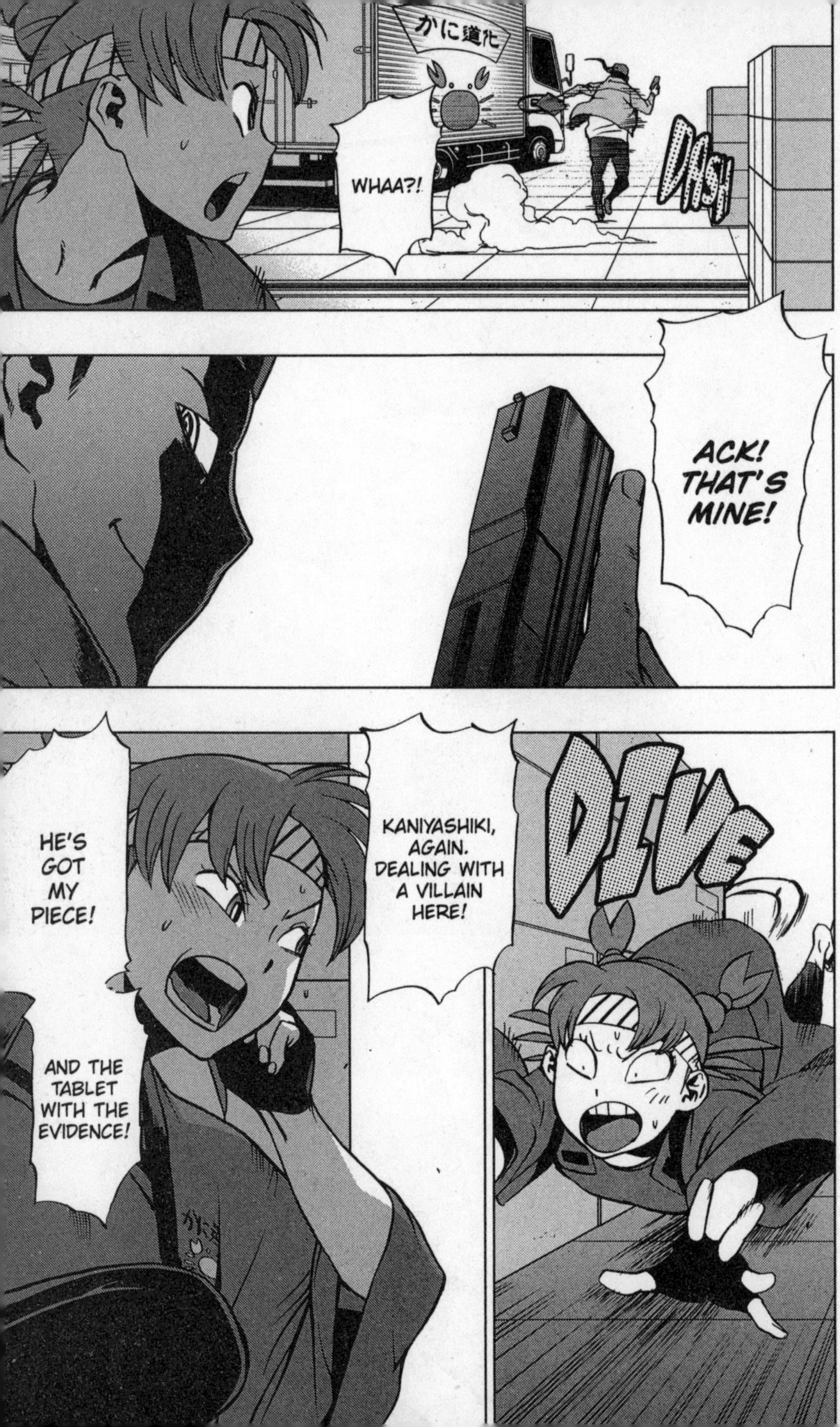
かに道化
WHAA?!
DASH
ACK! THAT'S MINE!
DIVE
KANIYASHIKI, AGAIN. DEALING WITH A VILLAIN HERE!
HE'S GOT MY PIECE!
AND THE TABLET WITH THE EVIDENCE!

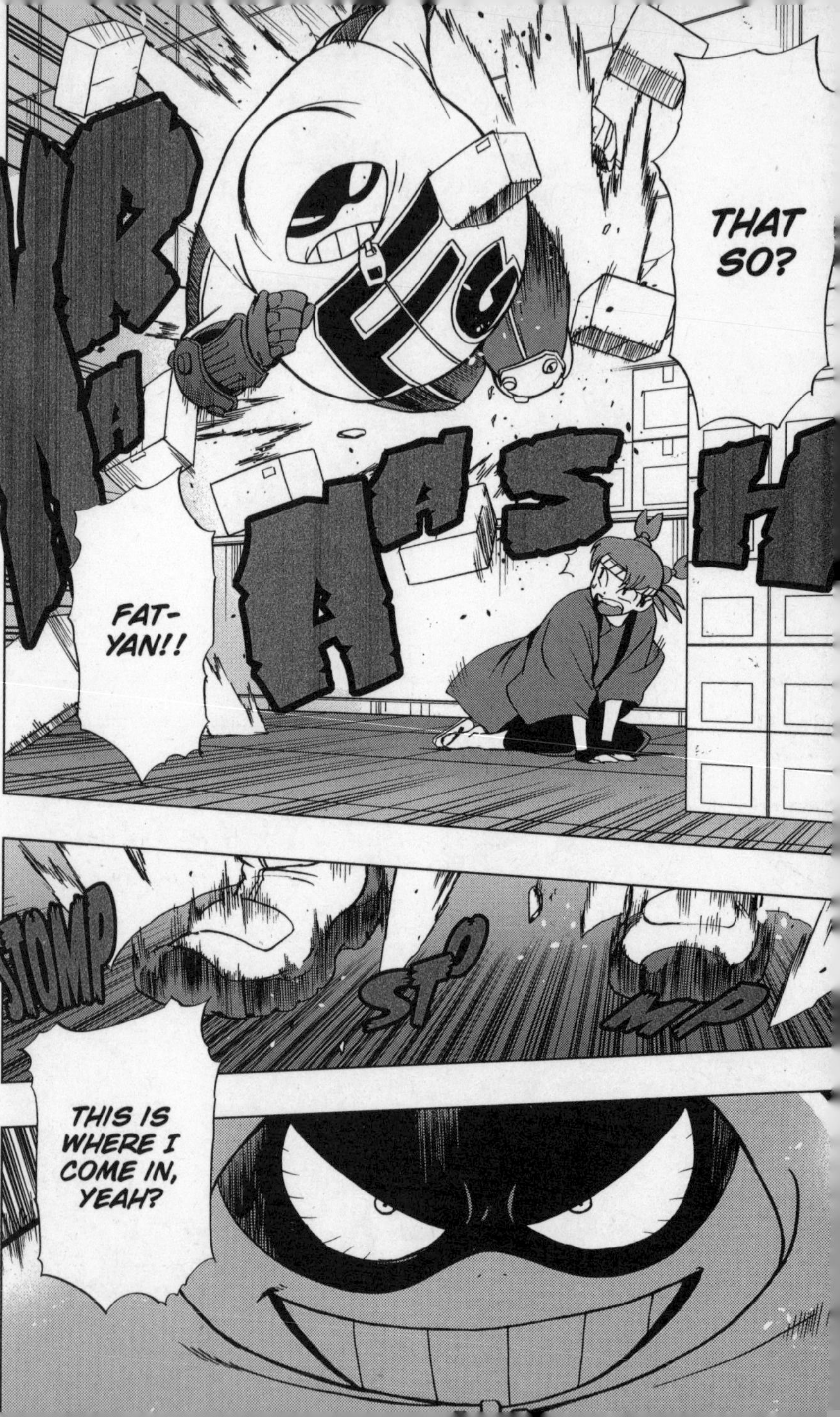
THAT SO?
FAT-YAN!!
STOMP
STOMP
THIS IS WHERE I COME IN, YEAH?

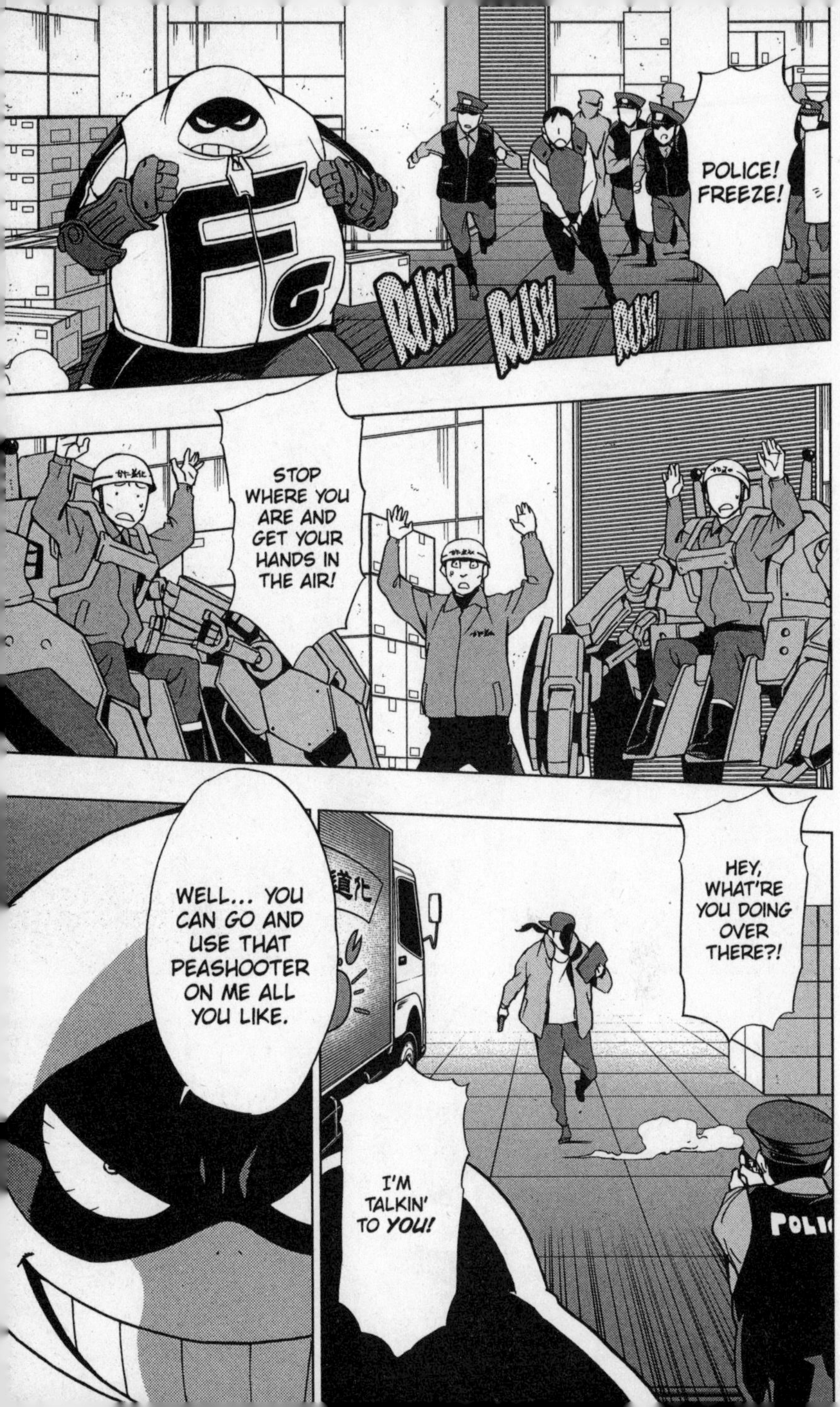
POLICE! FREEZE!
RUSH
RUSH
RUSH
STOP WHERE YOU ARE AND GET YOUR HANDS IN THE AIR!
HEY, WHAT'RE YOU DOING OVER THERE?!
I'M TALKIN' TO YOU!
POLIC
WELL... YOU CAN GO AND USE THAT PEASHOOTER ON ME ALL YOU LIKE.

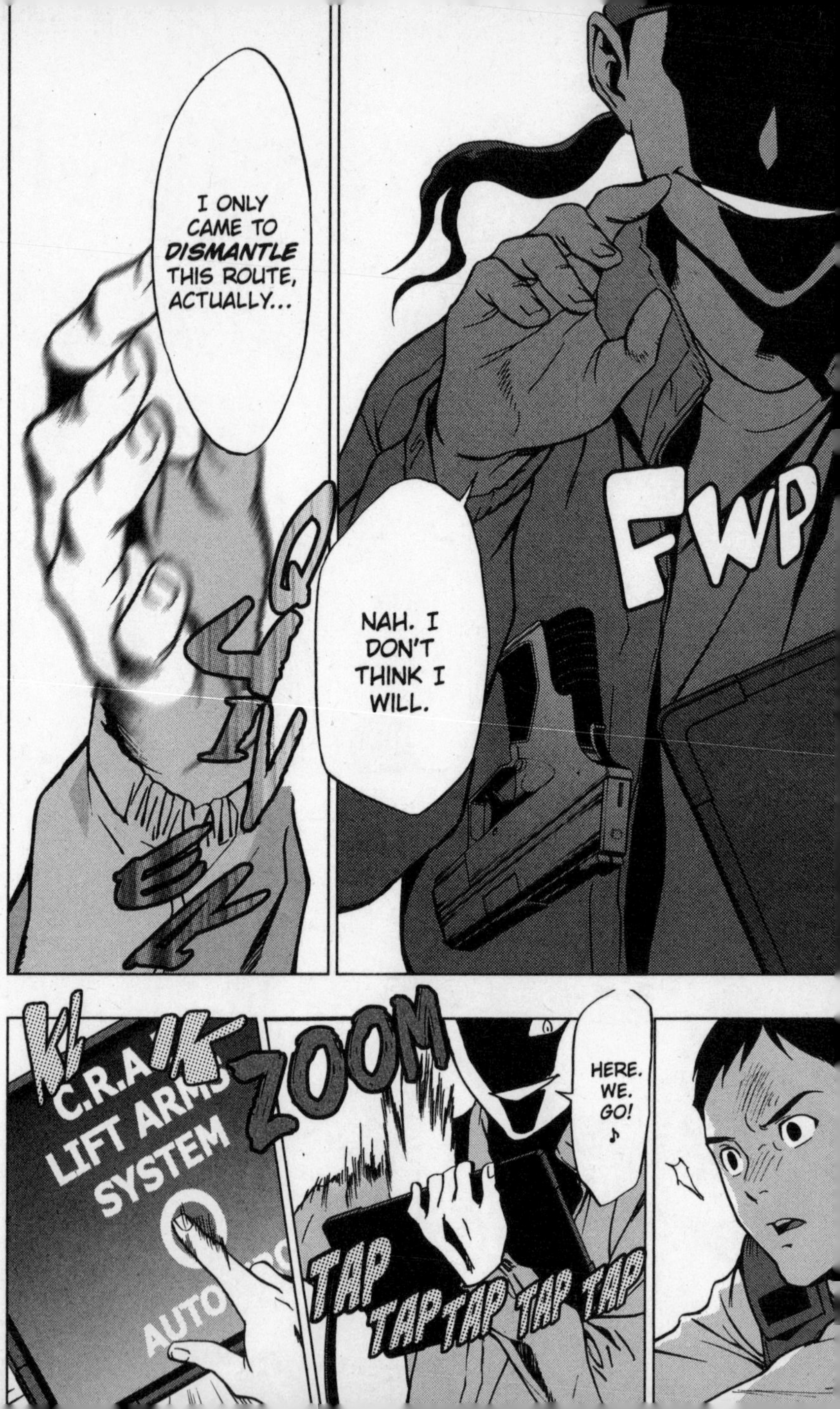
FWP
NAH. I DON'T THINK I WILL.
I ONLY CAME TO *DISMANTLE* THIS ROUTE, ACTUALLY...
HERE. WE. GO! ♪
ZOOM
TAP TAP TAP TAP TAP TAP
C.R.A
SYSTEM
AUTO

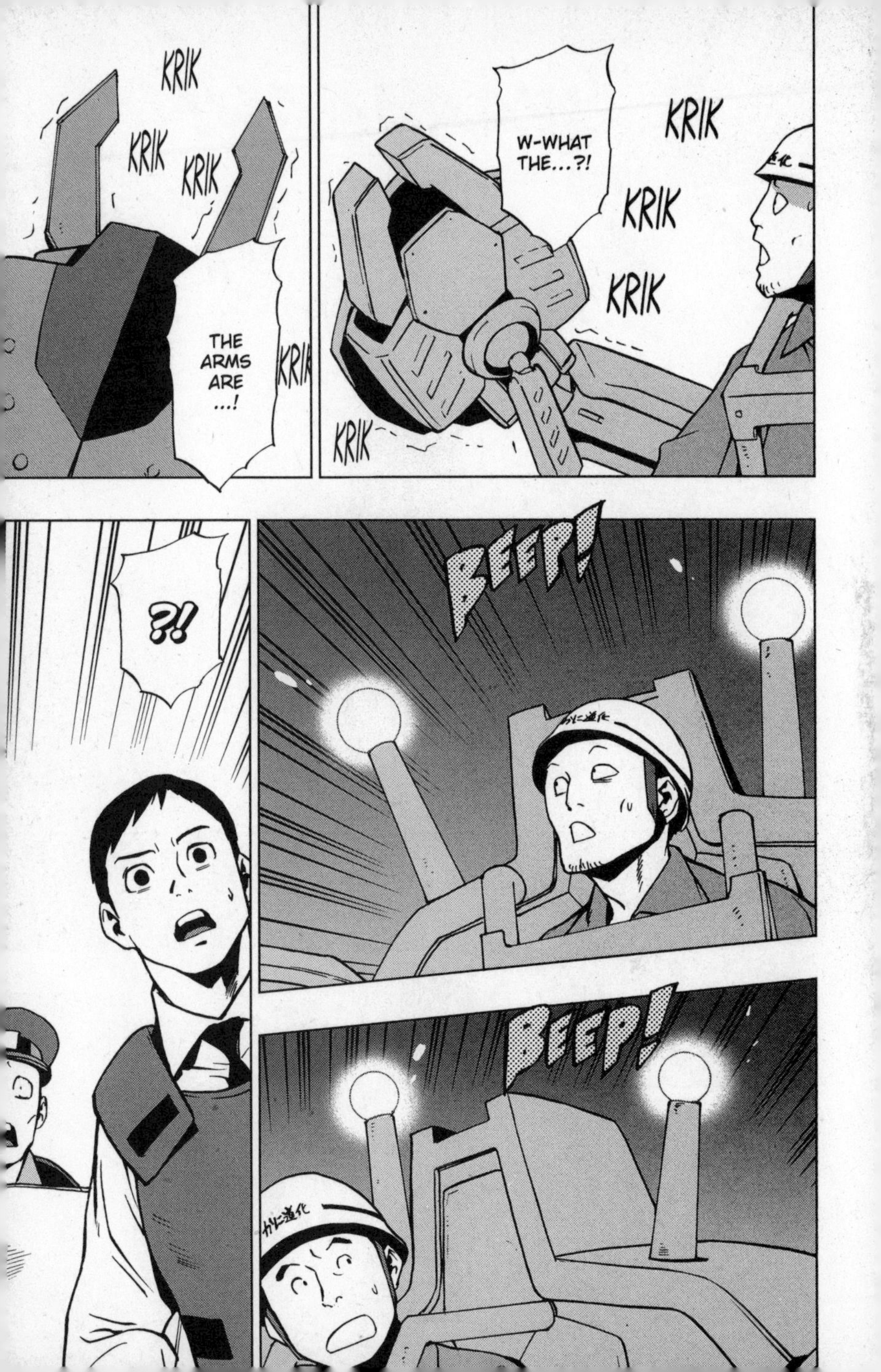
KRIK
W-WHAT THE...?!
KRIK
KRIK
KRIK
KRIK
KRIK
KRIK
THE ARMS ARE ...!
KRIK
BEEP!
BEEP!
?!

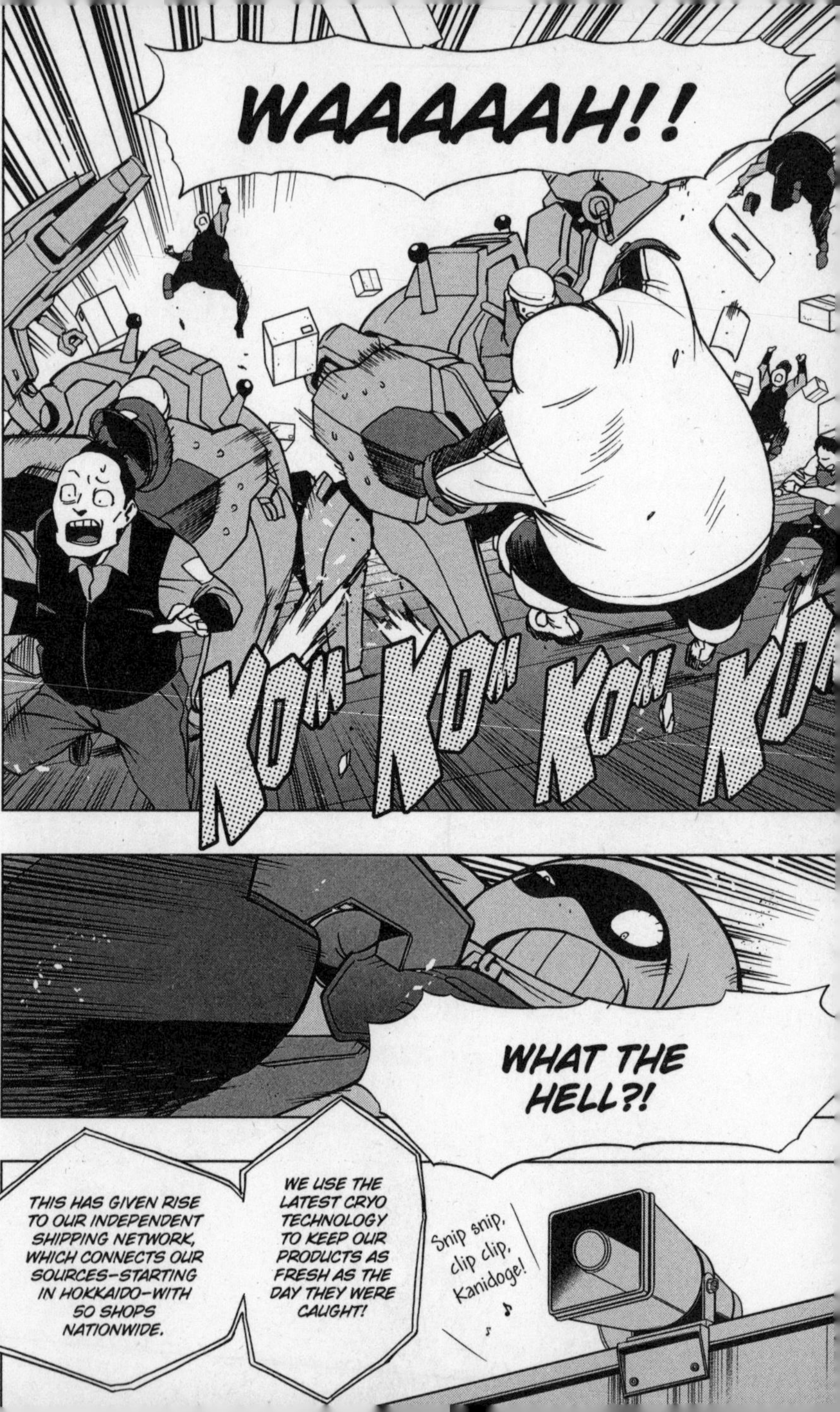
WAAAAAH!!
KOM KOM KOM KO
WHAT THE HELL?!
Snip snip, clip clip, Kanidoge!
WE USE THE LATEST CRYO TECHNOLOGY TO KEEP OUR PRODUCTS AS FRESH AS THE DAY THEY WERE CAUGHT!
THIS HAS GIVEN RISE TO OUR INDEPENDENT SHIPPING NETWORK, WHICH CONNECTS OUR SOURCES—STARTING IN HOKKAIDO—WITH 50 SHOPS NATIONWIDE.

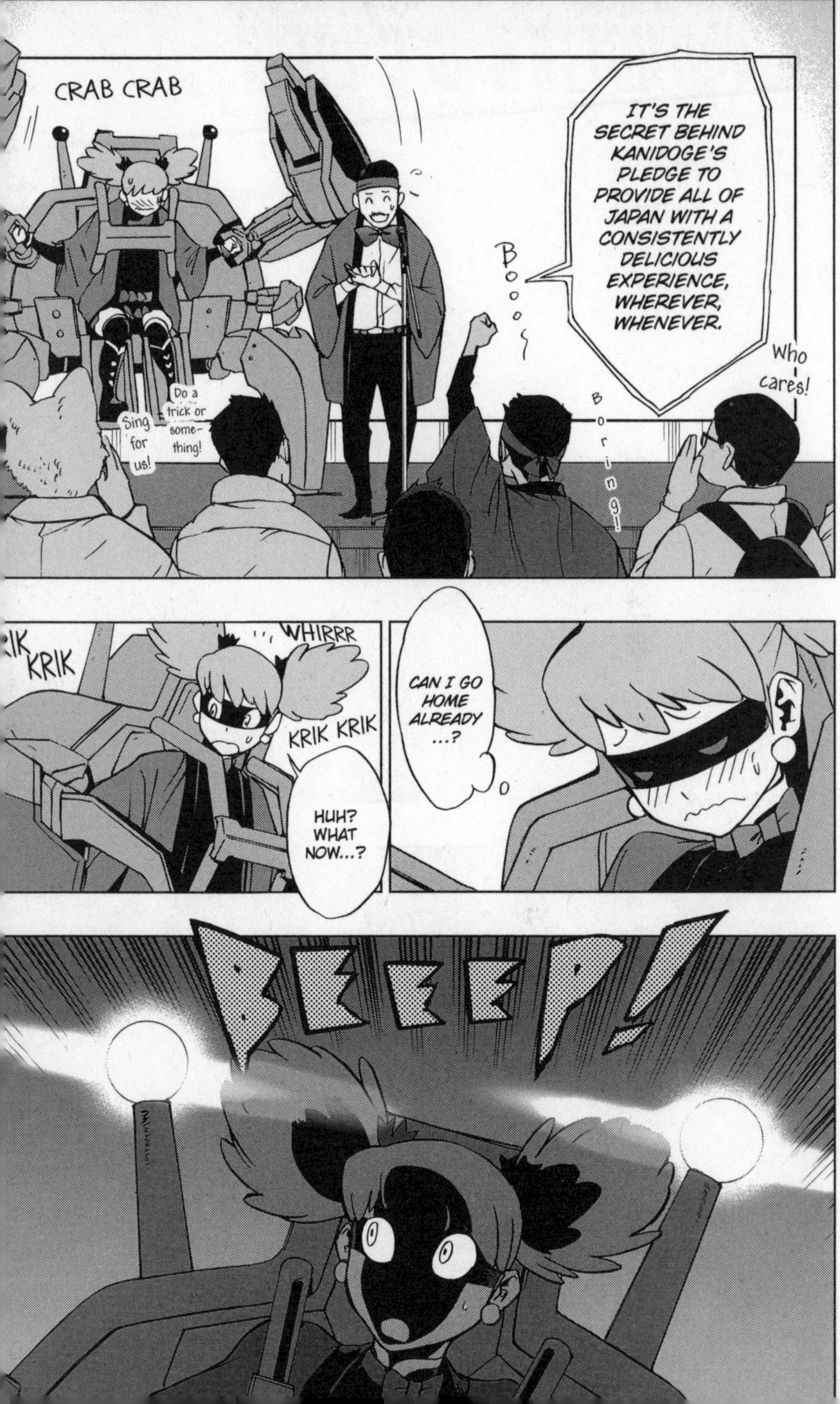
IT'S THE SECRET BEHIND KANIDOGE'S PLEDGE TO PROVIDE ALL OF JAPAN WITH A CONSISTENTLY DELICIOUS EXPERIENCE, WHEREVER, WHENEVER.
Who cares!
Boooo
Boring!
CRAB CRAB
Do a trick or some-thing!
Sing for us!
CAN I GO HOME ALREADY ...?
WHIRRR
KRIK KRIK
HUH? WHAT NOW...?
KRIK KRIK
BEEP!

ICHIRO HOTTA & JIRO HOTTA

THE ROUGH DESIGN

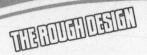

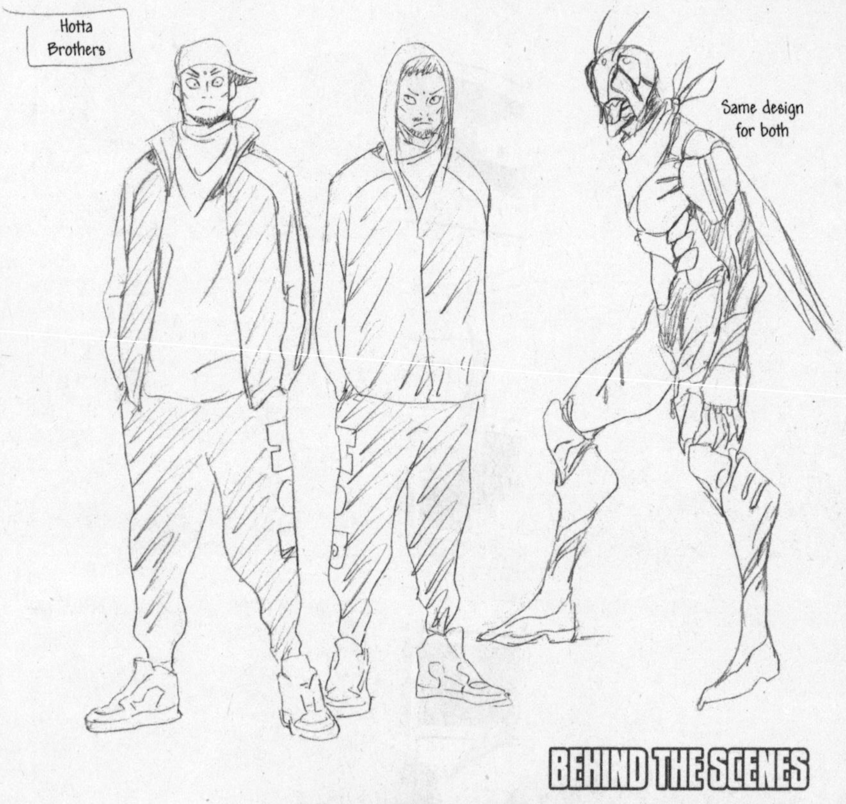
Hotta Brothers
Same design for both

BEHIND THE SCENES

These are some gray-zone types Aizawa interrogates. My thought process was as follows: crooked pawnshop (*battaya* in Japanese; *batta* also means "grasshopper") -> grasshopper monsters -> knockoff Kamen Riders. They're always together, and even their friends call them the Hotta Brothers, which contributes to that fun sense of a tight-knit community.

—Furuhashi

There are already so many bad Kamen Rider knockoff designs out there, so this was hard to pull off. The inspiration is clear at a glance, but the subtle differences in the insect elements are… Nah. Never mind, forget it. They're grasshoppers. It's fine. (LOL)

—Betten

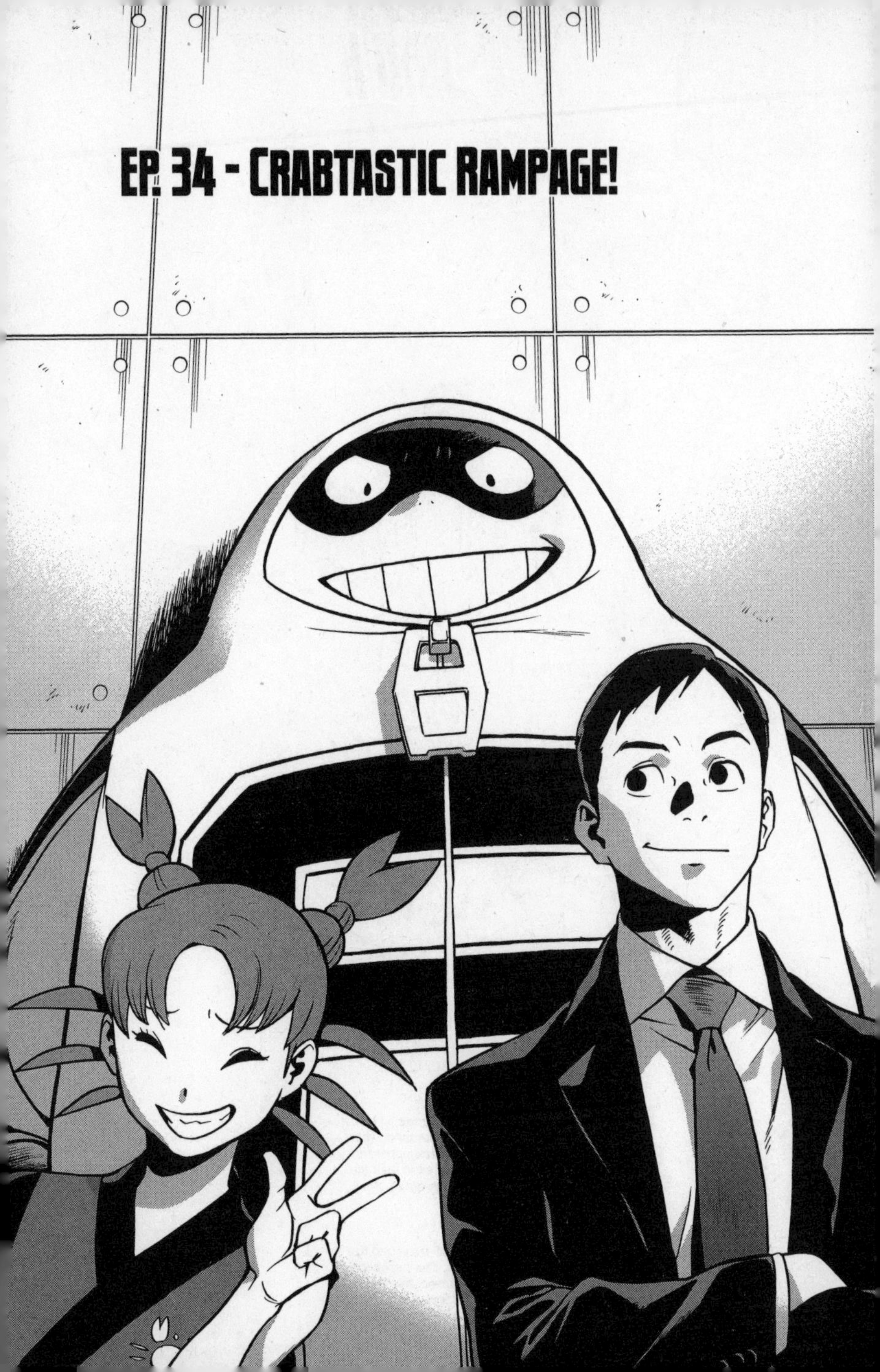
EP. 34 - CRABTASTIC RAMPAGE!

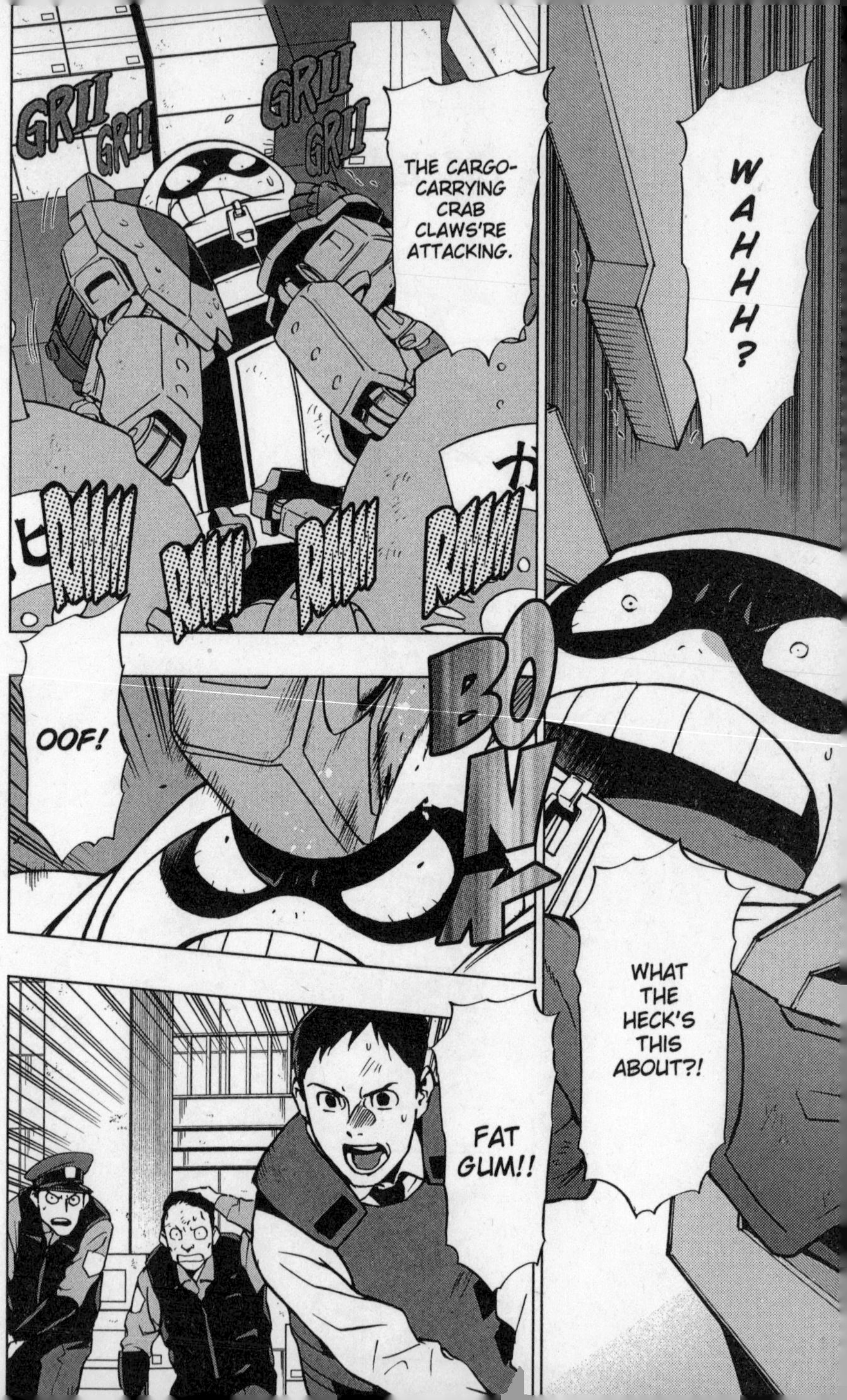
WAHHH?
THE CARGO-CARRYING CRAB CLAWS'RE ATTACKING.
GRII GRII
GRII GRII
BONK
OOF!
WHAT THE HECK'S THIS ABOUT?!
FAT GUM!!

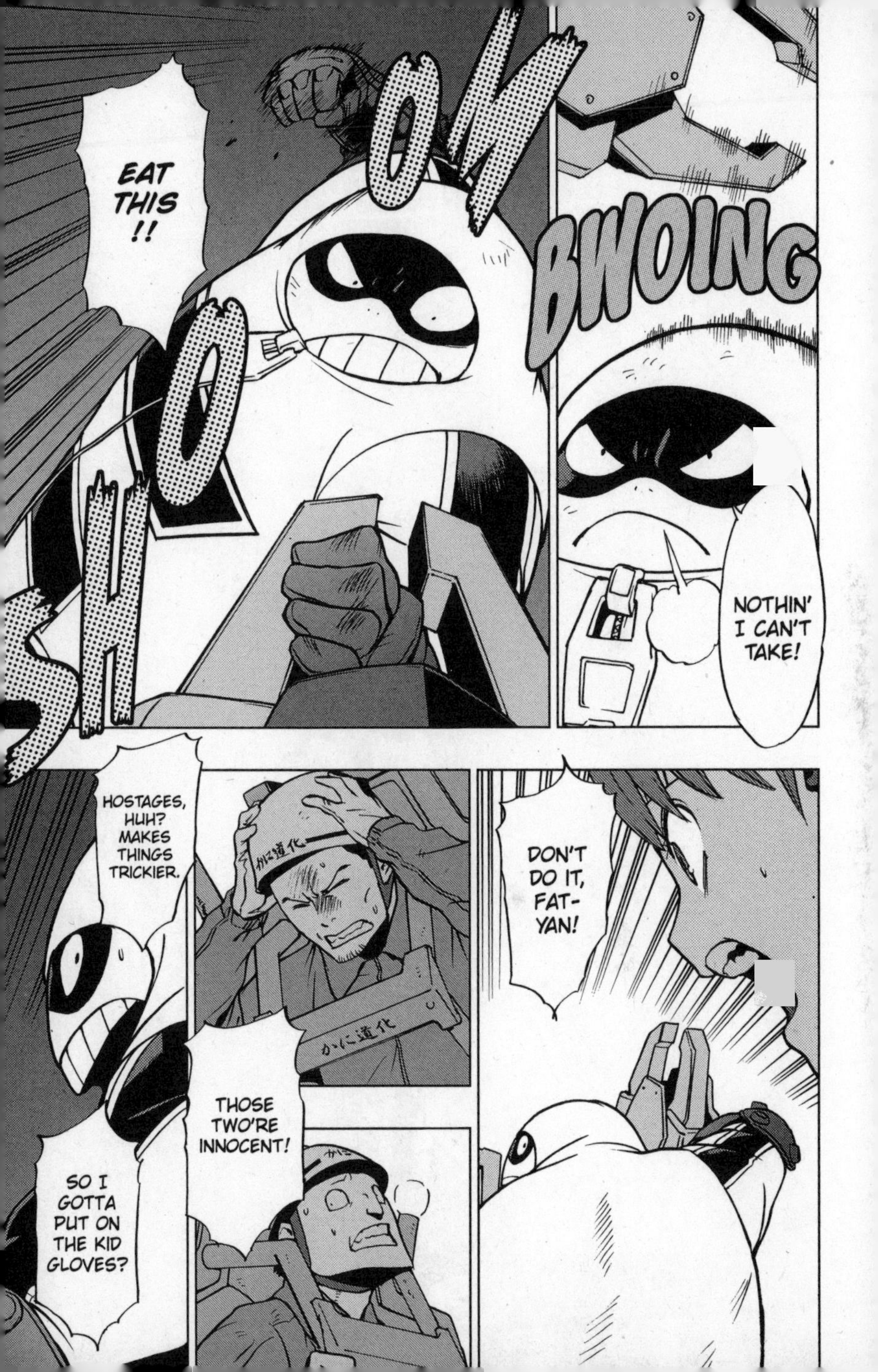
BWOING
NOTHIN' I CAN'T TAKE!
EAT THIS !!
DON'T DO IT, FAT-YAN!
かに道化
HOSTAGES, HUH? MAKES THINGS TRICKIER.
THOSE TWO'RE INNOCENT!
SO I GOTTA PUT ON THE KID GLOVES?

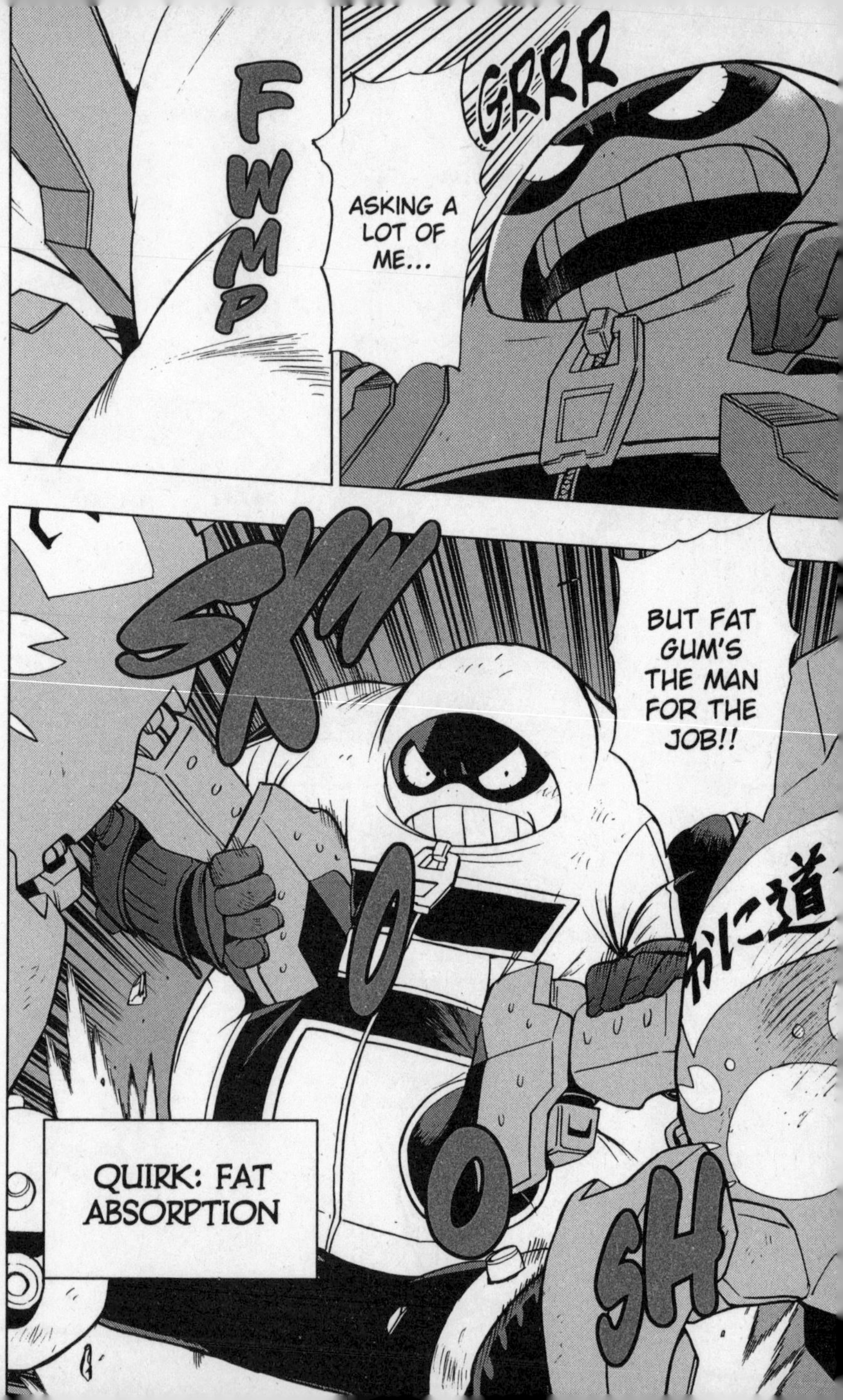
GRRR
ASKING A LOT OF ME...
FWMP
BUT FAT GUM'S THE MAN FOR THE JOB!!
SKW
かに道
QUIRK: FAT ABSORPTION
SH

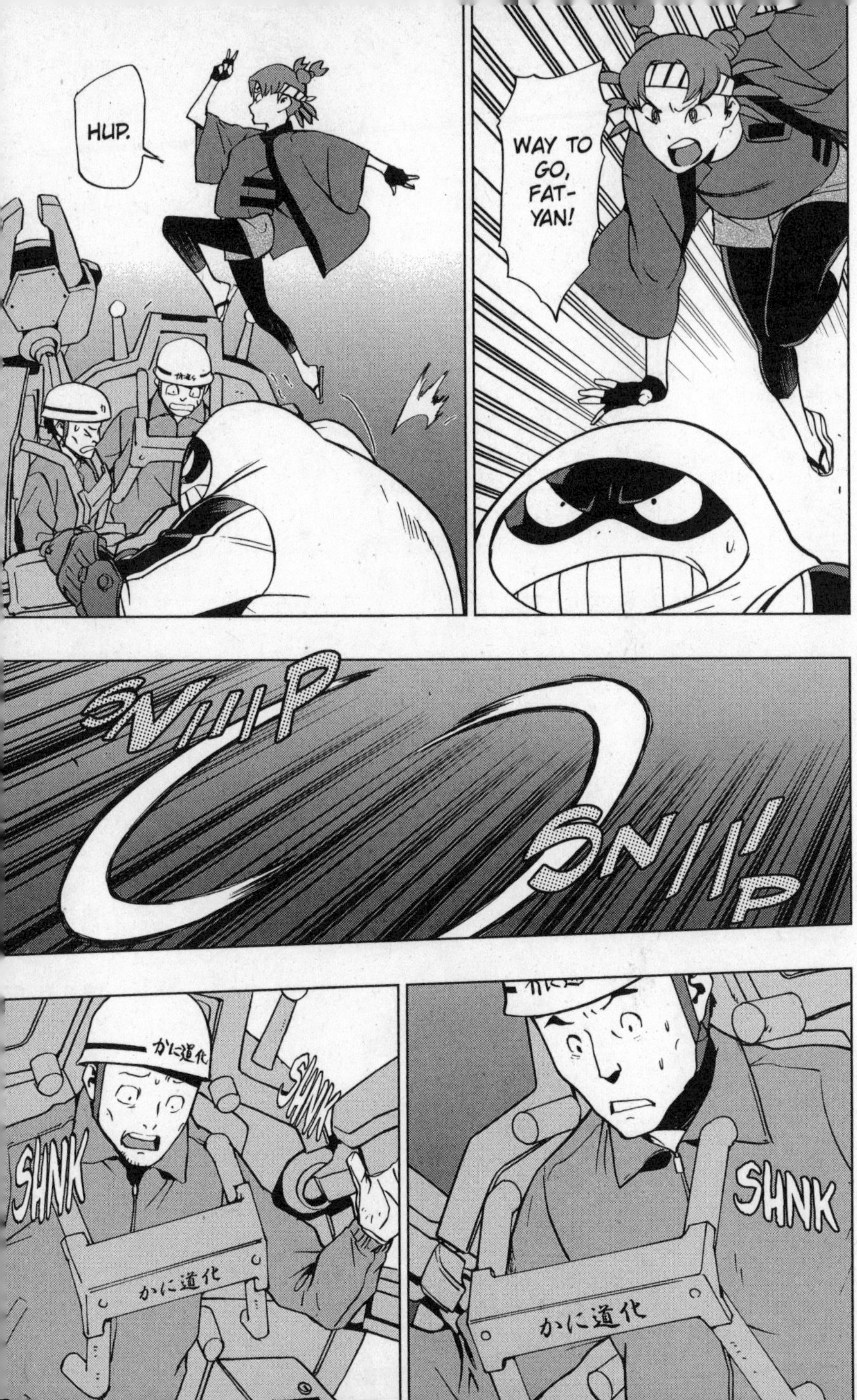
WAY TO GO, FAT-YAN!
HUP.
SNIIP
SNIIP
SHNK
かに道化
SHNK
かに道化
SHNK
かに道化

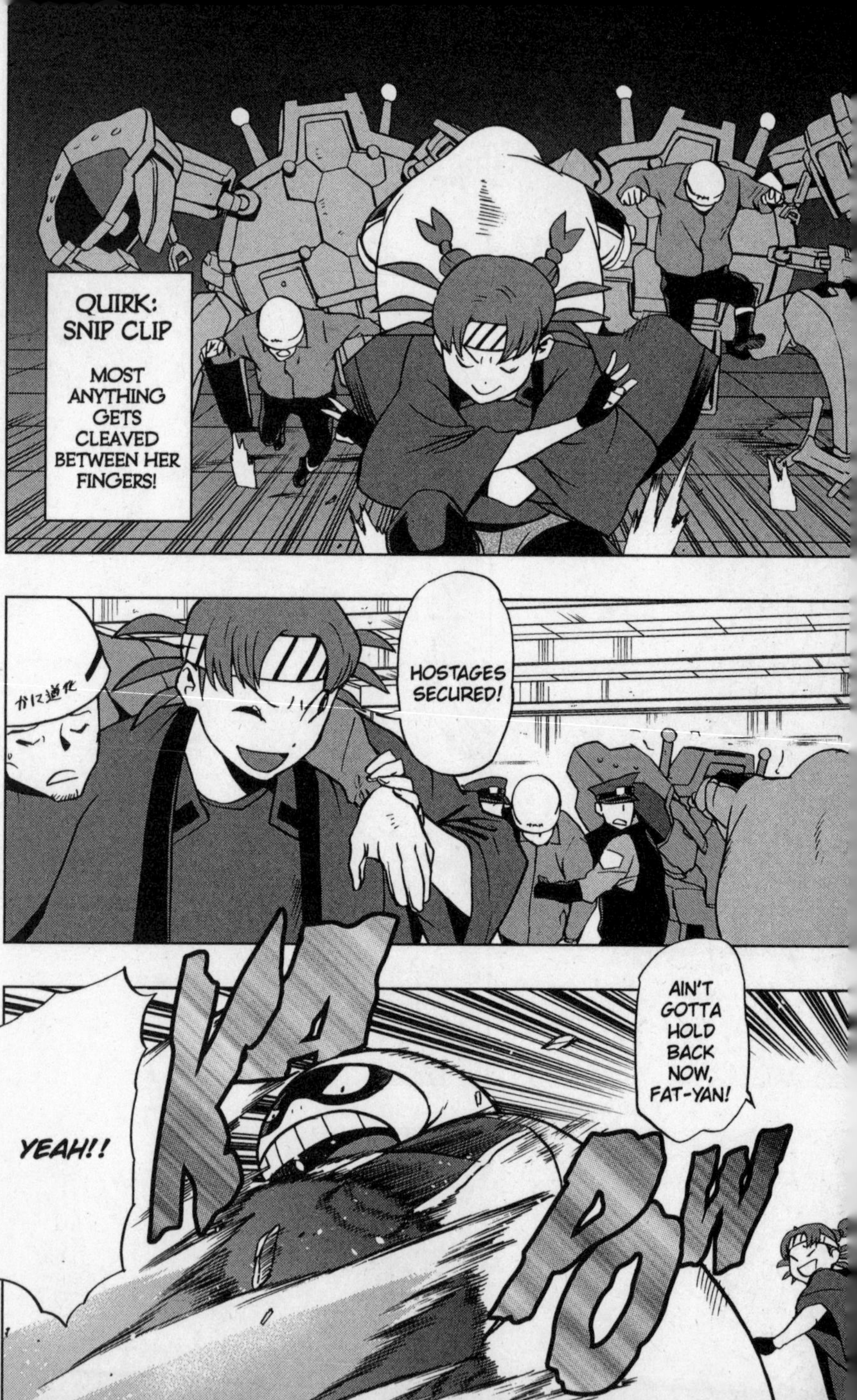
QUIRK: SNIP CLIP
MOST ANYTHING GETS CLEAVED BETWEEN HER FINGERS!
HOSTAGES SECURED!
AIN'T GOTTA HOLD BACK NOW, FAT-YAN!
YEAH!!

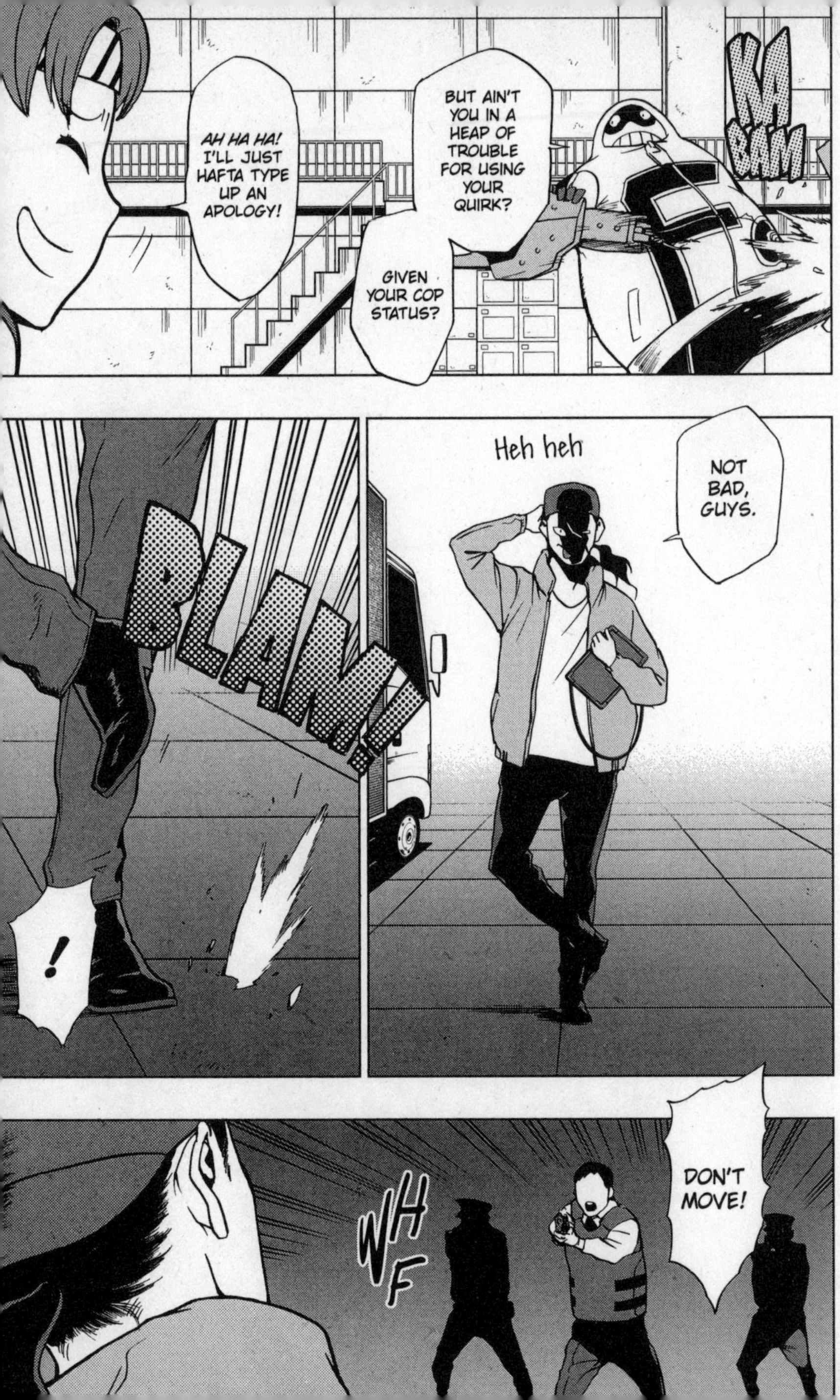
KA BAM
BUT AIN'T YOU IN A HEAP OF TROUBLE FOR USING YOUR QUIRK?
GIVEN YOUR COP STATUS?
AH HA HA! I'LL JUST HAFTA TYPE UP AN APOLOGY!
NOT BAD, GUYS.
Heh heh
BLAM!!
!
DON'T MOVE!
WHF

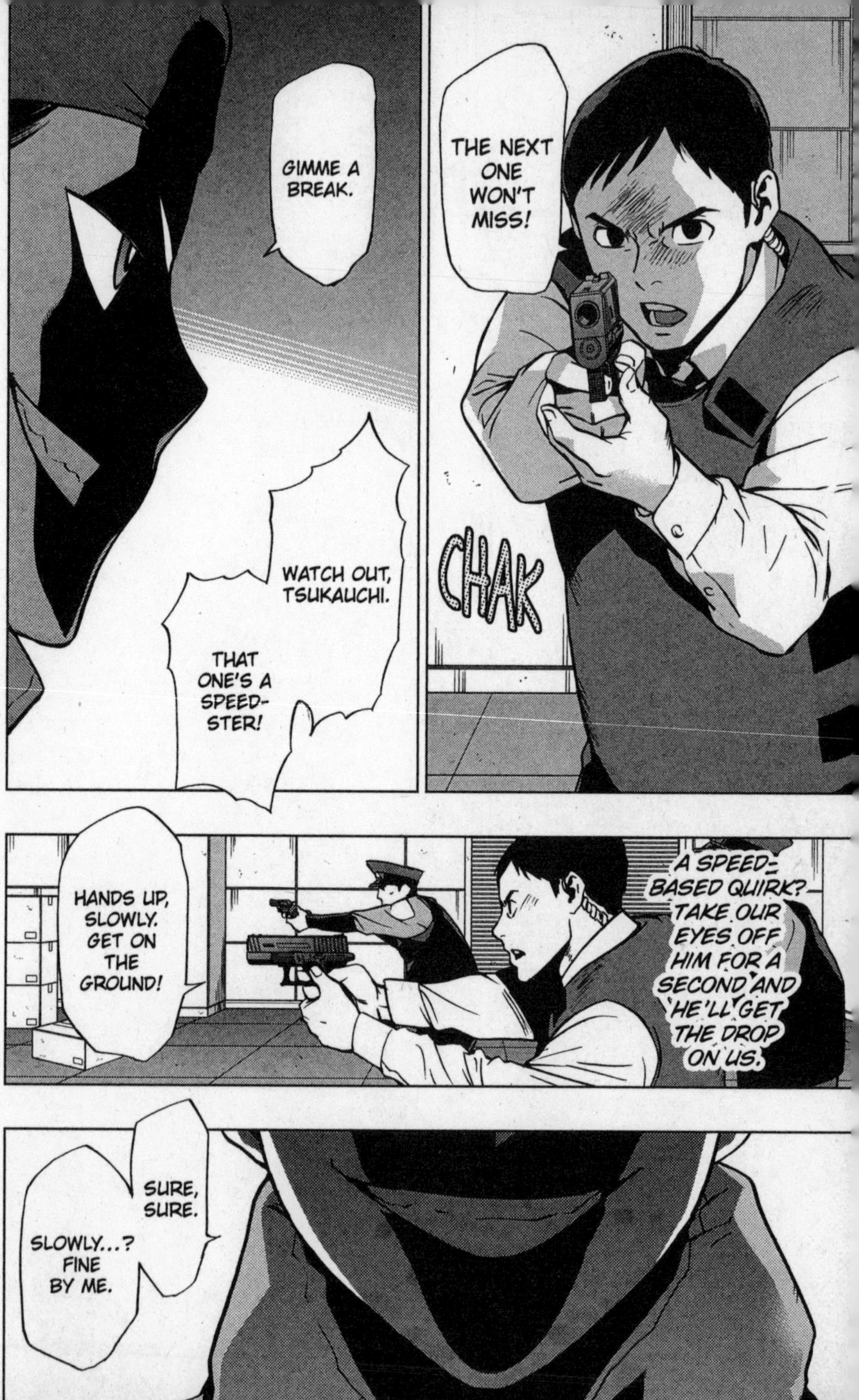
THE NEXT ONE WON'T MISS!
CHAK
GIMME A BREAK.
WATCH OUT, TSUKAUCHI.
THAT ONE'S A SPEED-STER!
A SPEED-BASED QUIRK? TAKE OUR EYES OFF HIM FOR A SECOND AND HE'LL GET THE DROP ON US.
HANDS UP, SLOWLY. GET ON THE GROUND!
SURE, SURE.
SLOWLY...? FINE BY ME.

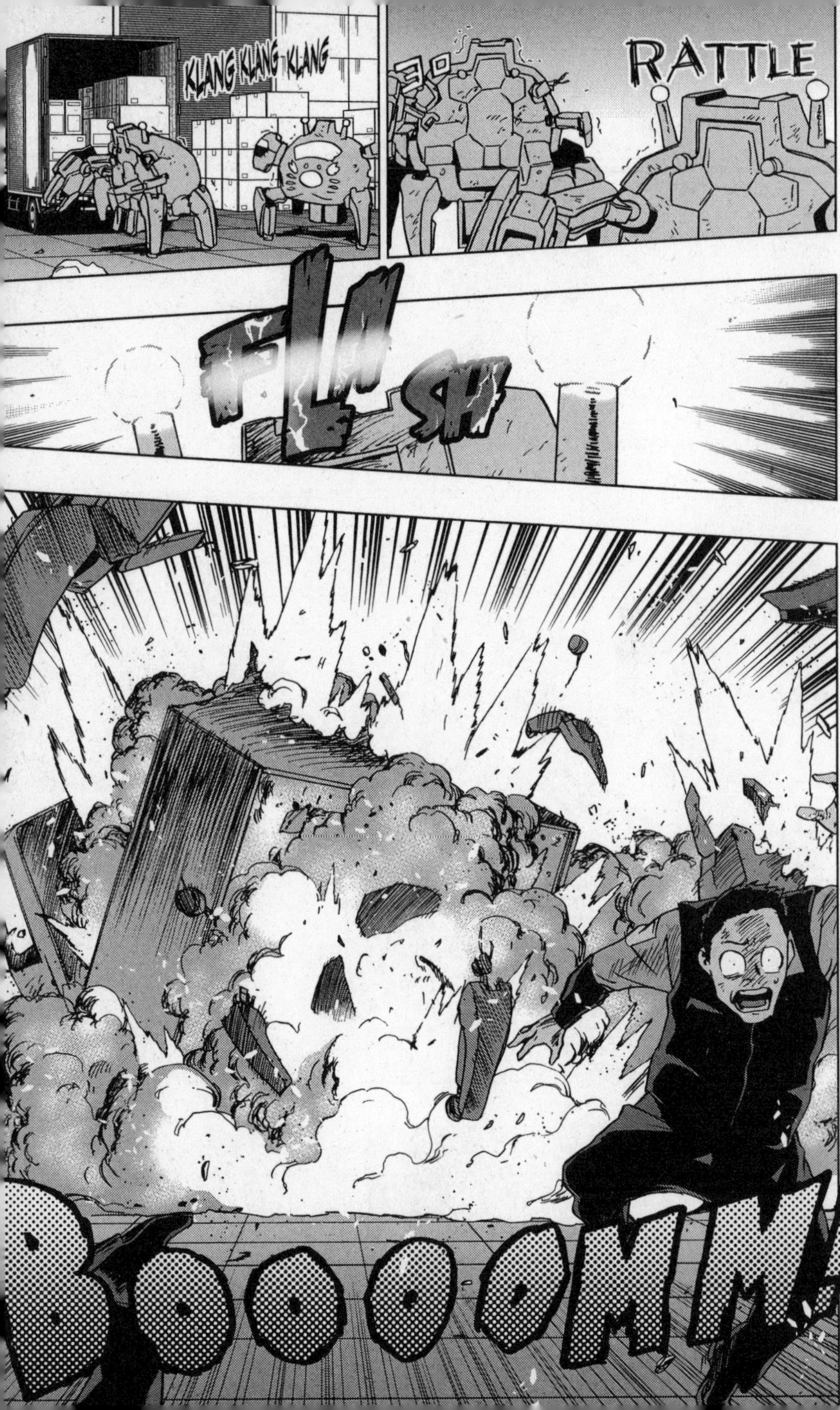
RATTLE
KLANG KLANG KLANG
FLASH
BOOOOMM!

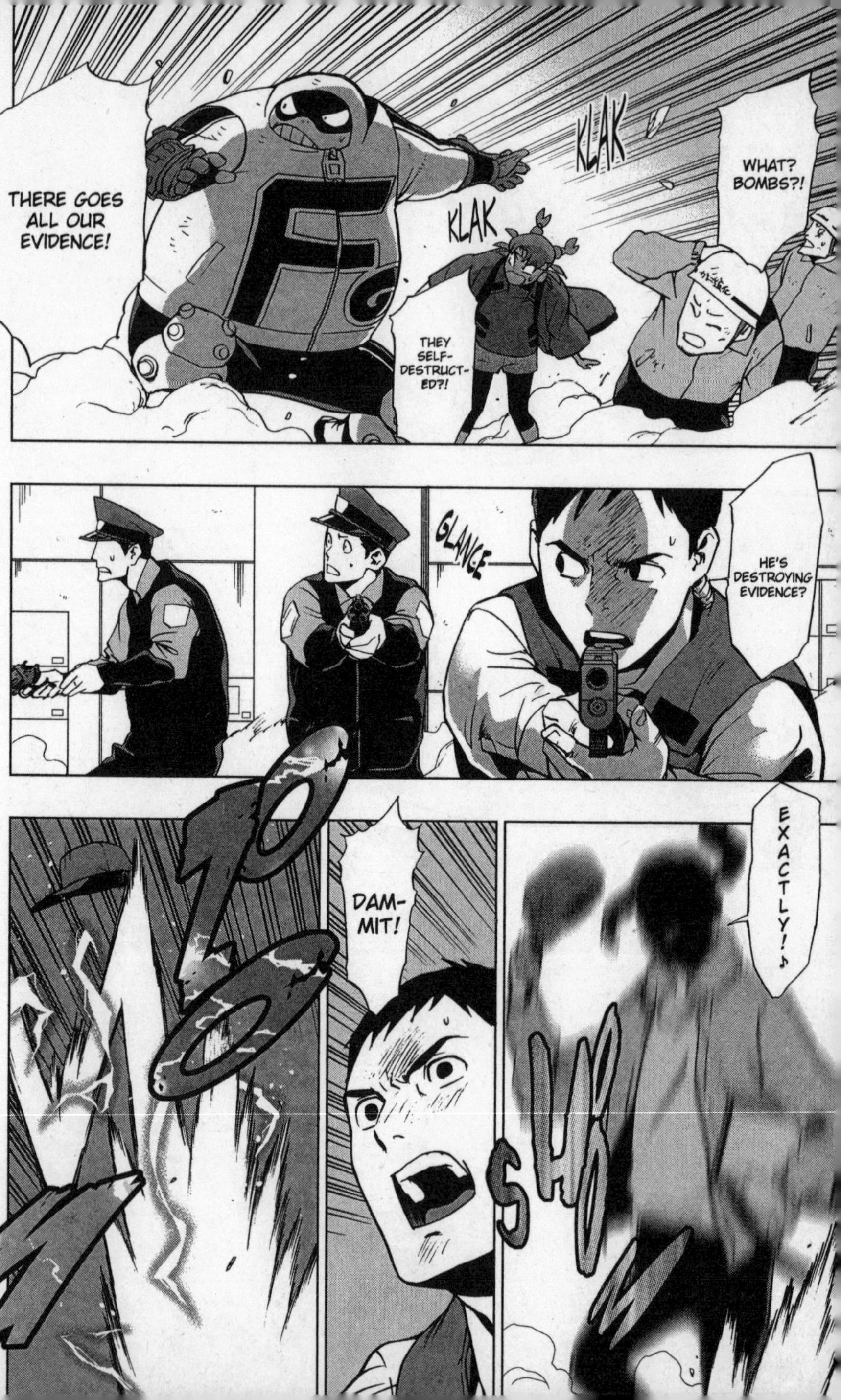
WHAT? BOMBS?!
KLAK
KLAK
THEY SELF-DESTRUCT-ED?!
THERE GOES ALL OUR EVIDENCE!
HE'S DESTROYING EVIDENCE?
GLANCE
EXACTLY!♪
DAM-MIT!

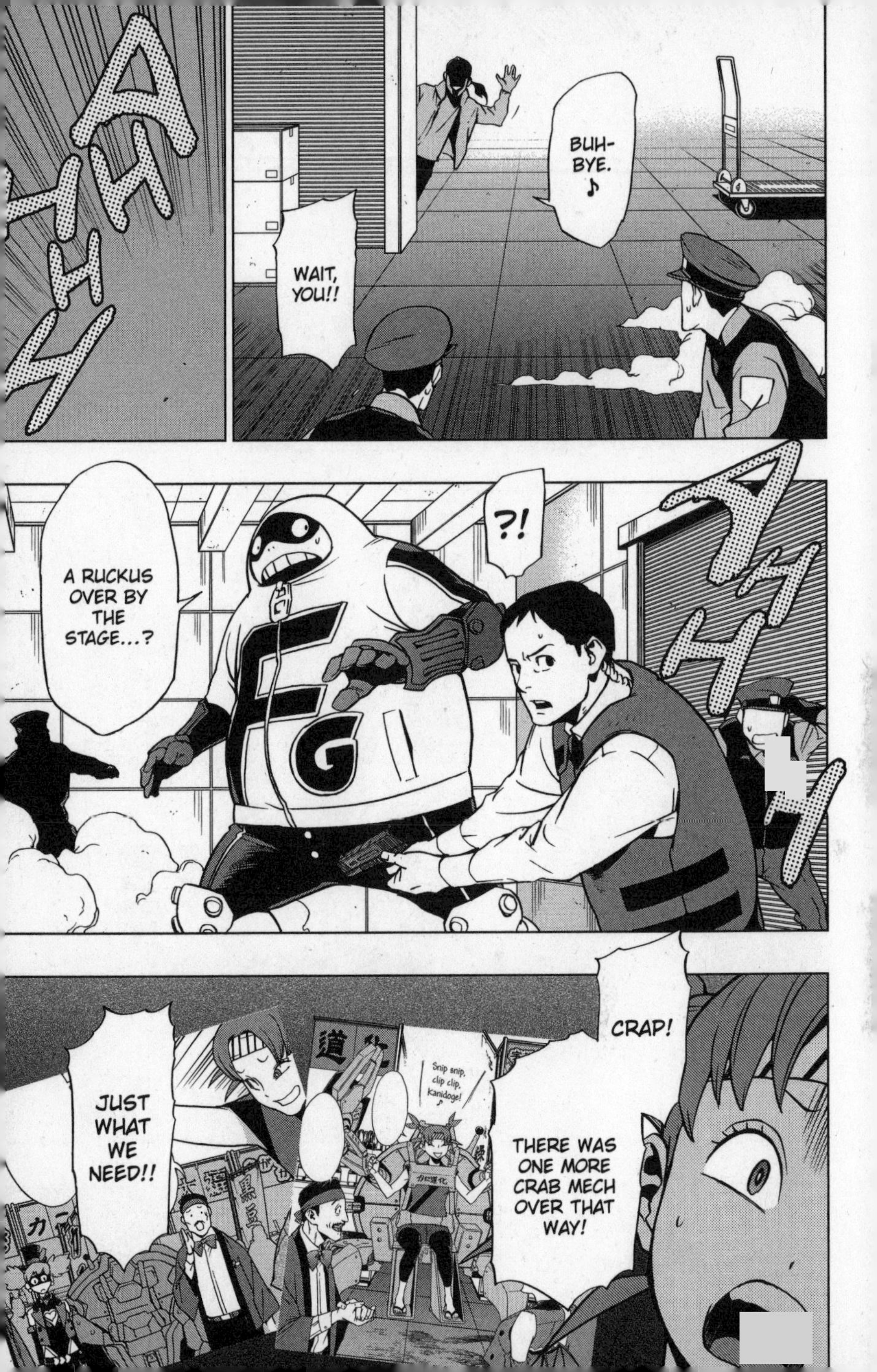
BUH-BYE. ♪
WAIT, YOU!!
AHHHH
AHHHH
?!
A RUCKUS OVER BY THE STAGE...?
CRAP!
THERE WAS ONE MORE CRAB MECH OVER THAT WAY!
Snip snip, clip clip, Kanidoge! ♪
JUST WHAT WE NEED!!

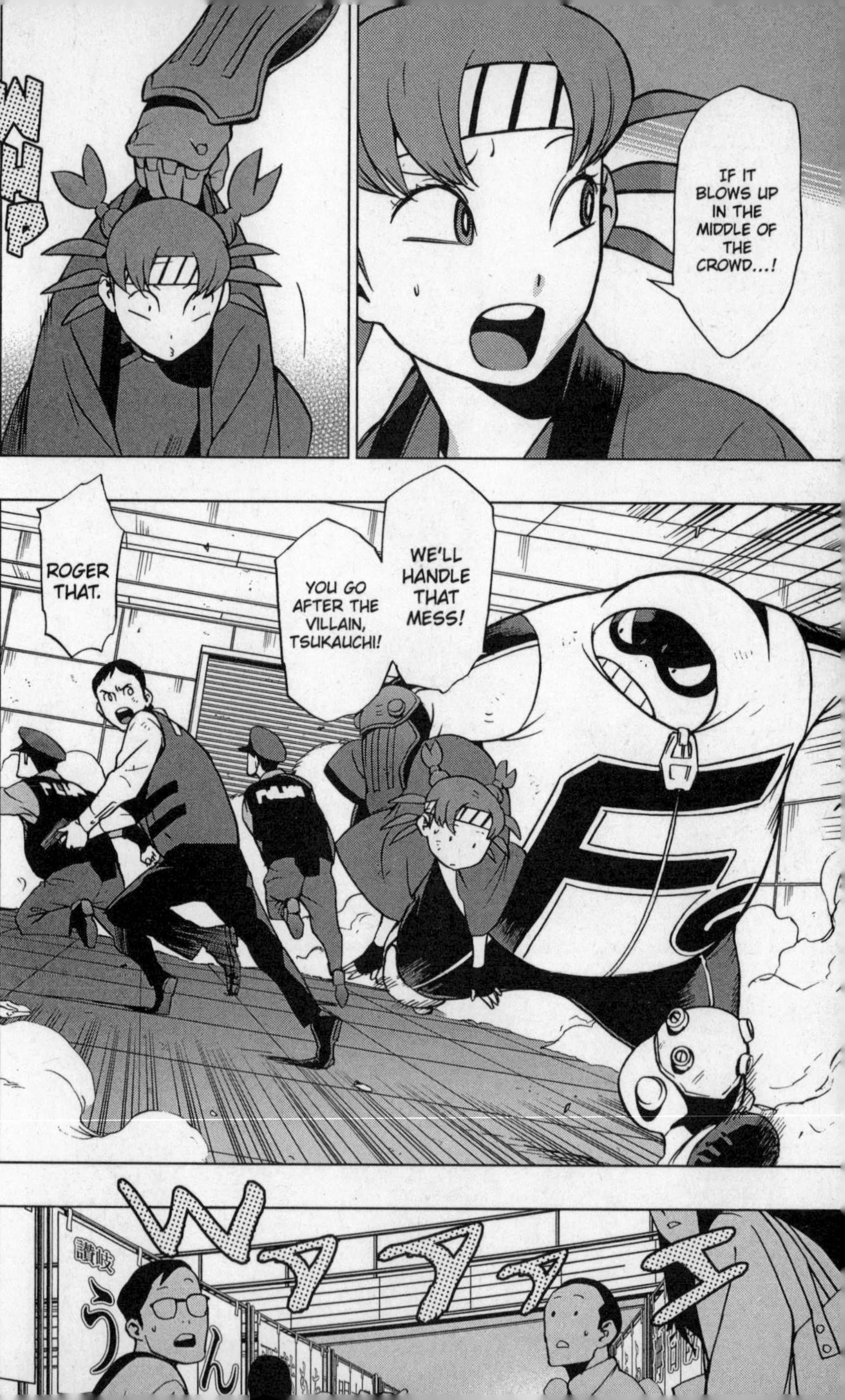
IF IT BLOWS UP IN THE MIDDLE OF THE CROWD...!
WHIP
WE'LL HANDLE THAT MESS!
YOU GO AFTER THE VILLAIN, TSUKAUCHI!
ROGER THAT.
讃岐

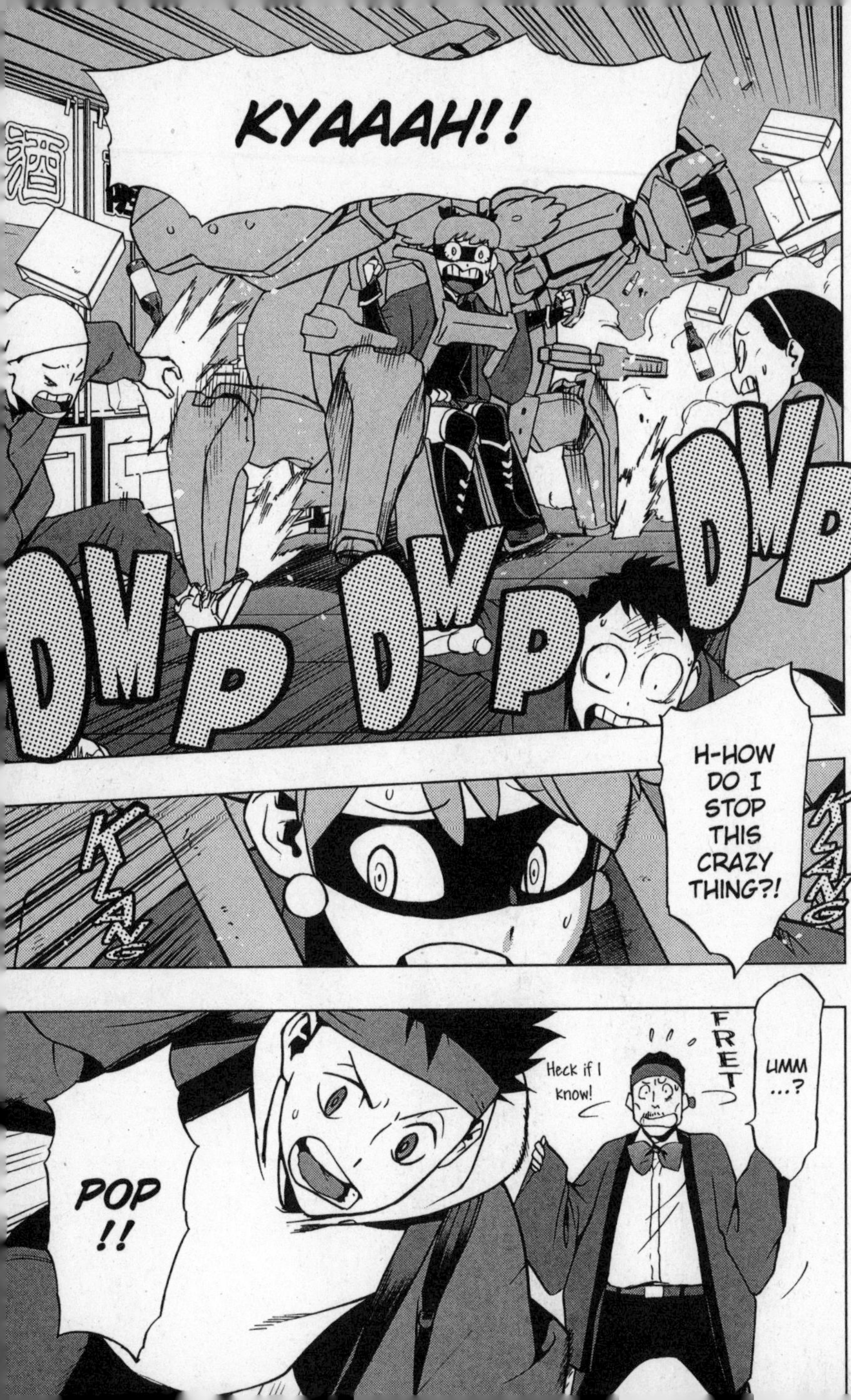
KYAAAH!!
酒
DMP
DMP
DMP
H-HOW DO I STOP THIS CRAZY THING?!
KLANG
KLANG
UMM ...?
FRET
Heck if I know!
POP !!

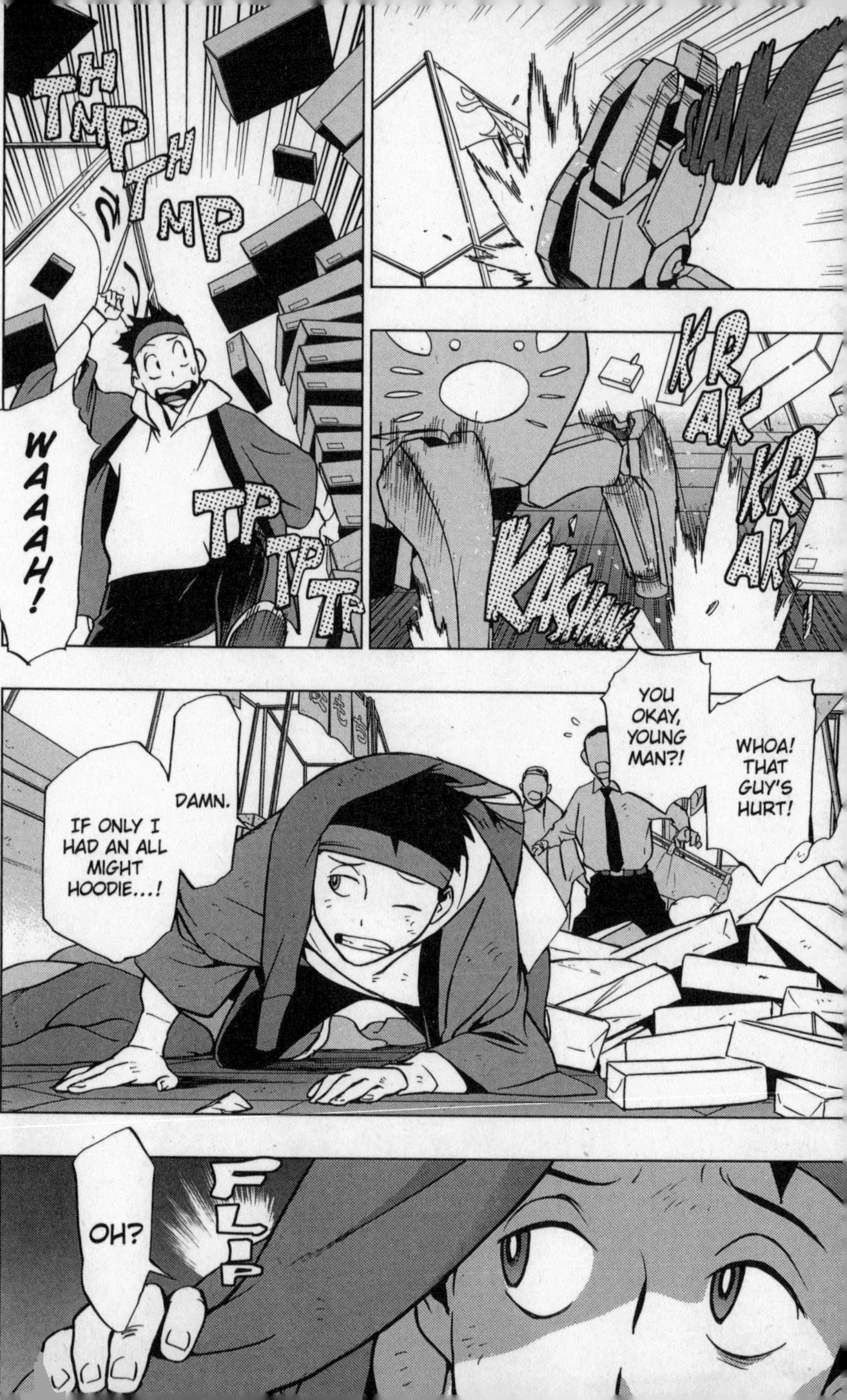
SLAM
KRAK
KRAK
KASHUNK
THTMP
THTMP
WAAAAH!
TP
TP
TP
WHOA! THAT GUY'S HURT!
YOU OKAY, YOUNG MAN?!
DAMN.
IF ONLY I HAD AN ALL MIGHT HOODIE...!
FLIP
OH?

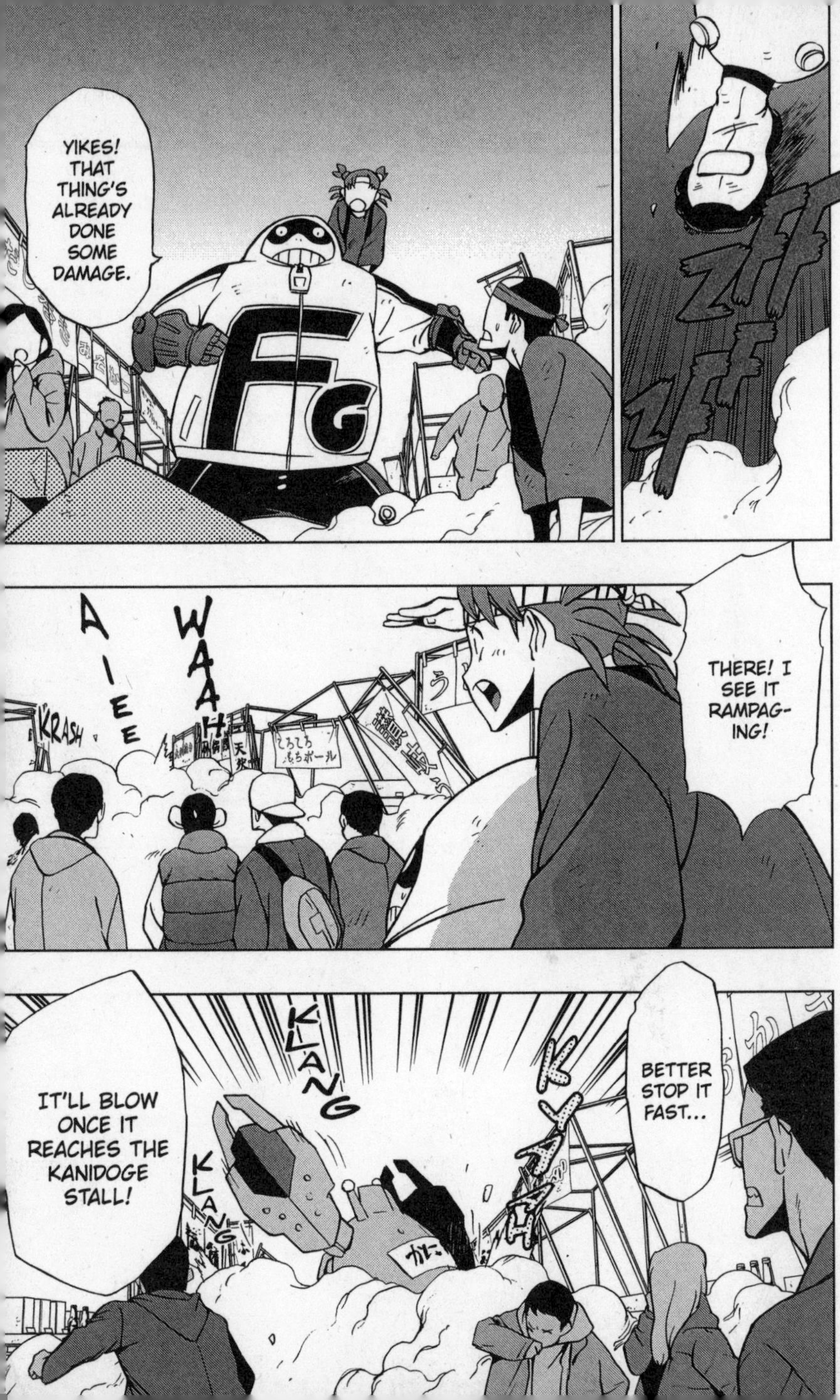
YIKES! THAT THING'S ALREADY DONE SOME DAMAGE.
THERE! I SEE IT RAMPAGING!
WAAAH
AIEEE
KRASH
BETTER STOP IT FAST...
KLANG
KLANG
IT'LL BLOW ONCE IT REACHES THE KANIDOGE STALL!

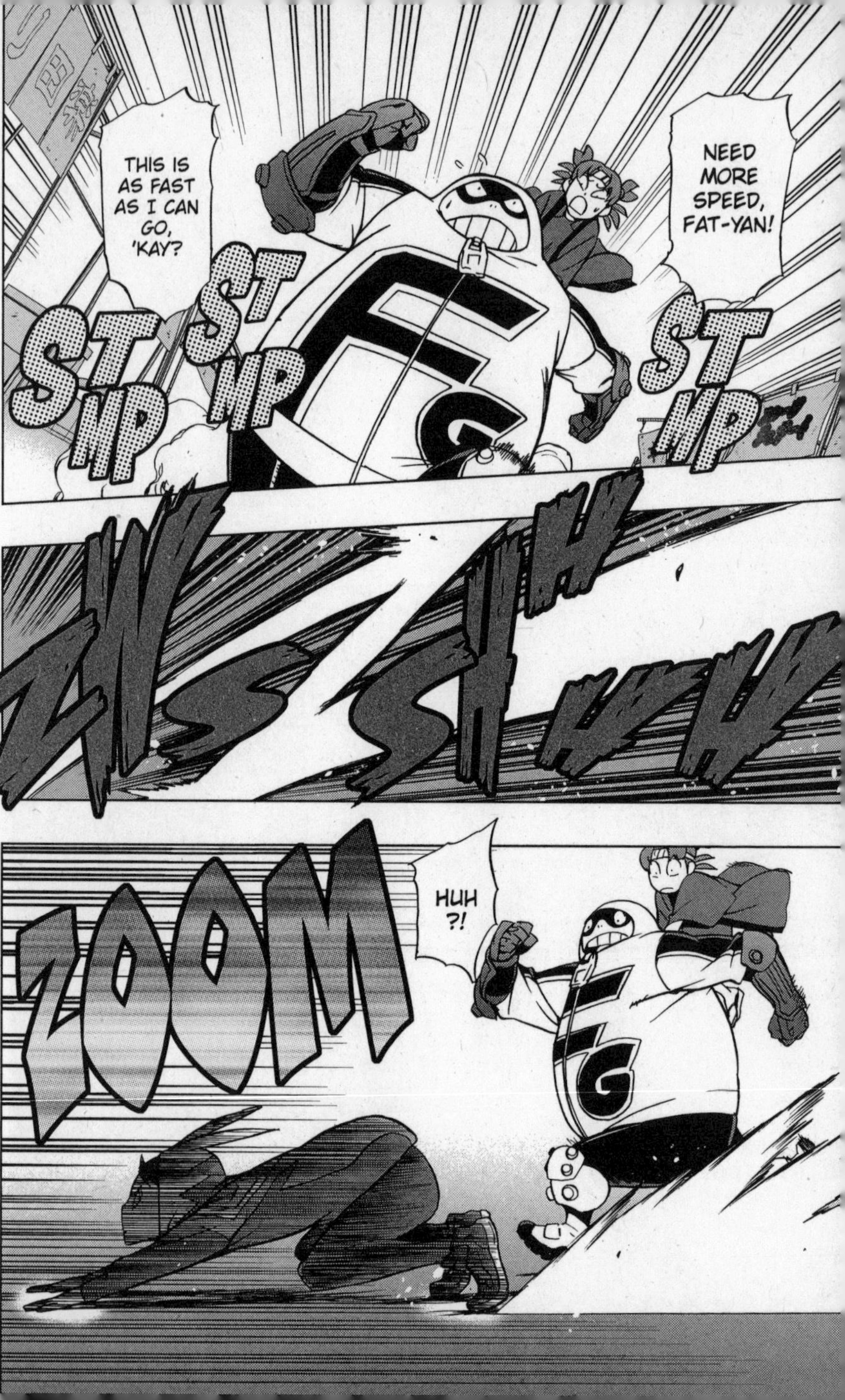
NEED MORE SPEED, FAT-YAN!
THIS IS AS FAST AS I CAN GO, 'KAY?
STMP
STMP
STMP
ZWSSHHHH
HUH ?!
ZOOM

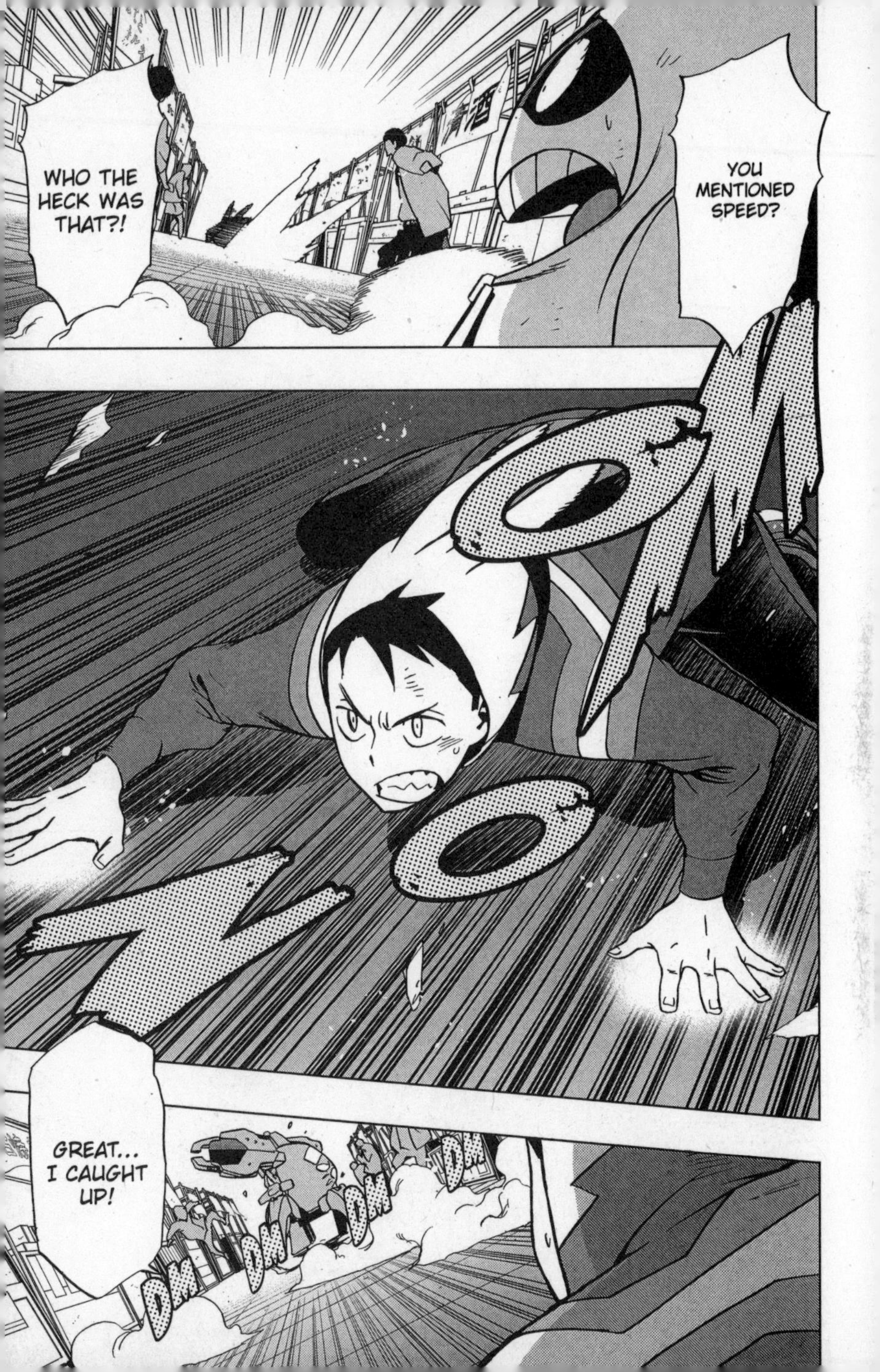
YOU MENTIONED SPEED?
WHO THE HECK WAS THAT?!
WOOM
GREAT... I CAUGHT UP!
DM DM DM DM DM

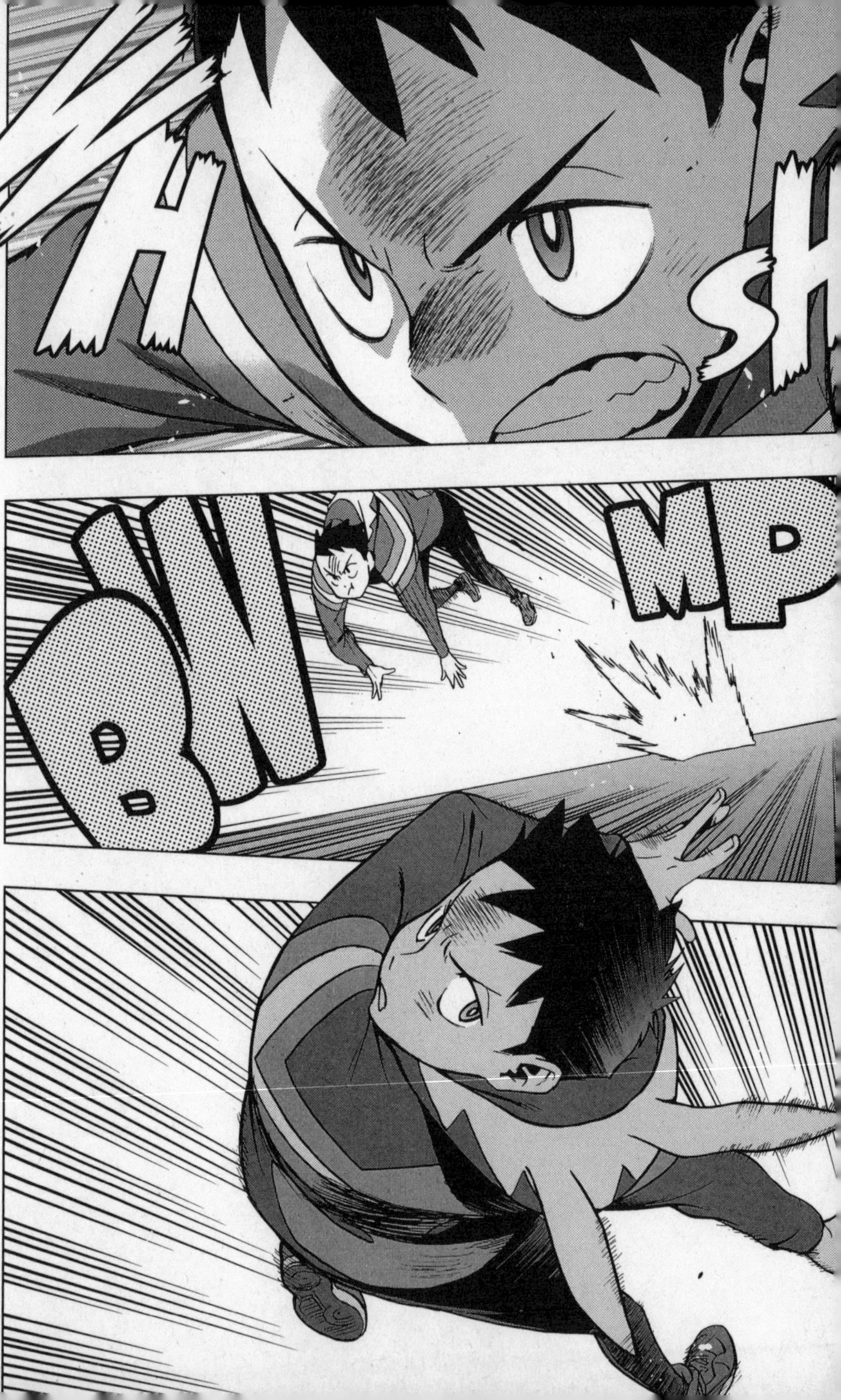
WHA
SH
BUMP

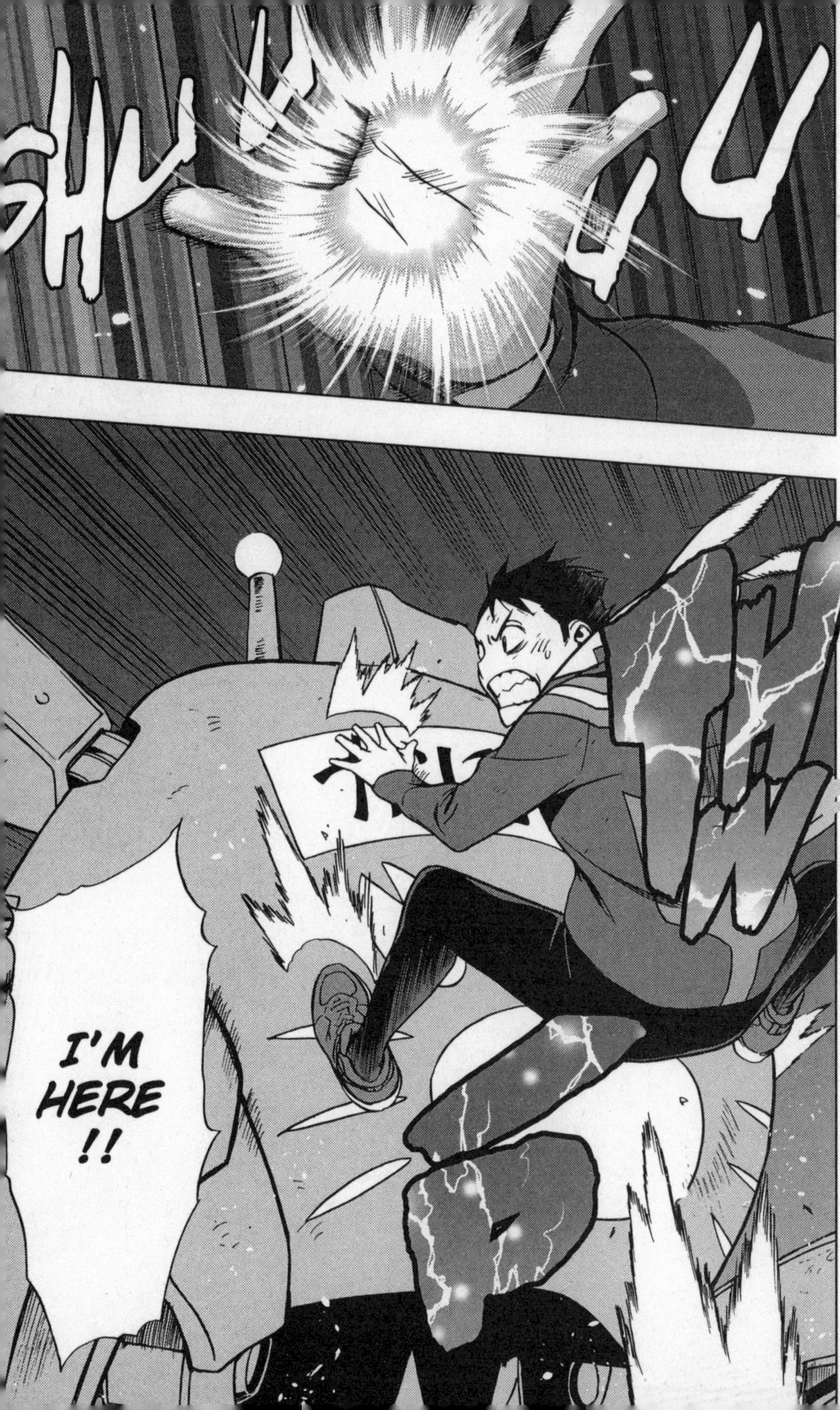
I'M HERE !!

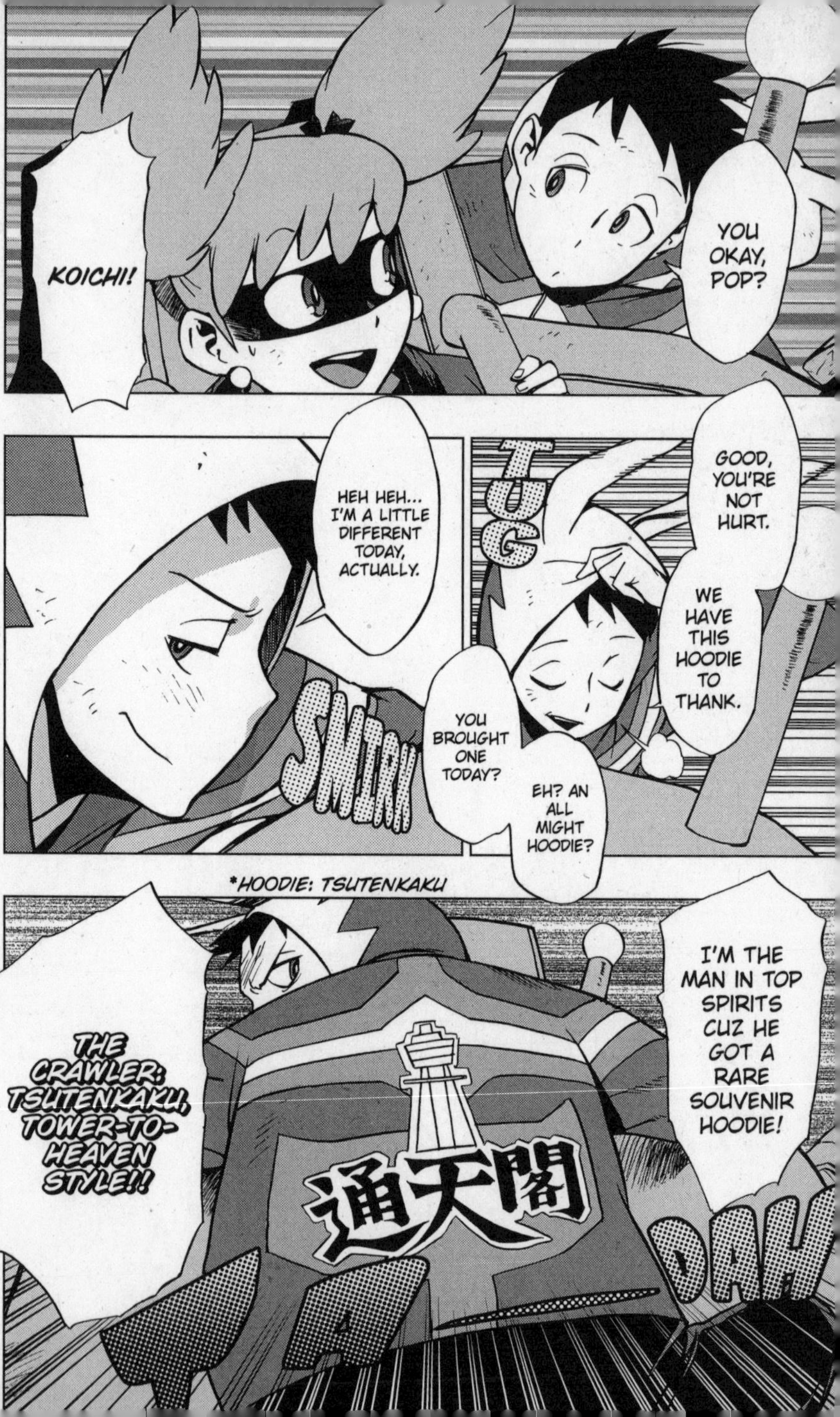
YOU OKAY, POP?
KOICHI!
TUG
GOOD, YOU'RE NOT HURT.
WE HAVE THIS HOODIE TO THANK.
EH? AN ALL MIGHT HOODIE?
YOU BROUGHT ONE TODAY?
HEH HEH... I'M A LITTLE DIFFERENT TODAY, ACTUALLY.
SMIRK
*HOODIE: TSUTENKAKU
I'M THE MAN IN TOP SPIRITS CUZ HE GOT A RARE SOUVENIR HOODIE!
DAH
通天閣
THE CRAWLER: TSUTENKAKU, TOWER-TO-HEAVEN STYLE!!

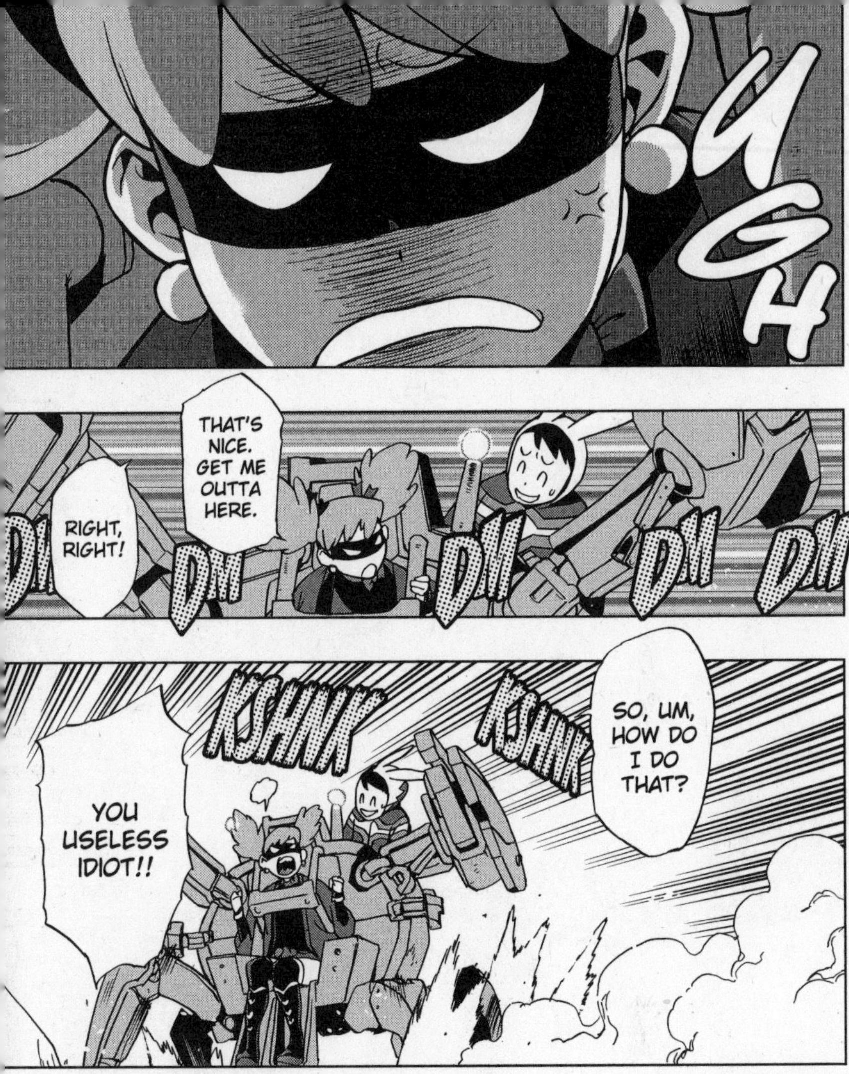
UGH
THAT'S NICE. GET ME OUTTA HERE.
DM DM
DM
RIGHT, RIGHT!
DM DM
KSHNK
SO, UM, HOW DO I DO THAT?
KSHNK
YOU USELESS IDIOT!!

*SIGN: LOCAL ALL MIGHT HOODIES

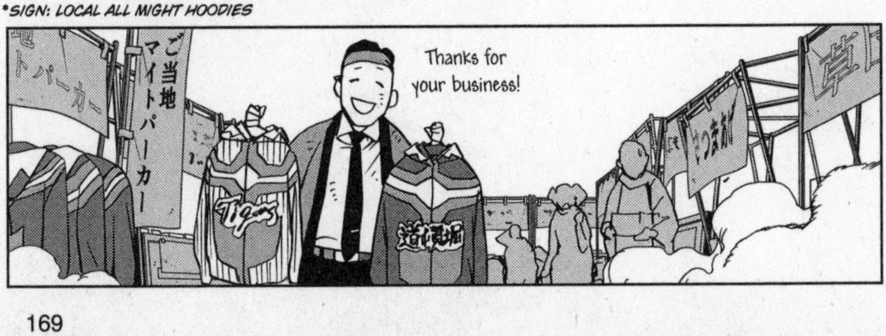
Thanks for your business!
ご当地マイトパーカー

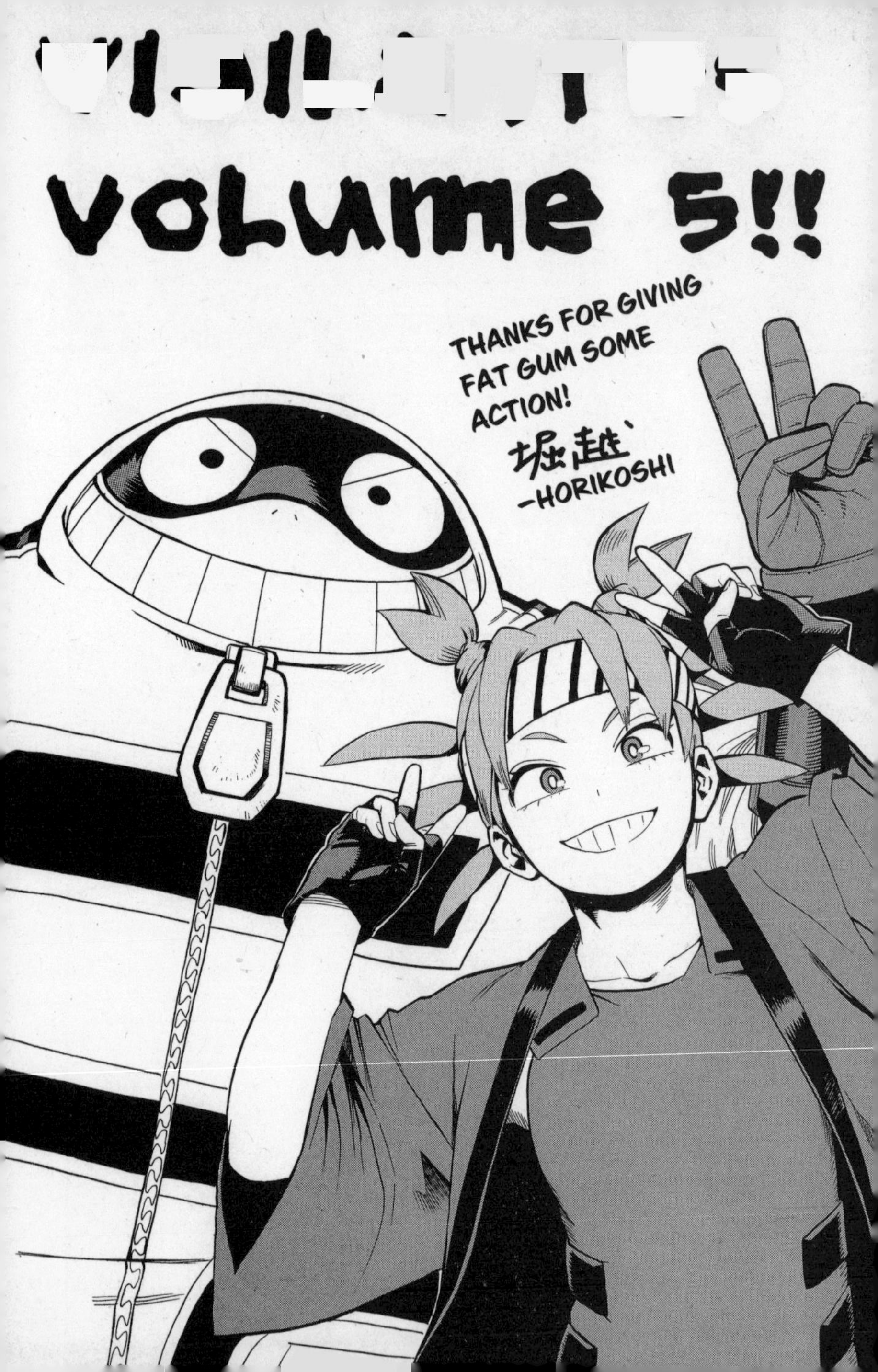
VOLUME 5!!
THANKS FOR GIVING FAT GUM SOME ACTION!
堀越
-HORIKOSHI

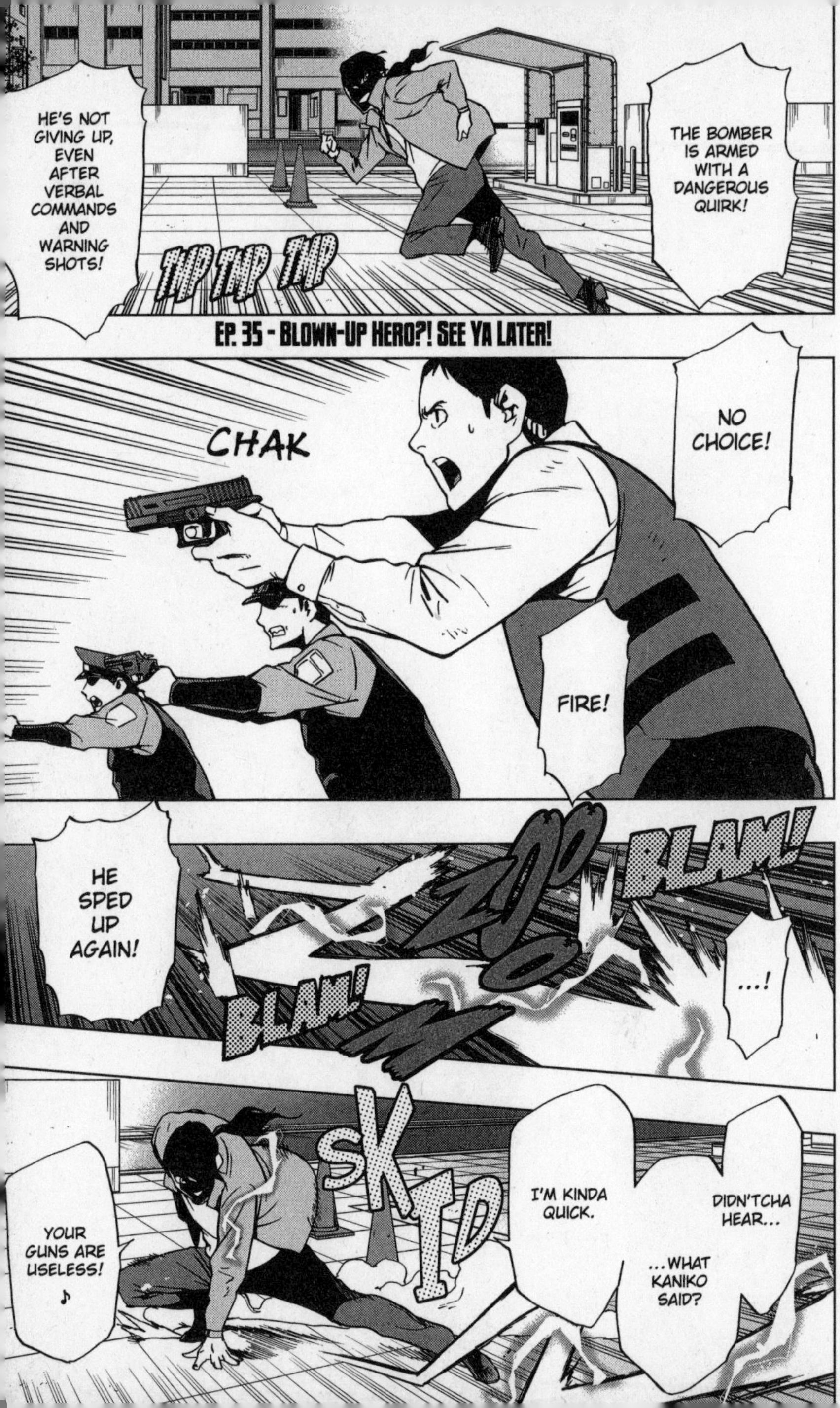
THE BOMBER IS ARMED WITH A DANGEROUS QUIRK!
TMP TMP TMP
HE'S NOT GIVING UP, EVEN AFTER VERBAL COMMANDS AND WARNING SHOTS!
EP. 35 - BLOWN-UP HERO?! SEE YA LATER!
NO CHOICE!
CHAK
FIRE!
...!
BLAM!
ZOOOM
BLAM!
HE SPED UP AGAIN!
DIDN'TCHA HEAR...
...WHAT KANIKO SAID?
I'M KINDA QUICK.
SKID
YOUR GUNS ARE USELESS! ♪

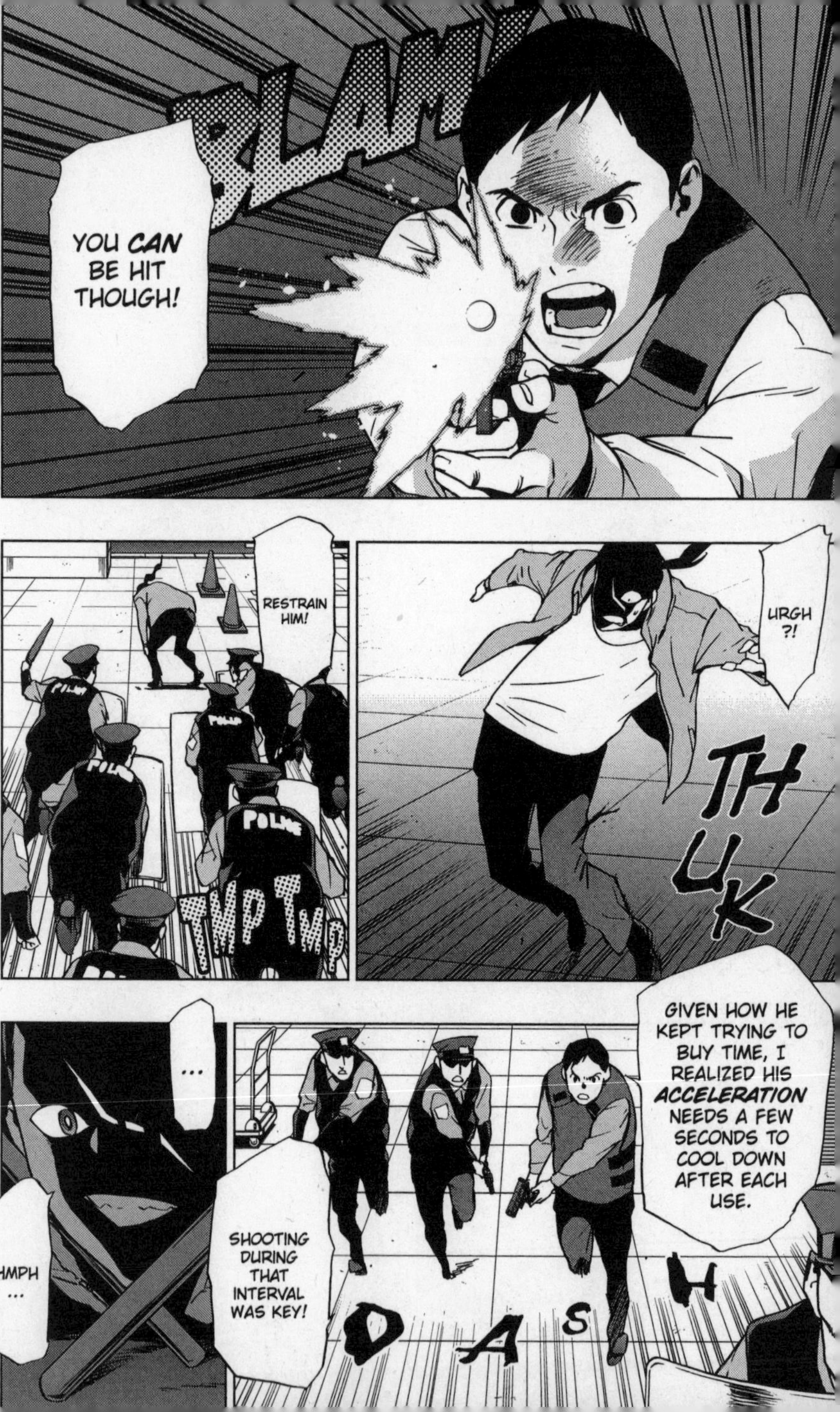
YOU CAN BE HIT THOUGH!
URGH ?!
THUK
RESTRAIN HIM!
TMP TMP
GIVEN HOW HE KEPT TRYING TO BUY TIME, I REALIZED HIS ACCELERATION NEEDS A FEW SECONDS TO COOL DOWN AFTER EACH USE.
SHOOTING DURING THAT INTERVAL WAS KEY!
DASH
...
HMPH ...

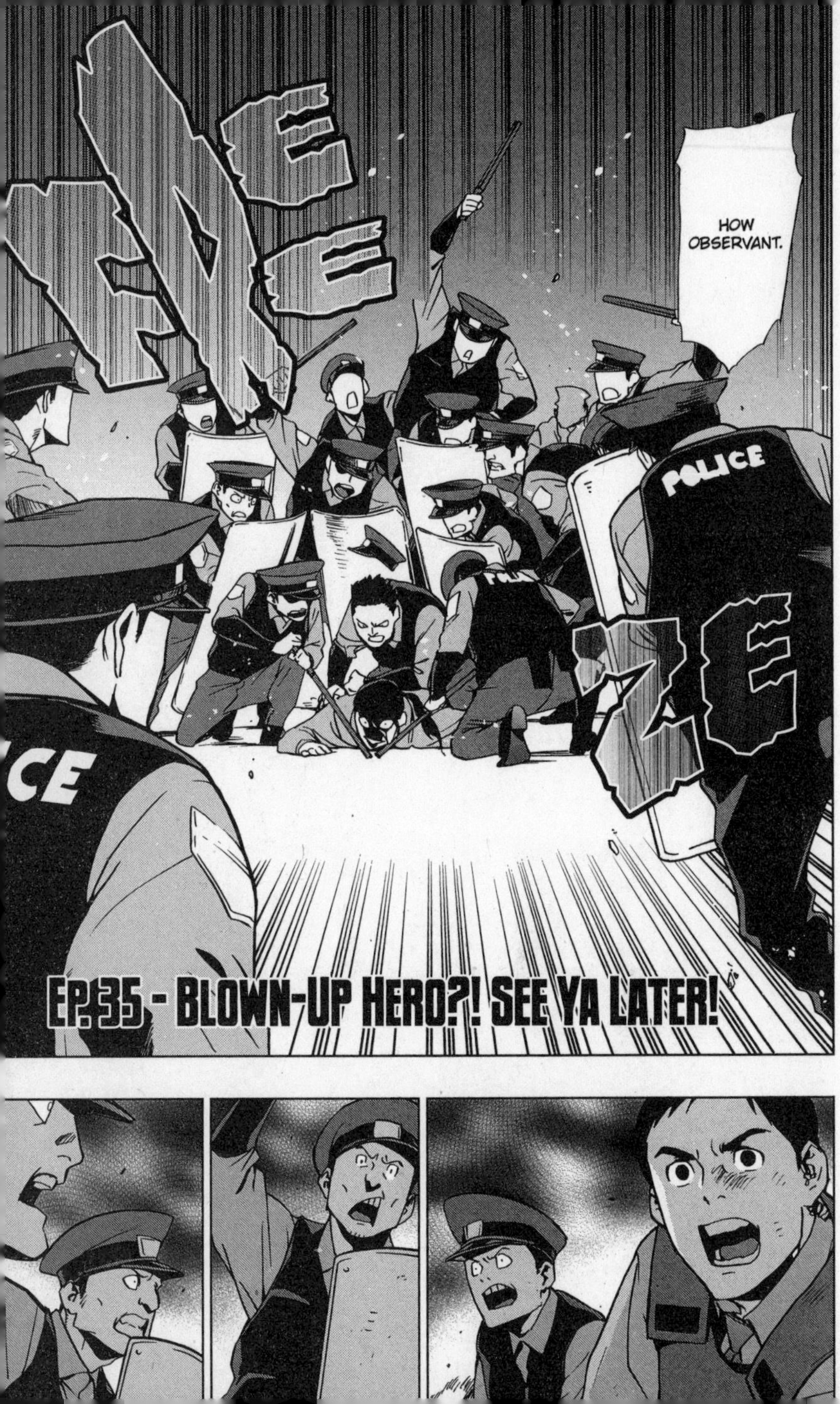
HOW OBSERVANT.
POLICE
CE
EP. 35 - BLOWN-UP HERO?! SEE YA LATER!

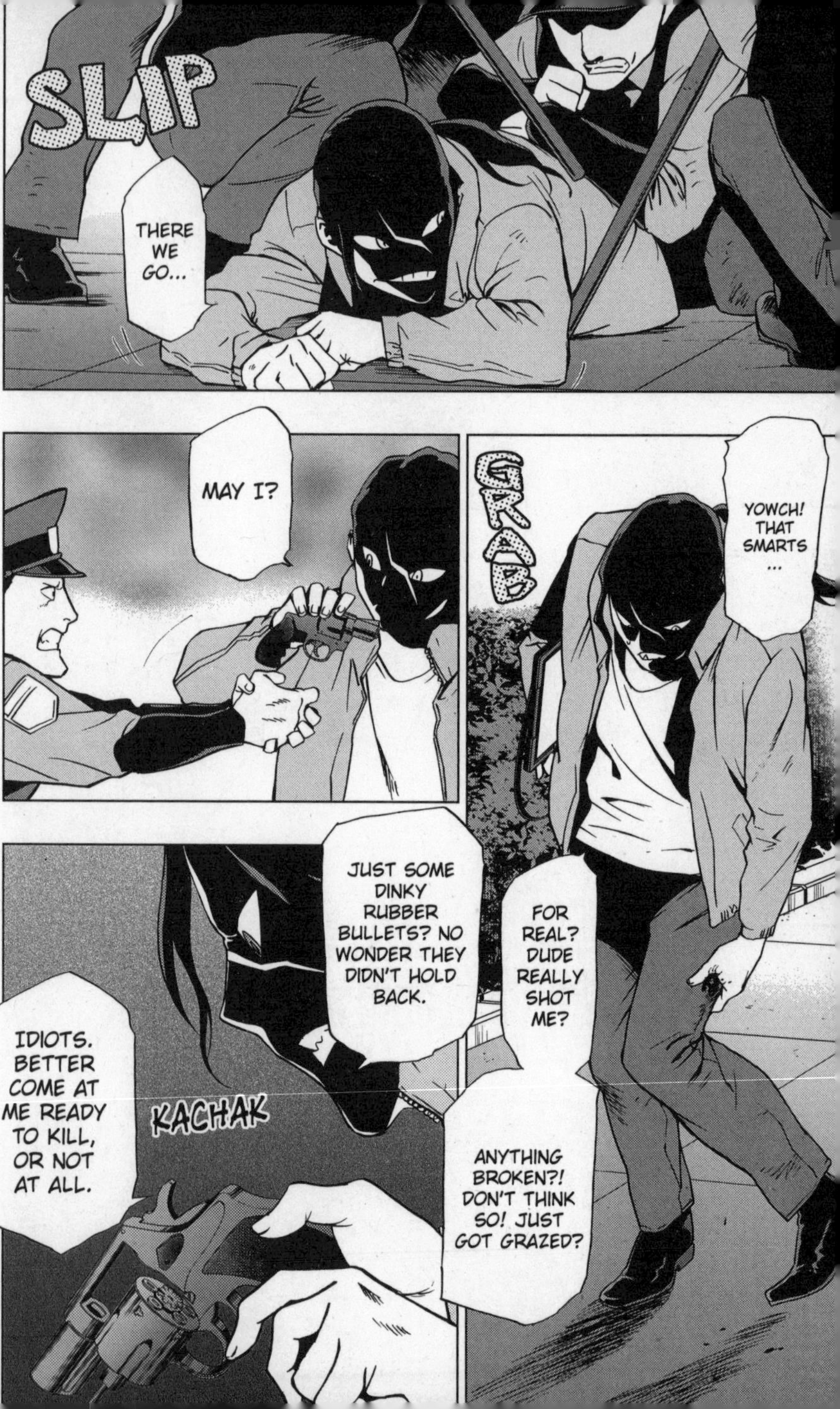
SLIP
THERE WE GO...
GRAB
YOWCH! THAT SMARTS...
FOR REAL? DUDE REALLY SHOT ME?
ANYTHING BROKEN?! DON'T THINK SO! JUST GOT GRAZED?
MAY I?
JUST SOME DINKY RUBBER BULLETS? NO WONDER THEY DIDN'T HOLD BACK.
IDIOTS. BETTER COME AT ME READY TO KILL, OR NOT AT ALL.
KACHAK

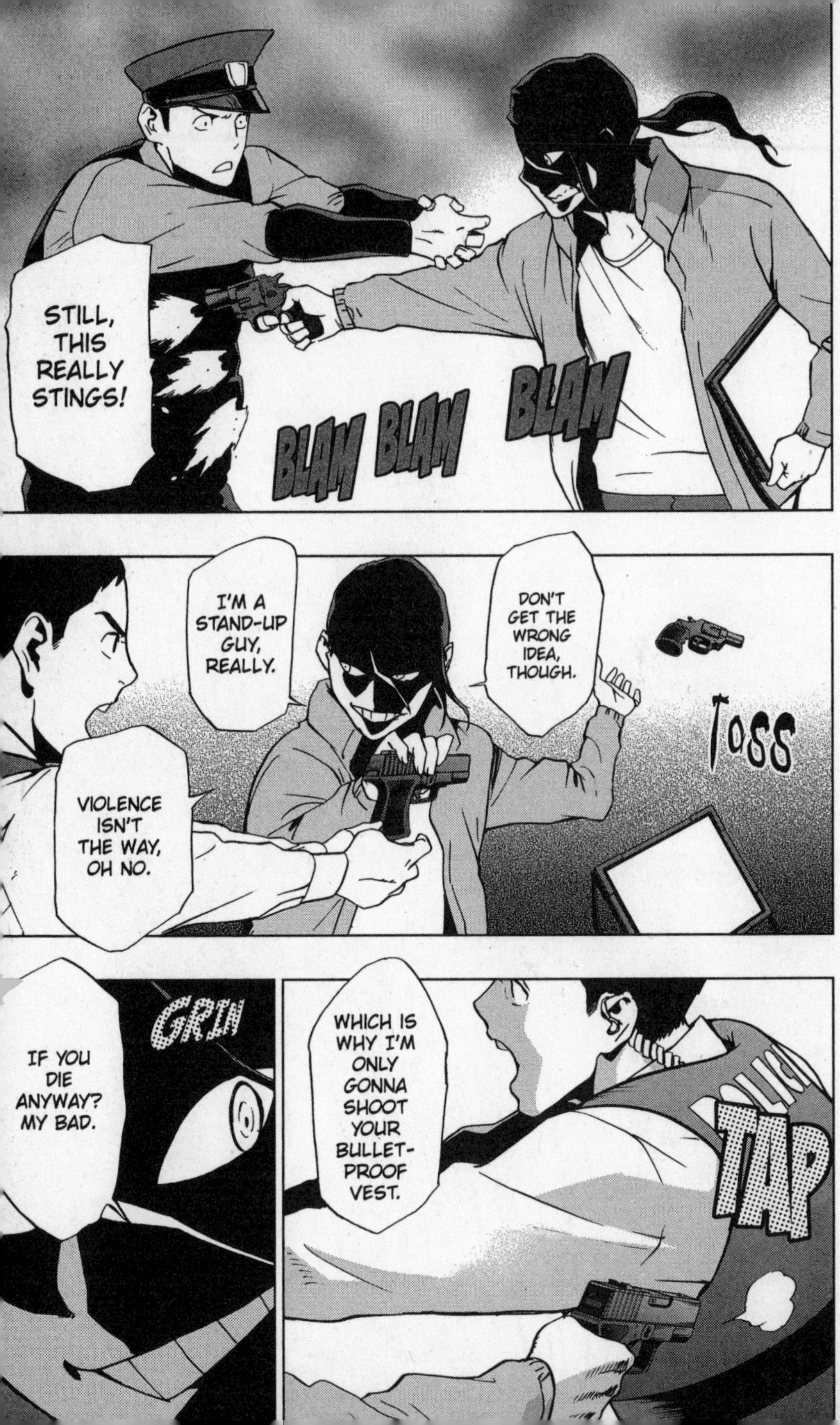
STILL, THIS REALLY STINGS!
BLAM BLAM BLAM
TOSS
DON'T GET THE WRONG IDEA, THOUGH.
I'M A STAND-UP GUY, REALLY.
VIOLENCE ISN'T THE WAY, OH NO.
TAP
WHICH IS WHY I'M ONLY GONNA SHOOT YOUR BULLET-PROOF VEST.
GRIN
IF YOU DIE ANYWAY? MY BAD.

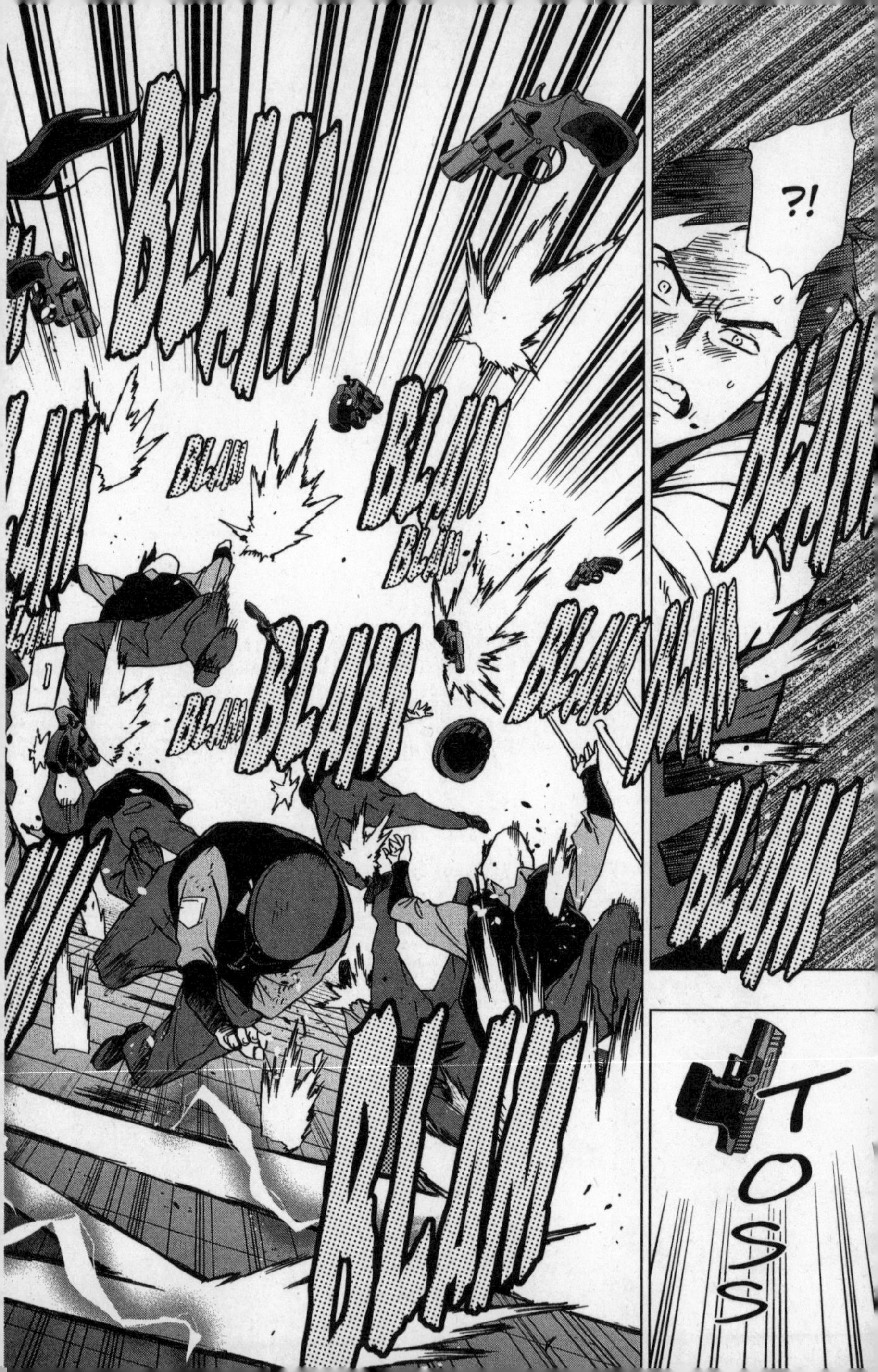
?!
BLAM
BLAM
TOSS
BLAM
BLAM
BLAM
BLAM
BLAM-
BLAM
BLAM
BLAM
BLAM BLAM
BLAM

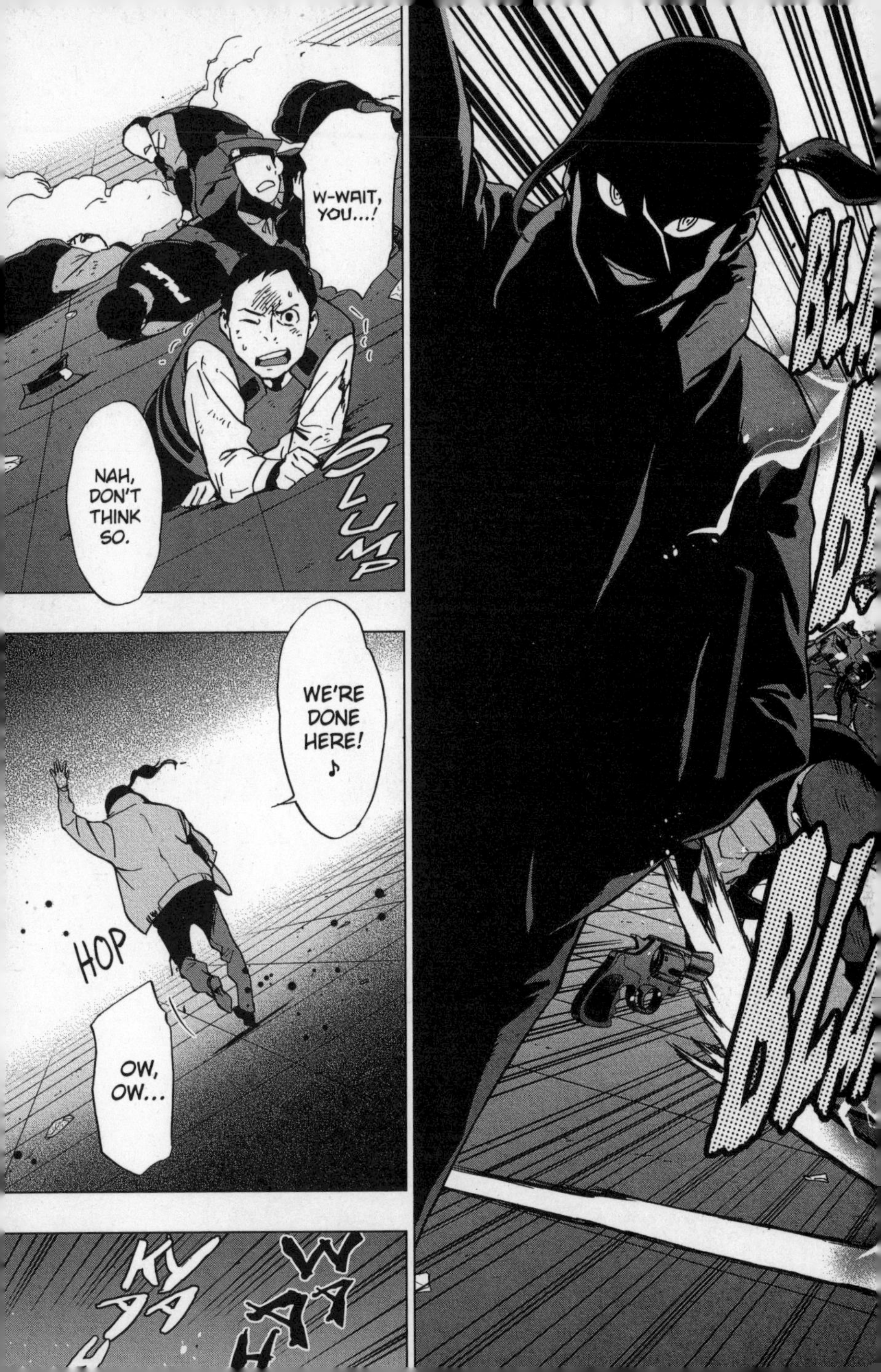
W-WAIT, YOU...!
NAH, DON'T THINK SO.
SLUMP
WE'RE DONE HERE! ♪
OW, OW...
HOP
WAAH
KYAAH

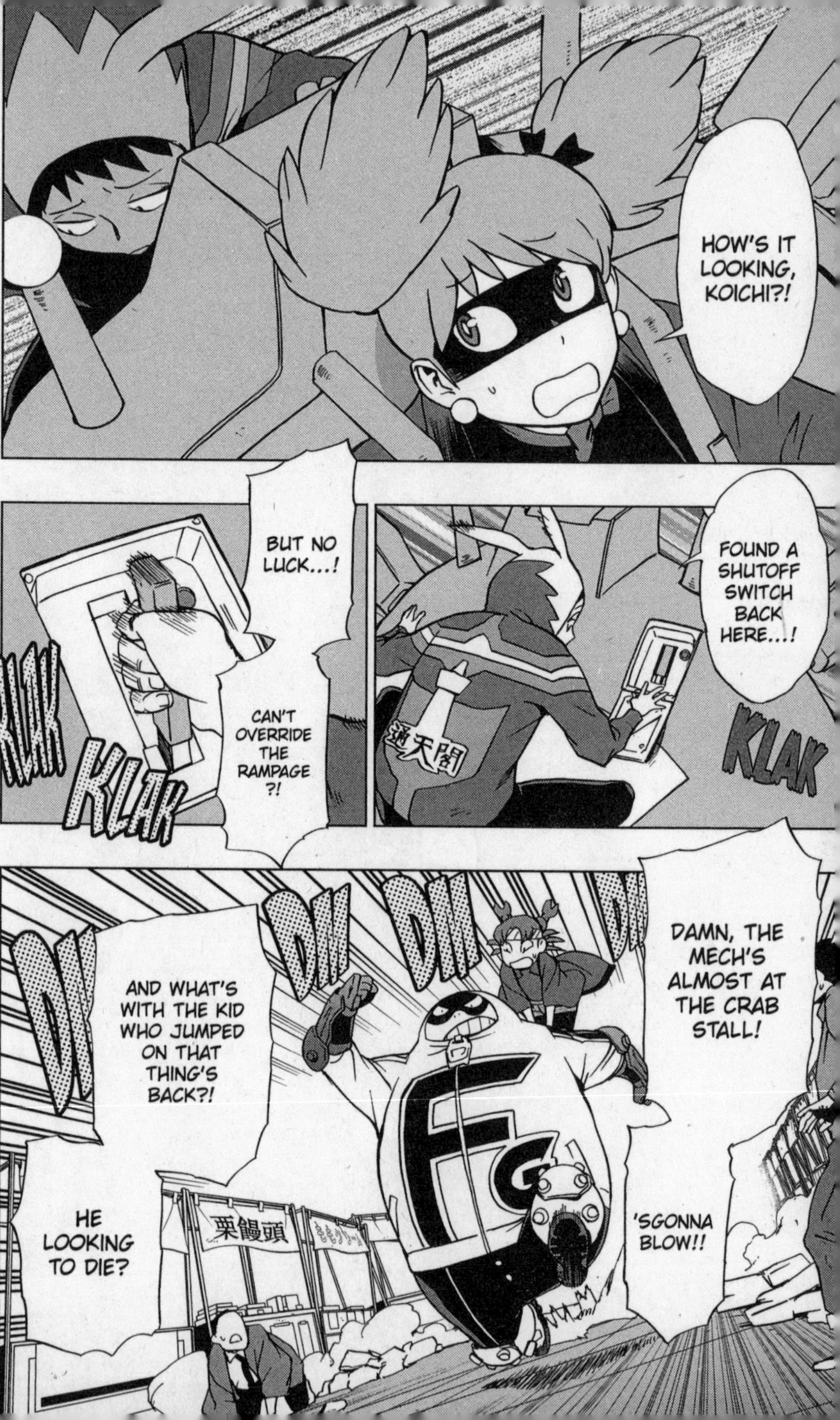
HOW'S IT LOOKING, KOICHI?!
FOUND A SHUTOFF SWITCH BACK HERE...!
KLAK
BUT NO LUCK...!
CAN'T OVERRIDE THE RAMPAGE?!
KLAK
KLAK
DAMN, THE MECH'S ALMOST AT THE CRAB STALL!
'SGONNA BLOW!!
DM
DM
DM
AND WHAT'S WITH THE KID WHO JUMPED ON THAT THING'S BACK?!
HE LOOKING TO DIE?
栗饅頭

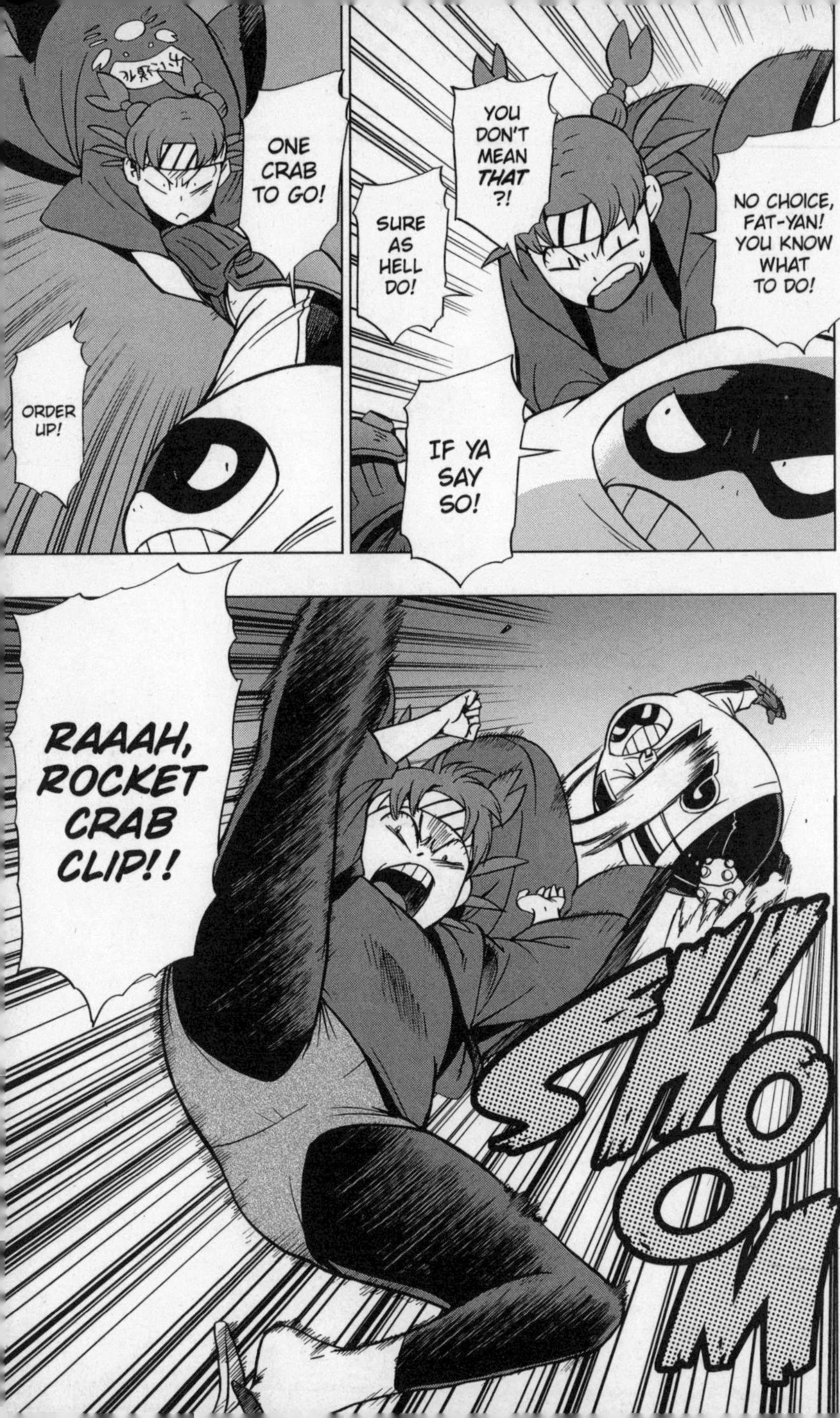
NO CHOICE, FAT-YAN! YOU KNOW WHAT TO DO!
YOU DON'T MEAN *THAT*?!
SURE AS HELL DO!
IF YA SAY SO!
ONE CRAB TO GO!
ORDER UP!
RAAAH, ROCKET CRAB CLIP!!
SHOOM

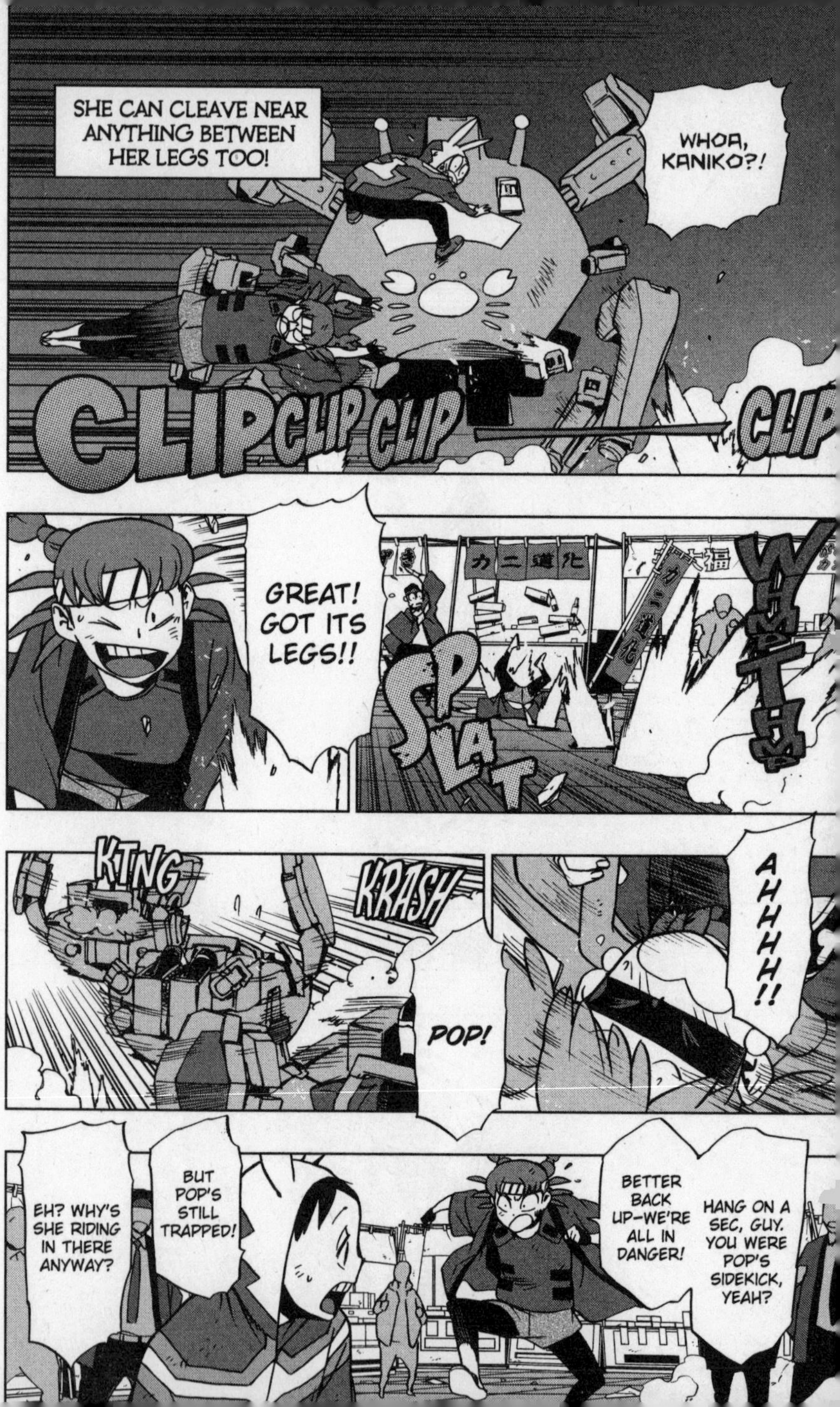
WHOA, KANIKO?!
SHE CAN CLEAVE NEAR ANYTHING BETWEEN HER LEGS TOO!
CLIP
CLIP CLIP CLIP
WHMP THMP
SPLAT
GREAT! GOT ITS LEGS!!
AHHHHH!!
POP!
KRASH
KING
HANG ON A SEC, GUY. YOU WERE POP'S SIDEKICK, YEAH?
BETTER BACK UP–WE'RE ALL IN DANGER!
BUT POP'S STILL TRAPPED!
EH? WHY'S SHE RIDING IN THERE ANYWAY?

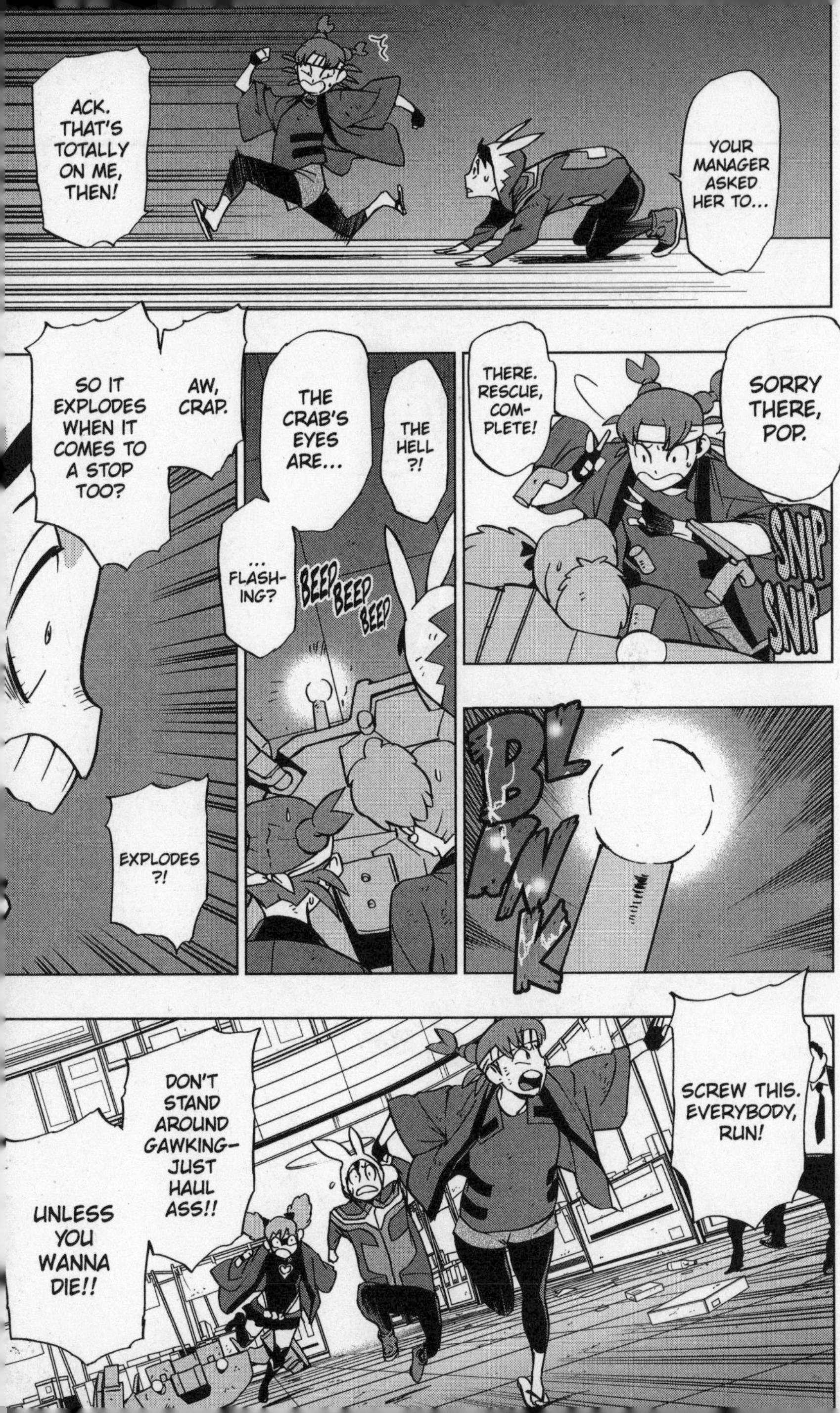
YOUR MANAGER ASKED HER TO...
ACK. THAT'S TOTALLY ON ME, THEN!
SORRY THERE, POP.
THERE. RESCUE, COMPLETE!
SNIP SNIP
BLINK
THE HELL ?!
THE CRAB'S EYES ARE...
...FLASHING?
BEEP BEEP BEEP
AW, CRAP.
SO IT EXPLODES WHEN IT COMES TO A STOP TOO?
EXPLODES ?!
SCREW THIS. EVERYBODY, RUN!
DON'T STAND AROUND GAWKING—JUST HAUL ASS!!
UNLESS YOU WANNA DIE!!

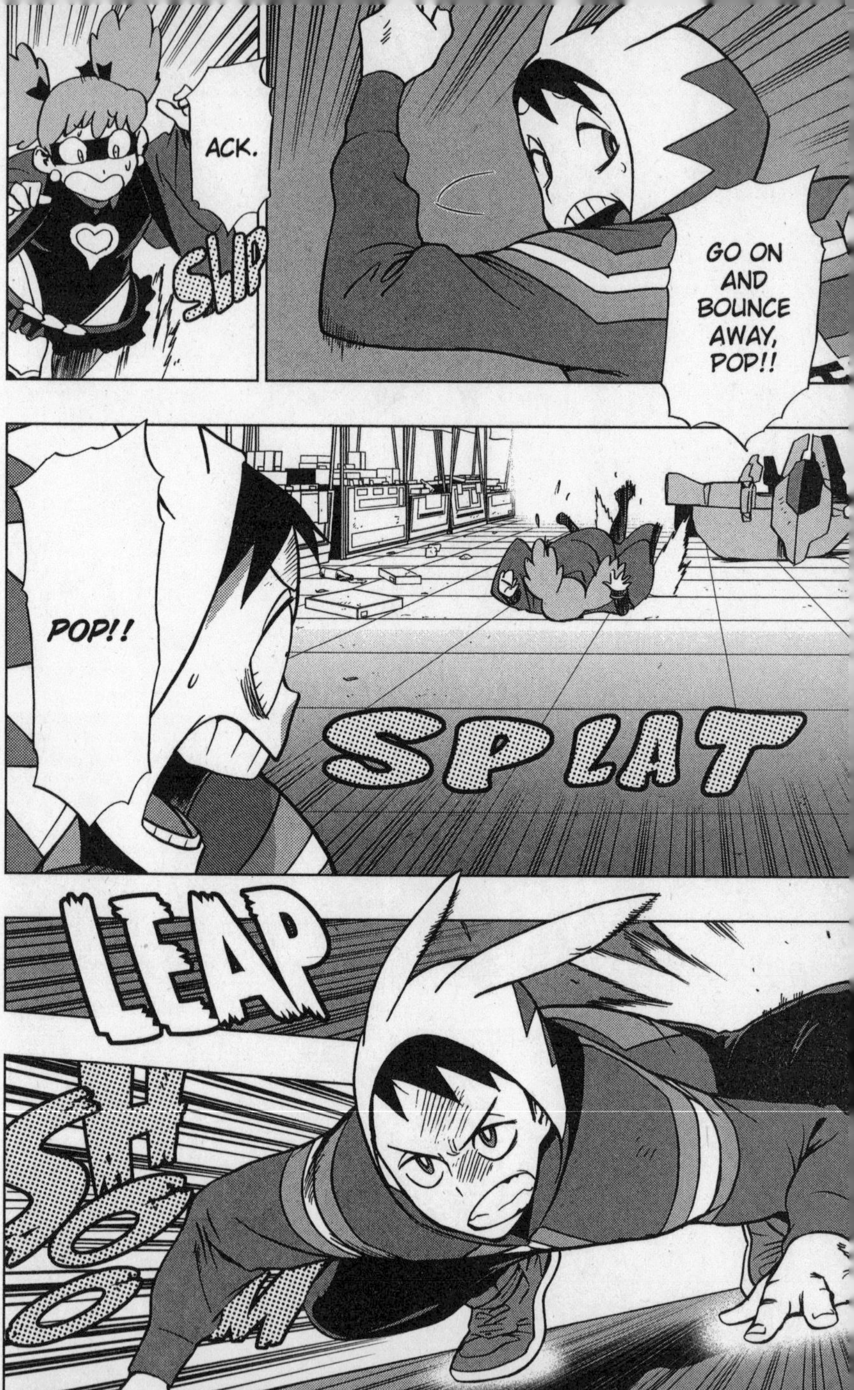
GO ON AND BOUNCE AWAY, POP!!
ACK.
SLIP
POP!!
SPLAT
LEAP
WHOOSH

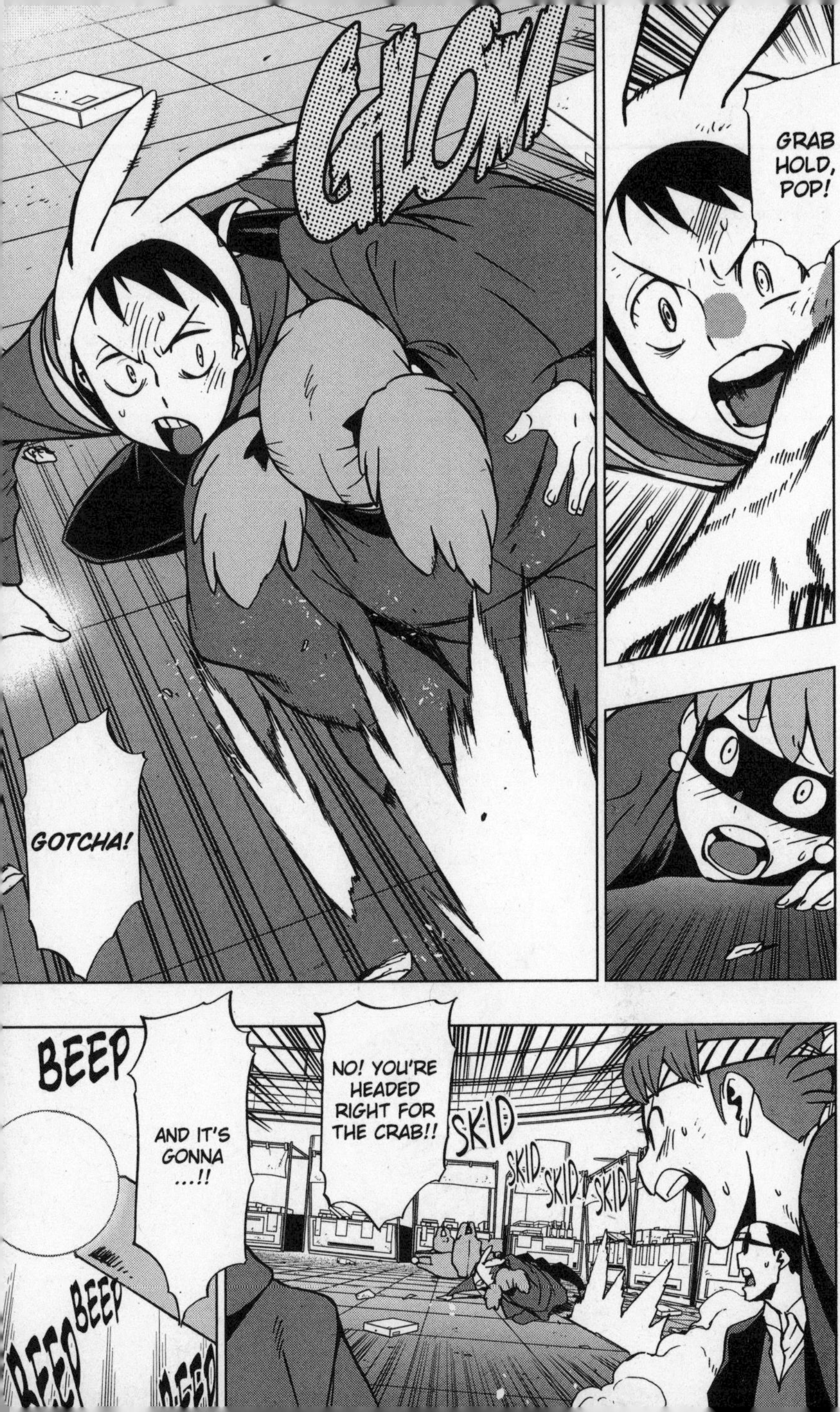
GRAB HOLD, POP!
GLOMP
GOTCHA!
SKID
SKID SKID SKID
NO! YOU'RE HEADED RIGHT FOR THE CRAB!!
AND IT'S GONNA ...!!
BEEP
BEEP
BEEP

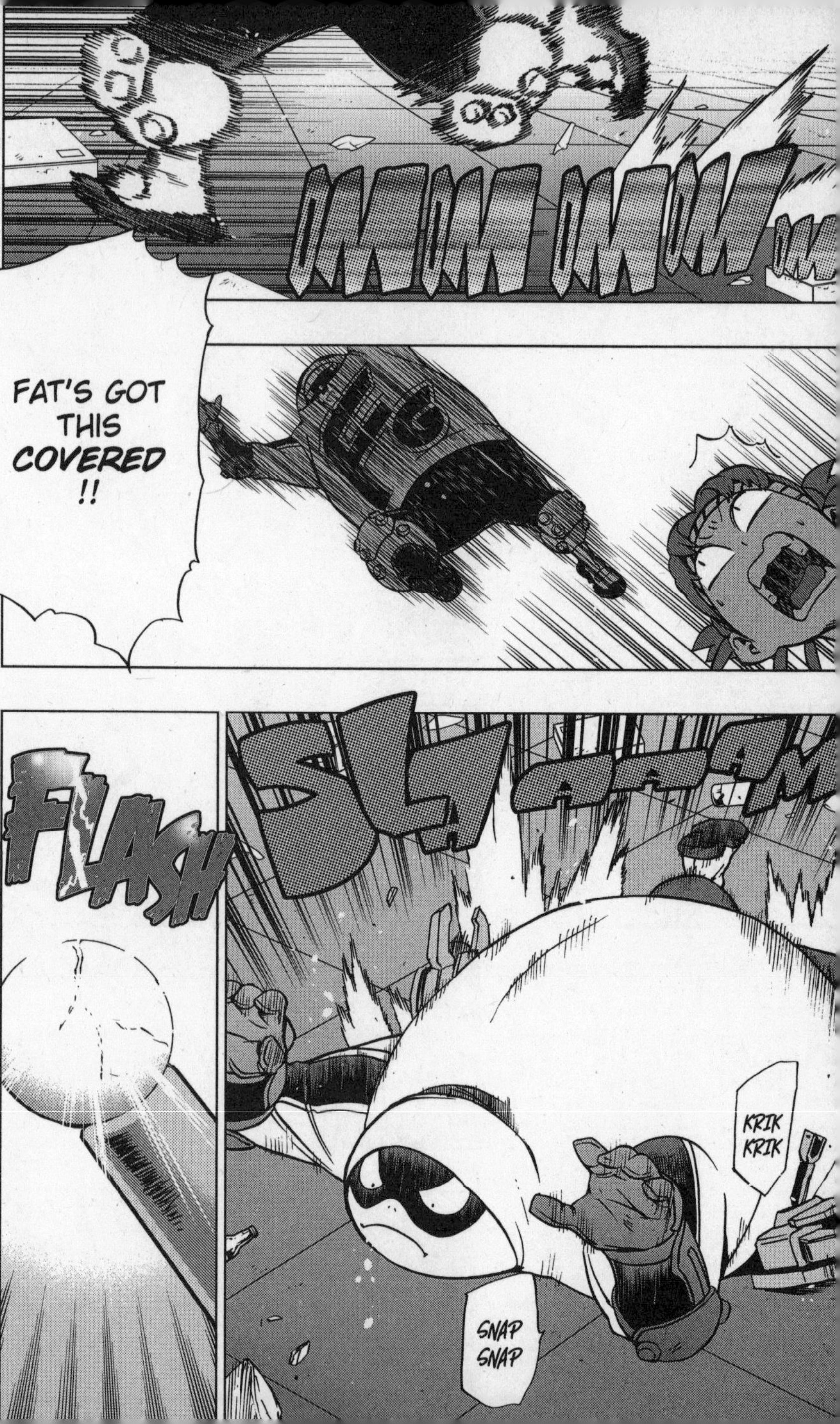
FAT'S GOT THIS COVERED !!
KRIK KRIK
SNAP SNAP
FLASH

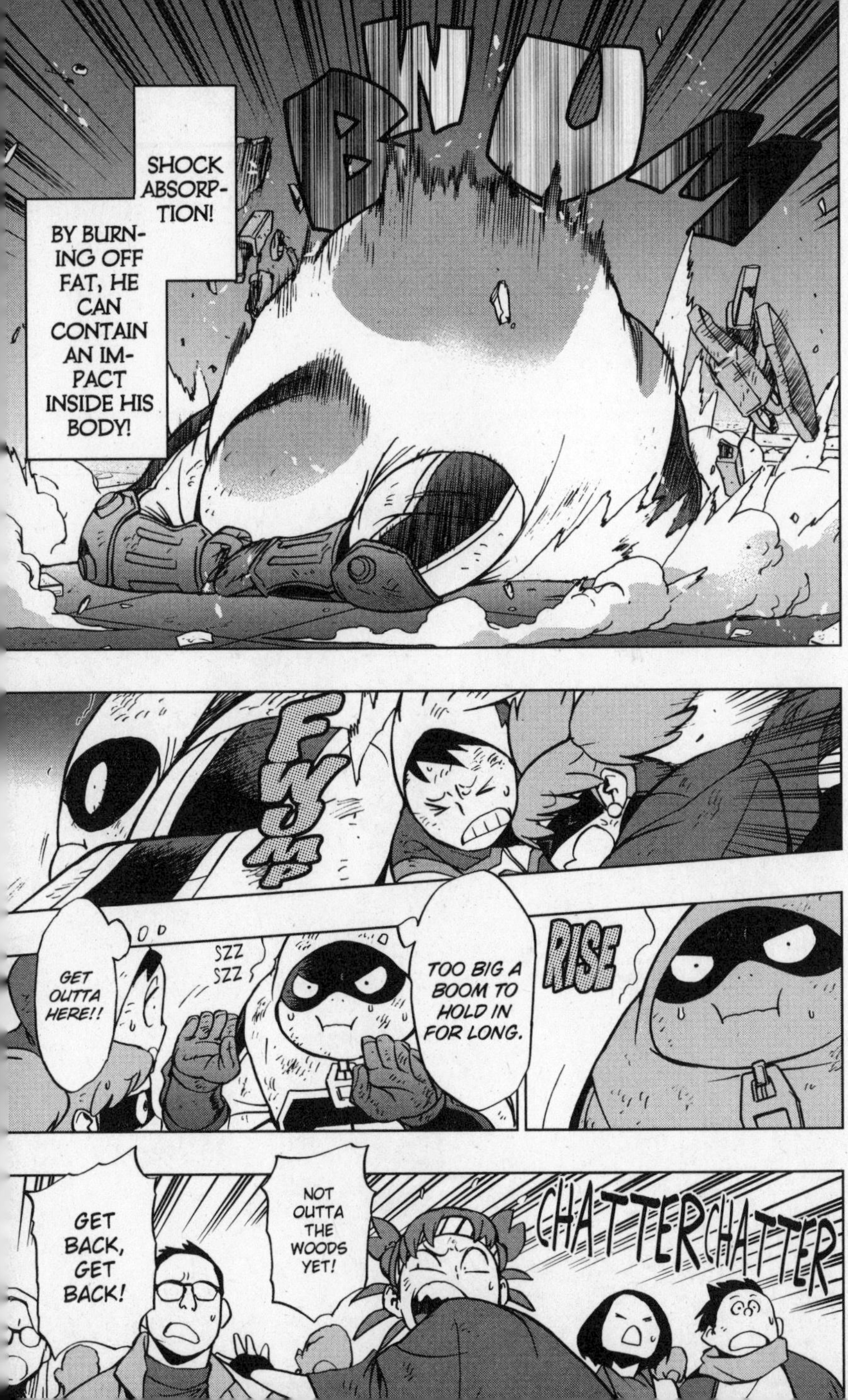
BWOOM
SHOCK ABSORP-TION!
BY BURN-ING OFF FAT, HE CAN CONTAIN AN IM-PACT INSIDE HIS BODY!
FWUMP
RISE
TOO BIG A BOOM TO HOLD IN FOR LONG.
SZZ SZZ
GET OUTTA HERE!!
CHATTERCHATTER
NOT OUTTA THE WOODS YET!
GET BACK, GET BACK!

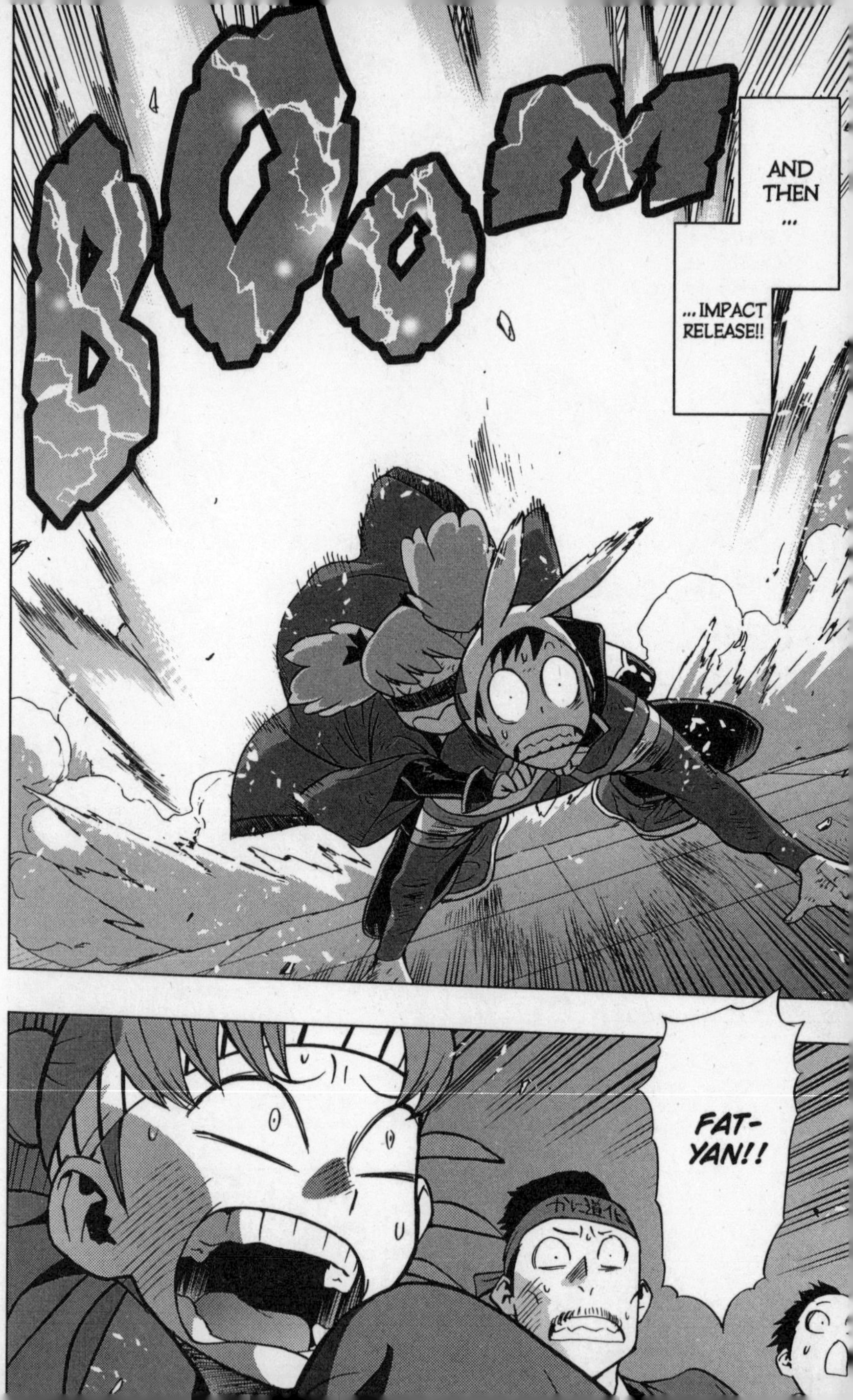
AND THEN ...
...IMPACT RELEASE!!
BOOM
FAT-YAN!!

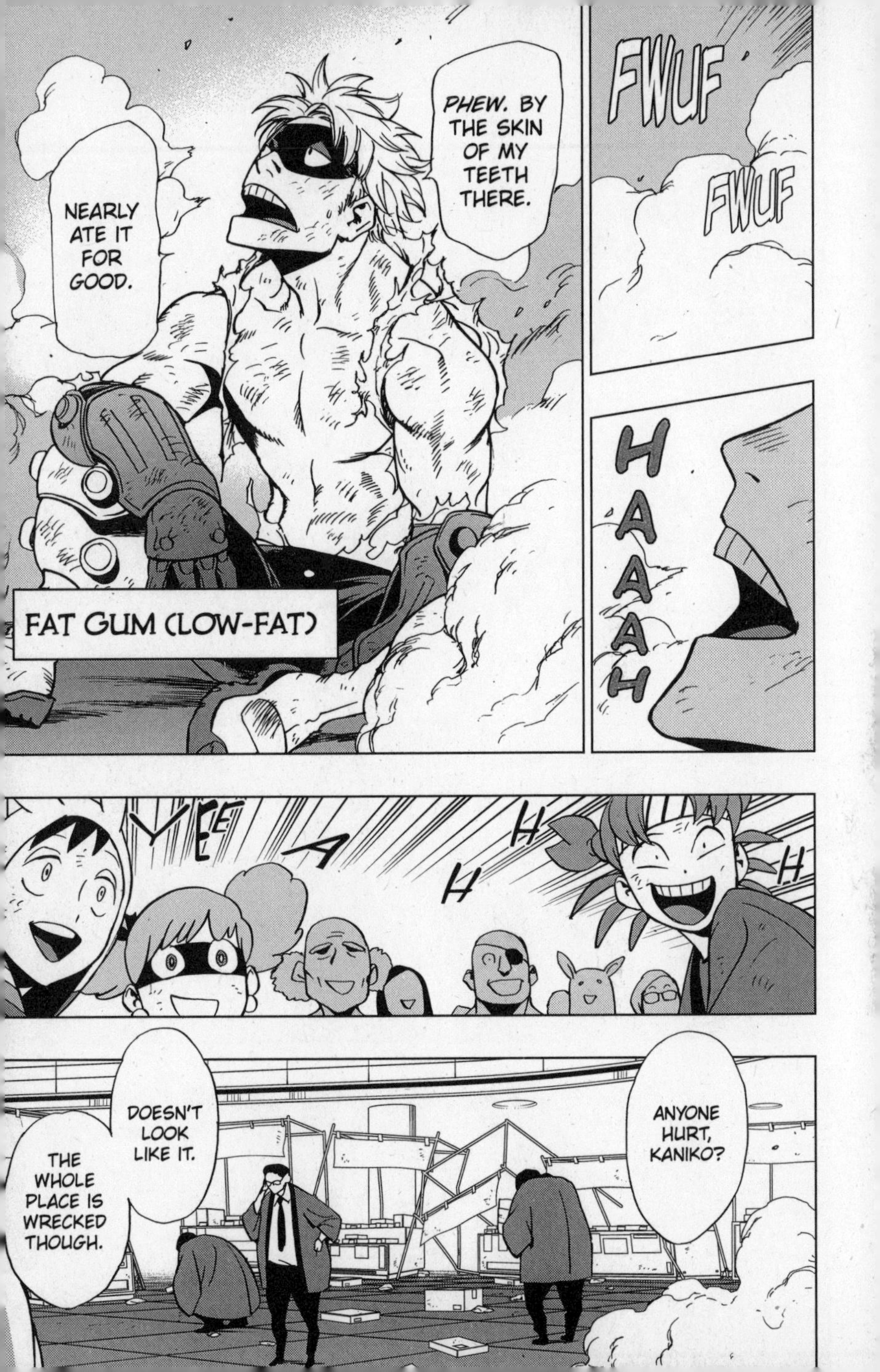
FWUF
FWUF
HAAAAH
PHEW. BY THE SKIN OF MY TEETH THERE.
NEARLY ATE IT FOR GOOD.
FAT GUM (LOW-FAT)
YEEAHHHH
ANYONE HURT, KANIKO?
DOESN'T LOOK LIKE IT.
THE WHOLE PLACE IS WRECKED THOUGH.

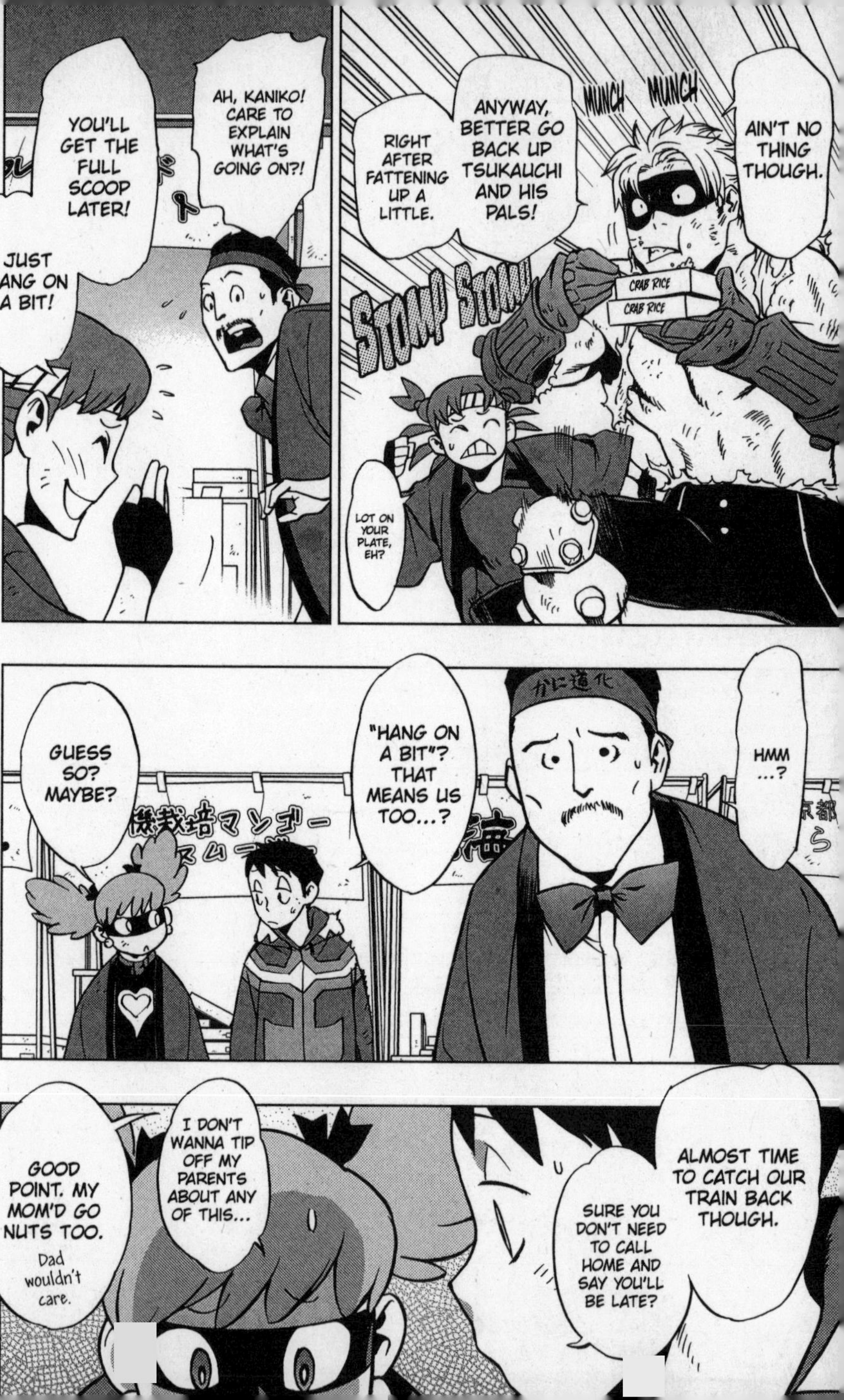
AIN'T NO THING THOUGH.
MUNCH MUNCH
ANYWAY, BETTER GO BACK UP TSUKAUCHI AND HIS PALS!
RIGHT AFTER FATTENING UP A LITTLE.
CRAB RICE
CRAB RICE
STOMP STOM
LOT ON YOUR PLATE, EH?
AH, KANIKO! CARE TO EXPLAIN WHAT'S GOING ON?!
YOU'LL GET THE FULL SCOOP LATER!
JUST HANG ON A BIT!
HMM ...?
"HANG ON A BIT"? THAT MEANS US TOO...?
GUESS SO? MAYBE?
ALMOST TIME TO CATCH OUR TRAIN BACK THOUGH.
SURE YOU DON'T NEED TO CALL HOME AND SAY YOU'LL BE LATE?
I DON'T WANNA TIP OFF MY PARENTS ABOUT ANY OF THIS...
GOOD POINT. MY MOM'D GO NUTS TOO.
Dad wouldn't care.

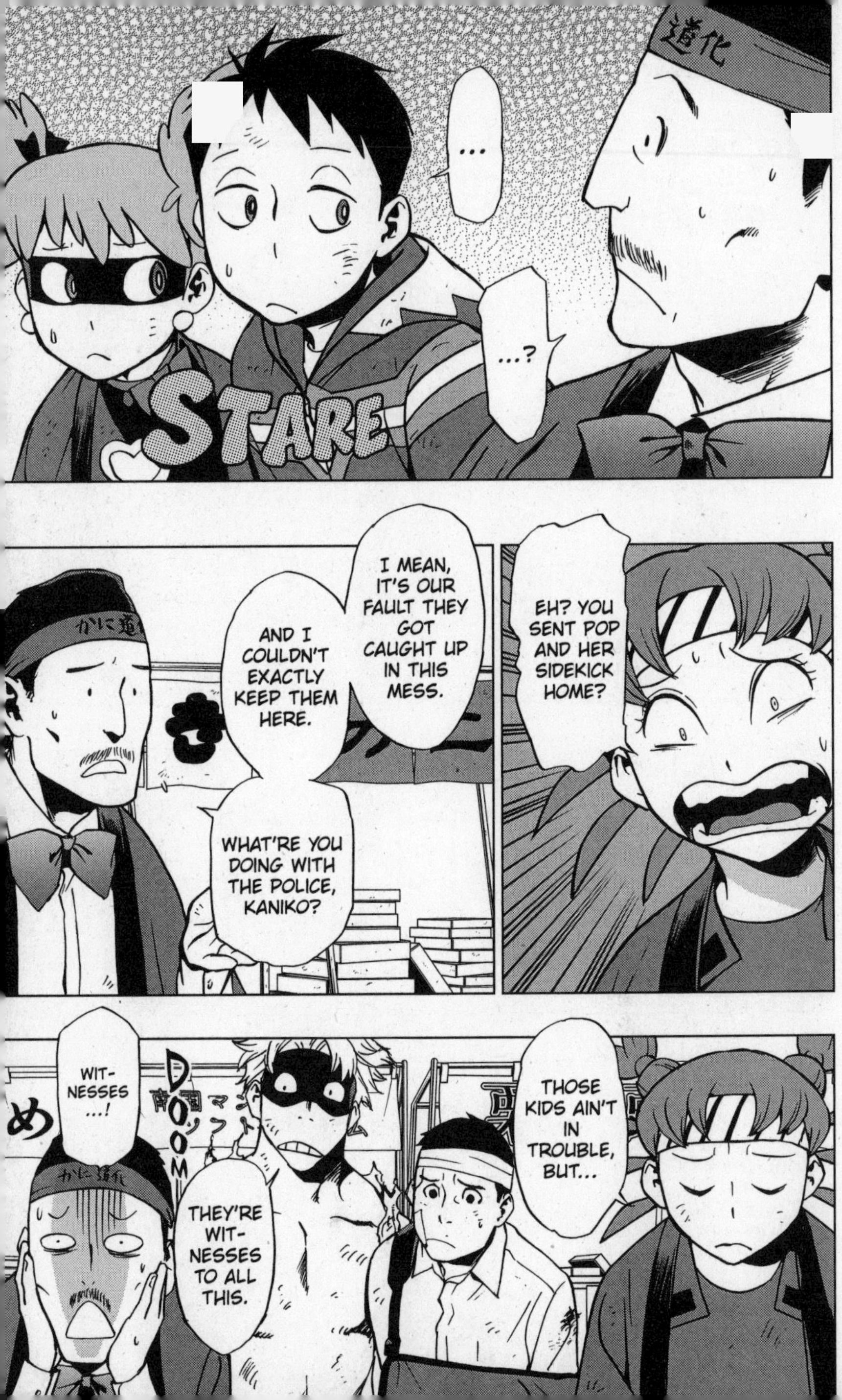
...
...?
STARE
EH? YOU SENT POP AND HER SIDEKICK HOME?
I MEAN, IT'S OUR FAULT THEY GOT CAUGHT UP IN THIS MESS.
AND I COULDN'T EXACTLY KEEP THEM HERE.
WHAT'RE YOU DOING WITH THE POLICE, KANIKO?
THOSE KIDS AIN'T IN TROUBLE, BUT...
THEY'RE WIT-NESSES TO ALL THIS.
DOOOM
WIT-NESSES ...!

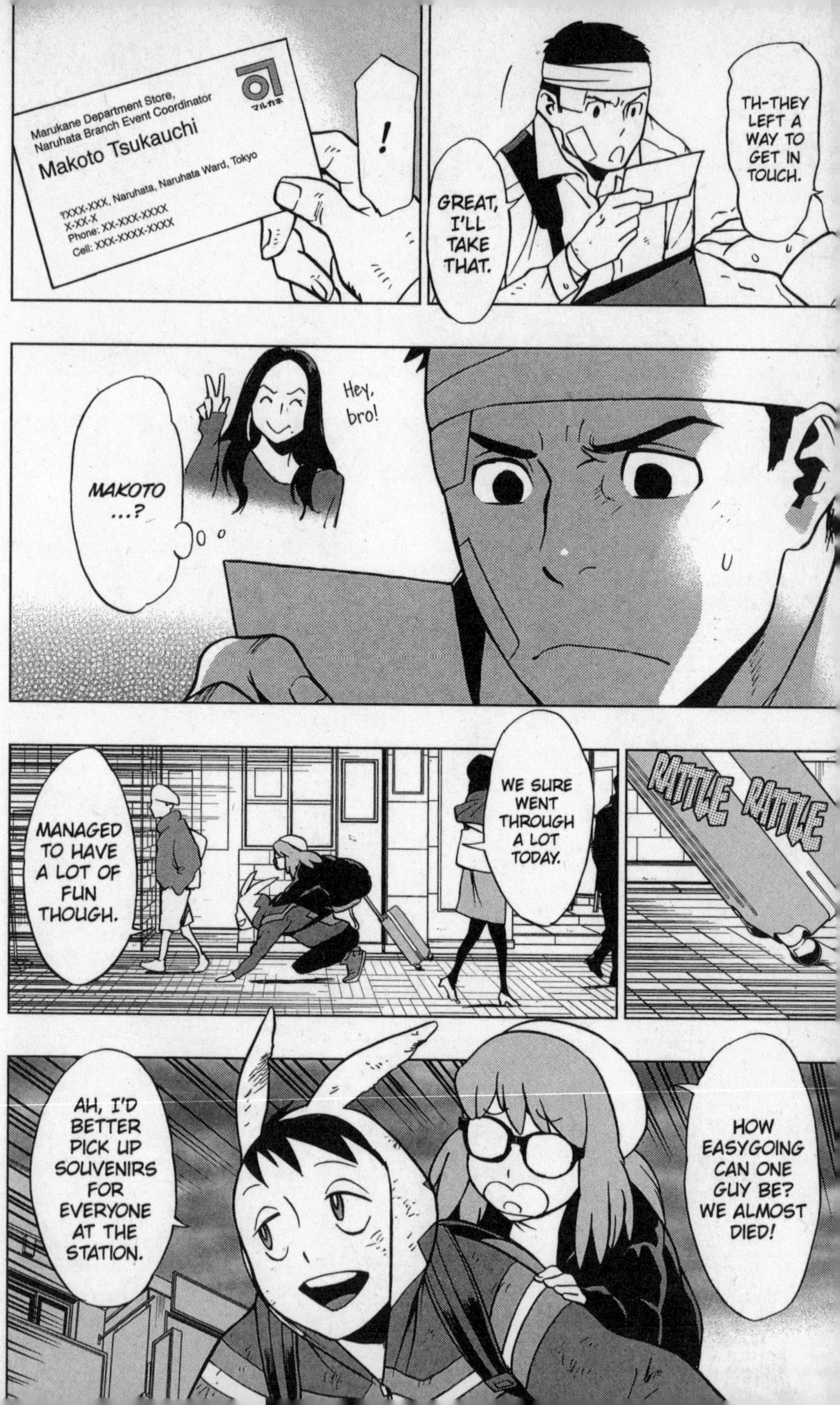
TH-THEY LEFT A WAY TO GET IN TOUCH.
GREAT, I'LL TAKE THAT.
!
Marukane Department Store, Naruhata Branch Event Coordinator
マルカネ
Makoto Tsukauchi
〒XXX-XXX, Naruhata, Naruhata Ward, Tokyo X-XX-X
Phone: XX-XXX-XXXX
Cell: XXX-XXXX-XXXX
Hey, bro!
MAKOTO ...?
RATTLE RATTLE
WE SURE WENT THROUGH A LOT TODAY.
MANAGED TO HAVE A LOT OF FUN THOUGH.
HOW EASYGOING CAN ONE GUY BE? WE ALMOST DIED!
AH, I'D BETTER PICK UP SOUVENIRS FOR EVERYONE AT THE STATION.

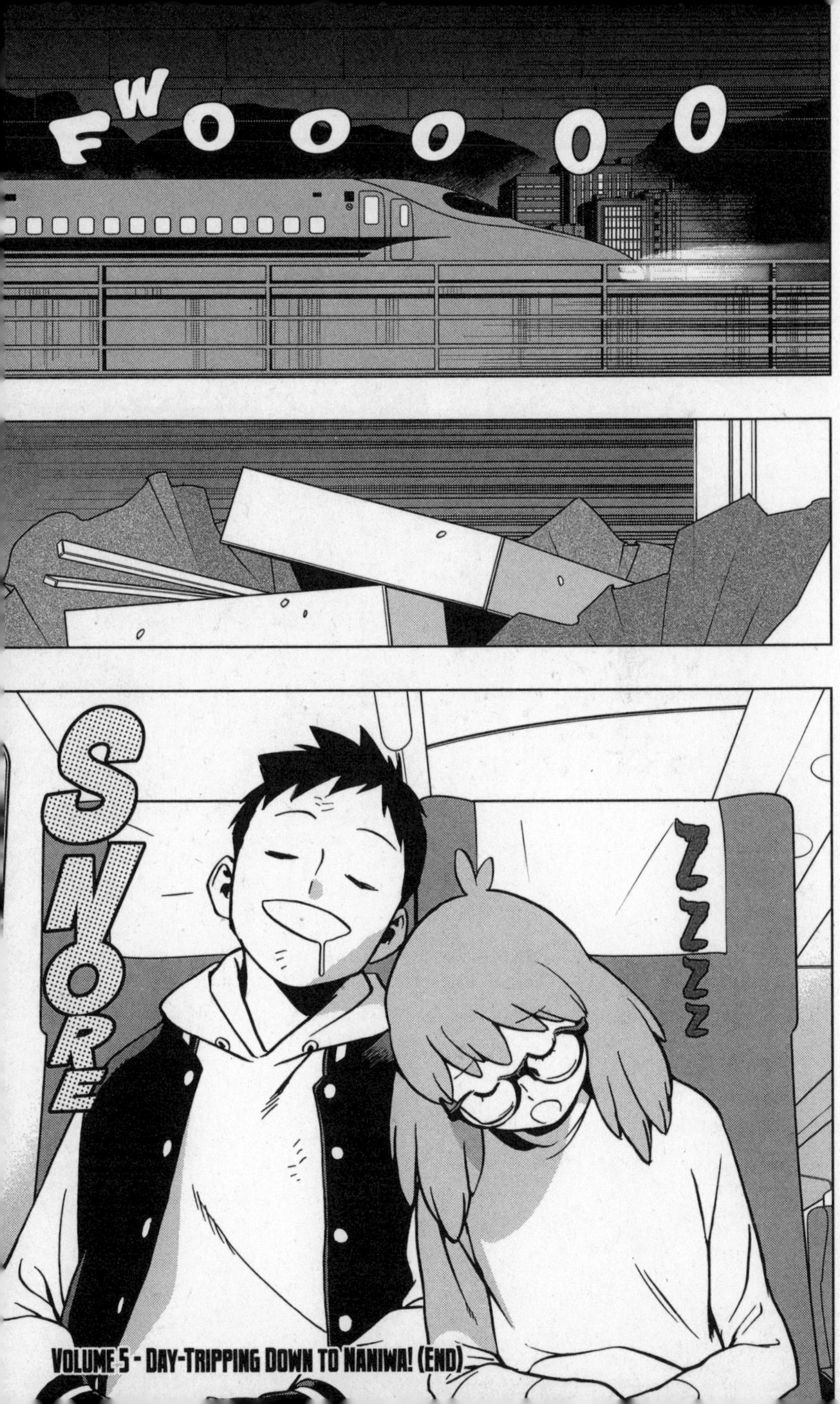
FWOOOOO
ZZZZ
SNORE
VOLUME 5 - DAY-TRIPPING DOWN TO NANIWA! (END)

YOU'RE READING THE WRONG WAY!!

MY HERO ACADEMIA VIGILANTES

reads from right to left, starting in the upper-right corner. Japanese is read from right to left, meaning that action, sound effects and word-balloon order are completely reversed from English order.

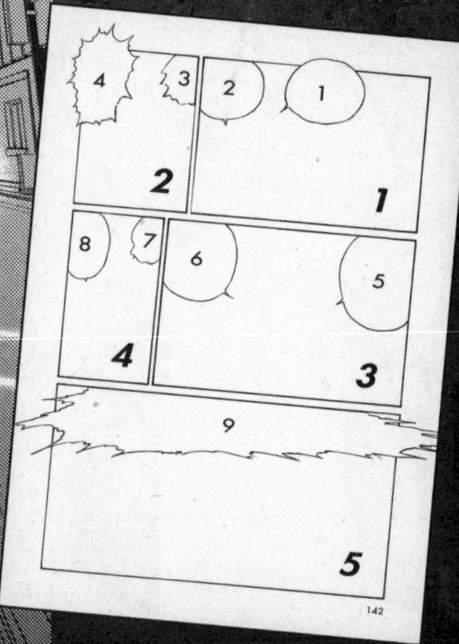

1
2
3
4
5
6
7
8
9
1
2
3
4
5
142

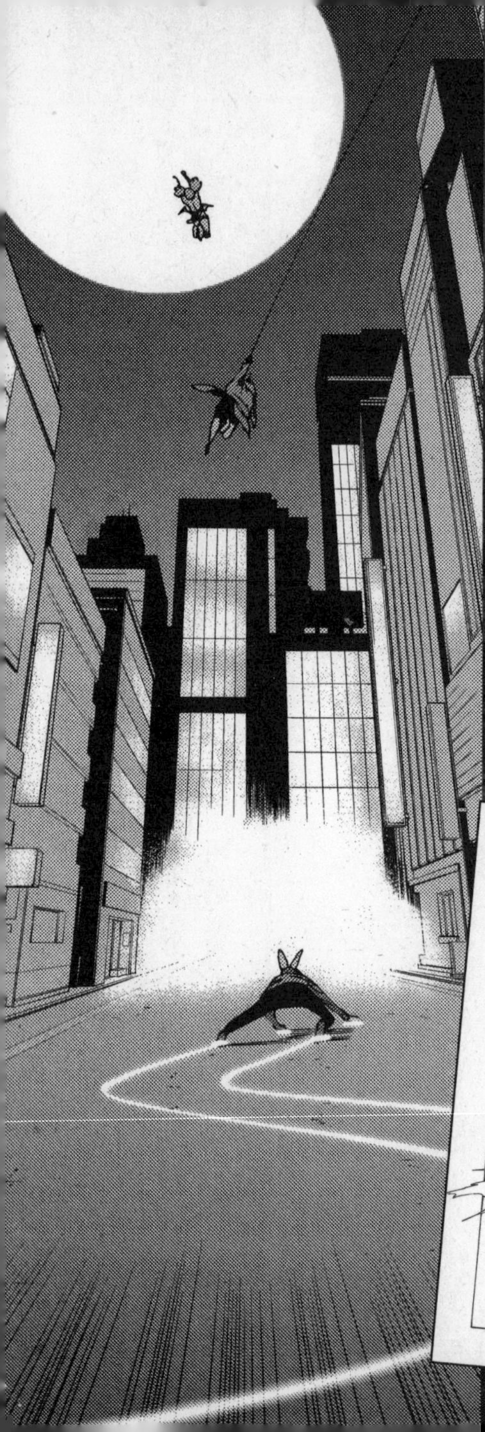

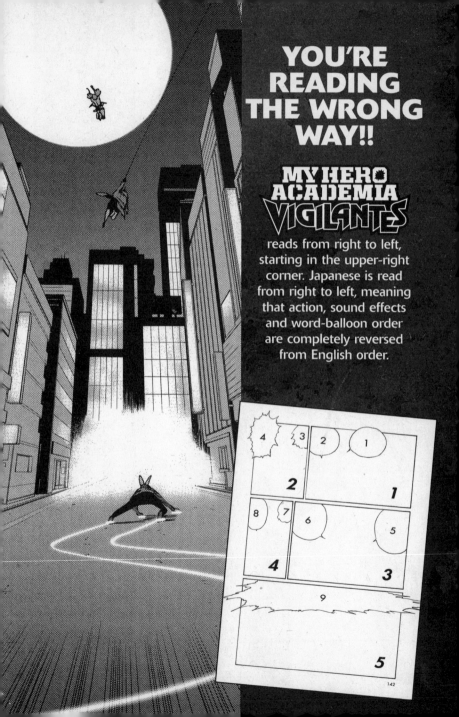